The 2020 Presidential Election in the South

Voting, Elections, and the Political Process

Series Editors: Shauna Reilly and Stacy Ulbig

Receptive to studies in the American and comparative settings, Voting, Elections, and the Political Process series examines the broadly defined electoral process. The series seeks scholarly monographs and edited volumes that investigate the ways in which voters, candidates, elected officials, parties, interest groups, the media, and others interact in the context of electoral politics. Works with a focus on individual attitudes and behavior, institutional and contextual influences, and the legal aspects of the electoral process are welcome. This series accepts interdisciplinary work using a variety of methodological approaches.

Recent Titles
The Trifecta in Voting Barrier Causation: Economics, Politics, and Race
    by Shauna Reilly
An Unprecedented President and the Prospect for American Democracy
    by Arthur Paulson
The Resilient Voter: Stressful Polling Places and Voting Behavior by Shauna Reilly and
    Stacy Ulbig
*Unconventional, Partisan, and Polarizing Rhetoric: How the 2016 Election Shaped the
    Way Candidates Strategize, Engage, and Communicate* edited by Jeanine E. Kraybill
The 2016 Presidential Election: The Causes and Consequences of a Political Earthquake
    edited by Amnon Cavari, Richard J. Powell, and Kenneth R. Mayer

The 2020 Presidential Election in the South

Edited by
Scott E. Buchanan
and Branwell DuBose Kapeluck

LEXINGTON BOOKS
Lanham • Boulder • New York • London

Published by Lexington Books
An imprint of The Rowman & Littlefield Publishing Group, Inc.
4501 Forbes Boulevard, Suite 200, Lanham, Maryland 20706
www.rowman.com

6 Tinworth Street, London SE11 5AL, United Kingdom

Copyright © 2021 The Rowman & Littlefield Publishing Group, Inc.

All rights reserved. No part of this book may be reproduced in any form or by any electronic or mechanical means, including information storage and retrieval systems, without written permission from the publisher, except by a reviewer who may quote passages in a review.

British Library Cataloguing in Publication Information Available

Library of Congress Cataloging-in-Publication Data

Names: Buchanan, Scott E., editor. | Kapeluck, Branwell DuBose, 1969- editor.
Title: The 2020 Presidential Election in the South / edited by Scott E. Buchanan and Branwell Dubose Kapeluck.
Description: Lanham : Lexington Books, [2021] | Series: Voting, elections, and the political process | Includes bibliographical references and index. | Summary: "This edited volume, written by the leading experts in their particular states, focuses on the historic 2020 presidential election in the South. The region has played a critical role in determining the occupant of the White House for the last 50 years, and the South once again was pivotal in the 2020 contest between Trump and Biden"— Provided by publisher.
Identifiers: LCCN 2021033524 (print) | LCCN 2021033525 (ebook) |
   ISBN 9781793646712 (cloth) | ISBN 9781793646705 (ebook)
Subjects: LCSH: Presidents—United States—Election—2020. | Elections—Southern States—History—21st century. | Southern States—Politics and government—1951-
Classification: LCC E915 .A135 2021 (print) | LCC E915 (ebook) |
   DDC 324.973/0905—dc23
LC record available at https://lccn.loc.gov/2021033524
LC ebook record available at https://lccn.loc.gov/2021033525

Contents

Acknowledgments — vii

Introduction: The South: A Region in Transition — 1

PART I: THE SETTING AND NOMINATING PROCESS — 5

1 The 2020 Southern Electorate: Demographics, Issues, and (In)Distinctiveness — 7
Patrick R. Miller

2 The 2020 Presidential Nomination Process — 33
Aaron A. Hitefield and M. V. Hood, III

PART II: ELECTIONS IN THE DEEP SOUTH — 51

3 Alabama: Politics of Personality in the Heart of Dixie — 53
Shannon L. Bridgmon

4 Georgia: Breakthrough to Blue — 77
Charles S. Bullock, III

5 Louisiana: Trump Support in This Swamp Runs Deep — 95
Robert E. Hogan and Anna R. Elinkowski

6 Mississippi: Republican Hegemony Persists — 111
Stephen D. Shaffer

7 South Carolina: Redder than Red for Now — 129
Branwell DuBose Kapeluck and Scott E. Buchanan

PART III: ELECTIONS IN THE RIM SOUTH — 153

8 Arkansas: Once More with Feeling for Trump — 155
   Jay Barth and Janine A. Parry

9 Florida: Kingmaker No More? — 173
   Jonathan Knuckey and Aubrey Jewett

10 Kentucky 2020: Bluegrass, Red State — 207
   Joel Turner, Scott Lasley, and Jeffrey P. Kash

11 North Carolina: Even More Deeply Divided in 2020 — 223
   J. Michael Bitzer

12 Tennessee: Trump Territory, Again — 245
   Vaughn May

13 Texas: Partisan Changes Finally Afoot — 261
   Seth C. McKee

14 Virginia: Trump Accelerates the Bluing of the Commonwealth — 279
   John J. McGlennon

15 Five Southern States That Could Change American Politics — 301
   H. Gibbs Knotts

Index — 315

About the Contributors — 327

Acknowledgments

This edited volume is the tenth in a series of analyses of presidential elections in the southern states beginning in 1984 and continuing through the 2000 election and published by Praeger. A state-by-state study of the 2004 presidential election was not published in edited book form, but rather appeared as a special double issue of the *American Review of Politics*. The 2008–2016 election analyses were published by the University of Arkansas Press. Due to a change in the University of Arkansas Press's content focus, we are happy to now be working with Lexington Books on the analysis of the 2020 presidential election in the South. We would like to gratefully thank the University of Arkansas Press for so generously allowing the chapter authors to use some of their chapter texts from *The Future Ain't What It Used to Be: The 2016 Presidential Election in the South*.

While the presidential election has been the focus of each volume, other important aspects of contemporary Southern electoral politics have also been addressed, including congressional and state elections and the overall status of party development and competition in the South. This volume continues the general organizational plan of the previous publications, including an introductory chapter, a chapter on presidential primaries, a chapter on issues in the 2020 presidential election, as well as chapters on each southern state and a conclusion summarizing lessons from the 2020 election cycle.

We are very appreciative of the support of those who have made this book possible or who have contributed to the atmosphere in which this work was created. The Citadel Foundation provided indispensable financial support for the Citadel Symposium on Southern Politics, a biennial conference that for over four decades has brought together a community of scholars engaged in the study of Southern politics and that has, in the process, helped to develop the network of contributors involved in this study. We would also like to thank the authors of the various chapters. Without you, we would never be able to complete a project like this in such a timely fashion.

Finally, we wish to thank our acquisition editor, Joseph Parry, and Carter Moran, the copyeditor, for their support, patience, and guidance during the publication process.

Introduction
The South: A Region in Transition
Scott E. Buchanan and Branwell DuBose Kapeluck

In the aftermath of the 2020 presidential election, many within the Republican Party entered a period of soul-searching as to their party's future, not only in terms of 2022 and beyond but also for what the party stands for. With former President Donald Trump still looming large within the Republican Party, the party's direction remains murky at this point. The South, sans Virginia, no longer looks nearly as monolithic in presidential politics. Much as Trump's future impact on the GOP remains unclear, so it is a bit uncertain what the role of the South will be going forward in presidential elections. In many ways, the region and Donald Trump are joined at the hip. While Trump was enormously popular in the rural South among white voters, the combination of Trump's rhetoric, campaign style, and the COVID-19 pandemic all led to high negative feelings for him among urban and suburban voters of all races. Simultaneously, Donald Trump was able to unite voters in one camp and divide them in another, all the while calling into question the traditional post–World War II Republican belief system. This was no small feat.

Democrats see new hope on the horizon when they look upon the South—a region that they had solidly controlled until the 1960s, only to see the region become steadily more Republican after 1964. Though Virginia had become a truly purple state in 2008 and 2012, the past two presidential elections witnessed Donald Trump transfer the Old Dominion into a reliable blue state. In his chapter on Virginia, John McGlennon describes in detail how demographic and migration shifts have transformed the Commonwealth. In many ways, Virginia might be a harbinger of new political trends to come. In 2020, Georgia joined Virginia, as former Vice President Joe Biden became the first Democrat to win the Peach State since 1992. Even more surprising to many is the fact that Democrats swept both U.S. Senate seats in Georgia. In doing so, Georgia voters elected Jon Ossoff, the first Jew to ever represent the state in the U.S. Senate, and Raphael Warnock, the first black candidate to ever be elected to the senate from Georgia. The elections of Ossoff and Warnock also tipped the Senate into Democratic control. As it has done often in history, the South played a pivotal role in national politics.

Time will tell what the region will look like in future elections, and trying to predict the future is fraught with danger. Looking back to the 2020 presidential election provides more than enough to analyze. In the lead-up to the 2020 presidential election, Bullock et al. (2019) argued that the traditional division of the region into Rim South and Deep South has become outdated and should be refocused. This dichotomy first developed by V. O. Key in 1949 was during a time in which race was truly the fulcrum on which Southern politics pivoted. While Professor Key was the first national political scientist to realize the distinctions within the region's politics, his division of the South has stood the test of time—until now. Increasingly, the South fits into a different division. While race is certainly still fundamental to understanding Southern politics, Bullock et al. argue that contemporary political trends in the region hinge a great deal on whether the state is undergoing economic growth and increasing in-migration. Put another way, Southern states that are seeing increasing diversity in their populations are showing much more willingness to vote Democratic than states that are becoming increasingly less diverse. This theme is present to some degree in all of the chapters in this volume. It will be apparent to the reader that high-growth states without exception demonstrate increased competitiveness in national-level election outcomes. Competitiveness between Democrats and Republicans is increasing, with the Democrats on the upswing in many cases. Meanwhile the low-growth states show signs of becoming even more Republican for the foreseeable future.

As with previous volumes in this series, the premise of this book is that the South constitutes a unique political and cultural region of the United States. The South continues to fascinate the nation, and studies of the region can be found not only in politics but literature, linguistics, and even cuisine. As has been studied by numerous other political scholars, the South is also more distinctly religious, at least outwardly, than other parts of the nation. This, too, has been studied as to its political impact, and many of the chapters to follow cover the influence of the region's religiosity on state politics.

Unlike past volumes in this series though, we include a new state in the coverage of the reason. For the first time, we add a chapter on Kentucky to our study of the presidential election in the South. While most studies of politics in the region follow V. O. Key's decision to focus on the eleven states of the former Confederacy, we felt that the time had come to include the Bluegrass State. While Kentucky has historically been considered a border state, it does have a star on the Confederate Battle Flag. In the twenty-first century, Kentucky looks "more Southern" in many ways politically than do some other states traditionally included in any political study of the region. In their chapter on Kentucky, Joel Turner, Scott Lasley, and Jeffrey Kash even provide evidence that a significant number of Kentuckians think of themselves as Southerners.

As the title suggests, the primary focus of this book is on the presidential election. However, even casual political observers are aware that presidents and presidential elections have a substantial impact on down-ballot offices. An examination of elections from the congressional level down to the state level makes clear that the Republican Party has made significant inroads in Southern state governments in the early twenty-first century. While Republicans had enjoyed intermittent success in some states prior to the early 2000s, Democrats were able to maintain their grip on governor's mansions and state legislatures long after they had ceded the presidency and to a great extent Congress to the Republicans. The early 2000s saw the Republicans rise to power in large part due to GOP strategists effectively "nationalizing" state politics, even down to the local level. The early 2000s saw the Republicans gain control of the majority of governorships in the South, and the remaining Democratic governors were more conservative than the national party. After the 2010 midterm elections, Republicans were in control of both chambers of nine Southern state legislatures, with split control in Kentucky and Virginia. By 2016, this number had risen to ten states with unified Republican control, with Virginia being the only split.

After Donald Trump's unlikely win in 2016, some political observers even felt that Republicans would begin to take supermajorities in state legislatures. However, the 2018 midterm elections and the 2020 presidential election have dampened Republican enthusiasm substantially. While the Republicans still control a majority of governorships, the Democrats can now boast four Democratic governors, and the Democrats gained control of both chambers of the Virginia legislature in the 2018 election cycle. Democrats are certainly eyeing the potential of Stacey Abrams to challenge Brian Kemp in 2022, after she nearly won in 2018. Still, Democrats were certainly disappointed in their inability to gain control of more state legislatures, especially with redistricting coming up at some point prior to the 2022 midterm elections.

All of these factors, both historic and contemporary, have made the South an area of significant academic scholarship. One of the preeminent academic conferences to focus solely on the politics of the American South has been the biennial Symposium on Southern Politics, which has been held since 1978. Sponsored by the Citadel Department of Political Science, the Symposium was founded by the late Tod Baker, Laurence Moreland, and Robert Steed, all professors at the Citadel. Every two years, academics from across the country meet in Charleston, South Carolina, to discuss the South's unique position in American politics. The conference has resulted in a number of books on southern politics, many of which were the product of collaborations among symposium participants. The *American Review of Politics* has also regularly published the best work presented at the conference. Since 1984, the organizers of the conference have published a book on the role of the South in each presidential election. Professor Scott Buchanan and Professor DuBose Kapeluck continued the tradition established by Baker, Moreland, and Steed with the publication of edited volumes on the 2008, 2012, and 2016 presidential elections, and now this volume.

All of the authors of the various chapters to follow are experts, both academically and otherwise, in the field of Southern politics. Almost all of them have presented research at the Symposium on Southern Politics, and untold numbers of journal articles, books, and other research have come from research these authors presented at the Symposium. We hope that the readers of this volume will gain a deeper knowledge and understanding of the context of the region and its politics, as well as the states that make up the region.

Part I

THE SETTING AND NOMINATING PROCESS

Chapter 1

The 2020 Southern Electorate

Demographics, Issues, and (In)Distinctiveness

Patrick R. Miller

The near Republican sweep of the South in the 2020 presidential election belies a far more compelling and critical year in the region. After the earliest contests in the Democratic primary suggested momentum behind Vermont Senator Bernie Sanders, former Vice President Joseph Biden decisively won the South Carolina Democratic primary and revitalized his campaign (van Wagtendonk 2020). He ultimately won every southern primary, securing the Democratic nomination with a broad voter coalition built upon deep support from black voters (Kilgore 2020).

The general election proved just as dramatic. Though just one southern state flipped from its 2016 presidential choice, handicapper *Cook Political Report* rated six southern states as competitive in the Electoral College, and actually rated more southern states as tossups than it did in 2016 (Miller 2018). Down ballot, southern races for U.S. Senate—especially the Georgia runoffs—and House proved critical to Democrats winning unified control of Congress by thin margins.

Donald Trump's victories in most southern states also obscure a complex and changing regional electorate, albeit one that has arguably lost much of its historical distinctiveness. Divisions along racial and religious lines remain prominent among southern voters, but an emerging divide along education lines among whites is reshaping the political map. This chapter examines the 2020 southern electorate, focusing on its political tenor, key demographics, and the issue attitudes that defined voters.

STATE VOTING AND TURNOUT PATTERNS

In 2020, Joe Biden won two southern states. He claimed the fourth straight Democratic victory in Virginia, which by 2020 had arguably become a blue state. Biden also flipped Georgia from Republicans, the first Democratic win there since 1992. Neither state was mathematically necessary for Biden's Electoral College win, given his victories in non-South states. As table 1.1 shows, Biden also held Trump to single-digit wins in Florida, North Carolina, and Texas, which *Cook Political Report* all rated as tossups with Georgia. Trump scored more convincing wins in every other southern state.

The national popular vote swung 3.3 points to Biden compared to Hillary Clinton's 2016 performance, netting him 51.3 percent of votes cast. Every southern state followed this pattern to some degree. Biden gained just 0.4 percent over Clinton in Florida but improved by over 4 points in Georgia and Virginia. Trump improved his 2016 performance by 0.9 points nationally. In 2020, Trump improved his performance in every Southern state. These aggregate data cannot show, however, how much turnout changes, swing-voting, or the collapse of third party and Independent candidates each contributed to these vote shifts.

Nationally, 66.7 percent of the voting-eligible population (VEP) voted in 2020, the highest VEP turnout in a presidential election since 1900 and an 8.6 percent increase from 2016 (U.S. Election Project 2021). While VEP turnout increased in every southern state, most experienced increases below the national rate. Indeed, VEP turnout in Alabama and Arkansas increased at half the national rate or less. Only Tennessee and Texas exceeded the national turnout increase.

Table 1.1 also provides raw vote changes. Biden gained 15.4 million votes over Clinton's vote total nationally, whereas Trump bested 2016 by 11.2 million votes. Both candidates gained votes in every southern state relative to 2016—most critically in Georgia for Biden and Florida for Trump—though in half Trump gained more raw votes than Biden did. Consequently, every southern state also saw an increase in its total vote from 2016, ranging from 88,000 in Arkansas to 2.3 million in Texas.

DATA

Voter data for analyses come from the Fox News Voter Analysis (FNVA) survey, conducted jointly with the Associated Press. The FNVA sampled roughly 110,000 registered voters nationally from October 26 to November

Table 1.1 State Voting and Turnout Patterns

	US	AL	AR	FL	GA	KY	LA	MS	NC	SC	TN	TX	VA
Presidential Vote 2020, Percentage													
Joseph Biden	51.3	36.6	34.8	47.8	49.5	36.2	39.9	41.1	48.6	43.4	37.5	46.5	54.1
Donald Trump	46.8	62.0	62.4	51.1	49.3	62.1	58.5	57.6	49.9	55.1	60.7	52.1	44.0
Presidential Vote 2020, Percentage Change from 2016													
Democratic Vote	+3.3	+2.2	+1.1	+0.4	+4.2	+3.5	+1.4	+1.0	+2.4	+2.8	+2.7	+3.4	+4.4
Republican Vote	+0.9	−0.1	+1.8	+2.5	−1.1	−.04	+0.4	−0.3	+0.1	+0.2	−0.1	0	−0.4
Other	−4.1	−2.2	−3.0	−2.9	−3.1	−3.0	−1.8	−07	−2.5	−2.9	−2.7	−3.3	−3.9
Turnout, Percentage													
VEP Turnout	66.7	63.1	56.1	71.7	67.7	64.9	64.6	60.2	71.5	64.5	59.8	60.4	73
VEP Change v. 2016	+8.6	+4.4	+3.6	+6.1	+7.7	+5.4	+4.7	+6.7	+6.9	+7.6	+8.8	+9.3	+7.5
Raw Vote Change from 2016 (in thousands)													
Total Vote	+21399	+200	+88	+1589	+851	+213	+119	+103	+783	+410	+546	+2321	+478
Democratic Vote	+15431	+120	+43	+792	+596	+144	+76	+54	+495	+236	+273	+1381	+432
Republican Vote	+11239	+123	+76	+1051	+373	+124	+77	+56	+396	+230	+330	+1205	+193

Source: "2020 Presidential General Election Results," *Dave Leip's Atlas of U.S. Presidential Elections*, November 3, 2020, accessed April 23, 2021, https://uselectionatlas.org/RESULTS/; "2020 November General Election Turnout Rates," United States Elections Project, November 3, 2020, accessed April 23, 2021, http://www.electproject.org/2020g.

3, 2020 (Fox News 2020). It combined respondents from a random sample from state voter files, a sample of self-identified registered voters using a probability-based panel, and a sample of self-identified registered voters from non-probability online panels. Interviews were in English and Spanish and completed via phone or web. Responses were weighted to adjustment targets based on Census and voter file data.

Though the FNVA is not a traditional exit poll, it does provide data for every state. The National Election Pool (NEP) did conduct more traditional exit polling but only sampled voters in eight southern states with key presidential or Senate races (CNN 2020). However, given the small sample sizes in some states in the FNVA, analyses of all voter subgroups are not available due to unreliable subgroup estimates.

POLITICAL DISPOSITIONS

A century ago, the southern electorate was almost homogeneously white, heavily rural, and reliably Democratic (Black and Black 1987). Modern southern voters are far more racially diverse, more urbanized, and less Democratic than their Solid South ancestors. The next two sections of this chapter document the political and demographic characteristics of southern electorates, plus voting patterns within key voter groups.

Partisanship is a potent predictor of both American voting behavior and partisan-driven attitudes like presidential job approval or candidate trait perceptions (Lewis-Beck et. al 2008). Table 1.2 provides the partisan breakdown of FNVA respondents. In reporting partisanship, the FNVA combines Independents who lean to a party with explicit partisans. This approach has merit since partisan leaners are often as partisan in their political behavior as overt partisans (Keith et al. 1992). However, it means that the Independents reported in table 1.2 are solely the small chunk of voters who consider themselves pure Independents.

Partisan loyalties were about equally divided among voters nationally, considering the margin of error in the survey. Republicans held a 1 point identification advantage over Democrats. Five percent of voters were identified as pure Independents. For comparability, the NEP national sample, which did not combine partisan leaners with overt partisans, showed the national electorate thus: 37 percent Democrats, 36 percent Republicans, and 26 percent Independents (CNN 2020).

FNVA respondents in every southern state except Virginia were more Republican than Democratic. However, like the national numbers, the reporting protocol in the NEP depicts electorates that are more divided for the states where data are available. In Georgia, for example, whereas the FNVA shows

Table 1.2 State Electorate Characteristics

	US	AL	AR	FL	GA	KY	LA	MS	NC	SC	TN	TX	VA
Partisanship													
Democratic/Lean Dem.	47	33	35	43	45	35	39	37	44	39	34	41	49
Republican/Lean Rep.	48	63	61	51	51	61	57	60	50	57	62	54	45
Independent	5	4	4*	6	4	4	4	3	6	5	4	5	5
Trump Job Approval													
Approve	47	64	60*	48	49	61	53	58	52	56	60	50	46
Disapprove	53	36	40*	52	51	39	47	42	48	44	40	50	54
Ideology													
Conservative	38	51	47	39	42	47	46	48	42	48	51	43	36
Liberal	33	20	21	26	26	22	21	22	26	21	22	24	30
Moderate	30	28	32	35	32	31	33	30	32	30	27	33	34
Race													
Black	11	22	13*	12	29	8	26	29	19	22	13	12	16
Latino	9	1*	2*	18	3	1*	2*	0*	3	2	1*	23	4
White	74	75	82	66	64	90	69	69	75	75	84	59	73
Other	6	2	3*	4	4	2	3	1*	4	2	2	5	7
White Evangelical													
Yes	23	53	49	20	39	44	30	54	35	37	47	28	24
No	77	47	51	80	61	56	70	46	65	63	53	72	76
Community Type													
Urban	20	13	15*	23	15	11	19	9	15	7	15	26	17
Suburban	45	32	26	56	50	31	36	23	38	46	38	44	50
Small Town/Rural	35	56	59	21	35	58	45	67	48	47	47	29	30

Notes: All table entries are percentages. Biden won voters in all italicized cells. Stars indicate that vote choice estimates are not available for respondents in that cell.
Source: "Poll Results," FOX News, November 3, 2020, accessed April 23, 2021, https://www.foxnews.com/elections/2020/general-results/voter-analysis.

a majority Republican-leaning electorate, the NEP has voters identifying as 34 percent Democrats, 38 percent Republicans, and 28 percent Independents (CNN 2020).

Voters were loyal to their partisan preferences. Nationally, Biden won 95 percent of Democrats, whereas Trump won 91 percent of Republicans. Biden also won pure Independents nationwide 52–38 percent over Trump. The same pattern generally replicated in the South, with both nominees winning about 90 percent of their own party identifiers in each state, and Biden winning pure Independents in most states where estimates are available.

For most Americans, presidential approval heavily reflects party preferences (Erikson et al. 2002)—approving when the President is a co-partisan, and disapproving when not. Thus, it should not surprise that Trump's job approval numbers tracked closely with aggregate partisanship both nationally and in the South. Though Trump's national job approval was −6 points, he earned even to net positive scores in nine southern states. Voters in Georgia and Virginia both disapproved of Trump's performance and preferred Biden for president, whereas Florida voters narrowly net disapproved of Trump but still preferred him over Biden.

Ideological self-labels are an often symbolic political identity, detached from issue preferences for many but strongly predictive for others (Ellis and Stimson 2012). Nationally, conservatives enjoyed a 5-point identification plurality. Trump won conservatives 88–11 percent, whereas Biden won moderates 61–36 percent and liberals 90–9 percent. In the South, conservatives were at least a modest plurality in every state and the majority in Alabama and Tennessee. These national voting patterns also generally replicated in the region, save for Trump winning moderates in Arkansas and Kentucky.

These partisan and ideological data suggest a southern electorate that leans Republican and conservative, but that Democrats can still win in certain states with a sufficiently broad coalition. Biden's narrow Georgia win illustrates this. He won 97 percent of Democrats and just 7 percent of Republicans but carried the small bloc of pure Independents by 27 points. Likewise, Biden won 88 percent of liberals and 12 percent of conservatives but crushed Trump 65–32 percent among moderates. With a large enough Democratic base in Georgia, Biden's landslide victories in the "political center" carried the state.

RACE

Race persists as a powerful electoral divide (White and Laird 2020), especially in the South where racially polarized voting appeared stronger than it

Table 1.3 Biden Vote Share by Demographic Group

	US	AL	AR	FL	GA	KY	LA	MS	NC	SC	TN	TX	VA
Race													
Black	91	91	--	89	92	84	88	94	94	92	88	88	90
White	43	20	26	39	29	32	22	18	38	29	29	32	45
Latino	63	--	--	54	59	--	--	--	46	--	--	62	57
Gender													
Female	55	40	36	51	54	39	43	43	52	49	41	49	57
Male	46	32	33	44	44	33	36	37	45	36	33	43	50
Race x Gender													
Black female	93	95	--	92	95	89	92	95	95	94	93	90	93
Black male	87	--	--	86	87	--	81	--	93	--	--	84	--
White female	46	20	24	41	30	34	22	16	39	32	31	33	46
White male	39	20	27	35	29	30	22	20	36	27	26	31	44
Latino female	66	--	--	57	--	--	--	--	--	--	--	63	--
Latino male	59	--	--	50	--	--	--	--	--	--	--	59	--
Whites: Education X Gender													
Female college grad	59	34	--	51	45	45	36	29	55	44	40	45	59
Female noncollege grad	39	15	16	38	21	30	16	11	31	26	28	26	39
Male college grad	46	29	--	37	34	35	26	28	44	29	31	32	51
Male noncollege grad	34	15	23	33	24	27	19	14	28	25	22	29	35
Evangelical													
Yes	18	12	11	17	11	16	9	11	14	9	12	18	18
No	58	52	50	53	58	51	52	41	58	53	58	58	62
Place Type													
Urban	65	59	--	55	68	61	67	61	64	54	67	58	63
Suburban	54	42	46	48	55	46	37	39	55	44	40	50	61
Rural	38	28	27	41	33	26	31	38	39	41	26	31	39

Notes: All table entries are percentages. Biden won voters in all italicized cells. Stars indicate that vote choice estimates are not available for respondents in that cell.
Source: "Poll Results," FOX News, November 3, 2020, accessed April 23, 2021, https://www.foxnews.com/elections/2020/general-results/voter-analysis.

was nationally in this analysis. As shown in table 1.2, non-Hispanic whites constituted 74 percent of voters nationally.[1] Trump carried them 55–43 percent, as table 1.3 shows, down from 57-37 percent in 2016 (CNN 2020). Whites were the majority of voters in every southern state. Six southern states had whiter electorates than the national average, led by Kentucky at 90 percent white. Texas, where whites were only 59 percent of voters, had the most racially diverse electorate. Like whites nationally, Trump won whites in every southern state, often by landslides. His best performance among whites came in Mississippi and his worst in Virginia, where he earned 81 and 52 percent, respectively.

Black voters were 11 percent of the national electorate and gave Biden 91 percent of their vote. In every southern state except Kentucky, they were a greater share of voters than they were nationally, peaking at 29 percent in Georgia and Mississippi—the latter more comfortably Republican thanks to stronger racially polarized voting. Biden hovered around 90 percent of the black vote across the South, though inferring too much from these cross-state differences is risky, given the larger margins of error that accompany estimates of voter subgroups.

Latinos were 9 percent of the national electorate. Though the Latino population is growing throughout the South (Krogs 2020), they were a low single-digit share of voters in all southern states except Florida and Texas. Indeed, in six states, their numbers were too small to derive reliable estimates of how Latinos voted. Biden won 63 percent of the Latino vote nationwide, and appeared to win them in all southern states where estimates were available except North Carolina where their 3 percent share of voters makes any estimate of their vote choice tenuous at best. Biden's support in the remaining states hovered within roughly a 10-point interval around 60 percent.

GENDER AND ITS INTERSECTIONS

Since the 1980s, Democrats have generally performed better with female than male voters (Winfrey 2018). This gender gap persisted in 2020. As table 1.3 shows, Biden won women nationally 55–44 percent over Trump, whereas Trump won men 52–46 percent. The South deviated somewhat from this pattern. Biden only won women in four southern states—Florida, Georgia, North Carolina, and Virginia—and tied Trump among women in South Carolina and Texas. He lost women in the remaining six states. Conversely, Biden won male voters 50–48 percent in Virginia but lost them in the other twelve states.

Biden performed 7 points better with white women than white men, losing them 52–46 percent and 59–39 percent, respectively. The strength and apparent direction of the gender gap varied more among white voters in the South, though. In every southern state where Biden earned a greater share of white female than male voters, the gender gap was smaller than it was nationally. Further, there was no gender gap evident among whites in Alabama and Louisiana, and the gap actually appeared reversed in Arkansas and Mississippi where Biden earned greater support among white men than white women. Given the margin of error in the state samples, it would be unwarranted to draw strong conclusions from these modest sex differences. However, the consistency of the pattern at least suggests that the gender gap was weaker among white southern voters than it was among whites nationally due to unknown factors.

Nationally, the gender gap persisted across races. Biden won black and Latino voters of both sexes, but with a similar intra-race gender gap as among whites. He did 6 points better with black women than black men, and 7 points better with Hispanic women than Hispanic men. This gender pattern persisted across southern states for minority voters. Given the small number of minority respondents in some state samples, reliable estimates of presidential vote by sex among black and Latino respondents are not available in all states. However, where data are available, Biden consistently performed modestly better among minority women than he did among minority men.

Gender also exhibits a powerful interaction with education, but primarily among whites (Montlake 2020). Specifically, whites with college degrees, especially women, have been becoming more Democratic in their voting behavior, whereas whites without college degrees, especially men, have been trending Republican. The education partisan gap among white voters has been evolving since 2000, but accelerated from 2016 onward (Suls 2016).

Nationally, Trump won voters without college degree, 51–47 percent, and Biden won college graduates, 57–41 percent. Among whites, Trump won noncollege voters 62–37 percent, whereas Biden won college graduates 52–46 percent. There was no education divide among minority voters. Biden won both non-whites without degrees and those with degrees by identical 73–25 percent margins. Isolating whites, as table 1.3 shows, Biden won female college graduates 59–39 percent, whereas Trump won male college graduates 52–46 percent, female noncollege graduates 60–39 percent, and male noncollege graduates 65–35 percent.

Where estimates are available, the education divide among whites largely replicated to the South. Biden performed best among southern white women with college degrees, winning them in Florida, North Carolina, and Virginia. His next best bloc was white men with college degrees, which he won only in Virginia. Among noncollege whites in the South, however, the gender gap that appeared nationally was not as consistently evident, and in five states the data suggest that Biden fared marginally better among noncollege white men than noncollege white women. It is unclear from these data why southern states tended to exhibit a smaller gender gap among noncollege whites than appeared nationally.

RELIGION

White Evangelicals have become overwhelmingly Republican (Wald and Calhoun-Brown 2018). Trump won them 81–18 percent, effectively unmoved from his 80–16 victory in this demographic in 2016 (CNN 2020). Across the South, Trump beat Biden among these voters, earning between 81 to 91 percent of their vote depending upon the state. Nationally, Biden won voters who are not white Evangelicals 58–40 percent. He also won them in every southern state except Mississippi, where he lost them 41–56 percent.

Critically, the FNVA does not disaggregate minority voters from non-Evangelical whites in its calculations. However, the NEP does. Nationwide, Biden won white non-Evangelical voters 56–43 percent in the NEP. He also won them in four southern states: 52–46 percent in Georgia, 54–44 percent in Kentucky, 51–48 in North Carolina, and 68–29 in Virginia. Biden and Trump tied 49–49 with these voters in Texas, whereas Trump won them 50–48 in Alabama and 54–45 in South Carolina. Evangelical identity was not included in the Florida exit poll, and NEP data are not available for the remaining southern states.

PLACE TYPE

Suburbia has become the key battleground territory in American elections (Aldrich et al. 2020). In 2020, the southern counties that Biden flipped from Trump were mostly more populous, and either entirely or heavily suburban: in Florida, Duval, Pinellas, and Seminole; in North Carolina, New Hanover; in Texas, Hays, Tarrant, and Williamson; and in Virginia, Chesapeake, Chesterfield, James City, Lynchburg, Stafford, and Virginia Beach. Conversely, Trump flipped some smaller population counties in 2020 and his margins improved in many rural communities where he already won landslide margins in 2016, but these changes were less dramatic than the suburban blue shift.

Even though Trump still won many southern suburban counties, some of the heaviest swings against him in 2020 came in those communities. For example, his vote margin shrunk 10 points in DeSoto County, Mississippi in the Memphis suburbs even as the statewide vote remained fairly similar to 2016. Other counties that Trump still won also saw his margin decline by double digits: Shelby County, Alabama, in suburban Birmingham; Rutherford County, Tennessee, in suburban Nashville; and Collin, Denton, Ellis, Kaufman, and Rockwall counties in suburban Dallas, Texas.

Suburban voters proved competitive. Nationally, Biden won them 54–44 percent over Trump. Likewise, he won suburban voters in Georgia, North Carolina, Texas, and Virginia. Trump managed single-digit wins among suburbanites in the remaining southern states except for Alabama, Louisiana, Mississippi, and Tennessee, where he won them more comfortably.

Biden won voters in urban communities both nationally and in every southern state double-digit margins. His weakest performances in that demographic were 11 point wins in Florida and South Carolina, where many urban communities—the Cuban-heavy sections of Miami-Dade County in Florida, for example—are still competitive to leaning Republican (Sessin 2020). Conversely, Biden lost rural voters nationally and in every southern state, breaking 40 percent only in Florida and South Carolina.

Critically, geography is often a visual representation of demographics (Hopkins 2017). For example, urban central cities often have larger nonwhite populations, so their typical Democratic lean may be more a function of race than urbanization, per se. Similarly, compared to rural communities, suburbs tend to attract younger, more educated, and more racially diverse populations. Both in the South and nationwide, the nature of this geographic realignment and its exact drivers merit further study.

THE COVID-19 PANDEMIC

The first COVID-19 case was diagnosed in the United States in late January 2020 (AJMC Staff 2021). As cases spread, states started enacting public health restrictions, such as business and school closures or mask mandates. Despite the more professional actions that his administration took, Trump downplayed the seriousness of COVID-19 in his often contradictory public comments. At times, Trump labeled concern about the virus a "hoax" (Holan 2020). On other occasions, President Trump commented that the disease would disappear or was under control, while also telling media privately that he was intentionally downplaying its seriousness (Holmes 2020). During the earlier phases of the pandemic, Trump promoted unproven and potentially dangerous treatments (Funke 2020; Solender 2020). Later, Trump mocked mask-wearing and mask requirements, while also calling mask-wearing "patriotic" (Cathey 2020).

Trump also attacked governors, especially Democrats, for the state-level COVID restrictions that they instituted (Montanaro 2020). Indeed, even as the virus was grabbing its early foothold, Trump called for ending business and school closures as mitigation measures (Breuninger 2020). In early October, Trump and the First Lady tested positive for COVID, leading to his hospitalization and quarantine (Gringlas and Sprunt 2020). By Election Day, over 9.4 million Americans had been diagnosed with COVID and nearly a quarter-million had died (Higgins-Dunn 2020).

The FNVA asked respondents to select "the most important issue facing the country" from a list of nine options. COVID and the economy dominated the list nationally: 41 percent chose COVID and 28 percent the economy. No other issues garnered double-digit endorsement as a top issue. Biden won "COVID voters" 73–25 percent, and Trump won "economy voters" 82–16 percent. This polarization may simply reflect voters echoing the issue priorities of their preferred candidates rather than voters arriving at these priorities through independent reasoning. In the South, this pattern consistently replicated, with COVID and the economy dominating voter priorities, and Biden and Trump, respectively, winning the two blocs by landslides.

Table 1.4 reports attitudes on COVID-related items. One item that demonstrated substantial partisan polarization measured the relative importance of the government's pandemic response to the presidential vote. Specifically, Democratic voters placed greater priority on that issue than Republican voters. Biden won voters who indicated that "the federal government response to the coronavirus" pandemic was "the single most important factor" to their vote by 78–21 percent nationally and by landslide margins in every southern state. Rather than totally dismissing the government's response, Republican-leaning voters tended to say that this was "an important factor, but not the most important." Trump won that group 57–41 percent nationally, and received 60–90 percent of their votes across the South. Just 16 percent of voters nationwide indicated that the government's pandemic response was either "a minor factor" or "not a factor" to them, though these voters backed Trump heavily.

Voters nationally disapproved of Trump's handling of the pandemic 55–45 percent. Given their more Republican-leaning nature, southern voters were generally more approving. The only southern states where voters gave Trump net disapproval on COVID were Florida, Georgia, North Carolina, Texas, and Virginia, though wherein most voters were still rather evenly divided.

Partisanship also likely drove responses to perceived candidate ability to handle the pandemic. Voters nationally gave Biden the advantage on this issue, though southern voters gave Trump at least a marginal advantage in every state but North Carolina, Texas, and Virginia. Across the national and state samples, the two candidates won nearly 100 percent of the voters who

Table 1.4 Attitudes about COVID-19 Pandemic

	US	AL	AR	FL	GA	KY	LA	MS	NC	SC	TN	TX	VA
Importance of "the federal government response to the coronavirus" to presidential vote													
Most important factor	39	33	34	42	39	32	34	36	39	35	32	39	40
One important factor	45	47	47	44	43	48	46	43	44	46	49	44	45
Minor factor	11	14	13	9	12	12	15	14	11	13	14	12	11
Not a factor	5	6	7	5	6	8	5	7	5	6	6	5	5
Approval of Trump's handling of the coronavirus pandemic													
Approve	45	61	59	48	47	58	56	56	47	53	59	49	43
Disapprove	55	39	41	52	53	42	44	44	53	47	41	51	57
Biden or Trump better able to handle the coronavirus pandemic													
Biden	47	34	44	43	45	36	35	37	47	42	38	48	54
Trump	38	56	49	44	47	49	51	52	40	44	49	41	34
Both equally	6	3	3	6	3	4	4	6	6	6	6	5	8
Neither	8	7	4	7	4	10	10	5	7	8	7	6	4
Coronavirus impact: lost job or income; missed out on a major event; close friend or family member died													
Yes	68	64	57	69	74	66	68	69	63	62	63	71	68
No	32	36	43	31	26	34	32	31	37	38	37	29	32
Do you think the coronavirus in the United States is:													
At least somewhat under control	49	60	55	53	53	55	60	57	51	56	57	55	48
Not at all under control	51	40	45	47	47	45	40	43	49	44	43	45	52
Which should be the federal government's higher priority?													
Limiting the spread, even if it damages the economy	60	49	49	58	58	51	50	59	58	49	54	57	65
Limiting additional damage to the economy, even if it increases spread	40	51	51	42	42	49	50	41	42	51	46	43	35
Requiring people to wear masks when around other people outside of their homes													
Favor strongly/somewhat	77	77*	73	77	74	71	65	70	78	69	78	78	79
Oppose strongly/somewhat	23	23*	27	23	26	29	35	30	22	31	22	22	21

Notes: All table entries are percentages. Biden won voters in all italicized cells. Stars indicate that vote choice estimates are not available for respondents in that cell.
Source: "Poll Results," FOX News, November 3, 2020, accessed April 23, 2021, https://www.foxnews.com/elections/2020/general-results/voter-analysis.

indicated that they would better manage the pandemic. Nationally, 6 percent of voters selected 'both equally" and 8 percent selected "neither," with Trump winning the two groups 82–15 percent and 70–21 percent, respectively. State-level estimates were not available for both and neither groups.

The FNVA asked whether COVID had affected respondents in any of three ways: "you or someone in your household lost a job or income," "you missed out on a major event, like a wedding or funeral," and "a close friend or family member died from the coronavirus." Nationwide, 38 percent of respondents indicated an economic impact, 52 percent indicated missing events, and 19 percent indicated a death in their social networks. Respectively, Biden won the three groups 55–43 percent, 55–44 percent, and 62–37 percent. Trump won each of the three groups not indicating an impact by 2–5 points.

While state-level COVID impacts are available in the FNVA, the smaller state sample sizes mean that estimating vote choice by type of COVID impact is frequently not possible at the state level. Fortunately, the survey includes a composite measure of all three impacts. In the national data, 68 percent of respondents indicated at least one of the three impacts, and Biden won them 55–43 percent. Trump won respondents indicating that COVID had not affected them in any way 56–43 percent.

In the South, the majority of respondents in each state sample indicated a COVID impact, ranging from 57 percent in Arkansas to 74 percent in Georgia. However, Biden only won impacted voters in Florida, Georgia, Mississippi, North Carolina, and Virginia, by margins ranging from roughly 5 to 10 points. Trump won unimpacted voters in all states except Virginia, earning up to 70 percent of their vote. If impact reports are truthful, then, especially in the South COVID impacts did not necessarily translate into Biden support, whereas unimpacted voters were far more unified in their support for Trump.

Respondents were fairly divided on whether COVID was "at least somewhat under control" or "not at all under control." Further, these responses were strongly polarized by party. Nationally, 49 percent of respondents said that COVID was under control to some degree, and they supported Trump 80–18 percent. Conversely, 51 percent said that COVID was not under control, and they supported Biden 83–15 percent. In the South, the majority of voters in every state except Virginia said that COVID was at least somewhat under control, typically margins of 5 to 20 points. Just like nationally, Trump won landslides among voters saying that COVID was under some control, and Biden won landslides among voters saying the opposite.

The FNVA also asked respondents about government policy priorities regarding COVID. Nationally, 60 percent indicated that "limiting the spread of the coronavirus, even if it damages the economy" should be the priority. Biden won those voters 77–21 percent. The remaining 40 percent indicated that "limiting additional damage to the economy, even if it increases the spread of the coronavirus" should be the priority. Trump won them 86–12 percent.

Among southern voters, the more conservative position of limiting economic damage was the preferred priority by identical 51–49 margins among voters in just three states: Alabama, Arkansas, and South Carolina. Louisiana voters were evenly divided, and voters in the remaining states leaned toward limiting spread. Only in Virginia were voters more likely than voters nationally to endorse limiting spread as their preferred priority. Across southern states, Biden consistently won voters who prioritized limiting spread, garnering 60–80 of their vote depending on the state. Trump consistently won voters who prioritized limiting economic impact, winning 80–95 percent of these voters depending on the state. Again, on this question, Trump voters were more consistent in matching their COVID attitudes with their presidential voting than were Biden voters.

Lastly, voters were asked about their opinion on masks. Strong majorities both nationally and in the South favored "requiring people to wear masks when around other people outside of their home." Seventy-seven percent of voters nationwide took that position, as did two-thirds or more of voters in every southern state. Nationally, Biden won voters who favored a mask mandate 63–36 percent, though he lost them to Trump 51–46 percent in Alabama. Mandate opponents were more politically unified, choosing Trump nationally 87–10 percent and favoring him by landslides across the South.

TURNOUT AND ELECTION SECURITY

With the COVID pandemic raging in 2020, many Americans opted to vote by mail rather than risking exposure by voting in person (Isaacs-Thomas 2020). Many states also modified their election procedures to accommodate the increased demand for mail voting (Kamarck et al. 2020). Trump responded to this, like he did in 2016, by declaring that Democrats were "rigging" the election against him and insinuating that he would only accept the election results if he wins (Panetta 2020). He continued to attack the integrity of the electoral process, calling mail voting inaccurate and fraudulent even while voting by mail himself, suggesting that mail ballots simply not be counted, and suggesting that the election be delayed until in-person voting was safe (Niedzwiadek 2020; Parks 2020; Sprunt 2020; Zucker 2020).

Table 1.5 details turnout patterns and attitudes about the election process. Given Trump's attack on voting, Republicans disproportionately voted in person and Democrats by mail (Garrison 2020). Trump won Election Day and early in-person voters 65–33 percent and 51–47 percent, respectively. More votes were cast by mail than either in-person format, and Biden won

Table 1.5 Attitudes about Voting

	US	AL	AR	FL	GA	KY	LA	MS	NC	SC	TN	TX	VA
Vote type													
Election Day	29	83	28	21	23	24	53	83	18	59	24	18	34
Early in-person	30	0	60	39	48	44	38	0	59	0	66	68	42
Mail	41	17	11*	41	29	32	9	17	23	41	10	13	24
Voted in 2016													
Yes	85	86	80	83	82	85	85	85	83	86	83	81	86
No	15	14	20	17	18	15	15	15	17	14	17	19	14
Confidence that votes will be counted accurately													
Very/Somewhat	69	59	63	71	66	65	63	59	68	65	65	67	66
Not too/Not at all	31	41	37	29	34	35	37	41	32	35	35	33	34
Confidence that people who are eligible will be allowed to vote													
Very/Somewhat	84	86	84	87	84	88	85	87	86	86	88	85	82
Not too/Not at all	16	14	16	13	16	12	15	13	14	14	12	15	18
Confidence that people who are NOT eligible will NOT be allowed to vote													
Very/Somewhat	64	56	58	65	63	61	58	58	64	58	60	61	63
Not too/Not at all	36	44	42	35	37	39	42	42	36	42	40	39	37
Concern that interference by foreign governments might affect election													
Very/Somewhat	69	65	60*	70	69	57	61	65	71	68	63	67	69
Not too/Not at all	31	35	40*	30	31	43	39	35*	29	32	37	33	31

Notes: All table entries are percentages. Biden won voters in all italicized cells. Stars indicate that vote choice estimates are not available for respondents in that cell.
Source: "Poll Results," FOX News, November 3, 2020, accessed April 23, 2021, https://www.foxnews.com/elections/2020/general-results/voter-analysis.

these voters 66–32 percent. This pattern replicated across the South, save for Biden also winning early in-person voters in Virginia. Neither Mississippi nor South Carolina offers early in-person voting (National Conference of State Legislators 2020).

Conventional wisdom holds that higher turnout favors Democrats, though that is a popular fallacy without strong empirical backing (Shaw and Petrocik 2020). Nationally, Biden won both those who had previously voted in 2016 by 50–48 percent, and those who had not by 56–42 percent. In the South, Biden lost 2016 voters in every state but Virginia, but won new voters in seven states. Even where he lost new voters, though, Biden still tended to perform better with them. In Alabama, for example, Biden lost 2016 voters 63–36 percent but lost new voters 57–41 percent. The FNVA does not give demographic profiles of new voters, so it is impossible to know how they differed from those who had voted in 2016.

The FNVA asked four items about election security. Both nationally and in the South, voters on balance expressed confidence in election integrity: net confidence that votes would be counted accurately, that people who are eligible to vote would be allowed to vote, and that those ineligible to vote would not be allowed to vote. However, perhaps given controversies related to Russian interference in 2016, majorities expressed concern that foreign government interference might affect the election outcome (Hosenball 2020). It appears that some voters may have adopted attitudes about election integrity that fit partisan narratives, perhaps responding to Trump's attacks on election integrity. Biden tended to perform better with voters who were confident in the vote count and that ineligible voters would not be voting, but who were also concerned that legitimate voters would not be able to vote and that foreign interference would occur.

VARIOUS CAMPAIGN ISSUES

Table 1.6 presents attitudes on various other campaign issues. The survey included two key economic items. With the country in recession thanks to the pandemic (Elving 2020), respondents nationwide rated the condition of the economy negatively 57–43 percent. Voters in half of southern states rated the economy net positively, typically by narrow margins, whereas voters in the other half rated the economy negatively. Trump won voters with positive economic perceptions and Biden won those with negative perceptions, likely reflecting the heavy role that partisanship has in shaping sociotropic economic evaluations (Hart 2016).

Most voters held less pessimistic attitudes about their pocketbook economics than they did national conditions. Roughly 70 percent both nationally

Table 1.6 Attitudes on Various Campaign Issues

	US	AL	AR	FL	GA	KY	LA	MS	NC	SC	TN	TX	VA
Condition of the national economy													
Excellent/Good	43	55	51	46	45	51	46	51	44	52	52	48	42
Not so good/Poor	57	45	49	54	55	49	54	49	56	48	48	52	58
Family financial situation													
Getting ahead	13	14*	8*	12	14	14	14*	10*	13	14	12*	15	15*
Holding steady	69	67	71*	69	68	70	66	65	68	72	69	67	66
Falling behind	18	19*	21*	19	17	16	20*	25*	19	14	19*	18	19
Affordable Care Act													
Repeal entirely or partly	49	60	60*	50	52	57	58	55	52	57	62	56	46
Leave as is/Expand	51	40	40*	50	48	43	42	45	48	43	38	44	54
Changing the health care system so that any American can buy into a government-run healthcare plan if they want													
Strongly/Somewhat favor	70	62	65*	72	63	64	70	66	70	62	64	66	71
Strongly/Somewhat oppose	30	38	35*	28	37	36	30	34	30	38	36	34	29
Concerned about effects of climate change													
Very/somewhat	70	62	59*	73	67	58	59	60	71	62	62	66	71
Not too/Not at all	30	38	41*	27	33	42	41	40	29	38	38	34	29
Abortion should be:													
Legal in all/most cases	60	40	37*	60	53	42	42	41	54	53	44	55	61
Illegal in all/most cases	40	60	63*	40	47	58	58	59	46	47	56	45	39
Roe v. Wade													
Leave it as is	70	57	56*	71	60	62	56	53	65	66	62	66	71
Overturn it	30	43	44*	29	40	38	44	47*	35	34	38	34	29
How serious a problem is racism in policing?													
Very/somewhat serious	72	64	64	72	73	64	72	67	70	66	66	71	73
Not too/Not at all serious	28	36	36	38	27	36	28	33	30	34	34	29	27
The criminal justice system needs…													
Complete/Major changes	67	63	67*	68	72	61	72	68	67	68	67	67	71
Minor/No changes	33	37	33*	32	38	39	28	32	33	32	33	33	29

Notes: All table entries are percentages. Biden won voters in all italicized cells. Stars indicate that vote choice estimates are not available for respondents in that cell.
Source: "Poll Results," FOX News, November 3, 2020, accessed April 23, 2021, https://www.foxnews.com/elections/2020/general-results/voter-analysis.

and in the South reported that their family financial situations were "holding steady." Nationwide, these voters preferred Biden 51–48 percent, though in the South, he won them only in Georgia and Virginia. Trump won them in the remaining states by margins ranging from 3 to 31 points. Trump consistently won voters who felt that their families were "getting ahead" financially, typically with 65–70 percent of their vote. Conversely, Biden won voters who felt that their families were "falling behind," taking 65–70 percent in this bloc nationally and across the South in all states where estimates were available—except Kentucky, where Trump won these voters by 7 points.

Health care was the third most important issue to voters nationally. Nine percent identified it as "the most important issue facing the country." Those voters supported Biden 66–32 percent nationally. This issue arose in different ways throughout the campaign. Trump continued to promote repealing the Affordable Care Act (ACA), even though Republicans had failed to do so legislatively, and his administration backed a Supreme Court challenge that could have invalidated the law, removing health coverage from nearly 25 million Americans (Stolberg 2020).

Americans favored either expanding the ACA or leaving it alone by 51–49 percent. Biden won those voters 87–12 percent, but and lost those favoring repeal to any degree 85–13 percent, suggesting strong party polarization around ACA attitudes. Southern voters tended to favor repeal, except in Florida, where voters were evenly divided on the issue, and Virginia. Curiously, over 1.1 million persons gained health insurance coverage through the Medicaid expansion provision of the ACA in Arkansas, Kentucky, and Louisiana (Kaiser Family Foundation 2019), yet those states were among the most supportive of repeal.

Progressives also pushed to expand health coverage through the Medicare for All (MFA) proposal, pressuring Biden unsuccessfully to move left on the issue (Higgins 2020). Americans favored "changing the health care system so that any American can buy into a government-run health care plan if they want to" by a 70–30 percent margin. Majorities in every southern state also favored that position. While this survey item does not perfectly capture MFA, the policy stated therein is arguably more liberal than the ACA, which is a "public option" for insurance. Given response patterns, some indeterminable portion of voters both nationally and in the South favored both repealing the ACA and creating a new health care policy to its political left. Except in Alabama, Biden consistently won voters who supported the public option statement, but lost voters opposed.

Climate change was a key issue in the Democratic primary, with candidates favoring aggressive action (Hood 2020). In contrast, Trump had called climate change a "hoax," withdrew from the Paris Climate Agreement, and championed fossil fuels (Giles and Song 2020). Only 4 percent of national respondents chose climate change as their top issue, and they supported Biden 86–11 percent. Despite the small number prioritizing the issue, 70 percent of respondents nationally and at least 58 percent in every southern state were somewhat or very concerned about the effects of climate change. Biden won these voters consistently, taking 55–70 percent of their vote nationally and across states. Voters who were not concerned about climate change generally voted Trump by 90 percent or more.

Abortion featured prominently in the campaign in the context of Supreme Court nominations, and whether the Court would overturn *Roe v. Wade*, the decision that established abortion rights (Crary 2020). Just 3 percent of voters nationally chose abortion as their top issue, and they voted for Trump 89–9 percent. Sixty percent of American voters indicated that abortion should be legal in all or most cases, whereas 40 percent said illegal. These groups respectively voted for Biden 71–27 percent and Trump 79–20 percent. Southern voters were more divided in their abortion attitudes. Majorities in six states leaned toward "legal" responses, and majorities in six leaned toward "illegal." Biden also consistently won southern voters saying legal, whereas Trump consistently won those saying illegal.

Importantly, most voters were not absolutist about abortion. Only 25 percent of voters nationwide said that abortion should always be legal, while 12 percent said it should always be illegal. The remaining 64 percent favored abortion rights under at least some undefined circumstances. Thus, it is equally accurate to say that 88 percent of American voters favored abortion rights in some form and that 75 percent favored at least some restrictions on the procedure.

This pattern replicated in the South, where majorities of voters in every state could be said to both favor the basic right to abortion and favor restrictions on it. Virginia and Texas were the most "pro-choice" states, taking the most extreme attitudes as an indicator, as roughly a quarter of voters in each favored no restrictions on abortion rights, whereas Alabama and Lousiaina were the most "pro-life" with slightly over 20 percent of voters in each always opposing abortion rights.

Most voters nationally and in the South also favored leaving *Roe v. Wade* "as it is" rather than overturning it. Seventy percent of voters nationally supported maintaining precedent on this matter, though support for that position was typically lower in the South. Support for overturning *Roe* was highest in Mississippi, where voters on balance still favored the ruling by 6 points. Biden tended to win voters who favored *Roe*, except in Mississippi where Trump won them 50–48 percent, whereas Trump consistently won voters who supported overturning it.

Criminal justice issues also played heavily in the campaign. In the aftermath of police killings of numerous African Americans, including Breonna

Taylor and George Floyd, protests aligned with the Black Lives Matter movement occurred in numerous cities (Altman 2020). Relatively few voters chose issues related to these events as their top issues, though—just 4 percent nationally selected law enforcement and 7 percent racism. These two groups were highly polarized. Voters prioritizing law enforcement voted Trump 86–11 percent and those prioritizing racism voted Biden 79–19 percent.

Strong majorities across surveys felt that racism is a serious problem in policing. Even in the most conservative southern states, roughly two-thirds of respondents identified racism as a problem. These voters generally supported Biden with 60–70 percent of their vote, whereas those who did not believe racism a problem in policing typically voted Trump by over 90 percent.

Similarly, large majorities across surveys expressed support for complete or major changes to the criminal justice system. Support for this position never fell below 61 percent in the South. This item proved less polarizing in how it mapped onto vote choice, however. While Biden generally won voters who favored reform, he narrowly lost them in Louisiana and Mississippi, and struggled to earn above 60 percent of these voters in southern states. Conversely, Trump consistently won voters who opposed substantial criminal justice reform, typically with over 70 percent of their vote across states.

WITHER SOUTHERN DISTINCTIVENESS?

Undoubtedly, the South in its most distinct historical form—conservative white Democratic domination built on the de jure subjugation of minority citizens—is long gone. The South now generally resembles the political, economic, and social trends that shape larger American life. For scholars of southern politics, finding ways in which the region remains politically distinct seems an increasingly challenging task.

Southern politics in 2020 cannot be homogenized in one statement, though. By many measures reported here, Virginia seems somewhat left of center in national politics. Other states—Florida, Georgia, North Carolina, and Texas—have credible status as competitive to swing states, each with its own unique demographic composites and trends that define them politically. South Carolina is rapidly growing but not obviously trending leftward. The remaining states in the region—Alabama, Arkansas, Kentucky, Louisiana, Mississippi, and Tennessee—seem politically stable, as defined as ever by the political divide between whites and blacks, plus the political muscle of white Evangelicals.

Though the South seems more Americanized today, there may still be ways in which it remains somewhat distinctive. Given that southern electorates are generally more Republican than the national average but not that substantially more conservative on issue attitudes, is there a stronger mismatch between partisanship and issues in the region than there is nationally that might matter in the future in some way? Racially polarized voting in this analysis seems stronger in the South than the non-South. White Evangelicals are more numerous in the South and may exercise their political power there in unique ways. The strong population and economic growth in the region also introduce a different dynamic than in states with more stagnant populations and economies. All of these trends merit study.

There are also important trends occurring in southern states, even ones that in aggregate seem stable politically. Latino and Asian populations are growing across the region. Suburban communities, with their stronger presence of college-educated whites, are trending Democratic, whereas rural communities are trending Republican. White Evangelicals are more Republican-leaning than ever. These trends, and how they play out mathematically with the demographic profiles of each southern state, will define politics in the region going forward.

NOTE

1. The 2020 NEP exit poll reported that non-Hispanic whites were 67 percent of voters. It is impossible to discern the source of that discrepancy with the FNVA survey, specifically whether it stems from random sampling error or a systematic difference with sampling, weighting, or some other methodological source.

REFERENCES

Aldrich, John, Jamie L. Carson, Brad T. Gomez, and David Rohde. *Change and Continuity in the 2016 and 2018 Elections*. Thousand Oaks: Sage, 2020.
Altman, Alex. "Why The Killing of George Floyd Sparked an American Uprising." *Time*, June 4, 2020. https://time.com/5847967/george-floyd-protests-trump/.AJMC Staff. "A Timeline of COVID-19 Developments in 2020." *American Journal of Managed Care*, January 1, 2021. https://www.ajmc.com/view/a-timeline-of-covid 19-developments-in-2020.
Black, Earl, and Merle Black. *Politics and Society in the South*. Cambridge: Harvard University Press, 1987.
Breuninger, Kevin. "Trump Wants 'Packed Churches' and Economy Open Again on Easter Despite the Deadly Threat of Coronavirus." *CNBC*, March 24, 2020. https://www.cnbc.com/2020/03/24/coronavirus-response-trump-wants-to-reopen-us-economy-by-easter.html.
Cathey, Libby. "Trump, Downplaying Virus, Has Mocked Wearing Masks for Months," *ABC News*, October 2, 2020. https://abcnews.go.com/Politics/trump-downplaying-virus-mocked-wearing-masks-months/story?id=73392694.

CNN. "Exit Polls: 2016 National Results." Accessed April 1, 2021. https://www.cnn.com/election/2016/results/exit-polls.

CNN. "Exit Polls: 2020 Georgia Results." Accessed April 1, 2021. https://www.cnn.com/election/2020/exit-polls/president/georgia.

CNN. "Exit Polls: 2020 National Results." Accessed April 1, 2021. https://www.cnn.com/election/2020/exit-polls/president/national-results.

Crary, David. "Ginsburg's Death Puts *Roe v. Wade* on the Ballot in November." *Associated Press*, September 20, 2020. https://apnews.com/article/virus-outbreak-ruth-bader-ginsburg-abortion-us-supreme-court-courts-577f2ad123b356b47c801525ea4688be.

Ellis, Christopher, and James A. Stimson. *Ideology in America*. New York: Cambridge University Press, 2012.

Elving, Ron. "Can This President Be Reelected In An Economy This Bad?." *NPR*, May 1, 2020. https://www.npr.org/2020/05/01/848318982/can-this-president-be-reelected-in-an-economy-this-bad.

Erikson, Robert S., Michael B. MacKuen, and James A. Stimson. *The Macropolity*. Cambridge: Cambridge University Press, 2002.

Fox News. "Fox News 2020 Voter Analysis Methodology Statement." Accessed April 1, 2021. https://www.foxnews.com/politics/fox-news-2020-voter-analysis-methodology-statement.

Fox News, "Poll Results: Georgia." Accessed April 1, 2021. https://www.foxnews.com/elections/2020/general-results/voter-analysis?state=GA.

Funke, Daniel. "In Context: What Donald Trump Said About Disinfectant, Sun and Coronavirus." *PolitiFact*, April 24, 2020. https://www.politifact.com/article/2020/apr/24/context-what-donald-trump-said-about-disinfectant-/.

Garrison, Joey. "Biden Voters Twice as Likely Than Trump Supporters to Vote by Mail in November, Survey Finds." *USA Today*, August 18, 2020. https://www.usatoday.com/story/news/politics/elections/2020/08/18/election-2020-biden-voters-twice-likely-vote-mail-survey-finds/3394795001/.

Giles, Christopher, and Wanyuan Song. "US Election 2020: What Is Trump's Record on the Environment?" *BBC News*, October 12, 2020. https://www.bbc.com/news/election-us-2020-54103861.

Gringlas, Sam, and Barbara Sprunt. "Timeline: What We Know of President Trump's COVID-19 Diagnosis, Treatment." *NPR*, October 5, 2020. https://www.npr.org/sections/latest-updates-trump-covid-19-results/2020/10/03/919898777/timeline-what-we-know-of-president-trumps-covid-19-diagnosis.

Hart, Austin. *Economic Voting: A Campaign-Centered Theory*. Cambridge: Cambridge University Press, 2016.

Higgins, Tucker. "Biden Suggests He Would Veto 'Medicare for All' Over Its Price Tag." *CNBC*, March 10, 2020. https://www.cnbc.com/2020/03/10/biden-says-he-wouldd-veto-medicare-for-all-as-coronavirus-focuses-attention-on-health.html.

Higgins-Dunn, Noah. "U.S. Reports Second-Highest Daily Number of Covid Cases on Election Day as Scientists Warn of a Dangerous Winter." *CNBC*, November 4, 2020. https://www.cnbc.com/2020/11/04/us-reports-second-highest-daily-n

umber-of-covid-cases-on-election-day-as-scientists-warn-of-a-dangerous-winter.html.

Holan, Angie Drobnic. "Ask PolitiFact: Are You Sure Donald Trump Didn't Call the Coronavirus a Hoax?" *PolitiFact*, October 8, 2020. https://www.politifact.com/article/2020/oct/08/ask-politifact-are-you-sure-donald-trump-didnt-cal/.

Holmes, Oliver. "What Donald Trump Has Said About Covid-19—A Recap." *The Guardian*, October 2, 2020. https://www.theguardian.com/us-news/2020/oct/02/what-donald-trump-has-said-about-covid-19-a-recap.

Hood, Grace. "What Climate Change Issues Mean To Democratic Primary Voters." *NPR*, February 27, 2020. https://www.npr.org/2020/02/27/809884853/what-climate-change-issues-mean-to-democratic-primary-voters.

Hopkins, David A. *Red Fighting Blue: How Geography and Electoral Rules Polarize American Politics*. Cambridge: Cambridge University Press, 2017.

Hosenball, Mark. "Factbox: Key Findings from Senate Inquiry into Russian Interference in 2016 U.S. Election." *Reuters*, August 18, 2020. https://www.reuters.com/article/us-usa-trump-russia-senate-findings-fact-idUSKCN25E2OY.

Isaacs-Thomas, Isabella. "How Risky Is Voting In Person? Here's How to Navigate Your Options During the Pandemic." *PBS*, October 13, 2020. https://www.pbs.org/newshour/health/how-risky-is-voting-in-person-heres-how-to-navigate-your-options-during-the-pandemic.

Kaiser Family Foundation. "Medicaid Expansion Enrollment." June 1, 2019. https://www.kff.org/health-reform/state-indicator/medicaid-expansion-enrollment/?currentTimeframe=0&sortModel=%7B%22colId%22:%22Location%22,%22sort%22:%22asc%22%7D.

Kamarck, Elaine, Yousef Ibreak, Amanda Powers, and Chris Stewart. "Voting by Mail in a Pandemic: A State-By-State Scorecard." *Brookings*, November 3, 2020. https://www.brookings.edu/research/voting-by-mail-in-a-pandemic-a-state-by-state-scorecard/.

Keith, Bruce E. David B. Magleby, Candice J. Nelson, Elizabeth A. Orr, Mark C. Westlye, and Raymond E. Wolfinger. *The Myth of the Independent Voter*. Berkeley: University of California Press, 1992.

Kilgore, Ed. "Joe Biden Owes It All to African-American Voters." *New York Magazine*, April 8, 2020. https://nymag.com/intelligencer/2020/04/joe-biden-owes-it-all-to-african-american-voters.html.

Krogs, Jens Manuel. "Hispanics Have Accounted for More Than Half of Total U.S. Population Growth Since 2010." *Pew*, July 10, 2020. https://www.pewresearch.org/fact-tank/2020/07/10/hispanics-have-accounted-for-more-than-half-of-total-u-s-population-growth-since-2010/.

Lewis-Beck, Michael S., Helmut Norporth, William G. Jacoby, and Herbet F. Weisberg. *The American Voter Revisited*. Ann Arbor: University of Michigan Press, 2008.

Miller, Patrick R. "The 2016 Southern Electorate: Demographics, Issues, and Candidate Perceptions." In *The Future Ain't What It Used To Be: The 2016 Presidential Election in the South*, edited by Branwell DuBose Kapeluck and Scott E. Buchanan, 3–22. Fayetteville: University of Arkansas Press, 2018.

Montlake, Simon. "As College Grads Flee the GOP, Political 'Diploma Divide' Grows," *Christian Science Monitor*, October 27, 2020. https://www.csmonitor.com/USA/Politics/2020/1027/As-college-grads-flee-the-GOP-political-diploma-divide-grows.

Montanaro, Domenico. "Coronavirus Latest: Trump's Fight with Governors Is One He Can't Win." *NPR*, October 2, 2020. https://www.npr.org/2020/04/20/837737368/trump-often-picks-fights-with-governors-but-americans-like-them-more.

National Conference of State Legislators. "State Laws Governing Early Voting." October 22, 2020. https://www.ncsl.org/research/elections-and-campaigns/early-voting-in-state-elections.aspx.

Niedzwiadek, Nick. "The 9 Most Notable Comments Trump Has Made about Accepting the Election Results." *Politico*, September 9, 2020. https://www.politico.com/news/2020/09/24/trump-casts-doubt-2020-election-integrity-421280.

Panetta, Grace. "Trump Hints That He Could Refuse to Accept the Results of the 2020 Election If He Loses." *Business Insider*, July 19, 2020. https://www.businessinsider.com/trump-suggests-that-he-wont-accept-the-2020-election-results-if-he-loses-2020-7.

Parks, Miles. "Trump, While Attacking Mail Voting, Casts Mail Ballot Again." *NPR*, August 19, 2020. https://www.npr.org/2020/08/19/903886567/trump-while-attacking-mail-voting-casts-mail-ballot-again.

Sessin, Carmen, "Trump Cultivated the Latino Vote in Florida, and It Paid Off." *NBC News*, November 4, 2020. https://www.nbcnews.com/news/latino/trump-cultivated-latino-vote-florida-it-paid-n1246226.

Shaw, Daron R., and John R. Petrocik. *The Turnout Myth: Voting Rates and Partisan Outcomes in American National Elections.* Oxford: Oxford University Press, 2020.

Solender, Andrew. "All The Times Trump Has Promoted Hydroxychloroquine." *Forbes*, May 22, 2020. https://www.forbes.com/sites/andrewsolender/2020/05/22/all-the-times-trump-promoted-hydroxychloroquine/?sh=28dbb30d4643.

Sprunt, Barbara. "FACT CHECK: Trump Falsely Claims That Votes Shouldn't Be Counted After Election Day." *NPR*, November 1, 2020. https://www.npr.org/2020/11/01/930140373/fact-check-trump-falsely-claims-that-votes-shouldnt-be-counted-after-election-da.

Stolberg, Sheryl Gay. "Trump Administration Asks Supreme Court to Strike Down Affordable Care Act." *New York Times*, June 26, 2020. https://www.nytimes.com/2020/06/26/us/politics/obamacare-trump-administration-supreme-court.html.

Suls, Ron. "Educational Divide in Vote Preferences on Track to Be Wider Than in Recent Elections." *Pew*, September 15, 2016. https://www.pewresearch.org/fact-tank/2016/09/15/educational-divide-in-vote-preferences-on-track-to-be-wider-than-in-recent-elections/.

United States Election Project. "National General Election VEP Turnout Rates, 1789-Present." Accessed April 1, 2021. Project, http://www.electproject.org/national-1789-present.

U.S. Election Atlas. "2020 Presidential Democratic Primary Election Results." Accessed April 1, 2021. https://uselectionatlas.org/RESULTS/national.php?year=2020&off=0&elect=1&f=0.

van Wagtendonk, Anya. "Biden Got Nearly Two-Thirds of the Black Vote in South Carolina." *Vox*, March 1, 2020. https://www.vox.com/policy-and-politics/2020/3/1/21160030/biden-black-vote-south-carolina-results.

Wald, Kenneth D., and Allison Calhoun-Brown. *Religion and Politics in the United States*. Lanham: Rowman & Littlefield, 2018.

White, Ismail K., and Chryl N. Laird. *Steadfast Democrats: How Social Forces Shape Black Political Behavior*. Princeton: Princeton University Press, 2020.

Winfrey, Kelly L. *Understanding How Women Vote: Gender Identity and Political Choices*. Chicago: Praeger, 2018.

Zucker, Anthony. "Donald Trump suggests Delay to 2020 US Presidential Election." *BBC*, July 30, 2020. https://www.bbc.com/news/world-us-canada-53597975.

Chapter 2

The 2020 Presidential Nomination Process

Aaron A. Hitefield and M. V. Hood, III

With a tumultuous four years having passed since President Trump was first elected, a term marked by impeachment and continual controversy, both Democrats and Republicans geared up for what would be a historic presidential election. President Trump was all but certain to be the Republican Party's nominee, with no serious candidate mounting a legitimate challenge against the sitting incumbent president. As a result, five states, including South Carolina, chose to cancel their Republican primaries or caucuses.

Alternatively, for Democrats, most candidates began announcing their candidacy by early 2019 (some entered as early as July 2017), with many citing perceived policy failures of the Trump administration and partisan politics as their reasons for running. In total, twenty-eight candidates emerged to vie for the nomination (three of which were from Southern states), resulting in one of the most crowded fields in history.[1] Amid the global COVID-19 pandemic and the unprecedented disruptions to the Democratic primary process, Joe Biden eventually succeeded in outdueling Bernie Sanders and a diverse candidate pool to become the Democratic nominee.

Finally, in a general election marked by the continued effects of the devastating pandemic as well as record levels of campaign spending, voter turnout, early in-person voting, and absentee-by-mail voting, Joe Biden successfully defeated Donald Trump to become the forty-sixth president. While no small feat, the story of Joe Biden's eventual success in 2020 begins with his revitalizing campaign victory in the South Carolina primary on February 29. Moreover, with the front-loaded nature of Southern primaries and Super Tuesday, the states of the former Confederacy played a disproportionate role in the presidential nomination process and signaled to the country the viability of the Biden candidacy.

The following chapter details the role that the South played in the 2020 presidential primaries. To do so, we first explain the underlying processes behind the nomination for each party, noting the rules governing the delegate allocation process. Concentrating on the Democratic primary, we examine the timing of election contests and the increased role that Southern states played due to their location within the process. We then discuss the results of the Democratic primary for the 2020 election cycle and also examine the pivotal role of South Carolina in the process, along with the ripple effects it had in spurring future President Biden's electoral success. Finally, we examine the makeup of the 2020 Democratic Primary electorate and support for Biden among various constituencies.

THE 2020 DEMOCRATIC PRESIDENTIAL PRIMARY

While both major political parties employ primaries and conventions to determine their presidential nominees, each party's delegate allotment process is notably different. On the Republican side, the RNC distributes ten at-large delegates to each state, as well as three delegates per U.S. House seat in each state. Additionally, they distribute another set of delegates based on several incentive-based rules, with states being rewarded additional delegates if they have a Republican governor, a majority-Republican congressional delegation or state legislature, a Republican senator, or if the state supported the Republican nominee in the previous election.[2] These delegates are then allotted to candidates in primaries or caucuses in three ways—either based on the proportion of each candidate's vote share in the state and each congressional district, a winner-take-all system in which the plurality winner receives the delegates of the state, or by a process combining both systems.[3] In total, the nomination process at the Republican National Convention in 2020 included 2,550 delegates or 2,443 pledged delegates based on their state's primary or caucus results and 107 unpledged delegates. Of those, President Trump won all but one delegate, with Former Massachusetts Governor Bill Weld securing one pledged delegate after receiving 1.3 percent of the vote in Iowa. With this monopoly of delegates, President Trump easily surpassed the required 1,275 delegate threshold, securing his second Republican nomination for president.[4]

To secure the 2020 Democratic nomination for president on the first ballot, candidates needed to receive 1,991, or a majority of the 3,979 pledged delegates. On the Democratic side, pledged delegates are awarded proportionally based on the share of vote received by a candidate in the primary or caucus.[5] If the nomination was contested and no candidate won on the first ballot, however, winning the nomination would require winning a majority of delegates (pledged and unpledged), which would equal 2,375. Pledged delegates are allotted by the DNC (Democratic National Convention) based upon the most recent 2010 Census, the state's Democratic share of the vote in the three most recent presidential elections, and the state's geographic proximity to other states simultaneously running their own respective primaries. Table 2.1 records the number of pledged delegates up for grabs in Democratic state primaries and caucuses. In total, there were 4,749 delegates, with 3,979 of those being pledged delegates. Of the available pledged delegates, 1,052, or 26 percent, were from the eleven states of the South.[6]

While the majority of the 4,749 total delegates in 2020 were pledged delegates, another 770 (16.2 percent) were unpledged, also known as superdelegates. Superdelegates, or those who are unpledged to any candidate, are distributed to states based upon the Democratic leadership, governorship, or elected national Democratic politicians (current or former) with voting addresses within each state.[7] While pledged delegates must follow the voting results of their respective states, superdelegates are not required to do so and have traditionally had a disproportionate influence on the outcomes of Democratic presidential nominations. In past elections, such as 1984 and 2008, superdelegates had a significant effect on the nomination of candidates. Both Walter Mondale and Barack Obama would have faced more narrow delegate margins if they had not won unpledged superdelegates in state primaries where they lost the popular vote (Southwell 1986; 2012). However, after the outcry from voters over superdelegate support for Hillary Clinton over Bernie Sanders in the 2016 nomination process, the DNC reduced the abilities of these delegates, no longer allowing them to vote on the first ballot at the convention (Kaplan 2018).

Timing of Primaries and Caucuses

The 2020 Democratic presidential nomination contest began on February 3 with the Iowa caucus and ended with the Connecticut primary on August 11. Table 2.1 lists the Democratic primary and caucus dates in sequential order, with Southern states presented in bolded text and underlined. Following Iowa, New Hampshire, and Nevada, South Carolina retained its position as the first in the South primary, with the Democratic primary held on February 29th. Only a few days later on Tuesday, March 3, six states in the region (Alabama, Arkansas, North Carolina, Tennessee, Texas, and Virginia) held their nomination contests along with eight non-South states and American Samoa. Referred to as Super Tuesday, this unique clustering of state primaries originated in 1988 (Hadley and Stanley 1989) and "was designed to attract more attention to the South from the presidential candidates and to improve the prospects of a moderate candidate in the Democratic party" (Abramowitz 1989, 982). Mississippi's primary contest was held later on

Table 2.1 The Timing of Democratic Presidential Primaries in 2020

Date	State	Pledged Delegates
February 3	Iowa	41
February 11	New Hampshire	24
February 22	Nevada	36
February 29	**South Carolina**	54
March 3	**Alabama**	52
	American Samoa	6
	Arkansas	31
	California	415
	Colorado	67
	Maine	24
	Massachusetts	91
	Minnesota	75
	North Carolina	110
	Oklahoma	37
	Tennessee	64
	Texas	228
	Utah	29
	Vermont	16
	Virginia	99
March 10	Idaho	20
	Michigan	125
	Mississippi	36
	Missouri	68
	North Dakota	14
	Washington	89
March 14	Northern Marianas	6
March 17	Arizona	67
	Florida	219
	Illinois	15
April 4	Wyoming	14
April 7	Wisconsin	84
April 11	Alaska	15
April 28	Ohio	136
May 2	Kansas	39
May 12	Nebraska	29
May 19	Oregon	61
May 23	Hawaii	24
June 2	District of Columbia	20
	Indiana	82
	Maryland	96
	Montana	19
	New Mexico	34
	Pennsylvania	186
	Rhode Island	26
	South Dakota	16

(Continued)

Table 2.1 The Timing of Democratic Presidential Primaries in 2020 (Continued)

Date	State	Pledged Delegates
June 6	Guam	7
	Virgin Islands	7
June 9	**Georgia** (originally March 24)	105
	West Virginia	28
June 23	Kentucky	54
	New York	274
July 7	Delaware	21
	New Jersey	126
July 11	**Louisiana** (originally April 4)	54
July 12	Puerto Rico	51
August 11	Connecticut	60
	Total	3,979

Source: The Green Papers, 2020 Presidential Primaries, Caucuses, and Conventions Chronologically, https://www.thegreenpapers.com/P20/events.phtml?s=c (Accessed April 27, 2021).

March 10 and Florida's on 17th. As can be seen, most of the Southern states, therefore, were originally scheduled early in the primary calendar. The frontloading of these contests has traditionally given the region an outsized influence in determining presidential nominees (Norrander 2014), a trend which continued in 2020 and influenced which Democratic would face President Trump in November.

Of particular note to this election cycle is the fact that a pandemic was raging in the United States, as well as other parts of the world, by mid-March. The coronavirus (COVID-19) outbreak did affect the timing of sixteen Democratic primaries—two of which were in the South.[8] Georgia was originally scheduled to hold its presidential preference primary on March 24. This election was delayed and combined with the statewide primary held on June 9, 2020. The other Southern state to delay its primary was Louisiana, moving the date from April 4 to July 11. The remaining nine states in the region, however, did not move their primary dates. With Bernie Sanders dropping out of the race on April 8, Georgia and Louisiana were effectively removed from playing any key role in the nomination process as Biden was the only remaining candidate in the race at that point.

Democratic Primary Results

Examined next are the Democratic primary results for the Southern states. Table 2.2 details the results in terms of popular votes accrued by state primary for the nine Democratic candidates still in the nomination contest at the time of the South Carolina primary. In these contests, Biden won a plurality of the vote for all eleven contests and a majority in six. On average, Biden's primary vote share was 57.5 percent, as compared to Sanders at 19.6 percent. No other candidates were able to break the 10-percent mark in terms of average vote share for states in the region. Michael Bloomberg came in a distant third with an average vote share of 9.4 percent.

Table 2.3 translates the popular votes won in the South by these nine candidates into pledged delegates. Delegate counts for the eleven states are presented along with regionwide summary figures. With the exception of Bloomberg (twenty-four) and Warren (nine), all of the delegates from Southern states went to Biden or Sanders. Of the available 1,074 delegates from the region, 739 (69 percent) were won by Biden and 302 (28 percent) by Sanders. For every delegate won by Sanders, Biden accumulated approximately 2.5 delegates. As will be demonstrated further, Biden's net delegate advantage over Sanders in the South certainly contributed to the former vice president's accumulation of a majority of delegates and his eventual nomination.

Figure 2.1 places the Biden-Sanders race within the context of the entire field of primaries and caucuses, beginning with Iowa on February 3 and ending with Wisconsin on April 7. Again, nine of eleven Southern states held their primary contests across this time period with Georgia and Louisiana being the exceptions. Sanders suspended his campaign for president on April 8. The figure presents the total cumulative delegate count for these two candidates as well as the cumulative delegate count for the South. One can reference table 2.1 for the timing of these contests, specific states, and the pledged delegate count at stake.

Although Iowa and New Hampshire are key contests, few actual delegates are at stake as witnessed in figure 2.1. As will be discussed further, to say that Biden got off to a slow start in the Democratic nomination would be an understatement. Following the South Carolina primary, however, Biden has nearly pulled equal with Sanders in terms of pledged delegates won, 54 versus 60, respectively.

After Super Tuesday on March 3rd that featured six Southern states, Biden overtakes Sanders in the delegate count, 715–635. As evidenced by the second and fourth bars, Biden's total count is the result of winning a lopsided share of delegates from Southern states. At this point in the race, more than half (54 percent) of Biden's overall delegate tally comprised delegates from Southern states, as compared to about a third (35 percent) of Sanders's total delegates. Post-Super Tuesday Biden's cumulative delegate count continues to rise, as does Sander's, albeit the gap between the two candidates grows over time. After the March 17 contests, which included the Florida primary, Biden's overall delegate count stood at 1,227 to 922 for Sanders. This would

Table 2.2 2020 Democratic Primary Results for the Southern States-Popular Vote

State	Biden	Sanders	Warren	Buttigieg	Klobuchar	Gabbard	Bloomberg	Steyer	Bennet
Alabama	63.3	16.5	5.7	0.3	0.2	0.2	11.7	0.2	0.5
Arkansas	40.6	22.4	10.0	3.3	3.1	0.7	16.7	0.9	0.3
Florida	62.0	22.8	1.9	2.3	1.0	0.5	8.4	0.1	0.2
Georgia	84.9	9.4	2.0	0.6	0.4	0.4	0.7	0.2	0.5
Louisiana	79.5	7.4	2.4	0.9	0.9	0.7	1.6	0.3	2.3
Mississippi	81.0	14.8	0.6	0.2	0.2	0.4	2.5	0.1	---
North Carolina	43.0	24.2	10.5	3.3	2.3	0.5	13.0	0.8	0.2
South Carolina	48.7	19.8	7.1	8.2	3.1	1.3	---	11.3	0.1
Tennessee	41.7	25.0	10.4	3.3	2.1	0.4	15.5	0.4	0.3
Texas	34.6	29.9	11.4	4.0	2.1	0.4	14.4	0.7	0.5
Virginia	53.3	23.2	10.8	0.9	0.6	0.9	9.7	0.1	0.1
Average	**57.5**	**19.6**	**6.6**	**2.5**	**1.5**	**0.6**	**9.4**	**1.4**	**0.5**

Notes: Entries are vote share received in Democratic Presidential Primary by state. Cells in gray indicate candidates had withdrawn from the race prior to the primary election in that state. A dashed line indicates the candidate was not on the ballot in a particular state.
Source: CQ Voting and Elections Collection, Election Results, https://library.cqpress.com/elections/index.php (Accessed April 27, 2021).

Table 2.3 2020 Democratic Primary Results for the Southern States-Pledged Delegates

State	Biden	Sanders	Warren	Buttigieg	Klobuchar	Gabbard	Bloomberg	Steyer	Bennet
Alabama	44	8	0	0	0	0	0	0	0
Arkansas	17	9	0	0	0	0	5	0	0
Florida	162	57	0	0	0	0	0	0	0
Georgia	105	13	0	0	0	0	0	0	0
Louisiana	54	6	0	0	0	0	0	0	0
Mississippi	34	5	0	0	0	0	0	0	0
North Carolina	68	37	2	0	0	0	3	0	0
South Carolina	39	15	0	0	0	0	0	0	0
Tennessee	36	22	1	0	0	0	5	0	0
Texas	113	99	5	0	0	0	11	0	0
Virginia	67	31	1	0	0	0	0	0	0
Totals	**739**	**302**	**9**	**0**	**0**	**0**	**24**	**0**	**0**

Notes: Entries are the pledged (hard) delegates won by state. Cells in gray indicate candidates had withdrawn from the race prior to the primary election in that state.
Source: The Green Papers, Presidential Primaries 2020, Democrat Hard and Soft Count Delegate Summary, https://www.thegreenpapers.com/P20/D-HS.phtml (Accessed April 27, 2021).

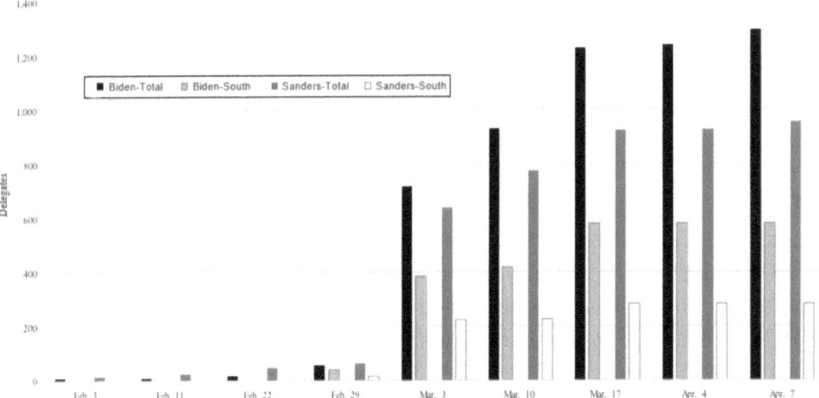

Figure 2.1 Biden and Sanders Cumulative Delegate Count. The Green Papers, Presidential Primaries 2020, Democrat Hard and Soft Count Delegate Summary, https://www.thegreenpapers.com/P20/D-HS.phtml (Accessed April 27, 2021).

be the final primary held in a Southern state until Georgia, which effectively occurred after the nomination was decided.

At the time that Sanders withdrew from the nomination race on April 8, he had amassed 954 delegates, 280 of which were won in the South. Biden's overall tally at the point was 1,293 delegates, with 580 being Southern in origin. At the effective conclusion of the race, 45 percent of Biden's cumulative delegate count to this point were won in the South, as compared to 29 percent of those for Sanders. Certainly, the region disproportionately helped propel Biden past Sanders to the nomination.[9] Although there were an additional twenty-five contests held after Sanders's departure, the fact that the Southern states were frontloaded in this process without a doubt aided Biden in his quest to face President Trump as the Democratic nominee. While one must win a majority of delegates to capture the nomination, one Southern state with only a small share of delegates played an outsized role in Biden's win. The next section will discuss the unique role of South Carolina in the 2020 Democratic presidential nomination contest.

THE PIVOTAL ROLE OF SOUTH CAROLINA IN THE 2020 NOMINATION CONTEST

Huffmon et al. (2017), as well as Graham and Buchanan (2018), highlight the importance of South Carolina in the presidential nomination process, especially in terms of selecting the Democratic nominee. In 2020, this was most certainly the case for Joe Biden. Only 54 delegates, or 1.4 percent of all pledged delegates, were up for grabs in South Carolina's Democratic primary. Far more important than the numeric count of delegates at stake was the timing of the South Carolina contest. Maintaining its place as the *First in the South*, the Palmetto State's primary was held on February 29 as the fourth contest after Iowa (February 3), New Hampshire (February 11), and Nevada (February 22).

Through the Nevada caucus Biden had certainly been underperforming, coming in fourth place in both Iowa and New Hampshire. It is a rare event for a candidate to not win or place in either of these first two contests and still capture the nomination. In fact, since the advent of the modern primary era in 1972, the eventual Democratic nominee in contested primaries has come in first or second place in Iowa or New Hampshire. Due in no small part to South Carolina, however, Biden was able to buck this trend and blaze a new trail to victory in the 2020 Democratic primary.

Figure 2.2 plots the Real Clear Politics poll average for Biden and Sanders in South Carolina from January 1st to February 29 (Election Day). Given his anemic start, Biden required not only a win but a decisive win in South Carolina. Throughout much of the time period plotted Biden does maintain a decisive lead over Sanders in the polls. Approximately two weeks out from the election, Biden's lead begins to decay, while Sanders's standing picks up. Then, about a week out from the election, Biden's numbers rose at an exponential rate. On Primary Day, the Real Clear Politics average had Biden at 39.7 percent versus Sanders at 24.3 percent, a 15-point gap.

What changed the trajectory of the Democratic Primary race in South Carolina? While Biden was going to win, based on the preelection polling

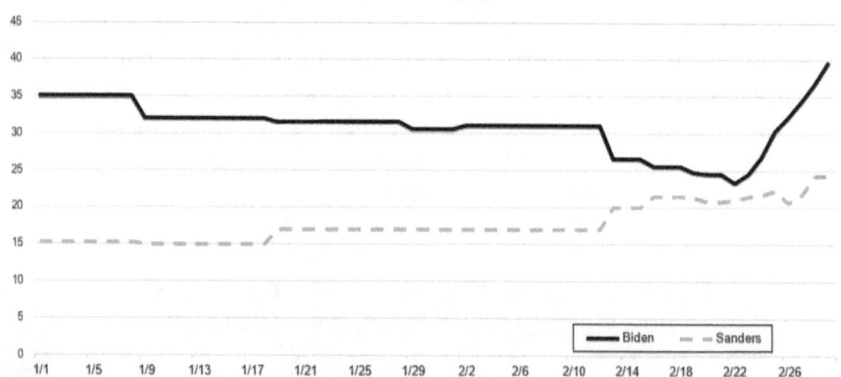

Figure 2.2 Real Clear Politics Poll Average-South Carolina. Real Clear Politics, South Carolina Democratic Presidential Primary, https://www.realclearpolitics.com/epolls/2020/president/sc/south_carolina_democratic_presidential_primary-6824.html#polls (Accessed April 27, 2021).

average, his margin of victory in South Carolina was likely propelled by the endorsement of Democratic Congressman James Clyburn (SC-6). Clyburn, an African American legislator, was the majority House whip in 2020. Well respected in Washington and a towering political figure in South Carolina, Clyburn's endorsement of Biden shortly before the election on February 26was monumentally influential (Oprysko and Caputo 2020). In his endorsement Clyburn remarked, "We know Joe. But more importantly, Joe knows us" (Owens 2020). Such was an especially important signal to black voters who, at 56 percent, comprised more than a majority of the Democratic primary electorate in South Carolina.[10] One source reported that Clyburn's endorsement influenced the vote of six in ten African American electors in the state.[11]

Of the race, a news synopsis stated the following, "when Democrats look back on their 2020 primary, Clyburn's endorsement of Biden will be viewed as a key inflection point, perhaps the moment that changed everything" (Owens 2020). In fact, there is empirical data to support the aforementioned statement. Figure 2.3 examines polling data in South Carolina before and after Clyburn's endorsement along with the actual vote outcomes from the primary. Here we take the average of polls conducted from February 26 and 27 and compare them to the average of polls conducted from February 12 through 25.[12] Biden's polling average increases fourteen percentage points, from 29 percent pre-endorsement to 43 percent post-endorsement. Sanders's numbers across the same time period increase from 20 percent to 24 percent.

With little time between Clyburn's endorsement and the date of the election, the polling average did capture the upward trajectory for Biden, but

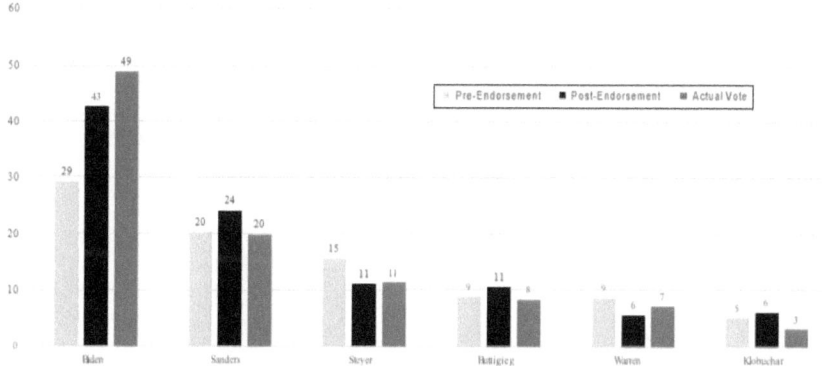

Figure 2.3 South Carolina Democratic Primary. Real Clear Politics, South Carolina Democratic Presidential Primary, https://www.realclearpolitics.com/epolls/2020/president/sc/south_carolina_democratic_presidential_primary-6824.html#polls (Accessed April 27, 2021).

not the total effect of the endorsement. This is evidenced by the fact that Biden's actual vote margin of 48.7 percent was 6 points higher than the post-endorsement polling average. Exit poll data from South Carolina indicates that more than a third (37 percent) of Democratic primary voters decided who to vote for in only the last few days before the election and, of this group, Biden tripled Sanders's support numbers—48 percent to 16 percent.[13] On the other hand, the post-endorsement polling average overestimated Sanders's vote share by 4 points.

THE SOUTHERN DEMOCRATIC PRIMARY ELECTORATE

In this section, we make use of the exit poll data from Edison Research conducted during the 2020 Democratic primary.[14] Eight of eleven Southern states were surveyed, with Arkansas, Georgia, and Louisiana being excluded. As is evident from the previous section, the black electorate can be a pivotal voting bloc in Democratic primaries. Table 2.4 details the percentage of African American voters that comprised various Southern Democratic primary electorates from 2004 through 2020. In some states, African Americans are capable of controlling the choice of candidate as they constitute a majority of all Democratic primary voters. In Alabama, Georgia, Mississippi, and South Carolina, black voters are typically a majority. In Mississippi, blacks now consistently constitute seven of ten Democratic primary voters. In the key state of South Carolina, African Americans have held a majority since the

Table 2.4 Percentage of Black Voters in Southern Democratic Primaries

State	2004	2008	2016	2020
Alabama	----	51	54	49
Arkansas	----	17	27	----
Florida	21	19	27	29
Georgia	47	51	51	----
Louisiana	46	48	----	----
Mississippi	56	50	71	69
North Carolina	----	34	32	27
South Carolina	47	55	61	56
Tennessee	23	29	32	26
Texas	21	19	19	20
Virginia	33	30	26	28
Average	37	37	40	38

Source: CNN, Entrance/Exit Polls, https://www.cnn.com/election/2020/primaries-caucuses/entrance-and-exit-polls (Accessed April 27, 2021).

2008 primary. Even if not in the majority, black support is required to win Democratic primaries in the South. Between 2004 and 2020, black voters made 37–40 percent of the region's Democratic primary electorate.

Table 2.5 shows the demographic characteristics of voters within the 2020 Democratic primaries. Besides black voters (see table 2.4), white voters made up the other major racial voting demographic within the Democratic primaries throughout the South. While they constituted a regionwide low of only 28 percent of Democratic voters in Mississippi, white voters in the remaining ten Southern states ranged anywhere from 40 to 70 percent of the primary electorate. Also of note, while only in single digits throughout the majority of the South, Latino voters constituted 19 percent of the primary electorate in Florida, and 32 percent in Texas.

In every Southern state, women constituted the majority of the Democratic primary electorate, never falling below 57 percent. Additionally, over 50 percent of voters in all Southern states were college graduates, earning an associate's degree or greater. In three states—Florida, North Carolina, and Virginia—between 62 and 66 percent of all Democratic voters received some manner of college degree. In Alabama and Mississippi alternatively,

Table 2.5 Characteristics of Voters in the 2020 Democratic Primaries in Southern States

Characteristic	AL	FL	MS	NC	SC	TN	TX	VA
White	46	49	28	62	40	70	44	61
Black	49	29	69	27	56	26	20	28
Latino	3	19	3	6	2	2	32	6
Female	61	59	58	57	59	57	57	57
17–29	10	11	13	14	11	11	15	13
30–44	23	17	19	22	18	25	22	23
45–64	38	36	42	37	42	40	38	40
65 and Older	28	37	26	27	29	28	25	23
HS or Less	18	13	21	15	18	17	13	15
Some College	28	21	27	22	27	26	28	20
Associate's	17	17	19	16	16	12	16	15
Bachelor's	19	29	18	25	20	23	24	26
Postgraduate	18	20	15	21	19	22	17	24
Independent	23	18	17	27	26	27	25	27
Liberal	54	54	46	59	50	58	58	53
Moderate	36	39	45	29	41	29	25	39
Conservative	9	7	8	12	9	13	17	8
Urban	41	58	24	40	21	50	56	25
Suburban	20	34	21	46	39	31	40	52
Rural	38	7	55	13	41	20	4	23

Source: CNN, Entrance/Exit Polls, https://www.cnn.com/election/2020/primaries-caucuses/entrance-and-exit-polls (Accessed April 27, 2021).

only 54 and 52 percent of voters respectively were college graduates, the lowest in the region. Overall, the results for gender, race, and education are not unexpected. Over the past two decades, women throughout the nation, and especially those with college degrees, have increasingly aligned with the Democratic Party. As of 2019, roughly two-thirds of women with college degrees identified as Democrats. Moreover, Democratic-leaning voters over the past two decades have become 40 percent non-white, as opposed to only 17 percent among Republican-leaning voters.[15]

The majority of the Democratic electorate was also comprised of middle-age voters, with at least 63 percent of the electorate in each Southern state being over 45 years old. In Florida, those over the age of 45 reached a region-high of 73 percent of the Democratic primary electorate. When examining the ideological leaning of the Democratic electorate, one can see that in all but Mississippi and South Carolina, liberal-leaning voters carry a majority share of the primary electorate, whereas moderate-leaning voters reach only a 39 percent high. In Mississippi and South Carolina, moderates were 45 and 41 percent, respectively, resulting in liberal voters failing to constitute a clear majority of the primary electorate.

Finally, when examining where voters reside, interesting patterns emerge. For instance, Mississippi is the only Southern state where a majority of Democratic primary voters (55 percent) live in rural areas of the state. Alternatively, in both Texas and Florida, a majority of Democratic primary voters reside in urban areas, or 56 and 58 percent, respectively. In Texas, 47 percent of voters reside in the Dallas, Ft. Worth, and Houston regions of the state. In Florida, 46 percent of voters reside in the Miami and Tampa Bay regions of the state, driving the dominance of urban voters in the Democratic primaries. Only in Virginia, does a majority reside in suburban areas within the state (52 percent). Such a result in 2020 was largely driven by the suburban areas outside of Washington D.C., which comprised 38 percent of the total Virginia primary electorate.

Table 2.6 shows the support that Biden received from these demographic groups. In every state in the South, a majority of black voters (over 57 percent in every state) supported Biden over the remaining pool of candidates. In Mississippi, for instance, 87 percent of black voters supported Biden over Bernie Sanders. Interestingly, while Biden won the majority of black support in the South, he was unable to match Clinton's vote share among black voters in 2016 where she garnered no less than 80 percent in every Southern state (McKee 2020). When examining white primary voters, Biden garnered a majority in only Alabama, Florida, and Mississippi.

Biden also attained slightly more support among women in the Democratic primaries, winning the majority of female support in four states versus three for men. Biden's primary support was also typically older than that of his

Table 2.6 Percentage of Demographic Group support for Biden, 2020 Primaries

Characteristic	AL	FL	MS	NC	SC	TN	TX	VA
White	57	61	70	34	33	37	30	48
Black	72	74	87	62	61	57	58	69
Latino	----	----	----	43	----	----	27	46
Male	61	60	78	42	48	38	33	49
Female	65	64	83	42	49	44	36	57
18-44 Years	47	39	68	29	30	22	16	34
45 and older	72	71	87	49	56	51	45	64
HS or Less	66	63	89	49	58	54	41	59
Some College	64	64	80	45	46	44	36	56
Associate's	64	62	80	46	49	43	35	54
Bachelor's	56	57	75	37	41	29	29	46
Postgraduate	67	67	82	37	51	42	36	54
Democrat	67	65	86	47	54	46	38	58
Independent	51	48	59	29	35	29	24	43
Liberal	55	55	74	37	42	35	30	45
Moderate	74	74	88	53	56	57	51	64
Urban	73	60	83	40	47	39	34	54
Suburban	66	66	77	39	43	44	34	49
Rural	52	----	82	58	55	46	----	61

Source: CNN, Entrance/Exit Polls, https://www.cnn.com/election/2020/primaries-caucuses/entrance-and-exit-polls (Accessed April 27, 2021).

opponents, with a majority of those above the age of 45 supporting Biden in all but two Southern states (Texas and North Carolina). Alternatively, Biden won a majority of younger voters in only Mississippi, garnering 68 percent of those between the age of 18 and 44. In Alabama, Florida, and Mississippi, Biden carried a majority of voters across all education levels, a trend that was fully reversed in both North Carolina and Texas. Given the number of candidates in these early states, however, Biden still successfully won a plurality of support in most educational categories across the entire region. Biden also had the most success among moderate voters, winning a majority of this group in every Southern state polled in the survey. While no strong patterns emerged related to place, Biden did receive a majority of support from rural, urban, and suburban voters in Alabama, Florida, and Mississippi.

CONCLUSION

Given the strategic timing of Southern primary elections, the region's primary voters held a disproportionate influence over the nomination process. Such a reality can be seen when comparing the voting populations within these Southern states to the entire U.S. population. By the end of Super Tuesday, states with less than 44 percent of the total U.S. population and 46 percent of the total Democratic primary and caucus vote were successfully able to force all but three of the ten candidates in the Democratic Primary to suspend their presidential campaigns. At the end of March, only two candidates remained with over twenty states still waiting to cast their primary ballots. While the South disproportionately influences primary results, it constitutes only 33 percent of the U.S. population. Moreover, the nine Southern states whose primaries were not rescheduled controlled 915 delegates or 23 percent of the total. In 2020, these states constituted 24 percent of all Democratic primary voters.

Nonetheless, while not representative of the entire U.S. population, the South has long played an important role in the nomination process of major party presidential candidates (e.g., Beachler 1996), and 2020 was no exception. Former Vice President Joseph R. Biden, Jr. was successfully able to reinvigorate his campaign with vital successes in South Carolina and in quick succession eight other Southern states, forcing the withdrawal of the majority of his opposition. Finally, with the suspension of Senator Bernie Sanders's campaign, Biden was able to secure the Democratic nomination and shift his focus toward President Trump and the November general election.

NOTES

1. The pool of candidates (with their respective states in parenthesis) includes: Joe Biden (Delaware), Bernie Sanders (Vermont), Tulsi Gabbard (Hawaii), Elizabeth Warren (Massachusetts), Michael Bloomberg (New York), Amy Klobuchar (Minnesota), Pete Buttigieg (Indiana), Tom Steyer (CaliforniaA), Deval Patrick (Massachusetts), Andrew Yang (New York), Michael Bennett (Colorado), John Delaney (Maryland), Cory Booker (New Jersey), Marianne Williamson (California), Julian Castro (Texas), Kamala Harris (California), Steve Bullock (Montana), Joe Sestak (Pennsylvania), Wayne Messam (Flordia), Beto O'Rourke (Texas), Tim Ryan (Ohio), Bill DeBlasio (New York), Kirsten Gillibrand (New York), Seth Moulton (Massachusetts), Jay Inslee (Washington), John Hickenlooper (Colorado), Eric Swalwell (California), and Richard Ojeda (West Virginia).

2. Based upon Rules established by the Republican National Committee. *Call of the 2020 Republican National Convention*, November 20, 2019, https://bit.ly/2NVoQDU.

3. Source: Republican Delegate Rules, 2020. https://ballotpedia.org/Republican_delegate_rules,_2020.

4. Source: "Presidential Primaries 2020, Republican Pledged and Unpledged Delegate Summary," www.thegreenpapers.com/P20/R-PU.phtml.

5. In order to be awarded pledged delegates from a primary of caucus, a candidate must exceed a 15 percent popular vote threshold. Source: "Delegate Selection Rules for the 2020 Democratic National Convention." FrontloadingHQ, https://cutt.ly/slKr6Sw.

6. Source: Presidential Primaries 2020, Democratic Pledged and Unpledged Delegate Summary, https://www.thegreenpapers.com/P20/D-PU.phtml.
7. Based upon Rules established by the Democratic National Committee. *Call of the 2020 Democratic National Convention*, August 25, 2018, https://bit.ly/3krIEuH.
8. The total number of states, sixteen, and two territories were forced to postpone their primary elections due to the threat of the pandemic were as follows: Alaska, Connecticut, Delaware, Georgia, Guam, Hawaii, Indiana, Kentucky, Louisiana, Maryland, Montana, New York, Ohio, Pennsylvania, Puerto Rico, Rhode Island, West Virginia, and Wyoming.
9. Including all primary and caucus contests from February 3rd through April 7th, there were a total of 2,409 pledged delegates at stake, with 37 percent (893) of these being from Southern states.
10. Edison Research Exit Poll of 2020 South Carolina Democratic Primary, https://rb.gy/x6ii3j.
11. Source: Edison Research. "2020 South Carolina Democratic Primary," https://rb.gy/ljd1uz.
12. Polling data are from Real Clear Politics (www.realclearpolitics.com). A total of ten polls were used to calculate the pre-endorsement average and two polls for the post-endorsement average. Two polls that were conducted across dates that spanned the endorsement were not included.
13. CNN Exit Poll of 2020 South Carolina Democratic Primary, https://rb.gy/x6ii3j.
14. Democratic exit poll data accessed from CNN (www.cnn.com/election/2020/primaries-caucuses/entrance-and-exit-polls).
15. "In Changing U.S. Electorate, Race and Education Remain Stark Dividing Line," Pew Research Center, June 2, 2020 (https://pewrsr.ch/2ZSLWO0).

REFERENCES

Abramowitz, Alan. 1989. "Viability, Electability, and Candidate Choice in a Presidential Primary Election: A Test of Competing Models." *The Journal of Politics* 51(4): 977–992.
Beachler, Donald W. 1996. "The South and the Democratic Presidential Nomination, 1972–1992." *Presidential Studies Quarterly* 26(2): 402–414.
Berg-Andersson, Richard E. 2021. The Green Papers, www.thegreenpapers.com.
"CQ Voting and Elections Collection." 2021. *CQ Press*, https://library.cqpress.com/elections/.
Graham, Cole Blease, Jr. and Scott E. Buchanan. 2018. "South Carolina: It's All about the Primary." In *The Future Ain't What It Used to Be: The 2016 Presidential Election in the South*, eds. Branwell DuBose Kapeluck and Scott E. Buchanan, 105–123. Fayetteville: University of Arkansas Press.
Hadley, Charles D., and Harold W. Stanley. 1989. "Super Tuesday 1988: Regional Results and National Implications." *Publius: The Journal of Federalism* 19(3): 19–37.

Huffmon, Scott H., H. Gibbs Knotts, and Seth C. McKee. 2017. "First in the South: The Importance of South Carolina in Presidential Politics." *Journal of Political Science* 45(1): 7–31.

Kaplan, Rebecca "Democrats Strip Power Away from Superdelegates." *CBS News*, August 25, 2018, https://cbsn.ws/3uywu7W.

McKee, Seth C. 2020. "The 2016 Presidential Nomination Process." In *The Future Ain't What It Used to Be: The 2016 Presidential Election in the South*, eds. Branwell DuBose Kapeluck and Scott E. Buchanan. Fayetteville, AR: The University of Arkansas Press.

Norrander, Barbara. 2014. *Super Tuesday: Regional Politics and Presidential Primaries*. University Press of Kentucky.

Putnam, Josh. 2021. FrontloadingHQ, www.frontloadinghq.com.

Owens, Donna. "Jim Clyburn Changed Everything for Joe Biden's Campaign." *Washington Post*, April 1, 2020, https://wapo.st/3rFL8YP.

Oprysko, Caitlin and Marc Caputo. "Biden Wins Crucial Jim Clyburn Endorsement Ahead of South Carolina Primary." *Politico*, February 26, 2020, https://politi.co/3rKUFOv.

Southwell, Priscilla L. 1986. "The 1984 Democratic Nomination Process: The Significance of Unpledged Superdelegates." *American Politics Quarterly* 14 (1–2): 75–88.

Southwell, Priscilla L. 2012. "A Backroom Without the Smoke? Superdelegates and the 2008 Democratic Nomination Process." *Party Politics* 18(2): 267–283.

Part II

ELECTIONS IN THE DEEP SOUTH

Chapter 3

Alabama

Politics of Personality in the Heart of Dixie

Shannon L. Bridgmon

While Alabama remained a reliable stronghold for the GOP in 2020, the state influenced presidential politics around the structures that defined the presidency of Donald Trump through the unwavering support of its own political leaders. Alabama's congressional politics, along with her influence in the Trump Administration and the aftermath of the election certification process, helped to define the parameters of presidential politics of 2020.

Perhaps no other political actor influenced the dynamics of presidential politics in Alabama during the 2020 election more than Jeff Sessions. His boomerang experience with the Trump administration elevated him from Alabama senator to Attorney General, and ultimately back to competing to regain his original seat. While superficially, such an experience may be an extension of conservative Alabama politics, Sessions's ill-fated sojourn to the Department of Justice set the stage for a chain of events that disrupted the balance of power and influence within the GOP itself. This move resulted in the unlikely election of a Democratic senator, backlash from both parties over family separations, the fallout from the 2018 midterm elections, and an eventual end to both his career and the Trump presidency itself.

Sessions's ascendancy to serve as attorney general was a combination of early support for then-candidate Donald Trump and a similar commitment to hardline immigration policies for which Trump campaigned.[1] His departure from the Senate did not signal a potential Democratic pick-up in the upcoming special election, with the election of another Republican almost guaranteed in the 2017 special election. However, Roy Moore's perpetual candidacy for statewide office finally achieved the political influence he sought, though not how anyone envisioned.[2] Moore's victory in the GOP primary reinforced Alabama's conservative voters' preference for political disrupters and hard-right policies. After securing President Trump's endorsement and the GOP nomination, allegations of pursuing underage girls and child abuse were enough for Alabama to narrowly elect Democrat Doug Jones to fill Sessions's vacated seat in the Senate. The first domino had fallen, shifting the partisan balance of the Senate and outlining the parameters of what Alabamians would tolerate in a candidate.

Sessions's ideological compatibility with President Trump failed to protect him from Trump's permanent ire after Sessions recused himself (as required by law) from the Mueller probe into the 2016 campaign. President Trump's view that this constituted a personal betrayal ensured his commitment to repay Sessions in kind. Following a season of public beratement via Twitter and public comments, President Trump finally retaliated by firing Sessions the day after the 2018 midterm elections. Trump largely blamed Sessions for the Mueller investigation, as well as for the political backlash against border separations that resulted in midterm electoral losses. By 2020, Jeff Sessions was once again a candidate for his old office, seeking both to capitalize on his early support of President Trump while simultaneously avoiding his wrath.

THE PRESIDENTIAL PRIMARIES

Presidential candidates of both parties focus on Alabama during the primary campaigns to court base voters. Alabama had moved party primary elections from June to Super Tuesday in March in order to increase the state's influence in the primary season. This proved to be an effective strategy for both the 2012 and 2016 primary cycles. However, the focus was not as intense as during the previous two cycles as Super Tuesday expanded to include California for the first time (Phillips 2020).

Republicans

President Trump's 2016 election worked to dramatically change the makeup of the Republican Party and its political agenda. Following the 2018 midterm elections, it became clear how much control he had over the national party organization itself. Despite consistent resistance among the staunchest establishment Republicans, the bulk of both the electoral party and the institutional party solidified behind Donald Trump. With a consistent approval rating among Republicans *of nearly* 90 percent, drawing a strong primary challenger was unlikely. This reality was reflected in the party as early moves in 2019 sought to change the RNC rules to eliminate any challenge to his nomination within the party (Mak 2019). The push began too late to affect the 2020 convention (Haberman and Karni 2019). By October 2019, the Trump campaign had successfully convinced 37 states to change their primary or delegate selection processes, with five states cancelling their primaries altogether (Gibson and Holland 2019).

Alabama Republicans proceeded with their 2020 primary election. This decision had less to do with serving the interests of a robust party competition within the presidential race than it did with fully serving the competitive Senate race. Former Massachusetts governor William Weld was the only Republican challenger to President Trump to make it on to the ballot. President Trump easily carried every county with 90 percent of the votes. Despite the lack of meaningful competition within the party, he drew more votes in the GOP primary than all other Democratic and Republican presidential candidates combined (Archibald 2020b).

Democrats

Several Democratic candidates made visits to the state during 2019, including Senators Elizabeth Warren, Bernie Sanders, Kamala Harris, and former Vice President Biden. As more than one-third of all Democratic delegates were contested on Super Tuesday, Alabama's relatively small share of delegates resulted in diminished campaign attention.

A crowded primary calendar is not the only obstacle for Alabama Democrats. The state party continued to struggle both electorally within the state and within the larger scope of the national party structure. As Democratic competitiveness plummeted over the past decade, the biracial party coalition that led the party during its dominance split. The first split occurred along racial lines and again in 2019 along generational lines. Doug Jones's unlikely victory helped energize younger progressives and push for more influence within the party. The party is now devolved into intraparty legal fights, including both state and federal cases over leadership. The party's black caucus (Alabama Democratic Caucus—ADC) accused the national party and Senator Doug Jones of attempting to dilute the ADC's influence in selecting the state executive committee. The federal suit claims the party bylaws are at odds with a 1991 consent decree. The latest version of the legal battle accuses the state party of racism under the leadership of its first black state party chair. Public statements from both sides accusing one another alternately of racism and "sour grapes" resurrected decades-old turf battles within the party (Cason 2021). This dysfunction has further crippled the state party's ability to carry out its basic functions—to recruit candidates and compete for elected office, as well as to serve as an effective opposition party when out of office. These conflicts further hamper the party's capacity to help presidential candidates as they seek the party's nomination.

Endorsements, fundraising, and momentum were somewhat fractured. Joe Biden picked up the endorsements of prominent Democratic leaders in the state including Sen. Doug Jones, Rep. Terri Sewell, and Birmingham Mayor Randall Woodfin. Also during February, former New York mayor Michael Bloomberg campaigned in the state and received the endorsement of the primary black caucus in the state, the Alabama Democratic Conference. Bloomberg's plan to revitalize black business communities and economic opportunities appealed to the caucus (Cason 2020a). Other candidates managed to achieve fundraising successes in the state. In terms of fundraising success in Alabama, Mayor Pete Buttigieg raised the most money in the state. Sen. Bernie Sanders had more individual donors, reflecting his strong grassroots appeal.

Alabama Democrats did not coalesce around a presidential candidate until the days immediately before Super Tuesday. As late as February 2020, Sen. Elizabeth Warren held a slight lead in the polls, followed closely by Joe Biden and Sen. Bernie Sanders. The most visible event during the primary season occurred as five candidates arrived in Selma the weekend before the primary to commemorate the Bloody Sunday attacks of 1965. Senators Warren and Klobuchar, along with Vice President Biden, Mayor Buttigieg, and Mayor Bloomberg participated in the events with compatible messages regarding civil rights (Herndon 2020).

Alabama Democratic voters followed the lead of South Carolina the week before Super Tuesday and supported Vice President Biden. Biden's sweeping win on Super Tuesday cemented his path to the nomination. He carried every county in the state, with 63 percent of the statewide vote. Senator Bernie Sanders received 17 percent of the vote and performed well in the more populous counties, while Bloomberg performed better in the rural counties of the Black Belt. Bloomberg's late candidacy may have prevented him from building a wider base of support among Alabama Democrats, 80 percent of whom are African American. Exit polls indicated Sanders performed well among younger white males, self-described liberals, and those with strong ideological commitments (Edison 2020).

CONGRESSIONAL PRIMARIES

The incumbency advantage in Alabama is almost unbreakable. Half of state legislative races were unopposed in the 2018 general elections, and half of the legislative primary races were also unopposed. Roughly 40 percent of legislative seats are unopposed in Alabama, allowing incumbents to sail to reelection (Cason 2019). The lack of competition is a combination of gerrymandering and one-party dominance in the state. As in most of Alabama's political history, electoral outcomes are determined at the primary. The tension between populist and anti-establishment elements continues to challenge older, more traditional Republican members, as they have since 2010. What started as the Tea Party movement has morphed into a new type of Republicanism in the state. Tea Party Republicans are now generally the norm, further splitting into more populist candidates and those "original" Tea Party actors who took over the old "establishment" in the primaries.

House of Representatives

Alabama's electoral competition is highest in primary races for open seats. Two House of Representatives districts opened up by retirements. Establishment Republicans Bradley Byrne and Martha Roby left their respective seats open in 2020. Byrne chose to leave his seat to compete for the U.S. Senate, while Roby had faced multiple challengers in 2018 following her criticism of President Trump. The backlash led her to announce her retirement from the seat after serving for ten years (Bowman 2019). Both parties fielded multiple candidates for those districts, and District 1 candidates had primary runoffs for each party.[3] Retiring incumbent Bradley Byrne (AL-01) endorsed Jerry Carl for the runoff, helping Carl ease to a win (Sharp 2020c). Of the remaining five incumbents seeking reelection in their district, only Rep. Mo Brooks faced a nominal primary challenger but no general election candidate. The other four faced no primary opposition, and only two drew an opponent in the general election. Ultimately, every incumbent easily won reelection, and the two open seats were filled with Republicans, as expected.

Senate

Doug Jones's surprise victory in the 2017 special election and Alabama Democrats' inability to recruit quality candidates in general left no challenge to Jones for the nomination. He found himself campaigning for other Democrats and occasionally landing some solid punches on his would-be opposition for the general election (Nilsen and Zhou 2020). However, the GOP primary election to determine his challenger proved to be a drawn-out process and the most competitive statewide race of 2020.

U.S. Rep. Bradley Byrne became the first candidate in the race in February 2019. He was well known throughout the state, having narrowly lost the GOP primary for governor in 2010. An establishment candidate, he represented traditional GOP interests but also remained supportive of President Trump. His early announcement should have shored up support and dissuaded other hopefuls, especially the newly unemployed Jeff Sessions. In 2010, he had been targeted by both Democrats and the right wing of his party, but he had since won a seat in Congress and proved to be an effective legislator for District 1. He consistently stressed his service to the state and demonstrated his ability to deliver pork to his district. His case to the voters hinged on his potential combined effectiveness with Sen. Richard Shelby to deliver for the state's interests (Sharp 2019).

Byrne's record and positive relationship with President Trump did not dissuade other candidates. Tommy Tuberville, the former Auburn football coach, had toyed with running for Alabama governor in 2018. He ultimately decided running against a GOP incumbent was too risky and officially entered the GOP primary for Senate in April of 2019. His early candidacy centered on name recognition and assumed support for half of the Alabama electorate who are Auburn fans. Beyond the ties to football, his political messages centered on general appeals to conservative values, faith, his political outsider status, and his fealty to President Trump (Cason 2020c).

Had Byrne and Tuberville remained the only two candidates, it may have been a typical race between an establishment career politician and an inexperienced celebrity newcomer. However, this is Alabama politics, so it had to be outlandish. As such, Roy Moore entered the Senate race in June 2019 to the horror of almost all Republican leaders. The controversial twice-removed state Supreme Court justice and perennially embattled candidate had publicly indicated his interest as early as March, stating the 2017 election had been "stolen" from him.[4] Although President Trump had endorsed him in the 2017 primary election, he personally discouraged Moore from running again (Dobuzinskis 2019). Party leaders quickly denounced his campaign. Ever defiant and drawing from an infinite well of self-confidence, Moore brushed aside the pushback as evidence of his electoral appeal and ultimate threat to the party establishment (Ax 2019).

As the filing deadline approached in November 2019, the Senate race had drawn several more minor candidates, with most attention focused on Byrne, Tuberville, and to a lesser extent, Moore. This focus changed the day before the deadline as Jeff Sessions finally entered the primary race. His announcement on Twitter was also accompanied by a video defending his loyalty to President Trump and did not refer to the actual race he was running. This indicated he was aware that his electoral success hinged on salvaging the relationship with the president—or at least stopping the continued attacks against him. It is unclear if he understood that his hopes were unrealistic or if his desire for "his" old seat were just too strong. The latter is likely, after running unopposed for the seat in 2014 and not facing any meaningful primary competition since his first run for Senate in 1996. Prior to his entry into the race, Sessions approached Byrne and Secretary of State Merrill regarding his candidacy. Merrill suspended his campaign following the phone call with Sessions. Byrne claims Sessions asked him to withdraw from the race for "his" seat (Sharp 2019b). The sense of entitlement to the seat and the president's animus toward him would be too much to overcome. Sessions never pulled ahead, focusing his campaign efforts on appeasing President Trump and producing negative ads on his rivals[5] (Gattis 2020).

The March primary election for Senate results resulted in a fractured party. Eight candidates appeared on the ballot, but clear divisions emerged among three candidates. Tuberville won forty counties and received 33 percent of the vote, with Sessions following behind with twenty counties and 32 percent. Byrne trailed in third place with 27 percent and Moore winning 7 percent. Byrne carried the seven counties in his home district, reflecting their support for the incumbent, while Sessions carried some counties in the southeastern Wiregrass region and others in southwestern Alabama near his home county of Dallas, along with the Huntsville metro area (Archibald 2020).

Tuberville and Sessions were to face off just four weeks later in a runoff but were delayed until July due to the COVID-19 outbreak. The runoff campaign would last four months and proved to be the most intense 2020 political campaign in Alabama. It also functioned as a proxy election for President Trump, who enthusiastically participated.

THE SENATE RUNOFF—THE TRUMP ELECTION

Considering Republican dominance in the state, the most competitive race Trump faced was the GOP runoff between two men who competed for his support. The campaign did not center on policy issues or on the personality of either candidate, but on the President himself. Immediately following the March 3 primary, President Trump immediately issued personal attacks against Session, labeling him disloyal and lacking courage. Sessions adopted a two-pronged approach to remind voters of his support for Trump and his influence on the agenda, as well as focusing on problems with Tommy Tuberville. The attempts to capitalize on his affiliation with the president backfired spectacularly. After drawing on the ties to Trump in fundraising activities, President Trump's campaign sent a letter instructing Sessions to stop "misleading" voters and explicitly expressed his opposition to Sessions's candidacy (Cason 2020b). Tuberville immediately capitalized on Trump's consistent anger at Sessions, and, one week after the primary, President Trump formally endorsed Tuberville over Jeff Sessions. The president's attacks on Sessions would continue and prove to be an albatross on the neck of his campaign.

Sessions also attempted to paint Tuberville as a carpetbagger whose only time in Alabama was during the nine years as the Auburn coach. He questioned Tuberville's residency and highlighted his ties to a financial scandal after his coaching years (Sharp 2020a). Tuberville's loyalty to his players was also questioned and his temperament toward students would resurface in the general election. In the end, these attacks did not seem to bother Alabama GOP voters. Southern Alabamians would have no problem identifying Tuberville as an Alabamian after spending almost a decade at Auburn. His name was synonymous with the state's most important activity and more importantly, with winning.

In terms of policy preferences, there is no discernable daylight between Sessions and Tuberville on policy issues. Sessions served as the policy architect of the Trump agenda, and Tuberville echoed support of those policies. The echoed support of President Trump became the defining issue of both campaigns. Tuberville's messages of support went so far as to have campaign signs and his campaign bus logo read "Tuberville + Trump 2020," advertising the president's endorsement. The few times Tuberville attempted to answer policy questions from reporters or voters ended badly, revealing his lack of familiarity with specific policies. Since he consistently polled ahead of Sessions by a wide margin, there was little need for Tuberville to engage with the media or debate the issues. Tuberville's campaign centered on traveling the state and having personal interaction with the voters, and he came across as approachable and relatable (Cason 2020c).

Sessions's campaign messages highlighted his early service to the president and his influence on the Trump administration. Nevertheless, he finally responded to President Trump directly after Trump endorsed Tuberville. That endorsement came at the end of a tweet accusing Sessions of letting the country down by recusing himself from the Mueller investigation. A brief Twitter back-and-forth ensued, full of insults and personal attacks. Sessions's response to the recusal reference and Tuberville endorsement was a sharp "you're damn fortunate I did. I protected the rule of law & resulted in your exoneration." Sessions also engaged in a side spat directly with Tuberville, calling him "weak" and Tuberville countering that Trump could not trust his own former attorney general. Sessions continued to press his adherence to the law in his recusal, but the president got the last word by tweeting at Sessions that he blew his chance, lacked courage (Sharp 2020b), and he hoped "this slime will pay a big price." Ultimately, it is difficult to both declare your loyalty and support for a man who lures you into a Twitter war of personal insults and curses.

The runoff election results are telling. Tuberville soundly beat Sessions, carrying all but three counties in the state. Sessions carried those three counties by a narrow margin. Based on the changes of support between the March primary and the runoff, it appears most Byrne supporters voted for Tuberville. Byrne, who represented the establishment wing of the party, cast himself as a friend to President Trump. Considering Tuberville and Sessions shared an ideology and general policy preferences, Sessions was still an establishment candidate. It is apparent that President Trump's continued hatred of Sessions mattered (Velasco 2020). Even in Tuscaloosa County, the home of the University of Alabama and no friend to anyone associated with Auburn University football, Sessions failed to carry the county in the runoff. This suggests even the home of the University of Alabama disliked Jeff Sessions more than Tuberville, who represented their arch-rivals. It is unclear if voters' rejection of Sessions is a direct result of the president's vitriol or if it harkens to the state's historic one-and-done support of fallen incumbents. Political comebacks in the state are not the norm, with the Alabama political graveyard littered with the foolhardy attempts of discarded former incumbents to win election again.[6]

THE GENERAL ELECTION

The general election reflected the lack of interparty competition in the state at all levels. Alabamians still proved engaged despite the low levels of competition at the general election. Overall voter turnout was 61.8 percent, down significantly from other modern elections in the state.[7] This is most likely due to the coronavirus and low levels of competition. Alabama consistently sends a Republican House delegation and one Democrat representing a majority-minority district, similar to other Deep South states. Congressional races benefited the district incumbents and Republicans in open seats. While the partisanship of each safe seat reflects voter preferences in the state, district lines reinforce both the partisanship of each district and protecting the incumbency advantage from general election threats.

An anticipated episode of interparty competition emerged in 2020. The most competitive race in the entire election cycle proved to be the U.S. Senate race between Democratic incumbent Doug Jones and political newcomer Tommy Tuberville. Given Tuberville's decisive runoff victory and Republican dominance in the state, the result was unsurprising. Nevertheless, Sen. Jones mounted a serious re-election campaign backed by impressive fundraising and his basic competence in office (Nilsen and Zhou 2020). Largely assumed to be a lame-duck Senator as soon as he was elected, Jones never really sought to quell his progressive instincts to win reelection. He voted consistently with the Democrats on policy but reached across the lines to work with Republicans. He voted with President Trump about 35 percent of the time, which was lower than his Democratic colleagues in Republican states. He also voted against President Trump's judicial nominees and voted to convict him in the impeachment trial of 2020.

Jones outspent Tuberville heavily and managed to outperform all other Democrats on the ballot with 40 percent of the vote. Tuberville continued to ride to the general election as the GOP nominee with President Trump's blessing. Like the primary runoff with Jeff Sessions, Tuberville polled in double digits ahead of his opposition, opted not to directly engage with his opponent, and largely ignored the press. Jones, on the other hand, utilized his impressive campaign war chest to wage heavy attacks against Tuberville's past behavior at various coaching posts. Doug Jones did enjoy some level of incumbency support, but not enough to win against Tuberville. The basic GOP to Democratic ratio in the state is roughly 2:1. Democratic House challengers pulled 33–35 percent of votes in the general election, which is consistent with overall Democratic performance in the last ten years.

Statewide elections in 2020 consisted of seven offices and six constitutional amendments on the ballot. All six of the judiciary races saw Republicans run unopposed. Two incumbents on Alabama's Supreme Court and four appellate justices faced no opposition, safely keeping all judicial seats in Republican control. The remaining statewide seat was for the president of the state Public Service Commission. Incumbent Twinkle Andress Cavanaugh faced Democrat Laura Casey, after previously running for reelection unopposed in 2016. She carried 62 percent of the votes to Casey's 38 percent. All Republican candidates for statewide office faced healthy primary opposition but only Cavanaugh drew a general election Democratic challenger.

Six constitutional amendments were on the general election ballot, with three appearing in order to boost turnout among conservatives. Amendments are placed at the end of the ballot and include voluminous language that quickly loses voters' interest. Legislatively referred amendments on valence issues are a routine strategy to mobilize turnout and encourage the voter to finish selecting candidates for all offices down-ballot. Amendment 1 was such an issue. It sought to change one word from restricting voting eligibility from "every" eligible citizen to "only" eligible citizens in Alabama. It passed overwhelmingly and did not change any eligibility requirements to vote. Participation in the constitutional amendments decreases as the list continues. Two amendments were identical in language to authorize "stand your ground' laws for churches in two counties. Two other amendments sought to make changes in the state judiciary system, with one passing to increase some judicial terms to two years (Burkhalter 2020).

RESULTS AND ANALYSIS

The electoral results for Alabama were unsurprising and consistent with previous elections of the past twenty years. Table 3.1 presents the election results. Incumbents fared well, but Republicans defeated Democratic Senator Doug Jones running a candidate not facing pedophilia accusations like Roy Moore. House incumbent vote margins remained stable from 2018, except

Table 3.1 Alabama Federal Election Results

Candidate (Party)	Vote (%)	Votes (#)	Incumbent Change (%)
President			
Joe Biden/Kamala Harris (D)	37	849,624	
Donald Trump/Mike Pence (R)*	62	1,441,170	−1
Joe Jorgensen (I)	1	24,886	
U.S. Senate			
Doug Jones (D)*	40	907,484	−10
Tommy Tuberville (R)	60	1,379,222	
U.S. House			
First District			
James Averhart	35	110,186	
Jerry Carl (R)	65	204,037	
Second District			
Phyllis Harvey-Hall (D)	35	104,592	
Barry Moore (R)	65	197,329	
Third District			
Adia Winfrey (D)	32	103,874	
Mike Rogers (R)*	68	216,700	4
Fourth District			
Rick Neighbors (D)	17	54,704	
Robert Aderholt (R)*	83	235,531	−3
Fifth District			
Mo Brooks (R)**	96	251,896	35
Write-In	4	11,028	
Sixth District			
Gary Palmer (R)**	97	273,205	23
Write-In	3	8,062	
Seventh District			
Terri A. Sewell (D)**	97	224,995	−1
Write-In	3	6,583	

Key: * = incumbent, D = Democrat, R = Republican, I = Independent.
** Incumbents Brooks, Palmer, and Sewell ran unopposed.
Source: Alabama Secretary of State election data website: https://www.sos.alabama.gov/alabama-votes/voter/election-data.

for Brooks and Palmer, whose increase in popularity coincided with running unopposed for the first time. President Trump won 62 percent of the votes, compared to Joe Biden's 37 percent. President Trump carried the same fifty-four counties as in 2016. These counties are reliably Republican, while Joe Biden carried the remaining thirteen counties in the Black Belt. These county patterns are identical in 2008, 2016, and 2020.

While Alabama's presidential preferences have remained solidly Republican for decades, overall Republican partisanship has risen and become more dominant over the past thirty years. While this top-down realignment took decades, it appears the partisan balance has finally settled after twenty years of Democratic decline. Republican and Democratic vote share at all levels remained remarkably consistent since 2016, saving Jones's razor-thin victory in 2017. Among contested elections, Democrats win an average of 35 percent of the vote, while Republicans take the 65 percent majority. These margins are consistent in all statewide and federal races since 2016. Straight party voting is again the norm in Alabama, reinforcing partisanship as the main influence on vote choice (Cason 2018). Of all votes cast in the general election, 67 percent were straight tickets. The party votes reflect the overall partisan margins in most contested elections in the state. Republican straight tickets make up 62 percent to the Democrats' 38 percent share of straight-party ballot votes (table 3.2).[8]

In terms of presidential voting, historical voting patterns based on geographic trends continue to persist. However, the trend since 2000 indicates rural areas composed of lower-income whites are voting more Republican at all levels. Support for Biden remained strongest in the Black Belt region. Democratic support significantly increased in all urban counties, especially Madison, home to the high-tech Huntsville area. Most Alabamians outside of urban areas and the Black Belt also remain solidly Republican.[9] Donald Trump's widest vote margins are found in northern Alabama Hill counties. Hill counties offered the weakest support for Biden, with outcomes much lower in comparison to those since 2000 but slightly better than in 2016. This region's support for Democratic candidates has plummeted since 2000 but appears to have at least leveled off. Republicans did not gain any significant support in any region but performed slightly better in the Coastal counties of Baldwin and Washington.

Racially aligned partisan voting remains a dominant characteristic in Alabama's political culture. White Alabamians voted overwhelmingly for Donald Trump. The Black Belt (named for its loam soil rather than its people) remains the lone Democratic region in the state. Enduring questions remain with regard to the intersection of race and politics in Alabama. Some questioned increased Republican strength in 2016 as a backlash against an African American president. The 2020 repeat of Donald Trump's 2016 performance may indicate several things. Perhaps Alabamians responded to Trump's particular campaign message and it is a function of candidate preference. This may indeed reflect racial conservatism inherent in Alabama's historical political culture or an attraction to his bombastic and disruptive style. There may also be a simpler explanation. Coupled with the overall partisan developments in the state, it appears there exists a lack of support for Democratic candidates in general. Nevertheless, partisan voting in Alabama is certainly correlated to race. Higher rates of white population lead to higher levels of Republican presidential voting. Biden's weakest electoral performance

Table 3.2 Alabama Democratic vote (in %) by County Characteristics

Characteristics Total	2020 Biden 37%	2016 Clinton 34%	2012 Obama 38%	2008 Obama 39%	2004 Kerry 37%	2000 Gore 42%
Median family income						
Less than $34,000	61.9	60.3	50.0	50.9	48.3	53.7
$34–43,000	25.1	24.5	28.5	31.4	33.7	42.2
> $43,000	29.6	29.1	37.3	40.3	36.7	40.8
Percentage of African American						
Less than 15%	16.6	16	22.4	24.3	27.5	35.5
15–40%	30.9	29.8	41.9	42.1	38.5	43.0
40% or more	56.5	59	48.0	59.0	53.2	55.9
Region of State*						
Tennessee Valley	23.1	22.1	30.0	31.8	36.9	44.1
Hill Country	21.8	21.2	57.0	26.8	7.7	35.6
Black Belt	62	61.9	63.0	60.9	56.7	60.5
Wiregrass	26.3	25.6	29.0	28.6	26.7	34.2
Coastal	32.5	33.3	28.0	29.1	27.5	31.4
Metropolitan	51.8	46.2	45.0	48.0	43.0	46.0

Notes: Regions of the state determined by the author and listed in text endnotes. All table entries are percentages.

Source: Computed by the author from data supplied by the Alabama Secretary of State and U.S. Bureau of the Census. Election data was obtained from the Alabama Secretary of State website: https://www.sos.alabama.gov/alabama-votes/voter/election-data. Demographic data for each county is found at: https://www.census.gov/quickfacts/fact/table/AL/RHI125219.

occurred in counties with less than 15 percent African American population. Counties with high levels of African American populations voted at higher levels for Joe Biden than white areas did (table 3.3).

Race is by far the strongest predictor for Trump votes in the 2020 election. College education indicates lower Republican support and higher Democratic support. Republican support also increases with income, consistent with class-based partisan cleavages. However, when analyzing support at the county level, support for President Trump is highest in those counties with a median income between $34,000 and $43,000, then levels off slightly in those counties above the threshold. These variations are still minor, as are those for education. Disparate political behavior is explained by racial group partisanship. Even geographic differences between the northern Hill counties and those in the Black Belt reflect the demographic differences by race, while controlling for other factors.

Results from 2020 indicate Alabama voters had firm preferences regarding both the Democratic and Republican presidential candidates. This marks a shift from 2016. Despite President Trump's strong performance in 2016, it is interesting to note that 4 percent of voters did not vote for any party candidate. Three percent of votes cast left the presidential race blank on the ballot and another one percent of voters wrote in another candidate.[10] This reflects

Table 3.3 Linear Regression: Determinants of Trump Vote at the County Level

Model	Unstandardized B	Std. Error	Standardized Beta	t	Sig.
1 (Constant)	−84.208	35.110		−2.398	.019
College	−.490	.103	−.180	−4.738	.000
PopulationLog	−1.758	1.642	−.039	−1.071	.288
IncomeLog	23.723	8.505	.119	2.789	.007
White	.869	.030	.917	28.753	.000

Note: Adjusted R^2: .970.
Source: U.S. Census Bureau demographic data website: https://www.census.gov/quickfacts/fact/table/AL/RHI125219.

many voters' distrust of both major parties' nominees as well as a general skepticism of Donald Trump. In 2020, undecided and protest voters declined dramatically, with only one-half of 1 percent not voting for a party candidate. Independent candidate Jo Jorgensen received 1 percent of the vote, down from the 3 percent support Independent candidates received in 2016.

While Alabama's partisan and racial voting patterns are consistent and unsurprising, interesting patterns emerge when examining the level of support for President Trump over time. President Trump took 62.0 percent of the presidential vote in 2020, down from 63.4 percent share in 2016. Democratic vote share increased from 34 percent support of Hillary Clinton to 37 percent for Joe Biden. County-level data reveals several trends consistent with overall state support as well as national trends. President Trump increased his support over 2016 in thirty-eight counties. In these counties, he increased his electoral margins by an average of 2.45 percent. His largest increases were in rural counties with large percentages of white voters. This is consistent with state voting patterns, in general. However, he also improved his performance in Black Belt counties that went for Joe Biden. This is consistent with national trends indicating increased support for the President among rural African American voters, especially men (Gurley 2020).

Other national trends emerged in Alabama among those groups in which Trump lost support. His vote margins dropped the most in the state's urban and suburban counties. Regression analysis of changing Republican vote share between 2016 and 2020 appears in table 3.4. These results indicate President Trump lost support among college-educated urban and suburban populations in Alabama. Shelby County had the largest drop in Trump support. As the main suburban county outside Birmingham, it is the wealthiest county with the highest percentage of college-educated residents. This is consistent with the results in table 3.4. Although Shelby County is overwhelmingly white and Trump still carried it by a 40 percent margin, his performance was still weaker than in 2016.

Table 3.4 Linear Regression: Changes of Trump Vote at the County Level, 2016 to 2020

Model	Unstandardized B	Std. Error	Standardized Beta	t	Sig.
1 (Constant)	43.697	22.329		1.957	.055
College	-.209	.066	-.446	-3.175	.002
PopulationLog	-1.781	1.044	-.231	-1.076	.093
IncomeLog	-7.466	5.409	-.217	-1.377	.174
White	.047	.019	.290	2.467	.016

Note: Adjusted. R^2: .594.
Sources: Vote margins calculated from data found at the Alabama Secretary of State election data website: https://www.sos.alabama.gov/alabama-votes/voter/election-data; U.S. Census Bureau demographic data website: https://www.census.gov/quickfacts/fact/table/AL/RHI125219.

The shifts in support reflect modern trends of both racialized voting patterns in the state and national trends reflecting lowered support in areas as population increases. The larger scope of these results indicates that Alabama's reluctance in committing to a candidate in 2016 was short-lived. Evaluations of President Trump's performance were decisive and reflected at the ballot box.

ELECTION CHALLENGE AND THE AFTERMATH

In the days following the general election, uncertainty over the results in late-reporting states and President Trump's refusal to concede would naturally draw attention to the contested states. Alabama's results were not in question, but firebrand Rep. Mo Brooks (AL-5) made a splash by jumping into the fray headfirst. Brooks immediately indicated he would be reluctant to certify votes as early as November 5—just two days after the election and a full two days before the election was called for Joe Biden (Brown and Wu 2020). In his appearance on a radio program, he went on to assert that "the Democrats are renowned for engaging in election fraud, voter fraud, election theft, however you want to categorize it" (Yaffee 2020). He alleged votes in other states that were processed after the polls closed were cast by unregistered voters and illegal aliens. This became his primary explanation of corruption in the 2020 presidential election that he used to mobilize most of the Republican caucus in the House of Representatives against certifying the Electoral College results. He repeatedly stated there was overwhelming and compelling evidence to his claims, but never provided any.

Brooks's early commitment to oppose certification was the first proposal of using Congress to assist President Trump in staying in office. His first suggestion toward this course sprang up alongside the president's commitment to pursue the results in multiple courts. Brooks's and President Trump's plans to resist the election results put Alabama's other Republican officials in an awkward position. Retiring Rep. Bradley Byrne (AL-01), Rep. Robert Aderholt (AL-04), and Governor Kay Ivey all reiterated President Trump's right to pursue recounts and court cases, if necessary (Nusbaum 2020). Senator Richard Shelby tweeted on November 10 that the "perception of fraud erodes confidence" in the electoral system but provided no other comment during the election challenge. Rep. Mike Rogers (AL-03) and Rep.-elect Barry Moore (AL-02) both cast doubts on the election integrity of the delayed results, but Moore pledged to work with the winner. Alabama's lone Democratic member, Rep. Terri Sewell (AL-07), dismissed claims of fraud and the pursuing challenges as "baseless" (Beck 2020).

As Republicans voiced support for President Trump's legal options, most looked toward December 14 as a natural endpoint for the extended campaign. The submission of Electoral College votes proved to only up the stakes for a congressional loyalty test. President Trump enthusiastically promoted Brooks's plan, leaning on Republicans in Congress to support the measure. A growing number of members, including the rest of Alabama's Republican delegation, were pulled toward officially contesting the Electoral College results of several states. Their votes functioned as a service to both the president himself and the GOP primary voters in their districts.

Brooks's campaign to stop the certification of the Electoral College results seemed far-fetched without a Senate cosponsor. Senate Majority Leader Mitch McConnell (R-KY) worked quickly to whip the caucus into ignoring what they saw as a stunt by Mo Brooks. Having no real relationship or history with incoming Senator-elect Tuberville—coupled with Tuberville's sole political identity as a Trump devotee—McConnell was unable to keep the campaign from seeping into the Senate. Three days after states formally cast their Electoral College votes, Senator-elect Tommy Tuberville indicated he was open to supporting Brooks's measure in the Senate (Garrison 2020). While cautioning he was holding back on his decision to do his "due diligence" (Ross 2020), President Trump appealed to Tuberville via Twitter and encouraged him to "take charge" (Durkee 2020). By December 20, it appeared Tuberville was all in on the effort. President Trump was pleased with both the loyalty and initiative of Alabama's Brooks and Tuberville. The mutual admiration was on display when President Trump recounted his phone call with Tuberville. "I spoke to a great gentleman Tommy Tuberville last night, and he's so excited . . . he said you made me the most popular politician in the United States" (Trump 2020). This opened the floodgates for other Republicans to join the effort as insurance for their own future primaries.

THE INSURRECTION AND IMPEACHMENT—ALABAMA'S ROLE

All of Alabama's Republican House delegation pledged to oppose the certification of the results. Tuberville and Brooks, however, personally coordinated their efforts with the White House in the hours before the certification. Senator Tuberville was the only member of Congress present at a meeting with Trump family members, Rudy Giuliani, and other committed supporters at the Trump International Hotel on January 5. One attendee posted on Facebook, "Fifteen of us spent the evening with Donald Trump Jr., Kimberly Guilfoyle, Tommy Tuberville, Michael J. Lindell, Peter Navarro, and Rudy Giuliani. We talked about the elections, illegal votes, court cases, the republics' status, what to expect on the hill tomorrow. TRUMP WILL RETAIN THE PRESIDENCY!!!" (Beck 2021). Tuberville denied attending the meeting, but pictures surfaced, confirming his participation (Burkhalter 2021). Mo Brooks was also accused of helping to organize and plan the March to Save America rally that ultimately turned violent.

Brooks categorically denied planning the rally, but he and President Trump both spoke at the rally. As election protesters gathered on January 6, Mo Brooks took to the stage. His much-scrutinized fiery speech including the following:

> I've got a message that I need you to take to your heart and take back home and along the way, stop at the Capitol . . . . Today, Republican senators and congressmen will either vote to turn America into a godless, amoral, dictatorial, oppressed and socialist nation on the decline, or they will join us and they will fight and vote against voter fraud and election theft and vote for keeping America great . . . . Today is the day that American patriots start taking down names and kicking ass. (Ramachandran 2021)

Despite the fallout from the ensuing violence, Brooks refused to apologize or walk back his remarks. He insisted he did not condone violence and the speech was not a call to violence (Chandler 2021).

As protesters stormed and breached the Capitol, President Trump still had Alabama on his mind. He made a call to Senator Tuberville as members and the vice president were being evacuated, asking Tuberville to raise additional objections in order to delay the final vote. Tuberville indicated the call lasted less than ten minutes, he notified President Trump the Vice President had been taken out, and that he hung up on the president (Cheney 2021). Rudy Giuliani also left a voicemail intended for Tuberville asking him to "slow it down" (Hayes 2021). It is unclear if President Trump and his team made any calls to other lawmakers, but it is apparent he considered further coordination with the Alabama Senator a given.

The deadly insurrection that followed also included Alabamians who traveled to Washington, D.C., to support the president's efforts. One of those who died in the attack was an Alabamian. Another Alabama man showed up to the Capitol with a truckload of explosives and was charged with seventeen federal weapons charges (Brown and Layman 2021). Multiple Alabamians were arrested for participating in the insurrection.

The fallout of the insurrection in Alabama's politics suggests a move away from a traditional establishment influence soon. House Republicans from Alabama proceeded to formally object to the certification on January 6 (Gattis and Koplowitz 2021). All of Alabama's Republican congressional delegation voted against impeachment and conviction, respectively. Senator Richard Shelby was the only Alabama Republican not to object to the election certification, and ultimately announced his retirement days before the conviction vote. Some speculated he may be persuaded to vote to convict President Trump, but he did not. Mo Brooks has remained defiant in the wake of formal moves to censure him in the House and indicated his interest in running for Shelby's seat in 2022. As the primary leader of the congressional resistance to certify Biden's win and his ensuing speech at the rally, Brooks has been catapulted into the national spotlight. While some donors have backed away from Brooks as he has grown more belligerent, he sees his notoriety as a boon to him for the 2022 primaries (Mosely 2021).

ALABAMA AND THE PRESIDENTIAL ELECTION

Alabama's experience in 2020 presidential politics was not characterized by the heavy campaigning of a swing state. Partisan-based voting remained stable down to the county level. Alabama evaluated President Trump's performance in office and local results mirror national lines of support and opposition since 2016. Instead, the state was instrumental in the nature of the political environment. The experience of Jeff Sessions as AG shaped the Trump Administration, its policies, and politics. Alabama's congressional influence on the aftermath of the election and events that culminated in the January 6 insurrection belied her electoral durability. Representative Brooks and Senator Tuberville's elections and subsequent actions tie Alabama to President Trump's interests long after the 2020 election cycle fades into history. Senator Richard Shelby's upcoming retirement and a possible open gubernatorial seat in 2022 will highlight the future of GOP politics in the state and the foundations for 2024 presidential politics in the south.

The extended and stabilized return to one-party competition strongly resembles the Alabama political system V. O. Key analyzed after World War II. While factional cleavages have emerged within the Republican Party in Alabama, it is unclear if the rift is ideological or personality-driven. Meanwhile, an equally dysfunctional minority party exists but is ineffective as the Democrats hover along eerily familiar fault lines of racial control. While each party engages in cannibalizing itself from within and one-party politics is the norm, Alabama seems comfortable in the habits of her long-established political culture.[11]

NOTES

1. For more background on Jeff Sessions's role in Trump's quest for the GOP nomination, see Shannon L. Bridgmon, "Alabama: Republican from Top to Bottom," in *The Future Ain't What it Used to Be: The 2016 Presidential Election in the South*, ed. DuBose Kapeluck and Scott Buchanan (Fayetteville: University of Arkansas Press, 2018), 43–58.

2. Although Moore had been elected and removed two times as the chief justice of the Alabama Supreme Court, he had intermittently been a candidate for Governor in 2006 and 2010, then again for U.S. Senate in both 2017 and 2020. His repeated defiance against secular authorities and flashy style gave him high levels of name recognition and a core of followers guaranteed to support his candidacy to any office he sought. For more, see Bridgmon, "Alabama," 2016 and Shannon L. Bridgmon, "Alabama: Republican Dominance and Democrats Fighting to Survive," in A Paler Shade of Red: The 2012 Presidential Election in the South, ed. DuBose Kapeluck and Scott Buchanan (Fayetteville: University of Arkansas Press, 2014), 37–50.

3. District 1 had five Republican candidates running for the open seat, while district 2's open seat saw seven candidates on the primary ballot. Support was evenly split among the candidates for district 2, which included former Alabama Attorney General Troy King placing fourth among the seven candidates.

4. Moore lost to Doug Jones by roughly 22,000 votes, with over 22,800 write in votes cast.

5. In an ironic twist, Sessions produced an ad highlighting footage of Bradley Byrne criticizing Donald Trump during the Access Hollywood scandal of October 2016.

6. The attempts of former incumbents were particularly rotten in 2020. There are a handful of politicos that resurrected their political career in Alabama—most notably, George Wallace. However, Moore is another. His defiance of a state order to remove a monument of the Ten Commandments from the state judicial building endeared him to Alabamians. After several years, he returned to the Supreme Court, only to be forcibly removed once again. The 2020 efforts of a comeback included not only Roy Moore and Jeff Sessions but also former Attorney General Troy King, who lost his second re-election bid in 2010. King's political, legal, and business dealings

follow a pattern of questionable associates destined for incarceration and bizarre schemes too shady even for Alabama's high tolerance for corruption.

7. The turnout of the year 2020 (61.8 percent) was slightly under the 1996 turnout (62.0 percent). These represent the lowest turnout rates in Alabama since 1988 (56 percent) when the U.S. turnout rate was 50 percent.

8. Straight ticket voting has risen from 48 percent in 2010 to 52 percent in 2012, 50 percent in 2014, 55 percent in 2016, 65 percent in 2018, and 67 percent in 2020.

9. Regions of the state are determined by the author. See Bridgmon (2018) for classification regions.

10. In 2016, 85,689 voters did not vote for any candidate nominated by a party, including Democrats, Independents, or Republican candidates. This reflects 4 percent of all votes cast. By 2020, those numbers dropped to only 13,144 voters not voting for any nominated candidate. Blank presidential votes only totaled 5,832 and only 7,312 voters wrote in a candidate.

11. Special thanks to Andree Reeves and Phillip Bridgmon for the helpful suggestions and feedback. My sincere hope is that our work over the years helps improve governance and democracy in the state I love.

REFERENCES

Archibald, Ramsey, "Senate Race Splits Alabama GOP, North vs. South." AL.com (Alabama Media Group), March 4, 2020, https://www.al.com/news/2020/03/senate-race-splits-alabama-gop-north-versus-south.html.

Archibald, Ramsey, "Trump Got More Votes in Alabama Primary Than All Democrats Combined." AL.com (Alabama Media Group), March 7, 2020, https://www.al.com/news/2020/03/trump-got-more-votes-in-alabama-primary-than-all-democrats-combined.html.

Ax, Joseph, "Alabama's Roy Moore launches 2020 Senate Bid Despite Republican Party Opposition." *Reuters*, June 20, 2019, https://www.reuters.com/article/us-usa-election-moore/alabamas-roy-moore-launches-2020-senate-bid-despite-republican-party-opposition-idUSKCN1TL159.

Beck, Caroline, "Ivey Says Votes Must be Counted, but Remains Confident in Delegation Working with Biden," *Alabama Daily News*, November 9, 2020, https://www.wbrc.com/2020/11/09/ivey-says-votes-must-be-counted-remains-confident-delegation-working-with-biden/.

Beck, Daniel. "The Trump hotel is Amazing!! Fifteen of Us Spent the Evening with Donald Trump Jr., Kimberly Guilfoyle, Tommy Tuberville, Michael J. Lindell, Peter Navarro." *Facebook*, January 5, 2021. https://www.facebook.com/danieljessbeck/posts/10158768287127432.

Bowman, Bridget, "Alabama GOP Rep. Martha Roby Not Running for Reelection," *Roll Call*, July 26, 2019, https://www.rollcall.com/2019/07/26/alabama-gop-rep-martha-roby-not-running-for-reelection/.

Bridgmon, Shannon L. "Alabama: Republican Dominance and Democrats Fighting to Survive," in *A Paler Shade of Red: The 2012 Presidential Election in the South*, eds. Scott E. Buchanan and Branwell DuBose Kapeluck, 37–50. Fayetteville: University of Arkansas Press, 2014.

Bridgmon, Shannon L. "Alabama: Republican from Top to Bottom," in *The Future Ain't What it Used to Be: The 2016 Presidential Election in the South*, eds. Branwell DuBose Kapeluck and Scott E. Buchanan, 43–58. Fayetteville: University of Arkansas Press, 2018.

Brooks, Mo (@RepMoBrooks) 2020. "As a U.S. House Member, I'm Going To Be Very Hesitant to Certify the Results of this Election if Joe Biden is Declared the Winner Under these Circumstances b/c I Lack Faith That This Was an Honest Election. Listen to My Interview on @WVNN Where I Explain Why." *Twitter*, November 5, 2020, https://twitter.com/RepMoBrooks/status/1324501794328875009.

Brown, Matthew and Nicholas Wu, "Alabama Rep. Mo Brooks Says He Will Challenge Electoral College Results," *USA Today*, December 3, 2020, https://www.usatoday.com/story/news/politics/elections/2020/12/03/rep-mo-brooks-challenge-electoral-college-results-congress/3808498001/.

Brown, Melissa and Brian Lyman, "Alabama Man With 'Particularly Lethal' Molotov Cocktails at US Capitol Riot Left Alarming Notes in Truck, Records Show," *Montgomery Advertiser*, January 12, 2021, https://www.montgomeryadvertiser.com/story/news/nation/2021/01/12/lonnie-coffman-alabama-man-molotov-cocktails-17-federal-charges/6647101002/.

Burkhalter, Eddie, "Breaking Down the Six Amendments on Alabama's November Ballot," *Alabama Political Reporter*, October 1, 2020, https://www.alreporter.com/2020/10/01/state-constitutional-amendments-alabama-ballot-november-2020/.

Burkhalter, Eddie. "Photos Put Tuberville in Trump's Hotel on Jan. 5 Despite Denying Meeting." *Alabama Political Reporter*, January 27, 2021, https://www.alreporter.com/2021/01/27/photos-posts-put-tuberville-in-trumps-hotel-on-jan-5-despite-him-denying-meeting/.

Cason, Mike, "65 Percent of Alabama Voters Cast Straight-ticket Ballots." AL.com (Alabama Media Group), November 7, 2018, https://www.al.com/news/2018/11/65-percent-of-alabama-voters-cast-straight-ticket-ballots.html.

Cason, Mike, "Competition Sparse in Many Alabama Legislative Districts." AL.com (Alabama Media Group), Updated Mar 06, 2019; Posted May 23, 2018, https://www.al.com/news/2018/05/competition_sparse_in_many_ala.html.

Cason, Mike, "Democratic Presidential Candidate Mike Bloomberg Says He'll Go 'Toe-to-Toe' with Trump." AL.com (Alabama Media Group), Feb 8, 2020, https://www.al.com/news/2020/02/democratic-presidential-candidate-mike-bloomberg-campaigns-in-alabama.html.

Cason, Mike. "Trump Campaign Tells Sessions to Quit Tying Himself to President," AL.com (Alabama Media Group), April 2, 2020, https://www.al.com/news/2020/04/trump-campaign-tells-sessions-to-quit-tying-himself-to-president.html.

Cason, Mike, "Tommy Tuberville Goes Low Profile to Run Out Clock in Runoff with Jeff Sessions," AL.com (Alabama Media Group), July 10, 2020, https://www.al.

com/news/2020/07/tommy-tuberville-goes-low-profile-to-run-out-clock-in-runoff-with-jeff-sessions.html.

Cason, Mike, "Federal Lawsuit Claims Alabama Democratic Party Diluted Black Influence With 2019 Changes," AL.com (Alabama Media Group), January 20, 2021, https://www.al.com/news/2021/01/federal-lawsuit-claims-alabama-democratic-party-diluted-black-voting-influence-with-2019-changes.html.

Chandler, Kim, "Mo Brooks Won't Apologize Despite Resolution for His Censure," *Associated Press*, January 13, 2021, https://apnews.com/article/donald-trump-censures-mo-brooks-capitol-siege-8a213b80ff208bb7f8588562f78e836c.

Cheney, Kyle, "Tuberville Says He Informed Trump of Pence's Evacuation Before Rioters Reached Senate." *Politico*, February 11, 2021, https://www.politico.com/news/2021/02/11/tuberville-pences-evacuation-trump-impeachment-468572.

Durkee, Alison, "Trump Urging Sen. Tuberville to Pursue Far-Flung Congressional Challenge to Biden's Win," *Forbes*, December 18, 2020, https://www.forbes.com/sites/alisondurkee/2020/12/18/trump-urging-senate-tuberville-to-pursue-far-flung-congressional-challenge-to-bidens-win/?sh=1920f4646d4a.

Dobuzinskis, Alex, "Alabama's Roy Moore, Undone by Allegations, Considers New Senate Run." *Reuters*, March 8, 2019, https://www.reuters.com/article/us-alabama-election/alabamas-roy-moore-undone-by-allegations-considers-new-senate-run-id USKBN1QQ024.

Edison Polling. "Edison Research Conducts Exit Polls on Super Tuesday 2020." https://www.edisonresearch.com/edison-research-conducts-exit-polls-on-super-tuesday-2020/.

Garrison, Joey, "Sen.-Elect Tommy Tuberville suggests He Might Challenge Electoral College Count; Other GOP Senators Mum." *USA Today*, December 17, 2020, https://www.usatoday.com/story/news/politics/elections/2020/12/17/republican-senators-mum-electoral-challenge-despite-mcconnell-plea/3940115001/.

Gattis, Paul, "Alabama Senate Race Turns Nasty with 2 Weeks to Go." AL.com (Alabama Media Group), February 18, 2020, https://www.al.com/news/2020/02/alabama-senate-race-turns-nasty-with-2-weeks-to-go.html.

Gattis, Paul and Howard Koplowitz. "Live updates: After Chaos, What Will Alabama GOP Lawmakers do in Election Challenge?" AL.com (Alabama Media Group), January 6, 2021, https://www.al.com/news/2021/01/live-updates-what-will-alabama-gop-lawmakers-do-in-election-challenge.html.

Gibson, Ginger and Steve Holland, "Trump Campaign Touts Republican Rule Changes Aimed at Unified 2020 Convention." *Reuters*, October 7, 2019, https://www.reuters.com/article/us-usa-election-trump/trump-campaign-touts-republican-rule-changes-aimed-at-unified-2020-convention-idUSKBN1WM236.

Gurley, Gabrielle, "Black Men Support Trump Again." *The American Prospect*, December 4, 2020, https://prospect.org/politics/black-men-support-trump-again/.

Haberman, Maggie and Annie Karni, "Republicans Changing Delegate Rules to Prevent Discord at Convention." *The New York Times*, October 2, 2019, https://www.nytimes.com/2019/10/02/us/politics/trump-republicans-delegates-convention.html.

Hayes, Steve, "Giuliani to Senator: 'Try to Just Slow it Down.'" *The Dispatch*, January 6, 2021, https://thedispatch.com/p/giuliani-to-senator-try-to-just-slow.

Herndon, Astead W, "Bloody Sunday' Commemoration Draws Democratic Candidates to Selma." *The New York Times*, March 1, 2020, https://www.nytimes.com/2020/03/01/us/politics/selma-bridge-march-2020-candidates.html.

Mak, Tim, "RNC Members Want To Block A Primary Challenge To Trump, But The Rules May Stop Them," *NPR*, January 4, 2019, https://www.npr.org/2019/01/04/681987077/rnc-members-want-to-block-a-primary-challenge-to-trump-but-the-rules-may-stop-th.

Moseley, Brandon, "Brooks Says Controversial Stand is Helping Him in the Polls." *Alabama Political Reporter*. January 27, 2021, https://www.alreporter.com/2021/01/26/brooks-says-that-his-controversial-stand-is-helping-him-in-the-polls/.

Nilsen, Ella and Li Zhou, "How the Senate's Most Endangered Democrat Thinks He Can Win, Again." *Vox*, September 21, 2020, https://www.vox.com/21428945/senate-most-endangered-democrat-doug-jones-alabama.

Nusbaum, Lydia, "Alabama Leaders Respond to Presidential Election." Montgomery: WSFA, November 9, 2020, https://www.wsfa.com/2020/11/09/ala-leaders-respond-presidential-results/.

Phillips, Amber, "What is Super Tuesday and Why is it Important?" *Washington Post*, March 4 2020, https://www.washingtonpost.com/politics/2020/02/19/what-is-super-tuesday/?arc404=true.

Ramachandran, Preetha, "An Electoral Challenge and a Speech at the pro-Trump Rally: A Duke Alum's Role in the Events of Jan. 6." *The Duke Chronicle*, February 4, 2021, https://www.dukechronicle.com/article/2021/02/duke-university-mo-brooks-election-2020-challenge-capitol-riots-censure.

Ross, Sean, "Exclusive: Tuberville doing 'due diligence' Before Making Decision on Congressional Challenge to Electoral College Votes." *Yellowhammer News*, December 17, 2020, https://yellowhammernews.com/exclusive-tuberville-doing-due-diligence-before-making-decision-on-congressional-challenge-to-electoral-college-votes/.

Sharp, John, "As Byrne Looks to 2020, He Confronts the Ghosts of 2010." AL.com (Alabama Media Group), February 21, 2019, https://www.al.com/politics/2019/02/as-byrne-looks-to-2020-he-confronts-the-ghosts-of-2010.html.

Sharp, John, "Bradley Byrne: Jeff Sessions Tried to Get Me to Drop Out of Senate Race." AL.com (Alabama Media Group), December 5, 2019, https://www.al.com/politics/2019/12/bradley-byrne-jeff-sessions-tried-to-get-me-to-drop-out-of-senate-race.html.

Sharp John, "Florida Man? Or Alabama's Next Senator? Tuberville's Residency Roils Campaign." AL.com (Alabama Media Group), March 10, 2020, https://www.al.com/news/2020/03/florida-man-or-alabamas-next-senator-tubervilles-residency-roils-campaign.html.

Sharp, John, "Trump Says Sessions Had His Chance and 'Blew it'; Urges Him to Exit Senate Race After Former AG Defends His Record." AL.com (Alabama Media Group), May 23, 2020, https://www.al.com/politics/2020/05/jeff-sessions-trump-twitter-battle-spills-into-saturday.html.

Sharp John, "Bradley Byrne Endorses Jerry Carl in District 1 Race; Continues to Stay out of Senate Contest." AL.com (Alabama Media Group), updated Jul 08, 2020; posted Jun 11, 2020, https://www.al.com/news/2020/06/bradley-byrne-endorses-jerry-carl-in-district-1-race-continues-to-stay-out-of-senate-contest.html.

Sharp, John, "Alabama GOP Juggles 'Mixed Bag' of Constituent Reaction to Electoral College Challenge, Trump's Anger." AL.com (Alabama Media Group), January 5, 2021, https://www.al.com/politics/2021/01/alabama-gop-juggles-mixed-bag-of-constituent-reaction-to-electoral-college-challenge-and-trumps-anger.html.

Thornton, Henry, "Two Alabama Democrats File Lawsuit, Claim Doug Jones Tried to 'Give Control of the Alabama Democratic Party to Whites'." *YellowHammer News*, January 13, 2021, https://yellowhammernews.com/tag/janet-may/.

Trump, Donald, Interview with Rudy Giuliani and Maria Ryan, *Uncovering the Truth with Rudy Giuliani & Dr. Maria Ryan*, WABC Radio, December 20, 2020, https://wabcradio.com/2020/12/20/exclusive-rudy-giuliani-dr-maria-ryan-uncover-the-truth-in-exclusive-interview-with-president-trump/.

Velsasco Eric, "Why Alabama Turned on Jeff Sessions." *Politico*, June 30, 2020, https://www.politico.com/news/magazine/2020/06/30/jeff-sessions-alabama-345067.

Yaffee, Micheal, Interview with Congressman Mo Brooks. "Afternoons With Yaffee & LT." NewsTalk, WVNN, November 5, 2020, https://twitter.com/i/status/1324501794328875009.

Chapter 4

Georgia

Breakthrough to Blue

Charles S. Bullock, III

For decades, Georgia elections had much in common with those of its Deep South neighbors. As in neighboring states, Barry Goldwater was the first Republican to score big in a presidential contest and his coattails ushered in the initial GOP member of Congress and held open the door to the state legislature for other Republicans. Georgia led the way to the first defections from the GOP by voting for home-grown Jimmy Carter in 1976. The Peach State stayed with its native son four years later even as the rest of the region climbed on Reagan's bandwagon. Georgia was slower than its neighbors to score other GOP victories, not putting a Republican in the statehouse until 2003. Nonetheless, while there were some differences in the ebb and flow of partisan fortunes, Georgia was only occasionally distinctive (Bullock et al. 2019).

All of this changed in 2020 when Georgia joined Virginia as the only southern state in Joe Biden's column. The Peach State was expected to be close but most prognosticators still expected it to remain a red state as it had been in every presidential election beginning with 1996, Biden's victory marked the first time that a northern Democrat had won Georgia since John Kennedy in 1960.

CHANGING DEMOGRAPHICS AND PARTISAN IMPLICATIONS

That Georgia voted for Biden was not the result of a dramatic shift in 2020. Rather Democratic strength had been gradually building for more than a decade. The GOP high-water mark came in 2004 when on his way to reelection George W. Bush took 58 percent of the vote in Georgia winning by more than half a million votes. Four years later, John McCain received 52 percent of the vote and won by 200,000 votes. In 2016, Donald Trump matched McCain's showing. The gubernatorial election of 2018 saw the stability of a 200,000-vote GOP cushion blow up when Brian Kemp won the governorship by just 55,000 votes. The erosion continued and Biden carried the state by 11,779 votes. Two months later, Democrats won both of the Senate seats in a runoff with Raphael Warnock knocking out Senator Kelly Loeffler by more than 90,000 votes as shown in figure 4.1. In the other runoff, thirty-three-year-old documentary filmmaker Jon Ossoff defeated Senator Perdue.

Multiple factors contributed to the erosion of Republican support. Foremost among these is the changing nature of the state's electorate. Georgia is a growth state and as such has attracted an increasingly diverse population (Bullock et al. 2019). This diversity is manifested both in its racial and ethnic makeup but also in the arrival of people from around the country attracted by the state's strong economy. In 1996, the audit done by Georgia's secretary of state of those who voted showed that whites cast 77.5 percent of the ballots. As recently as 2006, whites still accounted for more than 70 percent of those who went to the polls. By 2018, the last year for which the official audit is available as this is being written, whites accounted for less than 59 percent of the turnout. The audit done by Georgia's Secretary of State shows that the white share of the 2020 and 2021 vote was 58 percent.

The black share of the vote has increased from the low 20s in the 1990s. During Obama's two elections, blacks cast 30 percent of all votes. Hispanics and Asians are becoming larger components of the electorate. All these groups prefer Democratic candidates with the preference especially pronounced among African Americans who often cast about 90 percent of their

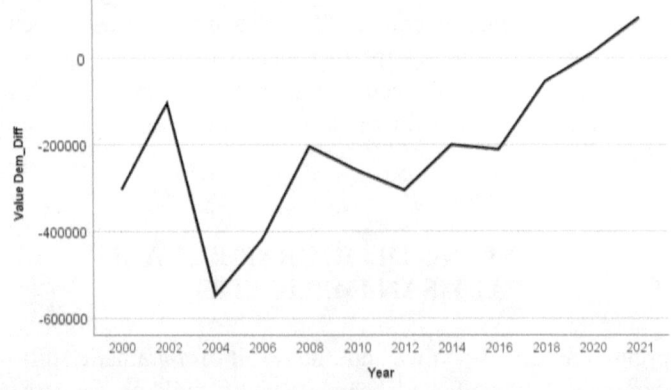

Figure 4.1 Size of the Democratic Loss or Win by Numbers of Votes in Top-of-the-Ticket Contests Since 2000. *Source*: Created by the author using official returns as reported by Georgia's Secretary of State.

ballots for Democrats (Bullock forthcoming; Fox News Democracy 2020; National Election Pool Exit Poll 2020).

A rule of thumb in recent Georgia politics has been that to win a Democrat needs for African Americans to cast 30 percent of the votes and for 30 percent of the whites to vote Democratic. As table 4.1 shows, the black vote has hovered around 30 percent and, except for Barack Obama who got 98 percent of that vote, Democrats have garnered about 90 percent support. Prior to 2020, Democrats lost because of poor performances with whites. The recent successful Democratic candidates have attracted right at 30 percent of the white vote augmented by strong support from growing ranks of other minorities.

The National Pool exit poll results for 2016 and 2020 presented in table 4.2 show that Trump ran five percentage points weaker than in 2020 among whites but picked up two more points of the black vote although that brought him just to 11 percent.

Estimates put Georgia's Hispanic population at about a tenth of the state's total but Hispanics have been slow to become politically active. The 2020 exit poll put the Hispanic vote share at 6 percent of the total, which Biden won 57–41 percent. An exit poll in Gwinnett County, however, found that 75 percent of that county's burgeoning Hispanic population lined up with Biden.

Slippage in Trump's white support came among the better educated. His share of the vote from white, college-educated women fell by eight points to 55 percent. An even more dramatic drop-off in support from white, college-educated men for Trump occurred as it went precipitously going from 76 percent in 2016 down to 56 percent in 2020. Stated alternatively, Biden doubled Clinton's share of the vote from better educated white men.

Table 4.1 Support for Democrats by Ethnic Group and Share of the Vote Cast by the Group

		White		Black	
Year		Support	% of Vote	Support	% of Vote
2008	Obama	23	64	98	30
2016	Clinton	21	61	89	28
2018	Abrams	24	59	92	29
2020	Biden	29	60	87	30
2020	Ossoff	28	60	87	29
2021	Ossoff	30	62	92	29
2021	Warnock	29	62	92	29

Note: Figures from 2020 Senate jungle primary are excluded because of the large field and fracturing of the vote.
Source: Created by the author using estimates of support from National Pool Exit Polls for 2008, 2016, 2018, 2020, and 2021. Percentage of the vote figures comes from the postelection audits done by Georgia's Secretary of State.

Table 4.2 Results of Exit Polls Comparing Trump Support in 2016 and 2020

	2016		2020	
	Share of the Vote	Trump %	Share of the Vote	Trump %
Race				
White	60	75	60	70
Black	30	9	30	11
Latino	4	27	6	41
Gender				
Female	55	43	55	44
Male	45	60	45	56
White Evangelical				
Yes	34	92	32	85
No	66	31	68	31
College Education				
White Female	16	63	13	55
White Male	15	76	12	56
Region				
Atlanta	18	22	19	22
Atlanta suburbs	28	46	28	44
North	19	69	19	73
Central	19	55	20	55
South	16	65	14	58

Source: Created by the author using National Pool Election Poll results.

White Evangelicals are the core Republican constituency. These voters made up 34 percent of Georgia's 2016 electorate and gave a near-unanimous 92 percent of their votes to Trump. While he continued to sweep these voters, his vote share sagged to 85 percent and their vote share slipped to 32 percent.

As in many states, urban centers support Democrats, while rural expanses flock to the GOP. The growth in Georgia's population has centered on urban areas, especially the Atlanta metro area which is geographically the largest in the nation. As the GOP advantage has diminished, the Democratic counties in the Atlanta area increased from three in 2004 to nine since 2016. Obama's 2008 campaign, while coming up short in Georgia, nonetheless flipped three Atlanta suburban counties. Another county went Democratic in 2014 but the big prizes came two years later when Gwinnett and Cobb, the second and third most populous counties in the state, went for Hillary Clinton. Democratic advantages were small in 2016 as Clinton carried Gwinnett by 19,000 votes and took a 7,000-vote plurality in Cobb. Four years later, these counties were solidly blue favoring Biden by 75,000 and 56,000 votes, respectively. Democratic gain in these counties is largely attributable to continuing changes in their ethnic makeup. Augmenting Democratic growth is the rightward drift of the GOP and the Trump message that alienated moderate suburbanites.

Table 4.3 shows the margins by which Democrats carried the state's four most populous counties. Clinton won the two that contain parts of the city of Atlanta by a combined 370,000 votes. She became the first Democratic presidential candidate in years to win the other two and did so narrowly. Biden improved and improved markedly on Clinton's performance in each of these counties adding more than 50,000 votes to his margin in all but Cobb where his winning margin was 49,000 votes larger than Clinton's. In DeKalb and Fulton, Biden's margin hovered around a quarter of a million votes each.

The exit poll data in table 4.2 do not seem to capture the decline in Trump's Atlanta vote that played a major role in flipping Georgia. The exit poll results show no change in Trump's Atlanta vote and only a two-point drop in Atlanta's suburbs. The rest of Georgia stuck with Trump. In twenty-three rural counties, Trump won more than 80 percent of the two-party vote, and in two counties, he topped 90 percent. Trump improved his performance in North Georgia where he got almost three-fourths of the vote. Fifteen of Trump's 80 percent counties were in the northern part of the state, many of them mountain counties hugging the state line. Trump held his own in the middle of the state but dropped by seven points in South Georgia.

Generational replacement also contributed to Biden's victory. Exit polls as far back as 2014 showed the under-thirty vote to be solidly Democratic. Even voters aged thirty to forty-four tended to prefer Democrats. Table 4.4 reports that Biden continued the Democratic success among the youngest voters although his margin was five points less than Clinton achieved. This less enthusiastic support among young voters was offset by Biden's stronger showing among other cohorts, especially retirees, 43 percent of whom voted for him probably in reaction to Trump's mishandling of the COVID pandemic. The National Pool exit poll found that of those who thought that efforts to handle the coronavirus were going badly, 87 percent voted for Biden. When confronted with a choice of whether it was more important to

Table 4.3 The Performances of Biden, Clinton, and Warnock in Georgia's Four Most Populous Counties

	Clinton		*Biden*		*Warnock*	
	Margin	%	Margin	%	Margin	%
DeKalb	199K	80	250K	83	238K	84
Fulton	171K	69	244K	73	220K	73
Gwinnett	19K	51	75K	58	79K	61
Cobb	7K	49	56K	56	49K	57

Source: Created by the author using official returns as reported by Georgia's Secretary of State.

Table 4.4 Candidate Support by Age, 2016 and 2020

Age	Clinton (%)	Trump (%)	Biden (%)	Trump (%)	Warnock (%)	Loeffler (%)
18–29	63	33	58	39	67	33
30–44	51	44	53	45	59	41
45–64	41	57	47	52	47	53%
>65	31	67	43	55	38	62

Source: Created by the author using National Election Pool Exit polls from 2016, 2018, 2020, and 2021.

try to contain the coronavirus or to rebuild the economy, 82 percent of the respondents who preferred the first option favored Biden.

Newer arrivals tend to be more supportive of Democrats than long-time residents. According to the 2020 Fox News Poll, most voters who had been in Georgia less than 20 years preferred Biden while Trump won a majority of those who had been in the state for more than 20 years.

None of these shifts in the composition of Georgia's electorate might have led to Democratic victory if the party had not made an investment in the state. Stacey Abrams (2019), whose 2018 gubernatorial campaign ended what she called "the 200,000 vote curse" losing by fewer than 55,000 votes, urged the Democratic Party to invest in Georgia. In 2008, the Obama campaign pulled its team out of Georgia in September (Galloway and Sheinin 2008). Clinton ignored the state in 2016. In response to Abrams's strong showing, Democrats put Georgia on their to-do list. In the closing weeks of the campaign, Biden, Kamala Harris, and Barack Obama all campaigned in Georgia.

Republicans also recognized Georgia's competitive status in 2020 although one of Georgia's senior Republican operative complains that the national party hesitated to share needed resources. President Trump made four trips to the state during the fall culminating with a rally in Rome two nights before Election Day. Vice President Mike Pence was a frequent visitor, as were various Trump offspring. While recognizing that Georgia had become competitive, only in the closing weeks did it dawn on the Trump team that they could actually lose Georgia. At that point, it invested heavily on pricey Atlanta television. Georgians responded to being in the national spotlight and set a record as five million trooped to the polls, an increase of almost 25 percent over the previous record set in 2016.

While Abrams and other Democrats have loudly criticized Georgia for suppressing the minority vote (Bullock et al. forthcoming), the state has taken steps to encourage voting. The GOP-controlled legislature approved no-excuse absentee voting in 2005 to facilitate voting among the elderly, usually a fountain of Republican support. The legislature also adopted an early voting format that allows voters to cast ballots in-person beginning twenty days before an election, ending on the Friday before Election Day. In the past, Democrats have dominated early in-person voting. The pandemic made early in-person voting less attractive. The GOP, like Democrats, continued the practice of encouraging supporters to cast absentee ballots. The party's message, however, clashed with Trump's warning that absentee voting was not secure. As a consequence, Democrats, many of them leery about crowds, sent in hundreds of thousands of absentee ballots, while Trump supporters heeded the president's warnings and waited to turn out on Election Day. In an effort to encourage his followers to show up on Election Day, Trump had a rally in Rome on the Sunday before the election.

Georgia counties do not begin counting absentee ballots until after the polls close on Election Day. Upon receipt, election officials check to see that the signature on the envelope containing the ballot matches the signature on file or on the voter's driver's license. The ballots can be scanned but not tabulated until the polls close.

The ballots cast on Election Day or early in-person using Georgia's new Dominion election equipment can be tabulated quickly and just a few hours after polls closed, Trump built a lead ultimately reaching about 300,000. Trump received 61.5 percent of the two-party votes cast on Election Day, but fewer than one in five voters went to the polls on November 3. He also won the early in-person voting with 53.2 percent.[1] But Biden dominated the absentee balloting taking 65.3 percent. In the days following the election, Trump's lead shrank, then disappeared and moving into the weekend, Biden inched ahead as absentee ballot counts slowly came in from the urban counties. Rather than acknowledging that his lead evaporated because Republicans heeded his warnings about the unreliability of voting absentee, Trump contended that the change occurred because Democrats were stealing the election.

Trump won Georgia by 211,000 votes in 2016. Biden improved on Clinton's performance across the four largest counties mentioned in table 4.3 by 229,000 votes, which wiped out the margin by which Trump won Georgia in 2016. Not only did Biden better Clinton's performance in terms of the number of votes in these vote-rich counties, but he also got larger shares of the vote in each of these counties. The Democratic advances in the four most populous counties are part of a larger trend. The Democratic percentage increased from 2008 to 2020 in *all* of the state's ten most populous counties (Todd 2021). Contributing to Democratic success all but one of the eight counties with the greatest increases in Democratic support is in Georgia.

Trump dominated rural Georgia. The only rural counties Trump lost were in the Black Belt, a swath across the middle of the state gradually shifting northward as it moves west from Columbus through Macon and on to Augusta. The Black Belt has rich soil and was the heart of the plantation economy prior to the Civil War. Some of these counties remain majority-black and others have black populations above 40 percent.

With Gwinnett and Cobb counties flipping to the Democratic Party in 2016, Republicans now score their largest winning margins in Atlanta's exurban counties but even here, Trump's edge shrank in 2020. Each of the four counties that provide Republicans with their largest winning margins in numbers of votes saw Trump's share decline in 2020. In Forsyth County, which gives Republicans their second-largest vote margins, Trump actually won by a smaller number of votes in 2020. Of concern for Republicans is the evidence that none of the counties that have had the greatest increase in GOP support over the last dozen years have gained population (Todd 2021).

Biden won despite having no ground game in Georgia. The state's Democrats followed their nominee's lead and avoided in-person campaigning. In contrast, the GOP engaged in traditional door-knocking carried out by paid workers augmented by volunteers.

CHALLENGES TO GEORGIA ELECTION

Georgia was the last state to be called. On November 7, Biden won the Peach State, equaling Trump's 2016 haul of 306 electors. When the Associated Press put Georgia in the Democratic column, that did not end the election but simply opened a new stage. In rejecting the outcome nationally, Trump directed much of his attack on Georgia. Some have speculated that Trump singled out Georgia as the site for his most aggressive efforts to reverse the results of the election because he could not believe that he might lose the state. Unlike, Michigan, Pennsylvania, and Wisconsin, which had been Democratic until 2016, Georgia had not supported a northern Democrat for president in sixty years. Even though the official overseeing Georgia elections, Secretary of State Brad Raffensperger is a Republican and a Trump supporter, the president repeatedly blamed Raffensperger for losing the state. Trump asked and even demanded that Raffensperger do something to alter the vote totals so that Georgia would end up in the Republican camp. Republican senators David Perdue and Kelly Loeffler, who would be competing in a January runoff since neither got a majority and desperate to curry Trump's favor, piled on. In a joint press release, devoid of specifics, they attacked their partisan colleague. "The Secretary of State has failed to deliver honest and transparent elections. He has failed the people of Georgia, and he should step down immediately" (Joint Statement 2020).

In 2020, Georgia replaced its eighteen-year-old voting machines with new touch screens made by Dominion. Among Trump's allegations was that in some instances, the machines awarded votes for Trump to Biden. To check out that rumor, Raffensperger ordered counties to hand count all five million ballots. In the course of this process, a few thousand uncounted votes were found but in Republican, not Democratic counties. When they were added in, Biden's plurality shrank from 14,000 to a little less than 12,000. The hand count did not uncover evidence of the machines misallocating votes. Since the margin was less than half a percentage point, Trump exercised the option to have another recount. This one was done by machine and did nothing to alter the result.

Because Biden had won the absentee votes convincingly, Rudy Giuliani and others in the Trump camp claimed that a number of these had been improperly cast (Judd 2020). U.S. Senator Lindsay Graham (R-SC) suggested that Raffensperger might exclude some of the absentee ballots from counties in which the process was heavily used. When this story became public, Graham denied the allegation and said that he had simply asked about the process (Walsh 2020). Trump claimed, with no evidence, that the signatures that must be on the envelopes containing the ballots had not been checked. One of the counties singled out in the complaints was Cobb which eight years earlier Mitt Romney won by 39,000 votes, but in 2020, Cobb favored Biden by 56,000 votes. The Georgia Bureau of Investigation drew a 10 percent sample of the envelopes and found no evidence of fraud with only two minor problems out of the 15,000 examined (Niesse 2020).

Another claim was that election workers in Fulton County mysteriously produced suitcases full of ballots. Videos, however, showed Fulton County election workers putting uncounted absentee ballots into the suitcases when they prepared to go home and then unpacking the suitcases when counting resumed (Corasaniti 2020b).

Other conspiracy theorists were certain that the temporary interruption in counting absentee ballots in Atlanta when a pipe burst at the facility had created a situation that allowed illegal ballots to be injected into the mix. Raffensperger rejected the claims of malfeasance by noting that his office had personnel there and, except when the Fulton County facility was closed after the pipe burst, representatives of the parties were on hand to witness the counting (Galloway 2020a).

President Trump did not hesitate to lean on Governor Brian Kemp, who he had endorsed in the 2018 GOP gubernatorial runoff. Trump's endorsement dramatically changed the trajectory of the contest in which then Kemp and then Lieutenant Governor Casey Cagle were competing (Bullock 2019). Trump and Kemp had never been personally close and the relationship deteriorated when Kemp tapped multi-millionaire businesswoman Kelly Loeffler to fill the Senate seat Johnny Isakson vacated at the end of 2019. Trump lobbied for Rep. Doug Collins who, as the ranking minority member of the House Judiciary Committee, led the president's defense at the first impeachment hearing. Although Kemp passed over Collins, the governor's support for Trump never wavered. When the president urged the governor to intercede and prevent the certification of the outcome, Kemp calmly responded that he did not have the authority to take that action. Kemp further alienated the president and some Republican legislators when he refused to convene a special session of the legislature, which Trump hoped would take the extraordinary action of ignoring the preference of Georgia's electorate and name a pro-Trump set of electors.

President Trump continued to press his claims that he had won a sweeping majority in Georgia. When speaking at rallies in Georgia, these claims elicited cheers from the crowd and his attacks on Kemp and Raffensperger intensified. He regretted his endorsement of Kemp in 2018 and called the governor a fool. Later, Trump called Kemp a "clown" and demanded that he resign (Bluestein 2020). Trump's final effort came in a phone call, four days before Congress would certify the results of the Electoral College. At times pleading and at times threatening, the president pressed his case that he had won Georgia and the election was being stolen by the Democrats. The president's demand boiled down to a request that the secretary of state "find" the 11,780 votes needed to shift Georgia from Biden to Trump. Unbeknownst to the president, Raffensperger recorded the hour-long phone call, which became public on the eve of the runoff.

TRUMP'S LOSS NOT A FLUKE

Everywhere but Georgia, the election season ended on November 3. Georgia, however, requires that, except for the presidency, candidates win with a majority. Because of the presence of a Libertarian candidate, Senator David Perdue fell 13,471 votes short of a majority. In the other Senate contest, a jungle primary with twenty-nine candidates, Raphael Warnock led with 32.9 percent of the vote. He would compete in a runoff against appointed Senator Kelly Loeffler who attracted 25.9 percent. These runoffs took on even greater significance since control of the Senate hung in the balance. Democrats had scored a net gain of a single seat on their quest to wrest three seats that, along with the vote of Vice President Kamala Harris, would have given them a majority. Republicans held fifty seats following the November election. If, somehow, Democrats could win both Georgia seats, then Harris's vote would allow them to organize the upper chamber, a major step toward enacting President Biden's agenda.

Georgia, in its unaccustomed role as a tossup state, received unprecedented attention leading up to November. That paled in comparison once it became clear that it would confer leadership of the Senate on either Chuck Schumer

(D-NY) or Mitch McConnell (R-KY). Tens of millions of dollars poured into the coffers of the four candidates. The parties ramped up their efforts sending both money and workers. Super PACs rushed in to pay top dollar to reserve the television ad slots that had not been purchased by other entities. When Georgia stations had no more ad slots to sell, space on stations in adjoining states whose signals beamed into parts of Georgia received a bonanza (Corasaniti 2020a). Incomplete filings showed $469 million spent on the Ossoff-Perdue contest with $362 million reported for the Warnock-Loeffler race (Martin and Fausset 2021), making these by far the most expensive Senate elections in history.

Since runoffs usually attract fewer voters than the contests that preceded them, they are seen as turnout elections rather than persuasion elections. The first priority of a turnout election is to remobilize those who voted for a candidate earlier and the way to do that is to attack the opponent and that was the playbook that guided the campaigns for the two Republican senators. Republican ads warned that should the Democrats, who were regularly referred to as radical socialists, win, then Democrats, in control of the Senate, House, and presidency would change America in frightening ways. In one ad, Perdue recited a litany of changes Democrats would impose: elimination of private health insurance, defunding the police, gutting the military, allowing illegal immigrants to vote, packing the Supreme Court.

Loeffler attacks on Warnock often took excerpts from his sermons. Statements taken out of context were used to claim that Warnock hated the military and the police. Another one showed Warnock praising Barack Obama's preacher Jeremiah Wright famous for the "Goddamn America sermon" that the GOP used unsuccessfully in the 2008 presidential campaign. The use of passages from Warnock sermons may have backfired and mobilized African Americans angered at what some saw as an attack on their religious institutions (Corasaniti 2020a; Sollenberger 2021). A Warnock ad countered that Loeffler had joined him in the pulpit where she said, "I am so humbled to be here with you today in this sacred place" (Galloway 2020b). Almost totally absent from the Republican advertising were indications of their policy initiatives if they won reelection.

The Democratic challengers included their share of attacks frequently chastising their opponents for using a briefing on the looming threat of a pandemic to improve their stock holdings rather than prepare Georgians for what was to come. They also offered a vision of change. They supported changes in the criminal justice system and called for voting rights legislation to reinvigorate the preclearance provision struck down by the Supreme Court in *Shelby County v. Holder* in 2013. Warnock and Ossoff urged more aggressive federal action against the pandemic. Warnock referred to the provision of adequate health care as a moral issue.

Republican media consultants found especially surprising Warnock's ads that injected a light touch rather than hammering his opponent. These television ads began in the first days of the runoff when Warnock warned that Republicans would launch attack ads that might, among other things, claim that he hated puppies and ate pizza with a knife and fork. The beagle puppy became so popular that a later ad had Warnock walking through a neighborhood with each frame showing him with a growing number of dogs pulling him toward a polling place (Goldmacher 2021). A third ad that many homeowners could identify with showed Warnock with a massive string of Christmas lights around his neck urging viewers to vote since that action would take less time than he would spend untangling the lights. These light-hearted ads humanized Warnock and helped deracialize the contest.

The Democratic Party sought to broaden its support by reaching out to individuals who had not voted in November, including teenagers who turned 18 between November and January 5. A top Democratic consultant explains that his organization identified a quarter-million African Americans who did not vote in November and bombarded them with phone calls and emails, and had canvassers visit their homes. He believes that 100,000 of these targeted individuals voted in the runoff. The runoff included almost a quarter of a million individuals who did not vote in November most of whom were minorities and 40 percent of whom were younger than thirty-five—components of the electorate that tend to favor Democrats (Niesse and Pebbles 2021). The Democrats who had avoided person-to-person campaigning returned to traditional grassroots efforts, albeit with masks in place, as the Ossoff staff mushroomed from 25 to more than 200, augmented by thousands of volunteers (Dawsey 2021).

Republicans also ramped up their door-knocking as the Republican National Committee sent 600 staffers just off the presidential campaign to Georgia (Hallerman 2020). But in contrast with new likely Democrats who turned out in January, the ranks of likely Republicans declined. An analysis done by the *Atlanta Journal-Constitution* identified 750,000 individuals who passed on voting in the runoff. The areas with the most dramatic drop-offs in participation are disproportionately White. Ironically, areas that experienced the most dramatic decline in participation were near where Trump held rallies (Niesse and Pebbles 2021). *New Yorker* writer Charles Bethea (2021), who attended the Dalton rally on the eve of the runoff, noted that many of the attendees were not Georgians, and they left before Senator Loeffler made her pitch. Some of those who go to Trump rallies are like political Deadheads who show up for the event even though they cannot vote in that jurisdiction. Some of the Georgians who attended the Trump rallies did not vote in the Senate runoff. Some Trump allies claimed that the senators were not doing enough to promote his claims of having won Georgia and therefore the Senate candidates did not deserve support (Garrison 2020). Other contributors to the disproportionate decline among Republicans are those who will turn out *only* when Trump is on the ballot.

Despite the reduction in participation, the runoffs attracted 4.5 million voters, a record for a runoff and a figure exceeded only by the five million who cast ballots in the previous November.

With Democrats united and surging, Ossoff overcame a November deficit of 88,000 votes and beat Perdue by 55,000 votes. Warnock maintained his jungle primary lead and beat Loeffler by 93,000 votes. While the margins in January exceeded those of two months earlier, the patterns were much the same with the Democrats winning the minority, youth, and urban votes, while the Republicans excelled with older, rural, and white voters. Table 4.4 shows that Warnock did especially well among younger voters, outpacing Biden by nine points with the youngest cohort.

Many attribute the defeat of the Republican senators and the GOP loss of the Senate to Trump. His unrelenting claims that Georgia's election system was corrupt convinced some Republicans that voting would be futile (Lerer et al. 2020; Fausset et al. 2021). While Trump dissuaded some Republicans from voting, his presence mobilized Democrats eager to deal him another defeat. A top official with one of the Democratic Senate campaigns stated that every time that Trump came to Georgia, their tracking poll registered an uptick. A Republican pollster acknowledged that Loeffler had a slight lead three days before the runoff, a lead that evaporated in the wake of the release of Trump's demands that Raffensperger find the votes needed to shift Georgia into the GOP column (Johnson 2021).

OTHER ELECTIONS

While Trump unquestionably mobilizes Republicans, he also energizes Democrats and their ranks are augmented by Republicans alienated by Trump. Evidence of the mixed Trump impact comes from the returns. While only Perdue got more votes than Trump, the president had the weakest performance in terms of vote share among Republican candidates. He trailed Perdue, two GOP candidates for the Public Service Commission, the vote share for the Republicans competing in the jungle primary for the other Senate seat and the vote share for the GOP congressional, state House, and state Senate candidates. Had Trump achieved the percentage of the vote attained by Perdue and the PSC candidates, he would have won Georgia's electors and not spent two months trying to force state officials to change the result.

Other evidence of relative GOP success comes in the returns for the state legislature. Democrats, who flipped fourteen metro Atlanta House seats and a pair of Senate seats in 2018 hoped that they might add the sixteen seats needed to achieve a majority in the lower chamber. Of a dozen House seats Republicans narrowly retained in 2018, Democrats flipped only three. Republicans managed to partially offset those losses by defeating the minority leader, the last white male Democrat representing a rural district. That GOP victory did not come cheaply as the party spent $1 million in a rural district with 22,250 voters (Prabhu 2020). The Democratic wins at the top of the ticket became attenuated at the level of legislative contests, which raises questions as to whether Georgia is on the verge of turning blue or it is simply that a critical component of the Republican electorate could not stomach Donald Trump. Nonetheless, the spin that Democrats put on their meager gains in the General Assembly is that Georgia is the rare state in which Democrats added seats in both chambers (Abrams 2020).

Compensating somewhat for disappointment in state House contests, Democrats had the only takeaway in the nation of a Republican congressional seat.[2] Carolyn Bourdeaux, who lost the Seventh District on the northeast side of Atlanta by 433 votes in 2018, won the now-open seat by 10,000 votes. Two years earlier, Democrat Lucy McBath won the adjoining Sixth District so that in the 117th Congress the GOP advantage fell to 8–6.

2020 AS A HARBINGER FOR 2022?

Georgia's Republican Party emerged from the 2020 election cycle at its weakest in more than a decade. It had been twenty-four years since the GOP lost a presidential contest and twenty years since it lost a Senate election. Republicans held fewer U.S. House seats than at any time since 2010. Potentially more troubling for the GOP was the division in the party's ranks triggered by Trump's baseless claims that he lost unfairly. The vitriol that Trump directed at Governor Kemp and Secretary of State Raffensperger seemed likely to fuel primary challenges in 2022. As the former president, cut off from Twitter, stewed in his Mar-a-Lago exile, defeating Kemp in 2022 reportedly became his top priority (Haberman and Epstein 2021). At the rally in Valdosta, Trump encouraged Doug Collins, his preference for the vacancy filled by Loeffler, to challenge Kemp. Early in 2021, a University of Georgia survey found Kemp upside down with 51 percent disapproval and 43 percent approval (Bluestein 2021). By a margin of 58–39 percent, Georgians reject Trump's claim of widespread voter fraud. While the survey found 40 percent of Georgians approving of Donald Trump but 57 percent disapproving, he had a much more favorable evaluation among Republicans, 66 percent of whom strongly approved with 19 percent somewhat approving. Endorsements by Trump may loom large in 2022 but to get that pat on the back, Republican candidates risk moving too far to the right as Loeffler and Perdue did.

Kemp may be Trump's least favorite Republican but other Georgians may find themselves challenged in the 2022 primary by individuals who claim the former president's favor. Trump repeatedly attacked and threatened Secretary of State Raffensperger as he sought to overturn the result of the presidential vote in Georgia. Lieutenant Governor Geoff Duncan who, like Kemp, stood by Raffensperger and rejected the president's baseless claims of election irregularities, could also become a target. Attorney General Chris Carr drew Trump's ire by opposing the lawsuit filed by the Texas attorney general that sought to block certification of the electors from Georgia and the other states that Trump claimed were stolen from him. If Trump continues along the path of retribution and that results in acrimonious GOP primaries, Republicans may be unable to reunite to face challenges from a united and confident Democratic Party. Democratic turnout often dips in a midterm election but Stacey Abrams countered that trend in 2018, and, if as expected, she heads the Democratic ticket in 2022, the GOP may see more prizes slip from its grasp.

The success registered by Joe Biden and the Democratic Senate candidates may become a model for aspiring Democrats in other southern states. Democratic wins in Georgia came about as a result of two factors. First, came the efforts of Stacey Abrams and others to mobilize the latent African American vote. The years that Abrams invested in this project came to fruition in 2020. Registering and then turning out record numbers of blacks alone does not suffice. The other element is attracting a sufficient share of the white vote. That part is trickier. Some candidates may find it easier than others to broaden their appeal to whites. The most important feature increasing white support for Democrats may be in-migration to the state. As Perry Bacon observed, the 2020 outcome differed from that of 2016 because "these aren't people shifting to the Democratic Party because of Trump—these are Democrats who just happened to show up in Atlanta's electorate at the time of Trump's rise" (Bacon 2020).

If recent trends continue, Georgia will remain competitive but with Democrats ratcheting upward. Abrams's supporters continue efforts to bring more minorities and younger citizens into the electorate. Each month sees more people moving to the state to take advantage of the economic opportunities and these new residents tend to lean more Democratic than Republican. Republicans in the legislature have seemingly conceded the Democratic tilt as one of their top priorities in 2021 is to make voting, especially absentee voting where Democrats ran up insurmountable majorities, more difficult (Niesse 2021). Other bills would reduce the availability of early voting. One proposal bans Sunday voting, famous for souls to polls efforts in black churches. Not all of the work by the GOP seeks to make voting more difficult. Loeffler, who as this is written, is contemplating a rematch with Warnock in 2022, has taken a page from Abrams's playbook, and launched a mobilization program directed as expanding the ranks of conservative voters (Bluestein 2021). Loeffler claims the state has two million potential conservatives who, if mobilized, would benefit Republicans who play on voter fears of change. Those kinds of messages have succeeded in rural Georgia. Staking out far-right positions comes with a cost as they can drive suburban voters toward the Democratic Party.

NOTES

1. Percentages here are exclusive of the small share received by the Libertarian candidate.
2. The only other gains scored by Democrats in 2020 came in two North Carolina redrawn to become more Democratic prior to the election.

REFERENCES

Abrams, Stacey. 2019. "The Abrams Playbook: The Strategy and Path to Victory in 2000."
Abrams, Stacey. 2020 "How Georgia Went Blue." *Democracy Docket* (December 11).
Bacon, Perry, Jr. 2020. "How Georgia Turned Blue." 538 (November 18).
Bethea, Charles. 2021. "Trump and the G.O.P. Lost Georgia. Black Voters Won It." *New Yorker* (January 5).
Bluestein, Greg. 2020. "As Runoffs near, Trump Says Kemp Should Resign." *Atlanta Journal-Constitution* (December 31).
Bluestein, Greg. 2021. "Republicans in Dicey Political Territory Now." *Atlanta Journal-Constitution* (January 31).
Bullock, Charles S., III, Susan A. MacManus, Jeremy D. Mayer and Mark J. Rozell. 2019. *The South and the Transformation of U. S. Politics*. New York: Oxford University Press.
Bullock, Charles S., III, Susan A. MacManus, Jeremy D. Mayer and Mark J. Rozell. Forthcoming. *African American Candidates in the New South*. (New York: Oxford University Press).
Bullock, Charles S., III, and Mark Rozell, editors. Forthcoming. *The New Politics of the Old South*, 7th ed. Lanham, MD: Rowman and Littlefield.
Bluestein, Greg. 2021a. "Loeffler Launches GOP Voter Drive." *Atlanta Journal-Constitution* (February 23).
Corasaniti, Nick. 2020a. "Ad Spending Soars in Georgia Races with Stakes Far Beyond State." *New York Times* (December 21).
Corasaniti, Nick. 2020b. "'Ridiculous': Election Official Debunks Claims of Fraud." *New York Times* (December 8).

Dawsey, Josh. 2021. "'Always about Him': How Trump's Obsession with Baseless Election Claims Cost Republicans in Georgia." *Washington Post* (January 10).

Fausset, Richard, Jonathan Martin and Stephanie Saul. 2021. "For Democrats, Victory amid Tumult." *New York Times* (January 7).

Fox News Democracy. 2020. Georgia President Exit Poll.

Franco, Marisa. 2020. "Latinos Sent a Warning Sign to Democrats," *New York Times* (November 20).

Galloway, Jim. 2020a. "Secretary of State Stands Up for the Facts." *Atlanta Journal-Constitution* (November 11).

Galloway, Jim. 2020b. "Taking Sen. Kelly Loeffler to Church." *Atlanta Journal-Constitution* (December 2).

Galloway, Jim, and Aaron Gould Sheinin. 2008. "Obama to Trim Staff in Georgia." *Atlanta Journal-Constitution* (September 10).

Garrison, Joey. 2020. "'They Have Not Earned Your Vote': Trump Allies Urge Georgia Republicans to Sit Out Senate Runoffs." *USA Today* (December 2).

Goldmacher, Sheldon. 2021. "A Puppy So Cute He Helped Tug Georgians Left." *New York Times* (January 21).

Haberman, Maggie, and Reid J. Epstein. 2021. "As Kingmaker, Trump Can Target Disloyalty." *New York Times* (January 26).

Hallerman, Tamar. 2020. "Runoffs Flood Georgia with Volunteers, Attention." *Atlanta Journal-Constitution* (November 16).

Johnson, Eliana. 2021. "Inside the GOP's Week from Hell." *Politico Playbook* (January 10).

Joint Statement from Senators David Perdue and Kelly Loeffler. 2020. (November 9).

Judd, Alan. 2020. "Judge Rejects Bid to Black Results." *Atlanta Journal-Constitution* (November 20).

Lerer, Lisa, Richard Fausset, and Maggie Haberman. 2020. "Trump Attacks Unsettle G.O.P. amid a Runoff." *New York Times* (December 2).

Martin, Jonathan, and Richard Fausset. 2021. "Georgians Vote, Charting Course of the Senate." *New York Times* (January 6).

National Election Pool Exit Poll. 2020. Georgia President Exit Poll.

Niesse, Mark. 2020. "Authenticity of Absentee Ballots Confirmed in Audit." *Atlanta Journal-Constitution* (December 30).

Niesse, Mark. 2021. "GOP Senators Introduce Measures to Restrict Absentee Voting in State." *Atlanta Journal-Constitution* (February 2).

Niesse, Mark, and Jennifer Peebles. 2021. "Lower GOP Turnout Helped Flip Senate." *Atlanta Journal-Constitution* (February 3).

Prabhu, Maya T. 2020. "Democratic Leader's Loss a GOP Win." *Atlanta Journal-Constitution* (November 30).

Sollenbeger, Roger. 2021. "Kelly Loeffler's New Facebook Ad Darkens Skin of Raphael Warnock, Her Black Opponent." *Salon* (January 4).

Todd, Chuck. 2021. "First Read." NBC News (February 24).

Walsh, Joe. 2020. "Report: Lindsey Graham Suggested Tossing Out Legal Main-In Ballots in Georgia, Secretary of State Say." *Forbes* (November 16).

Chapter 5

Louisiana

Trump Support in This Swamp Runs Deep

Robert E. Hogan and Anna R. Elinkowski

INTRODUCTION

The 2020 presidential election in Louisiana was extraordinarily similar to the 2016 election with respect to the outcome and level of support received by each party's nominee across regions of the state. Of the more than 2.1 million votes cast in Louisiana, Republican nominee Donald Trump won with 58.5 percent of the total vote to Joseph Biden's 39.9 percent. The two-party vote margin favoring Trump was 59.5 percent, which was only slightly lower than his 2016 margin (60.2 percent) but slightly higher than Romney's margin in 2012 (58.8 percent). All this suggests that Donald Trump's campaign appeals and priorities were highly attractive to the state's voters. Republicans have won Louisiana in every presidential election since 2000 and the high percentage sustained in 2020 bodes well for continued GOP success in the Pelican State (Louisiana Secretary of State, 2021).

BRIEF HISTORY

Changes in Louisiana politics over the past several decades are not unlike patterns observed in other southern states (Kapeluck and Buchanan 2018). As the allegiance of white voters shifted from Democratic to Republican candidates, the state's politics were altered dramatically. Republicans had some early successes in Louisiana at the presidential level (Dwight Eisenhower in 1956 and Barry Goldwater in 1964), but it was the 1970s before Republicans became an established presence. In 1972, voters elected a Republican congressman to the U.S. House, and in 1979, they elected a Republican governor (both firsts since Reconstruction). Table 5.1 traces these changes across various offices since 1980.

At the beginning of this period, Republicans were winning a sizeable percentage of the vote in presidential elections but constituted only a minority of the congressional delegation. At the state legislative level, they held only a handful of seats in each chamber, but Republican fortunes began to climb steadily in subsequent years and the pace accelerated dramatically about fifteen years ago. Along with winning strong majorities in presidential contests, Republicans currently hold all but one of the state's six U.S. House seats. Since the 2014 election, both U.S. Senate seats are occupied by Republicans. The GOP advantage in the legislature is now extensive as they control 69.2 percent of state Senate seats and 63.8 percent of State House seats (Louisiana Secretary of State 2021).

Table 5.1 Rising Support for the GOP in Louisiana 1980–2020

Year	Presidential Vote (%)	U.S. Senate Vote (%)	U.S. House Delegation (%)	Vote for Governor (%)	State Senate Seats (%)	State House Seats (%)
1980	51.2	1.6	25.0	50.3	9.5	0.0
1982			25.0			
1984	60.8	9.0	25.0	36.3	10.5	2.6
1986		47.2	37.5			
1988	54.3		50.0	18.6	16.2	12.8
1990		43.5	50.0			
1992	41.0	8.0	42.9	38.8	15.2	15.4
1994			42.9			
1996	40.4	49.8	42.9	63.5	26.6	33.8
1998		31.6	71.4			
2000	52.6		71.4	62.2	29.5	33.3
2002		48.3	57.1			
2004	56.7	51.0	71.4	48.1	38.5	35.2
2006			71.4			
2008	58.6	45.7	85.7	53.8	35.9	41.0
2010		56.6	85.7			
2012	57.8		83.4	65.8	61.5	55.2
2014		55.9	83.4			
2016	58.1	60.7	83.4	43.9	64.1	58.1
2018			83.4			
2020	58.5	59.3	83.4	48.7	69.2	63.8

Note: Election results represent the percent of the total vote for president, U.S. senator, and governor. *Note* that governors and state legislators are elected every four years and results are noted in the year following their election. Results for U.S. House, State Senate, and State House represent the percentage of seats won by Republicans.
Source: Louisiana Secretary of State.

Given the widespread support for Republicans for so many offices, one might be surprised to observe that Louisiana's last two gubernatorial elections were won by a Democrat. Staking out conservative positions on hot button issues such as abortion and guns, John Bel Edwards artfully exploited the vulnerabilities of his runoff opponent in 2015, U.S. Senator David Vitter, who faced continued allegations about his involvement with a prostitute in the so-called DC Madam scandal. Edwards won that race in a runoff against Vitter with 56.1 percent of the vote (Hogan 2018). In his bid for reelection in 2019, Edwards faced two major Republican opponents and prevailed with 51.3 percent in a runoff where he faced a weak, although well-funded opponent (Louisiana Secretary of State 2021). Such back-to-back wins by a Democrat for the state's highest office indicates that Democrats who take conservative positions on social issues and who can campaign hard on their opponent's weaknesses can have a shot at winning major office. But the fact that the GOP holds the six other statewide constitutional offices, all but one of the congressional delegation seats, and expanding majorities in both state legislative chambers, all suggest that Democratic successes will be exceptions to the general pattern of GOP dominance.

PRIMARY ELECTIONS

Prior to the start of the primary season, some presidential contenders and their surrogates made campaign stops in Louisiana. Donald Trump visited the state twice in November 2019 to hold rallies touting the candidacy of Republican gubernatorial candidate Eddie Rispone (Hilburn 2019). Joe Biden visited New Orleans earlier in the summer of 2019 to attend the Youth Empowerment Project and later joined Congressman Cedric Richmond for a fundraising dinner (WWLTV.com 2019). But given Louisiana's late place on the primary calendar, the state received relatively little attention from those seeking the presidential nomination.

Due to an oddity of Louisiana's election laws, the state was required to move its presidential preference primary from the first Saturday in March. In June of 2019, Governor Edwards signed an omnibus elections code bill changing the date to the first Saturday in April, which meant it would coincide with the Democratic primaries scheduled in Alaska and Hawaii. This was the latest date for a Louisiana presidential preference primary since 2000 and some party officials worried that placing the contest so late in the process would diminish Louisiana's influence in the crowded Democratic contest (Karlin 2019).[1] Of course, this was to be only the first of several changes in Louisiana's election calendar in 2020. As the severity of the COVID crisis unfolded, states began to consider altering the timing and manner of their presidential contests. On March 13, Louisiana became the first state to postpone its presidential primary, moving it to April 4 (Pramuk 2021). However, this date was later pushed back to June 20 and then moved once again to July 11. This late primary date meant that the nomination battle was a foregone conclusion before Louisiana voters could have an opportunity to register their preferences. Additional changes implemented by the Secretary of State expanded the eligibility of absentee voting by mail for the July primaries. These voting expansions were criticized by Republican lawmakers who successfully reduced mail-in ballot eligibility for the fall elections (Karlin 2020).

In presidential primaries, Louisiana restricts participation to registered party voters, and in 2020 approximately 471,581 voters participated. This was down significantly from the turnout of 613,017 in 2016 when the nomination was heavily contentious in both parties. Approximately 276,286 voters voted in the Democratic contest and 204,295 in the Republican contest. This resulted in a turnout rate of 21.3 percent for Democrats and 21.5 for Republicans. It should be noted that while Republican turnout was down significantly from where it was in 2016 (35.9 percent), Democratic turnout was not that much lower (23.5 percent). It makes sense that turnout was down among Republicans given the nominal opposition to the incumbent president. Perhaps turnout among Democrats was influenced by the many political party offices that were also on the ballot that provided incentives for party activists to participate. Whatever the case, it seems that turnout in both parties was relatively high, given that the nomination had effectively been decided already and fears over COVID continued to loom large (Louisiana Secretary of State 2021).

Regarding the outcome of the vote, table 5.2 shows that within the Democratic primary, Joseph Biden won 79.5 percent, Bernie Sanders received 7.4 percent, and the remaining twelve candidates on the ballot received a combined total of 13.1 percent. Among the Republicans, Donald Trump

Table 5.2 2020 Louisiana Presidential Primary Results

	Votes	%
Democratic Primary		
Joseph Biden	212,555	79.5
Bernie Sanders	19,859	7.4
Others	34,872	13.1
Republican Primary		
Donald Trump	195,910	95.9
Bill Weld	3,320	1.6
Others	5,065	2.5

Note: There were 12 additional candidates for the Democratic nomination and 3 additional candidates for the Republican nomination.
Source: Louisiana Secretary of State.

received 95.9 percent, Bill Weld received 1.6 percent, and the three additional candidates received 2.5 percent (Louisiana Secretary of State 2021). Given that Louisiana's primaries occurred at the end of the primary period, when both Trump and Biden had already passed the delegate threshold for securing the nomination, it is little wonder that the vote count was so lopsided.

Although both Biden and Trump won their primaries handily, their level of support varied by region of the state. Within the Democratic primaries, Biden's highest level of support was in the North-Central region while Sanders's highest support was in the Greater New Orleans region. Both Biden and Sanders received greater support where blacks comprised a larger portion of the population and where a higher share of whites have a college degree.[2] Biden's support was higher in urban parishes (a parish is Louisiana's equivalent to a county). while Sanders's support was greater in rural and suburban areas.[3] Even within the Republican primary where Trump won nearly 96 percent of the primary vote, some variation could be observed. Trump did best in the North-Central region, which is highly rural and in parishes where there are lower percentages of blacks and larger numbers of white voters without a college degree.

GENERAL ELECTION

Given voters' strong sentiment favoring Republicans, Louisiana's electoral votes were never considered up for grabs by the presidential campaigns. Campaign advertising and candidate visits (few were made due to COVID restrictions) were focused instead on a limited number of battleground states (Corasaniti, et al. 2020). Louisiana voters were therefore relegated to watching the campaign unfold on their television screens or digital devices. To the extent that presidential politics had any effect in the state, some local candidates attempted to utilize national politics to energize their bases of support.

Louisiana citizens did play an important auxiliary role in the presidential campaigns through their financial contributions to candidates. During the election cycle, both political parties and presidential campaigns raised substantial sums from Louisiana citizens. Federal Election Commission reports indicated that Louisiana citizens contributed approximately $11.8 million during the 2019–2020 cycle. In combination, the Republicans raised $7.6 million, nearly all of which flowed to the incumbent President's campaign. The Democrats' combined fundraising total was substantially less at $4.1 million with Biden's campaign raising over 70 percent of these funds (Federal Election Commission 2021). The substantial imbalance favoring Republicans is not too surprising, given the sentiments of state voters and the fact that incumbent presidents have an easier time raising funds.

Approximately 70.1 percent of registered voters in Louisiana cast ballots for president, an increase of over two percentage points from 2016 (Louisiana Secretary of State 2021). Nearly one-third of these votes were cast during the ten-day early voting period or by mail-in absentee ballot, a level breaking previous records by a sizable margin (Karlin 2020). Table 5.3 displays the rates of participation by various subgroups in the three most recent presidential elections. Participation varied by racial classification, as in previous years. In 2020, voters classifying themselves as white turned out at rates higher (74.5 percent) than voters classified as black (63.1 percent) or other (60.7 percent). For whites, this represented an increase from the two previous elections, perhaps reflecting the high degree of support for President Trump. For blacks, it represents a continuation of lower turnout than what had been observed in 2012 when President Obama was last on the ballot. Regarding gender differences, we see a continued pattern of women turning out to vote at higher rates than men. However, turnout among men was higher in 2020 than in the previous two elections (Louisiana Secretary of State 2021).

Large differences in turnout exist based on party registration. Turnout among Republicans was over 10 points higher than turnout among Democrats and over 20 points higher than turnout among "other" voters (unaffiliated voters or those registered with minor parties). Examining the party categories by race, one finds white Democrats voting at rates higher than black Democrats (72.1 to 67.9 percent). White Republicans had a turnout rate of 81.7 percent, the highest among any of the categories examined. Black Republicans voted at the lowest rate of any group examined at 51.3 percent; however, it should be noted that only about 2.2 percent of Republican registrants are black (Louisiana Secretary of State 2021).

Table 5.3 Voter Turnout in Louisiana Presidential Elections in 2012–2020

	2012	2016	2020
Total	67.9	67.8	70.1
White	69.4	71.5	74.5
Black	67.2	62.0	63.1
Other	52.9	56.5	60.7
Men	65.2	65.3	68.3
Women	70.2	69.9	71.7
Democrats	69.8	68.0	69.2
Republicans	76.4	78.0	80.6
Unaffiliated/ Other Parties	54.7	55.6	58.5
White Democrats	69.3	70.6	72.1
Black Democrats	70.9	66.6	67.9
White Republicans	77.6	79.2	81.7
Black Republicans	54.3	51.0	51.3

Source: Louisiana Secretary of State.

ELECTION RESULTS

The number of votes received by each major party candidate and the percentages of the two-party vote won by Republican nominees since 2012 are provided in table 5.4. Overall, Donald Trump received 1,255,776 votes to Joseph Biden's 856,034 votes. Trump's two-party vote total was 59.5 percent, slightly less than his winning percentage in 2016 (60.2 percent) but slightly more than Romney's margin in 2012 (58.8 percent). Comparing the support across the four regions of the state one finds that Trump did best in the Acadiana region (67.0 percent) and in the North-Central parts of the state (64.0 percent) and worst in the Greater New Orleans area (47.3 percent). Overall, the sources of Trump's support by region in 2020 weres nearly identical to what he received in 2016. Compared to Romney, Trump's support was lower in the Greater New Orleans region and higher in the Acadiana and North-Central regions. Such patterns comport with our general understanding that Trump's greatest strengths lie among rural voters (Louisiana Secretary of State 2021).

An additional perspective on candidate support throughout the state can be obtained by examining votes by the parish. Postelection analyses conducted nationally following the 2020 elections indicated that a variety of factors differentiate Republican and Democratic supporters. Among the more prominent are race, level of educational attainment, and urbanization. Trump's support was strongest among white voters with low levels of educational attainment and those residing in rural areas. Biden's support was greatest among minority voters, especially black voters, citizens with higher levels of educational attainment, and those living in urban areas. In addition, national analyses showed that many suburban areas shifted toward Biden in 2020 (Frey 2020). An aggregate-level analysis of the 2016 elections in Louisiana

Table 5.4 Louisiana Votes for Present by Region

Parish Region	Trump Votes	2020 Biden Votes	2020 Trump Two-Party %	2016 Trump Two-Party %	2012 Romney Two-Party %
Greater New Orleans	250,870	279,642	47.3	48.9	49.9
Acadiana	460,848	227,072	67.0	67.0	63.9
Florida Parishes	207,051	159,607	56.5	57.4	57.0
North-Central	337,007	189,713	64.0	64.0	61.4
Statewide	1,255,776	856,034	59.5	60.2	58.8

Source: Louisiana Secretary of State.

showed similar patterns across Louisiana's sixty-four parishes. Increases in Republican support were greatest in rural areas, where a high percentage of whites have no college degree (Hogan 2018). A comparable approach is employed here to link population characteristics to partisan support in presidential contests. Table 5.5 shows the Republican percentage of two-party support received across three elections in parishes on three dimensions. Parishes are grouped into high, medium, or low categories on the percentage of whites with at least a BA degree and percent black voters in the highest third, middle third, and lowest third (U.S. Census 2021). Residential characteristics of the district are designated as urban, suburban, and rural (National Center for Health Statistics 2021).

The results in table 5.5 indicate that support for Republican presidential candidates is quite strong in those parishes where a large percentage of white voters do not hold a college degree. In 2020, parishes ranked in the highest third of education attainment of whites supported Trump with 54.0 percent of the vote, but those ranked in the lowest third supported him with 71.9 percent. Looking across the three election cycles, one sees that these differences becoming more pronounced over time. The vote margin between the highest third and lowest third parishes was 11 points in 2012, 15 points in 2016, and nearly 18 points by 2020. Parishes with large numbers of whites without college degrees are a major source of strength for Republican presidential candidates in the state.

Looking at the percentage of black residents by parish, we also find major differences in support for the two parties. In 2020, support for Trump was 39.8 percent among parishes ranked in the top-third of black population

Table 5.5 Support for Republicans Presidential Candidates by Population Characteristics of Parishes (Two-Party Vote 2012–2020)

	2012 (%)	2016 (%)	2020 (%)
Whites with BA Degree			
High	55.3	55.4	54.0
Medium	65.2	69.0	69.7
Low	66.4	70.8	71.9
Percentage of Blacks			
High	41.4	40.6	39.8
Medium	62.7	64.5	63.7
Low	75.4	77.7	76.3
Characteristics of District			
Urban	49.8	49.2	47.7
Suburban	61.7	63.5	62.9
Rural	62.7	67.0	68.1

Source: Louisiana Secretary of State; U.S. Census Bureau, American Community Survey five-year average, 2015–19; National Center for Health Statistics, Urban-Rural Classification Scheme for Counties.

percentage but 76.3 percent among those ranked in the bottom third. This amounts to nearly a 36-percentage point difference and is consistent across all three election periods examined.

Major differences also exist across parishes depending on their urban, rural, or suburban designation. In 2020, rural parish support for Republicans was the highest where 68.1 percent of voters supported Trump. Support among suburban districts was only slightly lower at 62.9 while support within urban parishes was the lowest at 47.7 percent. Across the time periods, it appears that urban support for Republicans fell slightly while rural support grew a moderate amount. Support within the suburbs remained steady but fell slightly from 2016.

The general pattern to emerge is that Republican presidential candidates do very well in rural parishes where there are large percentages of white voters who have low levels of educational attainment. It would appear that these associations are getting more pronounced over time, particularly if we compare 2016 and 2020 to 2012. Such differences could be attributable to Donald Trump's candidacy and they may dissipate when he is no longer on the ballot. It is important to note, however, that while rural parishes and those with small black populations are a large source of strength for Republican presidential candidates, the total population of these parishes constitutes a relatively small percentage of the state's voters. Parishes with the smallest percentages of black voters (lowest third) account for only 28 percent of the state's population. Parishes designated as rural account for only about 16 percent of the state's total population. While these areas represent bastions of support, to remain successful, Republicans will need to continue winning a sizeable portion of the urban and suburban parishes.

Another way to assess voting patterns in Louisiana is to examine the individual-level responses of voters. Using publicly released data from a reputable polling firm that surveyed voters in late October, table 5.6 displays the distribution of several relevant characteristics by support for Trump and Biden (Chervenak and Licciardi 2020).

National polls conducted in 2020 indicated that party identification plays a major role in how citizens vote in presidential elections. Simply put, voters identifying with a particular party are much more likely to support that party's candidates for office (CNN 2020). However, we also know that partisanship has been less useful in explaining patterns of voting in southern states. This is particularly true for Democratic identifiers who have tended to cast ballots for Democrats running for state and local offices while at the same time also casting ballots for Republicans at the presidential level. Analyses of voting patterns in Louisiana's 2016 elections indicated that Democratic identifiers were far less loyal to their party's presidential nominee than Republican identifiers (Hogan 2018). While nearly 92 percent of Republican registrants supported Trump, only

Table 5.6 Poll Results of Likely Voters in Louisiana 2020

	Trump (%)	Biden (%)	Other (%)	Undecided (%)
Base support	59	36	4	1
Party Identification				
Democrat	18	77	3	2
Republican	90	8	1	1
Independent/Other	57	28	13	2
Race				
White	73	23	2	2
Black	28	65	5	1
Other	42	39	17	3
Age				
Under 35	50	45	5	0
35–54	59	31	7	2
55+	62	35	1	2
Gender				
Men	59	32	7	2
Women	59	39	1	1
COVID serious				
Yes	43	51	4	2
No	92	5	3	1
Don't Know	82	4	11	4

Source: University of New Orleans Survey Research Center. The interactive voice response (IVR) telephone survey contacted 755 respondents on October 22, 2020. The sample was chosen from a list of all registered voters who voted at least once in one of the past 10 state-wide elections. The poll had a margin of error of ± 3.6% with a 95% level of confidence.

slightly more than 60 percent of Democratic registrants supported Clinton. Do we see a similar pattern in 2020? Results in table 5.6 indicate that Democratic identifiers are indeed much less loyal to their party's nominee than Republican identifiers. Whereas 90 percent of Republicans said they intended to vote for Trump only 77 percent of Democrats said they planned to vote for Biden.[4]

What about those voters who identify with a different party or who say they are "independent"? A 2016 study of Louisiana voters found these voters supported Trump by a 2–1 margin (Hogan 2018). Here we see a very similar pattern in 2020 with Trump's support being nearly double that of Biden's among independents and other party identifiers.

Race is another prominent voter characteristic that is likely to impact candidate support. Analyses from Louisiana's 2016 presidential election showed that white support was much higher for the Republican nominee (68 percent for Trump and 20 percent for Clinton), while black voters were more supportive of the Democratic nominee (73 percent for Clinton and less than 7 percent for Trump) (Hogan 2018). Table 5.6 shows a similar pattern in 2020. Approximately 73 percent of white voters supported Trump, while 23 percent supported Biden. Among African Americans, 65 percent supported Biden and 28 percent supported Trump. Such a sizeable percentage of the black vote for a Republican seems much larger than one might expect and certainly much larger than it was in Louisiana in 2016 when Trump received approximately 6.5 percent of the black vote (Hogan 2018). Exit polls and surveys conducted nationally indicated that Trump improved upon his support from some minority groups, including African Americans (Frey 2020). His campaign clearly made appeals to African Americans by emphasizing enhanced economic prosperity during his administration. In addition, the Trump campaign used negative and largely misleading claims aimed at Biden to draw support from this group. For example, on more than one occasion, Trump falsely accused Biden of referring to black youth as "super predators," a reference that was actually made by Hillary Clinton (Collins 2020). The results in Louisiana suggest that these strategies were effective.

Another characteristic associated with voting is age. National polling in 2020 indicated that younger voters preferred Biden, while older voters were more favorable to Trump (Frey 2020). In Louisiana, voters aged fifty-five or over preferred Trump to Biden by nearly a 2–1 margin (62 to 35 percent). For those under 35, Trump was still the preferred candidate, but the margin was much smaller (50 for Trump and 45 percent for Biden). That Trump topped Biden even among this group of younger voters is testimony to the depth of his support in the state.

National exit polls indicated the presence of a gender gap in voting with men heavily preferring Trump and women favoring Biden by wide margins (CNN 2020). The results in table 5.6 show there is far less of a gender gap among Louisiana voters than what is typically observed at the national level. Approximately 59 percent of men prefer Trump but so do 59 percent of women. However, it is true that women prefer Biden (39 percent) to a greater extent than men do (32 percent). Such a finding has some parallels with polling from 2016 in Louisiana, although in that election, the gap in support among women for Trump over Clinton was much wider.

A final consideration involves perceptions of the COVID crisis. Specifically, did citizens' view about the seriousness of COVID have any relationship with their voting? Among those who said they felt the issue to be serious, a slight majority voted for Biden over Trump (51 to 43 percent). However, among those who said COVID was not serious, 92 percent supported Trump while only 5 percent supported Biden. Additionally, among those who weren't sure of the seriousness of COVID, support for Trump over Biden was also extensive (82 percent to 4 percent). Such findings indicate a clear association between COVID perceptions and voting; however, the exact nature of this relationship is unclear (e.g., whether there is a causal connection and, if so, which direction it flows).

In combination, these survey responses indicate that voter characteristics associated with voting in Louisiana are not exceptionally different from what we see at the national level. Factors such as party identification, race, age, and gender are generally having an influence as we might expect; however, the magnitude of the associations is not as pronounced among Louisiana voters. For example, while Democratic identifiers are clearly more supportive of Biden than they are of Trump, these differences are not nearly as large as those observed at the national level. The same patterns hold for race, age, and gender and reflect, in part, the deep level of support Trump enjoys among the state's voters.

OTHER ELECTIONS

Statewide elections and state legislators in Louisiana are elected to four-year terms in odd-numbered years with the last election being in 2019. As mentioned in the introduction, Governor John Bel Edwards faced opposition in 2019 from five candidates, two of whom were well-funded Republicans. Under Louisiana's open-election system, all candidates regardless of party compete in a first-round election with a runoff needed if no candidate receives a majority. One of Edwards's opponents was three-term Congressman Ralph Abraham who campaigned on his staunch conservative values and experience in Congress. Another major contender was Eddie Rispone, a businessman and first-time candidate who campaigned as a loyal ally of Donald Trump. Both Republicans took aim at Edwards's term as governor, criticizing his priorities and accusing him of being a tax-and-spend liberal.

As one might expect from an incumbent, Edwards's campaign focused primarily on his accomplishments as governor. Given that he is a Democrat in a Republican voting state, his campaign also emphasized his ability to work with members of both political parties, including President Trump. Edwards came close to winning outright with 46.6 percent of the vote but was pushed into a runoff with Eddie Rispone. Rispone's campaign had significant levels of funding, and he received not only a Trump endorsement but also campaign visits by the president himself. Still, Rispone had difficulty articulating a vision for what he would do as governor. Many complained that his stump speeches were little more than repackaged Trump talking points and some noted that his campaign was managed by out-of-state consultants who lacked the experience needed to successfully navigate the state's political terrain. In the end, Edwards won the runoff with 51.3 percent of the vote with many attributing his success to support he received from suburban voters. Although Edwards was an incumbent, and a popular one, his journey to reelection was perilous given his party affiliation (Bridges 2019, Rojas and Alford 2019).

In 2020, the highest office up for grabs was the U.S. Senate seat held by first-term Senator Bill Cassidy. Shreveport Mayor Adrian Perkins was the most prominent Democratic candidate to emerge in a crowded field to challenge Cassidy. He raised significant amounts of funding ($2.8 million to Cassidy's $11.5 million) and his campaign drew substantial interest, at least initially (Federal Election Commission 2021). Perkins faced difficulty getting his message to resonate in a media environment focused on presidential politics (Joseph 2020). Moreover, Senator Cassidy's refusal to meet him in a one-on-one debate (Cassidy would only agree to a debate if all fifteen candidates were invited) meant that Perkins was deprived of a major opportunity to make his case to voters (Deslatte 2020). Ultimately, Perkins's campaign never gained sufficient traction and Cassidy won the first round of elections outright with 59.3 percent of the vote (Louisiana Secretary of State 2021).

Of the six U.S. House seats in the state, five featured incumbent representatives (four Republicans and one Democrat) who all faced multiple opponents. However, each of the incumbents won reelection handily with anywhere from 60 percent to 72 percent of the vote. The only real competitive election was for the open seat in the Fifth Congressional District being vacated by Ralph Abraham who decided to retire from Congress after losing the governor's race a year earlier. Nine candidates (five Republicans and four Democrats) competed in the race that advanced two Republicans to a runoff. Luke Letlow, the Chief of Staff to the outgoing Congressman Abraham, faced Lance Harris, a businessman and member of the Louisiana House of Representatives in a runoff on December 5 that Letlow won with 62 percent of the vote. Tragically, the congressman-elect died of complications related to COVID a few weeks later before being sworn into office (Louisiana Secretary of State 2021). In March 2021, voters elected Republican Julia Letlow to represent the Fifth Congressional District. Letlow is the first Republican woman to represent Louisiana in the U.S. Congress.

While these congressional elections in Louisiana had little impact on presidential voting in Louisiana, Republican members of the Louisiana congressional delegation played prominent roles in the postelection saga in which Trump and his surrogates questioned the legitimacy of the results. Fourth District Congressman Mike Johnson led the effort to solicit fellow lawmakers to sign on to a friend-of-the-court brief asking the U.S. Supreme Court to delay certification of votes in four key states won by Biden (Quinn 2020). Congressman Clay Higgins from the Third District claimed to have inside data demonstrating that the election was compromised (Hilburn 2020). And, First District Congressman and House Minority Whip Steve Scalise insisted that all the legal avenues be allowed for appeal (Carrasco 2020). In the end, all Republican members of the Louisiana Congressional delegation, except for Senator Cassidy, voted to sustain objections to certifications of the votes of either Arizona or Pennsylvania

(Yourish, et al. 2021). While these efforts were ultimately unsuccessful, the situation enabled the Republican congressmen an opportunity to signal their continued backing of Trump where support for the President in their districts ranged from 61 to 68 percent in the 2020 elections (Fiddler 2021).

CONCLUSION

The patterns of voting observed in Louisiana elections did not differ greatly from those of previous elections. Donald Trump's margin of victory was similar to what it had been four years early and the distribution of support across the state's regions deviated very little from previous elections. Rural parts of the state, particularly those where smaller percentages of whites have a college degree, are a major source of strength for Republican candidates. The major drivers of voting patterns such as party identification, race, age, and gender continued to shape voting in a manner observed in past elections. In combination, these findings make it clear that the majority of Louisiana voters are likely to remain steadfast supporters of Republican presidential candidates for the foreseeable future.

NOTES

1. State law requires that municipal elections be held five weeks after the primary, which would have scheduled these elections within three days of a holiday (Easter), something that is prohibited under Louisiana election laws. Moving the presidential primary earlier was not possible given national party rules prohibiting early primaries (possibly jeopardizing Louisiana's delegates from being counted).
2. Parish information obtained from the U.S. Census Bureau, American Community Survey five-year average (2015–2019) (https://www.census.gov/).
3. The urban, suburban, and rural classifications are taken from the National Center for Health Statistics classification scheme (https://www.cdc.gov/nchs/data_access/urban_rural.htm). Recent findings indicate that these designations are highly correlated with how respondents characterize their residential communities Wieder 2019).
4. It is important to recognize that the 2016 poll asked about party registration while the 2020 poll asked about party identification. The slippage between registration and identification is generally greater among Democrats and this may explain why Democratic identifiers in 2020 were more loyal to Biden than party registrants were to Clinton in 2016.

REFERENCES

Carrasco, Maria, "Scalise: 'Let the Legal Process Play Out," *POLITICO* (December 13, 2020) https://www.politico.com/news/2020/12/13/house-minority-whip-scalise-legal-election-444849.

Chervenak, Edward E., and Anthony Licciardi, "The 2020 Presidential Election in Louisiana," *University of New Orleans Survey Research Center* (October 2020) https://www.uno.edu/academics/colaehd/la/political-science/survey-research-center/studies.

CNN Election Coverage: Exit Polls, https://www.cnn.com/election/2020/exit-polls/president/national-results.

Collins, Sean, "Trump Made Gains with Black Voters in Some States, Here's Why," *Vox* (November 4, 2020) https://www.vox.com/2020/11/4/21537966/trump-black-voters-exit-polls.

Corasaniti, Nick, Weivi Cai, and Denise Lu, "Flush with Cash, Biden Eclipses Trump in War for the Airwaves," *New York Times* (October 17, 2020) https://www.nytimes.com/interactive/2020/10/17/us/politics/trump-biden-campaign-ad-spending.html.

Deslatte, Melinda, "Senator Bill Cassidy Won't Debate Shreveport Mayor Adrian Perkins, Others in Senate Race," *Shreveport Times* (October 20, 2020) https://www.shreveporttimes.com/story/news/politics/2020/10/20/sen-bill-cassidy-wont-debate-adrian-perkins-other-opponents/5993941002/.

Federal Election Commission Presidential Election Louisiana, Accessed March 1, 2021. https://www.fec.gov/data/candidates/president/presidential-map/.

Federal Election Commission Senate Elections Louisiana https://www.fec.gov/data/elections/senate/LA/2020/. Accessed March 1, 2021.

Fiddler, Carolyn, "Daily Kos Releases 2020 Presidential Results for All 435 Congressional Districts," *Daily Kos Press* (February 22, 2021) https://www.dailykos.com/stories/2021/2/22/2017496/-Daily-Kos-releases-2020-presidential-results-for-all-435-congressional-districts.

Frey, William H., "Exist Polls Show Both Familiar and New Voting blocs Sealed Biden's Win," Bookings Research (November 12, 2020) https://www.brookings.edu/research/2020-exit-polls-show-a-scrambling-of-democrats-and-republicans-traditional-bases/.

Frey, William H., "Biden's Victory Came from the Suburbs," *Bookings Research* (November 13, 2020) https://www.brookings.edu/research/bidens-victory-came-from-the-suburbs/.

Hilburn, Greg, "Will President Donald Trump Return to Louisiana in 2020?" *Monroe News Star* (December 31, 2019) https://www.thenewsstar.com/story/news/2019/12/31/president-donald-trump-return-louisiana-2020/2782416001/.

Hilburn, Greg, "Louisiana Congressman Class Higgins Says He Has 'Inside Data' Election Compromised," *Lafayette Daily Advertiser* (November 8, 2020) https://www.theadvertiser.com/story/news/2020/11/06/rep-clay-higgins-says-he-has-inside-data-election-compromised/6194886002/.

Hogan, Robert E, "Louisiana: Trump Wins Big on the Bayou," in *The Future Ain't What It Used to Be: The 2016 Presidential Election in the South*, eds. Branwell Dubose Kapeluck and Scott E. Buchanan (Fayetteville: The University of Arkansas Press, 2018), 73–88.

Joseph, LeBron, "U.S. Senate Race Heating Up with Cassidy, Perkins, and Others," WGNO (October 21, 2020) https://wgno.com/news/moving-new-orleans-forward/u-s-senate-race-heating-up-with-cassidy-perkins-and-others/.

Kapeluck, Branwell Dubose, and Scott E. Buchanan. *The Future Ain't What It Used to Be: The 2016 Presidential Election in the South.* Fayetteville: The University of Arkansas Press, 2018.

Karlin, Sam, "Louisiana Legislature Passes Election Plan After Rolling Back Access to Mail-In Ballots," *The Advocate* (April 28, 2020) https://www.theadvocate.com/baton_rouge/news/coronavirus/article_5d1b0542-895c-11ea-b75e-6bba365dcb80.html.

Karlin, Sam, "This Quirk in Louisiana Election Law Moved the State's Presidential Primary Date in 2020," The Advocate (June 9, 2019) 2theadvocate.com https://www.theadvocate.com/baton_rouge/news/politics/elections/article_663438ae-8969-11e9-adcf-cf68159dde49.html.

Karlin, Sam, "Early Vote Shatters Records in Louisiana, with Nearly 1 Million Casing Ballots Ahead of Nov. 3" *The Advocate* (October 28, 2020) https://www.theadvocate.com/baton_rouge/news/politics/elections/article_3127e732-193c-11eb-9723-ef39592aebf5.html.

Louisiana Secretary of State web site: "Find Results and Statistics" Accessed February 15, 2021. https://www.sos.la.gov/ElectionsAndVoting/GetElectionInformation/FindResultsAndStatistics/Pages/default.aspx.

National Center for Health Statistics, Urban-Rural Classification Scheme for Counties https://www.cdc.gov/nchs/data_access/urban_rural.htm.

Pramuk, Jacob, "Louisiana Postpones Democratic Primary Over Coronavirus, The First State To Do So," *CNBC* (March 13, 2021) https://www.cnbc.com/2020/03/13/louisiana-postpones-democratic-primary-over-coronavirus-the-first-state-to-do-so.html.

Quinn, Melissa, "GOP Lawmaker Soliciting Fellow Republicans to Back Texas Effort Challenging Election Results," *CBS News* (December 11, 2020) https://www.cbsnews.com/news/texas-lawsuit-supreme-court-106-house-republicans/.

Rojas, Rick and Jeremy Alford, "In Louisiana, a Narrow Win for John Bel Edwards and a Hard Loss for Trump," *New York Times* (November 16, 2019) https://www.nytimes.com/2019/11/16/us/louisiana-governor-edwards-rispone.html?searchResultPosition=111.

U.S. Census Bureau, American Community Survey Five-Year Average (2015–19) https://www.census.gov/

Wieder, Ruth Igielnik, "Evaluating What Makes a U.S. Community Urban, Suburban, or Rural, *"Decoded, Pew Research Center* (November 22, 2019).

WWLTV.com, "Biden Makes New Orleans Campaign Stop at YEP Center, Fundraiser Set for Tonight," WWLTV July 23, 2019.

Chapter 6

Mississippi

Republican Hegemony Persists

Stephen D. Shaffer

The Magnolia State approached the 2020 presidential election with a Republican Party in the most dominating position since Reconstruction. The last time that the Republicans had lost the state's presidential electoral votes was in 1976, when the national Democratic Party offered a centrist, born again Southern Baptist, Jimmy Carter, as their presidential nominee. That was in a very different era though, when Democrats in Mississippi had a very ideologically diverse and biracial coalition, that included such conservative whites as U.S. Senator John Stennis. As an increasing number of conservative white voters came to identify with the Republican Party, retiring Democratic Senators and House members were increasingly replaced by Republicans. Retirements by Senators James Eastland in 1978 and John Stennis in 1988 were immediately followed by GOP Senators Thad Cochran and Trent Lott, and after the turn of the century, they were followed by current Senators Roger Wicker and Cindy Hyde-Smith. Republicans had held all three of the majority white U.S. House districts since two Democratic incumbents had fallen victims to the 2010 national GOP tsunami, as Democrats became relegated to the majority-black Mississippi Delta district held by long-time incumbent and civil rights pioneer Bennie Thompson. Even at the state level, Republicans had become dominant, controlling both of the state legislative chambers since the 2011 elections and winning all statewide offices in 2019.

POLITICAL CONTEXT

The 2018 special U.S. Senate election had offered a glimmer of hope for Democrats, as they offered a strong former congressman known for building biracial coalitions, and Republicans warred among themselves over who was more ideologically pure with the victor then getting into trouble over politically insensitive humor. Two-term GOP Agriculture Commissioner Cindy Hyde-Smith had been appointed Interim Senator after Cochran's retirement in March 2018, but was immediately attacked by right-wing conservative state senator Chris McDaniel as a former Democrat lacking a commitment to the Republican Party's conservative platform. Appointing governor Phil Bryant and other Republicans defended Mississippi's first female U.S. Senator as a champion of business and of the state's agriculture industry, and pointed out that she had cochaired President Trump's Agriculture Advisory Committee. Joining McDaniel in challenging Hyde-Smith in the November special election was Democrat Mike Espy, who had first been elected to the U.S. House in 1986 by defeating a Republican incumbent, and who had then been reelected three times in landslides as his diligent constituency service work was rewarded by biracial support. Espy praised Republican Senator Cochran's work for all Mississippians, and pledged that he would put Mississippi's interests above that of any party or any politician. President Trump made two campaign visits to the state on Hyde-Smith's behalf, warning that a vote for Espy was a vote for "the Democratic agenda, for open borders, and for radical socialism" (Bedillion 2018, 5A). He also charged that Espy would "vote in total lockstep" with Nancy Pelosi, Chuck Schumer, and "the legendary Maxine Waters" (Colvin 2018, 5). Prominent senators also got involved with Democratic presidential hopefuls Cory Booker and Kamala Harris campaigning for Espy, and South Carolina Republican Senator Lindsey Graham backing Hyde-Smith.

The competitiveness of this special Senate election was reflected in Hyde-Smith making the runoff election with only 41.3 percent of the vote, as Espy won a hefty 40.9 percent and McDaniel was knocked out by garnering only 16.4 percent. Hyde-Smith had to fight off claims that she was racially insensitive, as she had joked in Tupelo that she so respected a supporter that "if he invited me to a public hanging, I'd be on the front row" (Pettus and Beaumont 2018, 3A). She also joked to a few students at Mississippi State University (MSU) that "there's a lot of liberal folks in those other schools who maybe we don't want to vote" (Phillips 2018, 1). Hyde-Smith stressed constituency service, presenting a $100,000 United States Department of Agriculture (USDA) grant to MSU, and noted her membership on Cochran's important committees of Appropriations and Agriculture. She also projected a "down-home" image, running an ad "showing her in blue jeans and boots at her family's cattle auction" and relating cattle ranching to service in Washington as she picked up a shovel, "You can't be afraid to put your boots on and clean up the mess" (Pettus 2018, 3A). The Republican won the runoff election with 53.6 percent, but Espy was emboldened by his substantial 46.4

percent, which was the best showing for a Democratic Senate candidate since Stennis's last re-election (even former Governor Musgrove had garnered only 45.0 percent in the 2008 special election against Wicker).

The state elections of 2019 also offered some faint hope for Democrats running the next year. Once again, Republicans were split, this time in the gubernatorial contest between the conservative lieutenant governor Tate Reeves and the pragmatic former state Supreme Court chief justice Bill Waller, whose father had been a Democratic governor. Fearing that Reeves had made too many enemies as leader of the state Senate, three former GOP state party chairmen promptly endorsed the personable Waller, whose pragmatism extended to expanding Medicaid under Obamacare to help save closing rural hospitals and to raising the gas tax to fix Mississippi's deteriorating highways. Horrified conservative leaders such as Governor Bryant, former governor Haley Barbour, and Chris McDaniel promptly endorsed Reeves, who won the primary runoff election with 54 percent of the vote. Meanwhile, Democrats offered their one remaining statewide officeholder, four-term Attorney General Jim Hood, who had successfully cultivated an image of being a true ideological moderate (as reflected in polls). Hood portrayed himself as a fighter for "working people . . . people that work every day, pay their taxes, follow the rules, go to church," and criticized the Republican-controlled state legislature for their failure to expand Medicaid under Obamacare and for their tax cuts that had taken money away from education and infrastructure needs (Bologna 2019, 6A). Republicans were now united, fired up, and on-message. Reeves targeted Hood's "liberal" policies, promising to "oppose the values of Hollywood and Washington D.C.," and the "liberal ideas of the party of Chuck Schumer, Nancy Pelosi, and Jim Hood" (Pettus 2019, 1A). Both President Trump and Vice President Pence visited Mississippi to campaign for Reeves with Trump praising Reeves for being "pro-jobs, pro-family, and pro-life," and Pence blasting Hood as an out-of-touch liberal who supported Hillary Clinton and was soft on gun rights (Vance 2019a, 2A). Former governor Haley Barbour in a guest editorial berated Hood as promoting an atmosphere of Jackpot Justice that made it harder to recruit jobs and derided his planned tax increases as real job killers. While Republicans ran as a team, Democrat Hood was criticized by other Democratic statewide nominees as ignoring them and just running his own campaign. Reeves did pull out a narrow 52.6 percent victory and Republicans easily won all other statewide races, but Democrats were emboldened by the close gubernatorial race, and prominent party leaders such as Espy took the lesson that Democrats could actually win if they stopped running away from liberal positions on popular economic issues.

The 2020 state legislative session suggested that there was some progressive streak running through the state, but that Democrats were not the only politicians able to show some leadership. Defying the national mood of partisan polarization and divisiveness, the new lieutenant governor Delbert Hosemann (who as secretary of state had successfully implemented the state's Voter ID law) promptly maintained the state Senate's bipartisan leadership tradition by appointing thirteen Democratic committee chairs (eleven of whom were African Americans) to join the twenty-two GOP chairs, with Democrats chairing such substantively important committees as Corrections, Housing, Labor, and Public Health. Addressing an election challenge in the Republican-controlled House by a defeated Republican incumbent, after a fair and thorough committee investigation a unanimous voice vote seated the Democrat. With only two dissenting votes among the 174 state lawmakers on each of two important issues, the Republican-controlled legislature rejected the governor's effort to control the spending of the $1.25 billion federal coronavirus money that the state received, and settled a federal lawsuit by proposing a constitutional amendment to voters to eliminate the "electoral college" method of selecting statewide officials (criticized as being racially biased) and move to a direct popular vote.

Two other issues that promised to enliven the 2020 election were a constitutional amendment proposed by a citizen initiative for medical marijuana, and a proposal to adopt a new state flag in place of the old flag that contained the Confederate battle emblem. The latter proposal was sparked by several racial justice protests in response to police brutality allegations across the nation, as well as the SEC conference's decision to ban all post-season athletic championships from Mississippi because of the flag. The growing chorus for changing the flag included the Mississippi Economic Council (MEC), a coalition of faith and civic groups (Working Together Mississippi), athletes and staff at all eight public universities, and most state officials. After a bipartisan group of lawmakers working on this issue got House Speaker Philip Gunn's support for suspending the rules to consider this issue late in the session, conservative state senator McDaniel criticized lawmakers for lacking a "backbone" and giving in to "a very slick and a very well-funded campaign," prompting a first-term senator Jeremy England (a fellow Republican) to stand up to him and urge timely action in dealing with this divisive flag issue (Bologna and Ramseth 2020a, 1A, 7A). A standing ovation ensued with long-time black Caucus member Hillman Frazier hugging his GOP colleague. Both legislative chambers easily achieved the two-thirds vote needed to set up a flag commission that would propose a new state flag that could not contain any portion of the Confederate battle flag, but that must have the motto "In God We Trust" on it. The votes were again marked with bipartisan and biracial hugs among lawmakers.

THE PRESIDENTIAL CAMPAIGN: A FLYOVER STATE

Given Mississippi's long history of voting Republican for president, national Democrats confined their attention to the state to the nomination season. Several presidential hopefuls visited the state even before the presidential election year. Bernie Sanders in 2017 visited Canton to fight for workers' rights and pay by backing the unsuccessful effort to unionize Canton's Nissan auto workers. In 2018, Sanders held a town hall meeting in Jackson with Mayor Lumumba as he called for economic justice reflected in universal health care and reduced childhood poverty. In 2019, Elizabeth Warren went on a walking tour with the mayor of Greenville to promote her affordable housing plan, which sought to close the racial gap in home ownership, and at a CNN town hall meeting telecasted from Jackson she endorsed a study of reparations for African Americans. The same year, Beto O'Rourke showed his concern for undocumented immigrants targeted by ICE (U.S. Immigration and Customs Enforcement) raids by visiting Canton and speaking with them in Spanish. That December, Michael Bloomberg visited two of the state's Civil Rights museums and at a roundtable stressed his commitment to criminal justice reform.

Joe Biden garnered the most significant endorsements for the state's March 2020 presidential primary. Espy touted Biden as "a man of high competence and integrity," and warned that Bernie Sanders's "socialism . . . would not help people down ticket like me" (Ganucheau 2020, 3). Homeland Security Committee chairman and chair of the 2020 Democratic national convention, Bennie Thompson, praised Biden's "character and unmatched skills to lead us and get things done" and his "moral leadership that can end today's division and hate" (Pettus 2020a, 2). Biden himself visited Jackson the Sunday before the primary, starting by asking to "worship" with the congregation of New Hope Baptist Church and "not just make a speech," and crediting such congregations in the South with saving his presidential bid (Bologna and Ramseth 2020b, 7A). At historically black (HBCU) Tougaloo College, Biden called the election a "battle for the soul of America," pledged to unite and heal America, and promised to invest $70 billion more in HBCUs (Bologna and Ramseth 2020b, 7A). Biden easily won the state's primary with 81 percent of the vote to 15 percent for Sanders and 4 percent for other candidates.

Trump administration officials also made a few visits to the state before the primary. In addition to his two campaign visits in 2018 on behalf of Senator Hyde-Smith, President Trump in 2017 toured the opening of the state's civil rights museums, commemorating "the brave men and women" who had sacrificed "so much so that others might live in freedom," and singled out the widow of Medgar Evers who was in the audience and who received a standing ovation (Superville 2017, 9A). In 2018, Ivanka Trump attended a Department of Labor panel in Gulfport on affordable child care for working women, and learned about the state's success in providing child care and job training programs. The same year Secretary of Education Betsy DeVos, who had previously touted Mississippi's vouchers for eligible special needs students, visited a Lexington high school to learn about its participation in the state's innovative Global Teaching Project that provided blended learning approaches to minority and rural communities. Facing two virtual unknowns, Trump won 99 percent of the vote in the GOP presidential primary.

With Mississippi's increasing reputation as a deep red state, state polls consistently showing Trump with a big lead over Biden, tight contests in battleground states, and a raging pandemic, the national parties virtually ignored the Magnolia state during the general election, so state and local political figures took up the slack. Senator Hyde-Smith lauded Trump's debate performance, touting his success in bringing "better-paying jobs to our communities" and praising him as "the leader to take us back to our pre-pandemic growth," while blasting Biden for moving "too far to the left" and "opening the door for Socialist ideals" such as "Medicare for All, the Green New Deal, and an activist judicial takeover" (Harrison 2020a, 2). Local columnist Daniel Gardner labeled Biden as a "career politician" while Trump's virtue was that "he doesn't act like a politician, he doesn't talk like a politician" (Gardner 2020, 4). The vice president of Tupelo-based American Family Association, Walker Wildmon, had also concluded (as early as March) that the national Democratic Party's platform "no longer allows for moderates," as it permits "the murder of a baby . . . throughout all nine months of pregnancy," and deems homosexuality "a human right" and threatens fostering a "totalitarian mentality on . . . faith-based business owners" (Wildmon 2020, 9A).

On the Democratic side, two-term Tupelo mayor Jason Shelton had previously announced his retirement but plans to tirelessly campaign for Joe Biden, and participating at a virtual phone bank event for Biden with four other mayors argued that the election was a battle "for the soul of the nation," and that unlike Trump, "Joe Biden is an honest, decent, and kind person" (*Daily Journal* reports, 2020a, 3A). State Democrats hailed the selection of Kamala Harris as his vice-presidential running mate, with Oktibbeha County Democratic Chair John Young calling her "a good pick" who would do an "outstanding job," and Starkville state Representative Cheikh Taylor pointing out that she would not only become the first African American vice president but also the first vice president from an HBCU, Howard University, which was also the alma mater of both Taylor and Mike Espy (Benton 2020, 1). Both parties operated local campaign offices with Congressman Trent Kelly speaking in Tupelo at the Lee County GOP election headquarters opening, Lowndes County GOP headquarters advertising available Trump signs, and the MSU College Democrats receiving favorable publicity in both the student newspaper and the local newspaper.

THE SENATE ELECTION: A LIVELY REMATCH

A rematch of the 2018 Senate contest occurred, as Senator Hyde-Smith was unopposed for renomination after state senator Chris McDaniel declined to run, conceding that a Trump endorsement of the incumbent Republican doomed his prospects. Democrat Mike Espy was renominated with 93 percent of the primary vote, beating two little-known candidates, one of whom was a self-described democratic socialist. Espy as he had done as a congressman reached out to all Mississippians, pledging to be "an independent voice in the Senate—whatever is best for Mississippi," and running a commercial showing how he had crossed party lines as a congressman and worked with President Reagan and Senator Cochran (Harrison 2020b, 10A). However, he was willing to embrace national Democrats and some progressive policies, as he endorsed Biden as having "the capacity, the empathy, the experience and the knowledge to return this nation to some sense of normalcy" (Harrison 2020c, 8A). Espy was, in turn, endorsed by Biden for having worked "to improve the lives of Mississippi's working families" and having "the experience to move Mississippi forward" (Daily Journal reports, 2020b, 3A).

Mike Espy's primary issues were health care and racial reconciliation. He promptly backed a federal requirement of state Medicaid expansion under Obamacare, pointing out that Mississippi remained fiftieth in health outcomes, that rural hospitals were closing, and that African Americans were especially disadvantaged. Espy sought to humanize the issue by relating how he had nearly died from an asthma attack when he was a child and his father had to beg help from a white hospital. Espy tore into Hyde-Smith claiming that she was "hurting Mississippi, our progress, and our reputation" as she "openly laughs about public hangings and makes statements supporting voter suppression" (Vance 2019b, 5A). Former President Obama also got into the act, cutting a radio ad and a fundraising appeal that pointed out, "You were finally able to change the flag. Now, you can change your Senator, too," and concluding that Espy could "keep Mississippi moving forward" (Pettus 2020b, 7A). Espy's criminal justice proposals included better police training, more African American and women police officers, and more reliance on social workers and mental health professionals to deal with social problems. Espy also fell in line with Democratic senators' desires to prevent Trump from filling the Ginsberg Supreme Court vacancy until a new President was elected.

Cindy Hyde-Smith touted her important committee assignments and her ability to deliver federal funds to Mississippi, while also stressing her conservative values. She mentioned her delivery of disaster relief funding for farmers at an MEC event, and funding for agriculture, rural health care, and military shipbuilding delivered to Mississippians at a Lowndes County

Republican Women's luncheon, while her spokesperson touted her delivery of federal funds to Mississippi health care providers, small businesses, and the unemployed. Hyde-Smith stressed her "conservative values," and her effort to protect "our religious freedoms" so that Mississippians could "raise our children and worship the way that we want to worship" (Pettus 2020c, 6A). President Trump praised her as "incredible. She's tough and smart and strong," while former governor Phil Bryant warned that "If Mike Espy and the liberal Democrats gain the Senate we will take that first step into a thousand years of darkness" (Pettus 2020d, 4A). Responding to the criticism that the Republican senator was doing little in-person campaigning or fundraising, Republican national committee member Henry Barbour pointed out that laying low was the usual strategy for a front-runner, and that while both candidates were "good people," Espy "unfortunately has taken on the positions of the liberal Democratic Party" (Pender 2020, 6A).

Espy continued to vigorously campaign, to raise considerable funds, and to draw national Democratic interest and support. At a town hall meeting in Starkville hosted by the Oktibbeha County NAACP, Espy stressed his backing of improved health care and made a local connection by reminding the audience that his daughter had graduated from MSU and that his Congressional papers were housed in its library. The MSU College Democrats hosted him as a virtual speaker, and were impressed by how personable and down-to-earth he was. In October alone, Espy raised over $3.8 million with help from Senator Cory Booker and Stacey Abrams, and even the Democratic Senatorial Campaign Committee donated the maximum of $49,000. At a Jackson luncheon of Democratic activists that included union members and civil rights workers, former Massachusetts Governor Deval Patrick lamented how the coronavirus pandemic had exposed the economic vulnerability and "measures of despair" of the "black and brown communities" and many poor people, and argued that "Mike Espy is the only one talking about solutions" (Pettus 2020e, 2).

HOT BUTTON ISSUES: THE FLAG AND MARIJUANA

The state flag commission was a broad-based committee with members appointed by the governor, lieutenant governor, and House speaker, and its chair was the highly respected Reuben Anderson, the first African American on the state supreme court. The Committee solicited considerable public feedback regarding the design of a new flag, and out of the more than 3,000 designs submitted came up with five finalists, which flew on the flagpole of the old state capitol. The Commission's finalist was soon referred to as the In God We Trust flag because it featured this motto, or as the Magnolia flag because of Mississippi's official state flower being in its center. The business community launched an aggressive campaign supporting its adoption, pointing out that it would improve the state's image nationally and facilitate economic development and the attraction of more jobs to the Magnolia state. Supportive letters to the editor from the state's major utilities and banks soon appeared in newspapers across the state. The MEC established an In God We Trust Flag Commission for its advocacy campaign, and an associated Alliance for Mississippi's Future extolled the virtues of a new flag containing a magnolia blossom that symbolized the state's hospitality spirit along with a religious motto that represented its values and faith. The most visible opposition to the new flag was by an organization called Let Mississippi Vote, supported by state Senator McDaniel, which argued that voters should have more than one flag choice on the ballot, and that the old flag should be included as an alternative.

The medical marijuana issue became a more contentious one, as the citizen Initiative 65 permitted licensed physicians to prescribe the drug for "debilitating conditions," which included not only terminal illnesses but also a long list of conditions such as "post-traumatic stress disorder" and "chronic or debilitating pain." The legislature had therefore included an alternative Initiative 65A on the ballot which limited the prescription of medical marijuana to "terminal medical conditions" with the program to be designed by the "administering state agency." A well-organized and publicized campaign was launched by Mississippians for Compassionate Care, which blasted the legislative alternative as providing insufficient guarantees to patients and as an attempt to confuse voters so that they would defeat the more liberal measure. The group proceeded to publicize the stories of people who would be helped by medical marijuana and of other supporters, such as a medical resident who had multiple sclerosis, a doctor whose friend had cancer, and even a former lieutenant in a sheriff's department. One reporter even invoked the Bible's command to love thy neighbor, which would be obeyed by marijuana reducing the pain that people had. Opponents included former governor Phil Bryant, a progressive former Secretary of State Eric Clark, the state health officer Dr. Thomas Dobbs, members of local joint narcotics task forces such as the Columbus-Lowndes County force, and even the vice president of the Mississippi Association of Realtors. They made arguments about the potential dangers of marijuana, how it could serve as a gateway drug, how the initiative was a largely out-of-state effort to promote a multibillion-dollar industry, and how Initiative 65 would largely be free of state and local regulations.

Compared to these hot button issues, there was almost no publicity regarding House Concurrent Resolution 47, which was also on the ballot, to provide a direct popular vote for statewide offices. The state constitution of 1890 required statewide officials to receive not merely a majority of the popular vote but also a majority of the electoral vote, defined as winning a majority (by a plurality vote) of state house of representative districts. Civil rights advocates regarded this as a racially discriminatory device to ensure that an African American could never be elected to statewide office, and a federal district judge put a lawsuit against it on hold so that the state legislature could address this potential violation of the principle of one person, one vote. One time that this electoral college system came into play was in the 1999 gubernatorial election, when two minor candidates prevented Ronnie Musgrove from winning a majority of the general election vote, so the Democratic-controlled state house voted (on party lines) to confirm his victory. It was also in play in 1991 when in a three-person race, Republican Eddie Briggs won 49.5 percent of the vote to 41.5 percent for three-term lieutenant governor Brad Dye, though Dye graciously conceded even though his party controlled the legislature. Unlike the other two measures on the ballot, this constitutional amendment proposed by the legislature was viewed as a mere "housekeeping" matter.

ELECTION RESULTS AND ANALYSIS

The Magnolia State continued its streak beginning in 1980 of voting Republican for president, as Trump won 57.6 percent of the vote to only 41.1 percent for Biden, virtually identical to the 2016 election results (see table 6.1). Mississippi continued to be one of the most Republican states in the nation, as Trump's percentage of the two-party vote was once again at least 10 percent higher than it was nationally. The 2020 election results in the Magnolia State were therefore in line with the high level of presidential Republicanism that began in 1992, when Mississippi began to consistently exhibit an 8-11 percent margin of greater Republicanism than the nation as a whole.

County-level aggregate data provide some insight into an explanation for these results, given the absence of exit-poll data for Mississippi and the discontinuation of the statewide Mississippi poll project. The unit of analysis is the county with the dependent variable being Trump's percentage of the two-party vote and the independent variables being census data on the racial composition of each county, and attitudinal data on each county drawn from the pooled Mississippi Polls from 2002 through 2014. These attitudinal variables include party identification, abortion views, economic issue attitudes (a scale of health care and public jobs agree-disagree items), and a racial issues scale (combining affirmative action and minority aid items). The aggregate-level relationships among these attitudinal items using the county as the unit

Table 6.1 2020 Election Returns in Mississippi Federal Elections

Candidate (Party)	Vote (%)	Votes (#)
President		
Joseph Biden/Kamala Harris (Democratic)	41.06	539,398
Donald J. Trump/Michael Pence (Republican)*	57.60	756,764
Other candidates	1.34	17,597
Total presidential vote	100.00	1,313,759
U.S. Senate		
Mike Espy (Democratic)	44.13	578,691
Cindy Hyde-Smith (Republican)*	54.11	709,511
Jimmy L. Edwards (Libertarian)	1.77	23,152
Total Senate vote	100.00	1,311,354
U.S. House of Representatives		
First District		
Antonia Eliason (Democratic)	31.25	104,008
Trent Kelly (Republican)*	68.75	228,787
Total district vote	100.00	332,795
Second District		
Brian Flowers (Republican)	33.98	101,010
Bennie Thompson (Democratic)*	66.02	196,224
Total district vote	100.00	297,234
Third District		
Dorothy Benford (Democratic)	35.33	120,782
Michael Guest (Republican)*	64.67	221,064
Total district vote	100.00	341,846

Note: Results are complete and certified. The fourth district was unopposed.
Source: Mississippi Secretary of State website: https://www.sos.ms.gov/, accessed February 11, 2021.
* incumbent.

of analysis were quite consistent with the directions of the relationships and even their strengths when measured at the individual levels in each year of the Mississippi Poll, thereby minimizing the ecological fallacy possibility (Shaffer and Breaux 2018, 98).

Mississippi presidential voting patterns are amazingly stable over time, as the Pearson correlation by county of Republican percentage of the two-party presidential vote between 2016 and 2020 was an amazing .996. Race was most highly correlated with the 2020 Trump vote (−.974, with heavily black counties least likely to vote for him), party identification was second in importance (.583, more Republican counties in party identification most likely to vote for him), racial issues were third in importance (.462, conservative racial attitudes correlated to a Trump vote), and abortion views were fourth in importance (−.298, more pro-choice counties least likely to back him), while the economic scale was not statistically significant in these bivariate analyses (see table 6.2). However, when all of these predictors were placed into one multiple regression equation, all of them were statistically insignificant except

Table 6.2 Correlation Coefficients and Regression Results for County-Level 2020 Presidential Election Results

Predictors	Correlation coefficient	Unstandardized B-score	Std. error	Beta	t-score	Statistical significance
Black percentage of county	−.974***	−.009	.000	−.956	−32.329	.000***
Party identification	.583***	.007	.010	.028	.744	.459
Abortion attitudes	−.298**	−.028	.010	−.068	−2.811	.006**
Economic issue attitudes	.150	−.024	.010	−.067	−2.515	.014*
Racial issue attitudes	.462***	.000	.013	.000	−.008	.994

Source: Mississippi Secretary of State website, accessed February 11, 2021. U.S. Census Bureau website (2019 estimates): https://www.census.gov/quickfacts/fact/table/MS/PST045219, accessed February 11, 2021. Social Science Research Center, MSU (Mississippi Poll dataset).
Note: Adjusted R^2 = .957.
* $p < .05$
** $p < .01$
*** $p < .001$

for race and abortion (economic issues were weakly related, but in the incorrect direction). Furthermore, the standardized regression coefficient (Beta) for race was −.956, compared to a modest −.068 for abortion. The adjusted R^2 for the multiple regression equation was a robust 95.7 percent.

Republican Trump won an average of 73.2 percent of the vote in the 21 counties where African Americans made up 26 percent or less of the population, and he averaged 60.4 percent of the vote in the 35 counties with a black presence of 26-49.9 percent. However, in the twenty-six counties where African Americans comprised a majority, Trump earned an average of only 33.5 percent, and lost every black majority county to Biden (except for Panola, which over the past four years has just attained a bare 50.1 percent black majority). Biden's problem, though, was that he carried only three white-majority counties: Marshall and Warren, where blacks comprised a significant 47 percent and 49 percent, respectively, of the population, and Oktibbeha, home of Mississippi State University and its progressive faculty and staff, as well as a very active College Democrats chapter and county Democratic Party organization. The presidential election nationally was so heated that turnout rose for both political parties as the number of Democratic and Republican votes cast increased statewide and in both white- and black-majority counties relative to 2016. Indeed, Kamala Harris's position as the Democratic vice-presidential candidate may have helped Democrats slightly in black-majority counties, where the average number of Democratic votes increased by 238 compared to an increase of only 72 for Republicans.

The Senate election results were not only similar to the presidential results but also similar to the 2018 special Senate election, as Republican Hyde-Smith won reelection with 54.1 percent to 44.1 percent for Espy and the correlation between the presidential and Senate vote by county was .998. Similar to the county-level relations for the presidential vote patterns, race, party, abortion, and racial issues were correlated to the vote, with the multiple regression analysis showing the primacy of racial composition of the county and the Republican being slightly advantaged in more pro-life counties (see table 6.3). As in the presidential race, the Republican did best in counties 26 percent black or less (where she earned 69.1 percent of the vote), second best in the counties 26-49.9 percent black (57.3 percent), and weakest in black-majority counties (31.3 percent). The fact that these percentages are all 2–4 percent lower than they are for Trump likely reflects the fact that Mike Espy was slightly more popular among Mississippians than was Joe Biden. As such, Espy was able to not only carry every black majority county, but he also carried five white-majority counties. In addition to winning Marshall, Oktibbeha, and Warren counties which also went for Biden, Espy was able to win Chickasaw and Lowndes counties, counties where African Americans made up a sizable 45 percent of the populations.

Table 6.3 Correlation Coefficients and Regression Results for County-Level 2020 Senate Election Results

Predictors	Correlation coefficient	Unstandardized B-score	Std. error	Beta	t-score	Statistical significance
Black percentage of county	−.969***	−.008	.000	−.936	-29.203	.000***
Party identification	.598***	.013	.010	.053	1.291	.201
Abortion attitudes	−.300**	−.028	.010	−.071	−2.717	.008**
Economic issue attitudes	.156	−.023	.010	−.067	−2.346	.022*
Racial issue attitudes	.473***	.001	.013	.002	.047	.962

Source: Mississippi Secretary of State website, accessed February 11, 2021. U.S. Census Bureau website (2019 estimates): https://www.census.gov/quickfacts/fact/table/MS/PST045219, accessed February 11, 2021. Social Science Research Center, MSU (Mississippi Poll dataset).
Note: Adjusted R^2 = .949.
* $p < .05$
** $p < .01$
*** $p < .001$

This comparison of the presidential and Senate voting patterns illustrates how nationalized politics has become in Mississippi. Gone are the days when voters were quite willing to vote for a Democratic senator such as John Stennis and a Republican president such as Ronald Reagan, partly because the old-style conservative Democrat has vanished from the Magnolia State. A Civiqs survey of 507 likely voters from October 23–26, whose results were within 2 percent of the actual vote, showed the primacy of party identification, which itself is highly affected by race, to Mississippi voters (Civiqs Daily Kos 2020). Fully 96 percent of Republican identifiers planned to vote for Trump and 93 percent for Hyde-Smith, and 96 percent of Democrats planned to vote for Biden and 99 percent for Espy. This is a bleak situation for Magnolia state Democrats, since the same poll as well as a 2018 exit poll found that Republicans outnumbered Democrats by 16 percent (43 percent of likely voters were Republicans, 27 percent were Democrats, and 30 percent were Independents).

The congressional races as usual showed the power of incumbency, as fourth district Congressman Steven Palazzo ran unopposed in the general election after polishing off three GOP challengers, and the other three incumbents won over 64 percent of the general election vote (see table 6.1). First district GOP Congressman Trent Kelly beat a democratic socialist and University of Mississippi law professor Antonia Eliason. Second district Democrat Bennie Thompson and third district Republican Michael Guest were also easy victors. The fact that all three Republicans came from white-majority districts and the only victorious Democrat represented a black-majority district illustrated once again the high relationship between race and voting patterns. Repeating the multiple regression analysis for the U.S. House voting results by county but including party of the incumbent again illustrated the importance of race, though incumbency was second in importance in place of abortion which was third (data not shown). All of the incumbents were well known for constituency service and important committee assignments, illustrated by Congressman Guest's support for MSU's college students visiting Washington, D.C., on their annual Stennis-Montgomery Association trip, and his keynote address at a data summit where he praised the university's leadership in advanced technology.

Progressives did score three important victories, however. Reversing the 2001 popular referendum that saw 64 percent of Mississippi backing the old flag with the Confederate design over an alternative design, fully 71.3 percent of Mississippians voted for the new design. One big difference in the two election campaigns was that many Mississippians in 2001 appeared to resent (as shown in letters to the editor) how the election seemed to be an exercise in political correctness, while the 2020 campaign was a more positive one that produced an ideologically diverse winning coalition. Opponents of the old flag like Mike Espy who viewed it as "ugly . . . anachronistic," which "harkens back to an ugly time that I don't want my children and grandchildren to grow up under" could now vote for the new "In God We Trust" flag that was viewed by conservatives like Cindy Hyde-Smith as "boldly and publicly acknowledging our faith in God," showing Mississippians as "proud, hardworking, loving, innovative, and God-fearing Americans" (Pettus 2020f, 3A). Cities such as Jackson and Hattiesburg and universities such as MSU and Ole Miss promptly raised the new state flag, and some homeowners even began to fly it. Medical marijuana also passed, as the more liberal Initiative 65 garnered 57.9 percent of the vote to a mere 20.7 percent for the legislative Alternative 65A with other votes, including those voting against both measures making up 21.4 percent, again suggesting the wisdom of a positive marketing campaign, in this case, one stressing real people who were hurting and who could benefit from a pain medication being legalized in other states. Finally, removing the Electoral College element for statewide offices and moving to a direct popular vote won a landslide 74.4 percent, winning in every county.

REPUBLICAN DOMINANCE PERSISTS

Given the ideological chasm between the two national parties and the increased nationalization of Mississippi elections as shown by Mike Espy's and Jim Hood's basically left-of-center campaigns, winning a more conservative state like Mississippi has become a long-shot for Democrats not only in presidential elections, but also in U.S. Senate and statewide offices. The typical Mississippi voter tends to view Democratic presidential candidates as "somewhat liberal" and Republican candidates as "somewhat conservative," while their own ideological views are nearly identical to their perception of the Republican nominees (Shaffer and Breaux 2018, 103). Given the strong relationship between race and ideology, this ideological split between the parties has also produced a racial gulf between the two parties in Mississippi. Some of the most competitive races today are in the Republican party primaries themselves (or in special elections), as shown by former Supreme Court justice Bill Waller's spirited centrist challenge to Lieutenant Governor Tate Reeves in the 2019 gubernatorial race, conservative state senator Bill McDaniel's challenges to Senator Thad Cochran in 2014 and to Senator Cindy Hyde-Smith in 2018, and lively right-wing efforts to upend two first-term GOP congressmen in 2012 (Shaffer and Breaux 2014, 91). Republican ideological splits offer some hopes for Democrats, though so far Republicans have been able to nominate electable candidates who can unify their party. In 2020, Congressman Palazzo fended off three GOP challengers accusing him of such sins as being a "career politician," of "flooding the swamp far too long," and of not balancing the federal budget, winning an easy 66.8 percent first primary nomination (Ramseth 2020, 6A).

Democrats do have some strengths, particularly in district, city, and county elections. In a primarily rural state with 82 counties, many of which have low populations, Democrats can actually dominate many local offices. Even in the disastrous 2019 state elections, Democrats elected 248 county supervisors to 141 for the Republicans and 21 Independents. African Americans have made tremendous strides in the state's political arena, reflected by not only prominent congressmen Bennie Thompson and Mike Espy but also successful mayors like Vicksburg mayors George Flaggs Jr. and Robert Walker, and Hattiesburg mayor Johnny DuPree. And one can never discount the enthusiasm, optimism, and potential of the younger generation, embodied in MSU's College Democrats' president Georgie Swan, who provided significant publicity for her organization in the university's student newspaper, *The Reflector*.

REFERENCES

Bedillion, Caleb. 2018. "President endorses Hyde-Smith campaign." *Daily Journal*, October 3, 2018.

Benton, Charlie. 2020. "Area democrats react to VP announcement." *Starkville Daily News*, August 13, 2020.

Bologna, Giacomo. 2019. "Hood casts himself as fighter for working folks." *Clarion Ledger*, February 12, 2019.

Bologna, Giacomo, and Luke Ramseth. 2020a. "Tensions flare as legislators push off flag vote." *Clarion Ledger*, June 27, 2020.

Bologna, Giacomo, and Luke Ramseth. 2020b. "Push before the primary: Biden makes Jackson stop." *Clarion Ledger*, March 9, 2020.

Civiqs Daily Kos. 2020. "Mississippi survey, October 2020." Accessed February 7, 2021. https://civiqs.com/documents/Civiqs_DailyKos_MS_banner_book_2020_10_46eq84.pdf.

Colvin, Jill. 2018. "Trump sticks with old playbook to aid GOP in Senate runoff." *Starkville Daily News*, November 27, 2018.

Daily Journal reports, 2020a. "Tupelo Mayor participates in virtual phone bank for Joe Biden ahead of VP debate." *Daily Journal*, October 8, 2020.

Daily Journal reports, 2020b. "Biden endorses Democrat Espy in Mississippi US Senate race." *Daily Journal*, October 1, 2020.

Ganucheau, Adam. 2020. "Espy says Biden, not Sanders, can help Dems win the state's U.S. Senate seat in November. *Starkville Daily News*, March 10, 2020.

Gardner, David. 2020. "Biden politics but Trump produces." *Starkville Daily News*, October 30, 2020.

Harrison. Bobby. 2020a. "Gov. Reeves condemns white supremacy, but not Trump for refusing to do the same." *Starkville Daily News*, October 1, 2020.

Harrison, Bobby. 2020b. "Espy hasn't changed his strategy of reaching Mississippi voters. It's just nuanced." *Daily Journal*, October 25, 2020.

Harrison. Bobby. 2020c. "Espy's campaign will either be history-making or instructive for Mississippi Democrats." *Daily Journal*, August 9, 2020.

Pender, Geoff. 2020. "Up in the polls during pandemic, Sen. Cindy Hyde-Smith's campaign lays low." *Daily Journal*, August 26, 2020.

Pettus, Emily Wagster. 2018. "Ads pick up in Mississippi special election for US Senate." *The Dispatch*, October 25, 2018.

Pettus, Emily Wagster. 2019. "Reeves enters governor's race." *Daily Journal*, January 4, 2019.

Pettus, Emily Wagster. 2020a. "House homeland security chairman Thompson endorses Biden." *Starkville Daily News*, March 6, 2020.

Pettus, Emily Wagster. 2020b. "Obama endorses Espy; Trump backs Hyde-Smith." *Clarion Ledger*, October 22, 2020.

Pettus, Emily Wagster. 2020c. "Mississippi rematch: Espy challenges Hyde-Smith for Senate." *The Starkville Dispatch*, November 2, 2020.

Pettus, Emily Wagster. 2020d. "Miss. senator loyal to Trump is filing for reelection." *Clarion Ledger*, January 4, 2020.

Pettus, Emily Wagster. 2020e. "Analysis: Mississippi U.S. Senate race draws outside attention." *Starkville Daily News*, October 27, 2020.

Pettus, Emily Wagster. 2020f. "Analysis: Same names, some new dynamics in Senate contest." *The Dispatch*, October 19, 2020.

Pettus, Emily Wagster, and Thomas Beaumont. 2018. "Democrats eye US Senate seat in Republican-led Mississippi." *The Dispatch*, November 14, 2018.

Phillips, Ryan. 2018. "Video of Hyde-Smith at Starkville campaign event spurs backlash." *Starkville Daily News*, November 16, 2018.

Ramseth, Luke. 2020. "Who's running for Congress in Mississippi this year?" *Clarion Ledger*, January 26, 2020.

Shaffer, Stephen D., and David A. Breaux. 2014. "Mississippi: Democrats struggle in an increasingly dominant republican state." In *Second Verse, Same as the First*, edited by Scott E. Buchanan and Branwell DuBose Kapeluck, 83–99. Fayetteville: The University of Arkansas Press.

Shaffer, Stephen D., and David A. Breaux. 2018. "Mississippi: Republican Dominance Confirmed." In *The Future Ain't What It Used to Be*, edited by Branwell DuBose Kapeluck and Scott E. Buchanan, 89–103. Fayetteville: The University of Arkansas Press.

Superville, Darlene. 2017. "Trump hails civil rights heroes on visit to Jackson." *Daily Journal*, December 10, 2017.

Vance, Taylor. 2019a. "Trump urges support for Reeves in governor's election." *Daily Journal*, November 2, 2019.

Vance, Taylor. 2019b. "Espy announces 2020 Senate run." *Daily Journal*, November 13, 2019.

Wildmon, Walker. 2020. "Are there any moderate Democrats?" *Daily Journal*, March 1, 2020.

Chapter 7

South Carolina

Redder than Red for Now

Branwell DuBose Kapeluck and Scott E. Buchanan

In January 2016, then Lieutenant Governor Henry McMaster became the first major political figure in South Carolina to endorse Donald Trump for president. At a rally in Gilbert, South Carolina, McMaster announced his support for Trump by stating, "You know, we've got a saying in the South that says it's not the dog in the fight that's important, it's the fight in the dog that's important. Well, this dog's got plenty of fight—and it's gonna take some fighting" (Del Real 2016, para. 3). Much to the surprise of the state's Republican establishment, McMaster's support, and his unquestioned conservative pedigree, helped convince the state's Republican voters to cast their ballots for the New York billionaire in February 2016. Even though Trump's statewide victory was only 32.5 percent, he won forty-four of forty-six counties and all of the Republican convention delegates from the state.

Donald Trump's seemingly unlikely victory in 2016 was the launching pad for his eventual nomination and surprise White House victory later that year. In fact, Trump's victory is yet another example of how South Carolina, a state of roughly 5.1 million people, carries an outsized role in presidential elections, and not just for Republicans. Democrats also spend an enormous among of time and money courting the state's Democratic voters every four years. In this chapter, we will seek to understand the political landscape of South Carolina. Before analyzing contemporary political trends in the state, it is necessary to take a brief examination of the state's political background.

POLITICAL BACKGROUND

South Carolina politics has long been dominated by affinity to one political party, which in large part was born out of the legacy of Reconstruction in the state (Key 1949). In 1876, South Carolina, along with Florida and Louisiana, played a key role in the election of Republican Rutherford B. Hayes. Despite evidence of rampant irregularities, vote fraud, and outright violence, South Carolina delivered its electoral votes for Republican Rutherford B. Hayes as part of a political bargain. In exchange for the state's electoral votes, Republicans agreed to remove the last federal soldiers from the South and effectively ended Reconstruction (Morris 2003; King 2012). After 1876, South Carolina became one of the most loyally Democratic states in the Union until after World War II.

The first Republican breakthrough was in 1964. Though Barry Goldwater was the first Republican to win the state since Reconstruction, political trends were beginning to emerge as soon as 1948 that not all was well for the Democratic Party in the state at the presidential level. In 1948, delegates from some Southern states walked out of the Democratic Convention and formed the States Rights Party, better known as the Dixiecrats, to protest the national Democratic Party's adoption of a civil rights plank in the national party platform. The Dixiecrats nominated South Carolinian Governor J. Strom Thurmond and Mississippian Governor Fielding J. Wright as their nominees for president and vice president, respectively, and the Dixiecrat ticket would go on to win Alabama, Louisiana, Mississippi, and South Carolina.

Some evidence suggests that white South Carolinians' voting patterns were in flux throughout the 1950s and early 1960s (Buchanan 2003). Though he was not associated with the Dixiecrat movement, Jimmy Byrnes was elected governor in 1950 and played a role in helping to make the Palmetto state slightly more friendly to the GOP at the presidential level. Byrnes had been a national political figure in the 1930s and 1940s. Indeed, Byrnes rose to such prominence that he was considered to be a candidate for the vice presidency of the United States in 1944, but non-southern Democratic delegates opposed Byrnes's nomination due to the perception that he was anti-union. A committed segregationist, Byrnes was already considered to be outside the mainstream of the national Democratic Party by 1944. In the end, Harry S. Truman was chosen to be FDR's running mate. Once he became president, Truman named Byrnes as his Secretary of State, a position in which he would serve from 1945 to 1947 (McCullough 1993).

Byrnes ran for governor in 1950 and won easily in what one political commentator of the day described as a "coronation, not a campaign" (McGill 1950, 32). In 1952, Governor Byrnes invited Republican presidential nominee Dwight Eisenhower to speak at the Statehouse in Columbia and urged South Carolinian voters to cast a ballot for "Ike." Despite Byrnes's endorsement, Eisenhower failed to win the state, though he lost the state by less than two percentage points, making Eisenhower the most successful Republican nominee in the state since Rutherford B. Hayes. The Palmetto State returned to its Democratic form in 1956, but further Democratic erosion was evident when John F. Kennedy won the state in 1960, by a narrow margin, defeating Richard Nixon by only 10,000 votes.

After Goldwater carried the state in 1964, Republicans have dominated the presidential landscape. Between 1964 and 2020, the only Democratic nominee to win South Carolina was Jimmy Carter in 1976. Since 1980, the only Southern states Republicans have won in every presidential election cycle have been Alabama, Mississippi, Texas, and South Carolina. Despite Republican success at the presidential level though, political change was slower coming in down-ticket offices. With the exception of 1975–1979, Democrats continued to control the governorship until the 1980s. James Edwards was the first Republican governor, but he was elected largely as a result of an internal Democratic squabble (Bass and Poole 2009). Democrats continued to win most congressional seats and dominated the state legislature and most county level offices. Through the 1970s, most Republican strength in the state was found in the state's urban and suburban areas, with the Democrats having a firm grip upon the rural areas. As described by Lamis (1990), the state's Democrats continued to enjoy a firm grip on political power due to a biracial coalition of black voters and moderate to liberal white voters. The GOP's most noteworthy success was Senator Strom Thurmond's penchant for being constantly reelected to the U.S. Senate. Despite being a Democratic governor from 1947 and 1951 and the Dixiecrat nominee in 1948, Thurmond managed to get elected to the U.S. Senate in 1954 as a write-in candidate, largely over a controversy involving the state Democratic Party (Chodas 1993). In 1964, Thurmond defected to the Republican Party and went about the state campaigning with Barry Goldwater (Black and Black 1992).

The Palmetto State began to take on increased national prominence in the Republican presidential nominating process beginning in 1980. That year, South Carolinian Republicans began holding a primary that eventually came to be billed as the "First in the South" contest (Black and Black 1992). The contest was largely designed by state Republican leaders to give conservative southern Republicans a larger voice in the nominating process, and the plan worked. Despite having the support of Senator Thurmond and former Governor Edwards, former Texas Governor John Connally lost the primary, which ultimately doomed his chances for the Republican nomination. Yet, Ronald Reagan's win in the primary helped to cement his hold on the nomination, and it also began a trend that has been broken only once to date. From 1980 to 2020, the winner of the South Carolinian Republican presidential primary has gone on to win the Republican nomination, with the sole exception being former House Speaker Newt Gingrich's primary victory in 2012 before losing the nomination to Mitt Romney. Interestingly, the Republicans host this primary on a Saturday, and are the first Southern primary for either party. Though the state's presidential primary has the reputation for deciding Republican nominees, South Carolina also plays a crucial role for Democratic nominees as well. Since 1992, the winner of the state's primary eventually wins the nomination, with the sole exception being John Edwards's victory in 2004.

THE CURRENT POLITICAL LANDSCAPE

Historically, South Carolinian election results reflect at least three distinct internal political regions, the Upstate, Midlands, and Lowcountry, which has led to varying degrees of Republican success (Graham and Buchanan 2018). The Upstate is a ten-county region with a population of approximately 1.5 million residents, which accounts for approximately 30 percent of the overall state population (U.S. Census Bureau 2021). The area is home to both the Greenville MSA and the separate Spartanburg MSA. Greenville County accounts for over 33 percent of the region's population, while Spartanburg is the second-most populous county in the region. Republicans in urban and suburban counties tend to be both fiscal and social conservatives, while Republicans in the more rural sections of the Upstate tend to be much more focused on socially conservative issues. It is in the more rural upstate counties where Republicans perform the best of any counties in the state. Both rural and mountainous Oconee and Pickens County regularly support Republicans with at least 70 percent of the vote. The Upstate has seen significant growth in the last four decades due in part to more industry coming into the region. The construction of the BMW plant in Greer, South Carolina, in the 1990s helped to transform the region economically. From 2010 to 2019, the region's population expanded by approximately 10 percent (U.S. Census Bureau 2021).

Accounting for nearly 29 percent of the population are twelve counties known as the Midlands. In many ways, the Midlands are a tale of two regions. Some of the fastest-growing areas of the state are found in this region combined with rural outlying counties, which are losing population dramatically over the past two decades. In terms of sheer population, the two largest counties are Richland and Lexington with a combined total population of approximately 713,000 residents. Columbia, located mostly in Richland County with a portion of the city also lying in suburban Lexington County, is the second-largest city in the state. Being the state capital, much of the employment in the region is directly and indirectly related to state government. However, the fastest-growing Midland counties over the past decade are Lancaster, York, and to a lesser extent, Chester. The growth in these counties is directly due to the growth of Charlotte, North Carolina, in the past two decades. There is also a significant federal government presence, including both the former Savannah River Plant and a variety of military bases in the region.

Until the early 2000s, Democrats in the Midlands tended to be most competitive with Republicans due to much of the Black Belt running along the eastern edge of the region. In addition, voters who work directly for state government tend to be a more reliably Democratic vote. In the past two decades though, Republicans have become more competitive due partially to the suburban and exurban growth from Charlotte in the northern fringes of the Midlands. In the past few election cycles, Republicans have even made some in-roads into relatively rural Kershaw County, which is seeing some more exurban growth from the Columbia metropolitan area. In part, Republican growth in Kershaw can be attributed to President Trump carrying the county in 2016 and 2020. Indeed, Republican growth in Kershaw County became even more evident when state senator Vincent Sheheen, a moderate Democrat, who was the party's gubernational nominee in 2010 and 2014, was surprisingly defeated for reelection to the state senate in 2020.

The Lowcountry is a collection of twelve counties along the southern coast of the state and has seen significant changes in the past two decades and comprises approximately 23 percent of the statewide population. Much like the Midlands, counties in the Lowcountry fall into two dramatically different camps. Five counties are high-growth counties on the coast in the Charleston and Beaufort areas, while six interior counties are facing significant population declines. The median population increase between 2010 and 2019 in the five growth counties is 19.6 percent, while the median population decline in the declining counties is nearly 8 percent.

Charleston is the largest city in the state, and the Charleston MSA has a population of nearly 766,000 residents according to the 2019 Census estimates. Many of the newer residents of the Lowcountry have moved from other parts of the nation to the region. Republican voters there tend to be almost libertarian in their desire for lower taxes and smaller government compared to the greater importance of social issues in the Upstate. The Lowcountry is also the fastest-growing section of the state in part due to industrial development like Boeing and Volvo in the Charleston area.

The influx of new residents in the Charleston and Beaufort areas has resulted in the Democrats becoming more competitive in the region. Many who have moved to the area, especially retirees, tend to be Republican. New younger residents, who have moved in large numbers to the Charleston area, often are more likely to vote Democratic. This resulted in recent elections in the area being largely Republican in the Beaufort and suburban Charleston counties, while Charleston County is becoming increasingly a Democratic stronghold. Meanwhile, the more rural interior Lowcountry counties are generally friendlier territory for Democrats.

In the past two decades, the state arguably has a fourth distinct political region, the Pee Dee, with Myrtle Beach as the largest city in that region. The counties on the northern coast of the state were often historically placed in the Lowcountry area, but the creation of the Seventh Congressional District centered on Myrtle Beach has led political observers to increasingly categorize thirteen counties into the Pee Dee region. The least populous area of the state at approximately 18 percent of the state's population, the Pee Dee consists of two rapidly growing coastal counties, with ten inland counties that are losing significant population in recent decades. Home of the "Grand Strand," a stretch of nearly sixty miles of beach, the coastal counties Georgetown and Horry have seen significant population growth, largely due to tourism and retirees moving to the area. In fact, Horry County is the fastest-growing county in the entire state over the past decade.

Politically speaking, Horry and Georgetown are Republican strongholds in the region. Though historically Democratic, Darlington and Florence Counties have become competitive counties with Donald Trump carrying both counties in 2016 and 2020. The interior Pee Dee counties are either majority black or almost evenly divided between black and white voters, and these counties typically are carried by Democrats. The problem for Democrats is that the more populous Pee Dee counties have become increasingly Republican in recent election cycles.

THE DEMOCRATIC PRIMARY

When the South Carolina Republican Party effectively endorsed a second Trump term by canceling the GOP presidential primary, state Democrats feared that Upstate GOP voters might infiltrate the Democratic Presidential Primary in 2020. Some Republicans had even loosely organized a move to exploit the state's open primary system to "raid" the Democratic primary and vote for Bernie Sander in an attempt to undermine the Democratic primary. The group's likely ultimate motive was to encourage bipartisan support for switching to a closed primary system (Lovegrove 2020a). State Democratic Party Chair, Trav Robertson Jr., however indicated little concern over the effort.

Democratic candidates established a strong presence in the state leading up to the February 29th primary. Perhaps the biggest event of the primary season was Rep. Jim Clyburn's "World Famous Fish Fry," held in late June 2019. This annual event, which began almost three decades ago, brought twenty-one Democratic candidates to Columbia (Lovegrove 2019). Clyburn, the most influential Democratic politician in the state, declined to endorse anyone leading up to the event, claiming "I promised the party that I would help them make South Carolina relevant in the presidential [election], and I've been told by more than one person that if I were to make a formal endorsement in this campaign, the rest of the candidates would stay out of the state" (Davis 2019, para. 5). Ultimately Congressman Clyburn endorsed Biden at a National Action Network Breakfast in North Charleston three days before the 2020 primary, stating "I want the public to know that I'm voting for Joe Biden. South Carolina should be voting for Joe Biden" (Oprysko and Caputo 2020, para. 2). This endorsement came on the heels of Biden's significant losses in Iowa, New Hampshire, and Nevada and was widely seen as pivotal in reviving his sagging campaign for the nomination (Strauss 2020).

Eight contenders in the New Hampshire Democratic Primary garnered a combined 97.7 percent of the vote. These eight, in order of their vote tallies, were Bernie Sanders, Pete Buttigieg, Amy Klobuchar, Elizabeth Warren, Joe Biden, Tom Steyer, Tulsi Gabbard, and Andrew Yang. With Yang's departure from the field after New Hampshire, a seven-candidate field vied for in the South Carolina primary. With over 60 percent of the South Carolinian Democratic Presidential Primary vote African American, this was the first real test of Democratic candidate appeal among a diverse constituency. Voter turnout set a record at over 539,000, surpassing the previous record in 2008 by 7,000 votes. Clyburn's endorsement paid off handsomely with Biden winning decisively with 48 percent of the vote and all forty-six counties. Bernie Sanders, who polled within 5 percentage points of Biden five days before the primary (and two days before Clyburn's endorsement of Biden), came in a distant second with 19.9 percent of the vote (Pramuk 2020). Steyer and Buttigieg came in third and fourth with 11.3 and 8.2 percent of the votes, respectively. The loss was particularly bad for billionaire Tom Steyer who had saturated the state in advertising in a desperate bid to keep his campaign alive. Steyer spent $13.3 million, or $223 for each vote received, compared to Biden's $264,000 (Bohatch 2020). Biden's victory in South Carolina paved the way for his nomination. Immediately after the South Carolina Primary, Pete Buttigieg dropped out of the race the day after the primary and was followed by Amy Klobuchar the following day. Both Buttigieg and Klobuchar endorsed Biden before Super Tuesday, which proved a boost to Biden's strategy of attracting moderate Democratic voters.

Table 7.1 summarizes the CNN exit poll for the Democratic primary. African Americans composed 56 percent of the voters and gave Biden 61 percent of their vote. Almost 60 percent of voters were women and almost half cast their vote for Biden. Indeed, Biden won a plurality of votes in all demographic categories except for voters aged 17–44. Biden also won convincing pluralities in all issue areas. Notable is that Biden won twice the number of votes as Sanders, 45–23 percent, among voters that named income inequality as the most important issue area. He was the dominant choice for

Table 7.1 South Carolina Democratic Nominating Primary Exit Poll, February 29, 2020

	Biden	Buttigieg	Gabbard	Klobuchar	Sanders	Steyer	Warren
Demographics							
Male (41% of respondents)	48	8	2	2	24	10	5
Female (59%)	49	8	1	4	17	12	8
White (40%)	33	16	2	7	23	10	9
Black (56%)	61	3	1	1	17	13	5
17–44 years old (29%)	30	10	2	2	34	9	12
45 years and older (71%)	56	7	1	4	14	13	5
Issues							
Race Relations (17%)	54	9	1	1	12	14	9
Health Care (41%)	50	7	1	3	22	10	5
Climate Change (14%)	41	16	1	4	18	13	6
Income Inequality (21%)	45	5	2	4	23	11	10
Candidate Quality							
Cares about people like me (25%)	47	7	1	2	22	13	8
Can bring needed change (36%)	41	5	1	2	24	15	10
Can unite the country (29%)	59	13	1	6	11	7	3
Democrats should nominate someone who:							
Agrees with you on issues (43%)	43	7	3	4	24	12	6
Can beat Trump (54%)	52	10	0	3	17	11	8

Source: South Carolina Exit Polls," *CNN*, February 29, 2020, accessed March 8, 2020, https://www.cnn.com/election/2020/primaries-caucuses/entrance-and-exit-polls/south-carolina/democratic.

voters who wanted a candidate that cared for people, and could bring change. In an election occurring in a climate of bitter partisan polarization, 59 percent of voters thought that Biden was the best candidate for uniting the country. Moreover, Biden was the solid favorite among the 54 percent of voters that thought Democrats should nominate a candidate capable of beating Trump. Biden's triumph in South Carolina changed national perceptions regarding his ability to defeat Trump. A national poll on February 23rd found that only 17 percent of Americans believed Biden could beat Trump. By March 1st, this percentage doubled to 34 percent (Yokley 2020).

Biden entered the South Carolina Democratic primary as a candidate on the ropes. His dismal performance to that point cast serious doubts on his ability to secure the nomination. Biden had to outperform in South Carolina or it was likely the end of his candidacy. Clyburn's last-minute endorsement saved Biden in the state and led to the exit of Buttigieg and Klobuchar, key rivals for the moderate Democratic vote. This, coupled with a newfound belief in his chances against Trump in the general election, buoyed his flagging campaign leading to Biden winning ten of the fourteen Democratic state primaries (and all six southern state primaries) three days later on Super Tuesday. In sum, South Carolina was the linchpin for Biden's eventual nomination. It is interesting that this was a repeat of Clinton's 2016 nomination experience. She had only narrowly won Iowa (.02 percent) and lost New Hampshire decisively before reviving her campaign in the Palmetto State by beating Sanders 73 percent to 26 percent.

THE GENERAL ELECTION

Polls in the weeks and days leading up to the election were consistent in predicting a Trump win in South Carolina. In August, the Quinnipiac University Poll revealed 47 percent of registered voters-supported reelection of Trump compared to only 42 percent for Biden (Quinnipiac University Poll 2020). By early September, the same polling firm found Trump's lead had shrunk to a virtual dead heat at 48 for Trump versus 47 for Biden (Bustos 2020a). By mid-October, Trump had regained his advantage with The Sienna College/*New York Times* Poll indicating an 8 point advantage for the incumbent president (49 to 41) and this decisive advantage persisted through later polling (FiveThirtyEight.com 2020).

The wild card in the 2020 election was the impact of absentee ballots on the outcome. To reduce exposure to COVID-19, the state had relaxed absentee voting rules such that all voters were now qualified to vote absentee. In mid-September, a federal judge struck the requirement that ballots must be signed by a witness because of ongoing concerns regarding the coronavirus pandemic. This ruling, supported by the South Carolina Democratic Party, was appealed by the Election Commission and the state GOP and was ultimately struck down by a unanimous U.S. Supreme Court decision in early October. In the end, over 1.3 million South Carolinians cast absentee ballots, a substantial increase over the 503,000 that did so in 2016. Mirroring national trends, Biden enjoyed a substantial advantage among absentee voters, particularly mail-in absentee ballots. He received 60 percent of the mail-in votes and only 51 percent of in-person absentee votes. Republicans were much more likely to vote on Election Day, with Biden trailing Trump by 35 points among these South Carolina voters (Koeske 2020).

Overall, Trump handily won the Palmetto State by a 55–43 percent margin, well above the pollsters' prediction of 8 points. This was still less than his 14-point trouncing of Clinton in 2016, though modestly better than Romney's 10.5 percent margin over Obama in 2012. Turnout was high but not a record. In 2008, 76 percent of registered voters voted, while only 72.1 percent cast a ballot in 2020. This was still a marked increase from 2016's rate of 67.9 percent. The record for voter turnout was 1992, when 80.5 percent of registered voters cast a ballot. Given Trump's commanding margins in pre-election polls, South Carolina voters could be forgiven for believing that his victory was a foregone conclusion and staying home on Election Day.

Table 7.3 details voting and turnout margins in the four regions of the state and the most populous five counties in each region. Not unexpectedly, Trump did best in the conservative Upstate region of the state and even managed to slightly exceed his margin in 2016. He won 64 percent of the vote there and a whopping 74.6 percent of the vote in Pickens County, which retained its distinction as the most Republican county in the state. Trump saw some slippage in Greenville and Spartanburg, the two largest counties in the Upstate. Both counties have experienced significant growth, with Spartanburg County being the fifth fastest-growing county in the state. While it remains an open question whether newcomers to the state will diminish GOP hegemony, this trend should be concerning to Republican leadership.

The Midlands and the Lowcountry are the two regions most favorable to Democrats. In the Midlands, Democrats do well among minority voters in both Columbia and the rural counties. Biden won populous Richland County, home of Columbia, 68.4 to 30.1 percent, but lost suburban Lexington County by a similar margin. Lexington is the sixth fastest-growing county in the state and saw a two-percentage drop in Trump support from 2016. York County, outside of Charlotte, is another rapidly growing area that saw a decline in Trump's vote percentage since 2016. Overall, Trump carried the Midlands by a six-point margin. Biden's best performance was in the Lowcountry region of the state. Here he eeked out a 50.4 to 48 percent win, largely due

Table 7.2 Results of 2020 South Carolina Presidential and Congressional Elections

Candidate (Party)	%	Total Votes
President		
Donald J. Trump/Michael R. Pence (R) *	55.11	1,385,103
Joseph R. Biden/Kamala D. Harris (D)	43.43	1,091,541
Jo Jorgensen/Jeremy Spike Cohen (L)	1.11	27,916
Howie Hawkins/Angela Walker (G)	.27	6907
Roque Rocky De La Fuente/Darcy G. Richardson (ALN)	.07	1862
Total		2,513,329
U.S. Senate		
Lindsey Graham (R) *	54.44	1,369,137
Jaime Harrison (D)	44.17	1,110,828
Bill Bledsoe (C)	1.31	32,845
Write-in	0.09	2,294
Total		2,515,104
U.S. House		
1st District		
Nancy Mace (R)	50.58	216,042
Joe Cunningham (D) *	49.31	210,627
Write-in	.10	442
Total		427,111
2nd District		
Joe Wilson (R) *	55.66	202,715
Adair Ford Boroughs (D)	42.59	155,118
Kathleen K. Wright (C)	1.69	6,163
Write-in	.06	219
Total		364,215
3rd District		
Jeff Duncan (R) *	71.21	237,544
Hosea Cleveland (D)	28.69	95,712
Write-in	0.09	308
Total		333,564
4th District		
William Timmons (R) *	61.61	222,126
Kim Nelson (D)	36.89	133,023
Write-in	0.09	311
Total		360,550
5th District		
Ralph Norman (R) *	60.07	220,006
Moe Brown (D)	39.86	145,979
Write-in	0.07	273
Total		366,258

(Continued)

Table 7.2 Results of 2020 South Carolina Presidential and Congressional Elections
(Continued)

Candidate (Party)	%	Total Votes
6th District		
James E. "Jim" Clyburn (D) *	68.18	197,477
John McCollum (R)	30.82	89,258
Mark Hackett (C)	.91	2646
Write-in	0.09	272
Total		289,653
7th District		
Tom Rice (R) *	61.80	224,993
Melissa Ward Watson (D)	38.14	138,863
Write-in	0.06	235
Total		364,091

Source: South Carolina State Election Commission website at: https://www.enr-scvotes.org/SC/106502/Web02-state.264691/#/?undefined.
Note: R = Republican, D = Democratic, L = Libertarian Party, G = Green Party, C = Constitution Party, ALN = Alliance Party.
* = Incumbent.

to Trump's poor performance in Charleston County. Trump did well in Berkeley and Dorchester Counties, both of which are "bedroom" counties and rapidly growing in population. Berkeley County ranks second in growth and Dorchester County recently became home to Volvo's first American factory. Both counties saw declines in Trump's share of the vote compared to 2016.

The Pee Dee region is the smallest of the four regions, representing about 18 percent of the total vote cast. However, the Pee Dee is home to Myrtle Beach, which is located in Horry County. Horry County's population increased 31 percent from 2010 to 2019 and a 2020 article in the *Post and Courier* notes that in-migration to the county accounts for all population growth as the county has a negative birth rate. The area has become very popular for snowbirds and retirees. At 66 percent, Horry County registered the strongest support for Trump among the five largest counties in the Pee Dee, though it was the only one in which Trump got a lower percentage of the vote than he did in 2016.

Table 7.3 also demonstrates Trump and Biden's support in rural and urban counties. Clinton won 49.7 percent of the vote in rural counties in 2016, which was 1.7 percent more than Trump. This represented a deterioration in Democratic fortunes in rural areas where the higher concentrations of minority voters usually are solid victories for Democrats. In 2020, Trump continued GOP gains with rural voters, receiving 49.8 percent of the vote compared to 49.2 percent for Biden. Since so few African Americans voted for Trump, this vote illustrates how much the president resonated with white rural voters.

Table 7.3 Voting by Region and County in 2020 General Election

Region	Trump	Biden	Trump % Δ 2016	Percent of Total Vote Cast in State	Turnout Rate	Turnout Rate % Δ 2016
Upstate						
Greenville	58.1	39.9	-2.19	10.22	74.12	6.62
Spartanburg	62.9	35.6	-.09	5.91	73.01	6.11
Anderson	70.3	28.3	.64	3.83	74.43	8.67
Pickens	74.6	23.7	.93	2.28	74.25	3.23
Upstate Total	64.0	34.5	.11	28.62	73.89	6.62
Midlands						
Richland	30.1	68.4	-3.25	7.71	70.06	4.02
Lexington	64.2	34.1	-2.05	5.74	72.62	3.80
York	57.4	41.0	-1.62	5.72	73.32	6.25
Aiken	60.6	37.9	-1.51	3.39	69.85	2.58
Midlands Total	52.1	46.4	-.59	29.05	72.21	4.59
Pee Dee						
Horry	66.1	32.9	-1.59	7.19	71.04	8.47
Florence	50.6	48.3	-.96	2.57	71.19	6.83
Sumter	42.9	56	.96	1.95	67.44	4.15
Darlington	51.9	47	2.79	1.29	72.47	7.38
Pee Dee Total	55.9	44.1	2.30	18.45	70.83	7.46
Lowcountry						
Charleston	42.6	55.5	-.36	8.67	70.87	10.14
Berkeley	54.9	43.3	-2.01	4.14	72.54	6.66
Beaufort	54.4	44.4	-.53	3.90	71.09	.04
Dorchester	54.2	43.8	-3.01	3.06	68.66	8.51
Lowcountry Total	48.0	50.4	.45	23.88	70.88	6.68
Urban Counties (26)	56.4	42.2	-.48	85.64	72.06	6.96
Rural Counties (20)	49.8	49.2	4.75	14.36	72.34	5.77
Statewide Total	55.1	43.4	.36		72.10	6.25

Source: Computed by authors from data found at South Carolina State Election Commission website: https ://www.enr-scvotes.org/SC/106502/Web02-state.264691/#/access-to-races?undefined. County regional divisions are found here: https://sc.gov/government.

Trump was even able to flip two rural counties, Dillon and Clarendon, by the slimmest of margins: a combined 282 votes. Moreover, Trump received a higher vote share in each of the dozen counties he lost that have populations with less than 100,000 people. Furman political science professor, Danielle Vinson, speculated that perhaps this was driven by normally disillusioned blue county conservatives turning out to vote in what many thought was going to be a much closer race between Senator Lindsey Graham and challenger Jaime Harrison. Some support for that hypothesis is that the senate race garnered almost 2000 more votes than the presidential race (Koeske 2020). Whatever the case, Trump made serious inroads among the historically Democratic South Carolinian rural electorate.

The twenty-six urban counties combined were quite supportive of Trump. He gained 56.4 percent of their vote compared to Biden's 42.2. This statistic is misleading, as many counties classified as urban would be more accurately characterized as suburban. Table 7.4 reports key findings from the CNN 2020 South Carolina Presidential Exit Poll. That poll reveals that only 43 percent of self-identified urban respondents voted for Trump. Indeed, Biden won handily in Richland and Charleston Counties, the second- and third-largest counties in the state. These two counties combined account for roughly 16 percent of the total vote cast in 2020. Former GOP State Chairman, Katon Dawson, joked, "We ought to just offer Richland County up for sale to New York and Charleston County to California" (Wilks and Brussee 2020, para. 20). Trump, on the other hand, did very well in the suburbs. Gains among suburban respondents outpaced Biden 58 to 40 percent.

The exit poll sheds some light on individual-level determinants of vote choice in the 2020 election. It is clear that race was a predominant factor with 85 percent of black men and 96 percent of black women voting for Biden. Overall, 90 percent of African-Americans voted for Biden and only 7 percent for Trump. This compares to 94 percent support for Clinton and 4 percent for Trump in 2016 (CNN.com 2016). This is a small difference and not one that is likely to be part of a trend, though it does mirror modest increases in black support for Trump seen nationally. Analysis of national exit polls suggests that Trump's 2020 share of the vote improved by 4 percent among black women and 5 percent among black men (Jennings 2020). Biden won a narrow majority of the 30–44 age group (50 to 48 percent) but fell far short in the others, particularly the older respondents. In 2016, Trump tied with Clinton in the 18–29 age group and won in all other age categories. Biden did predictably well with relatively low-income South Carolinian voters, winning 62 percent of the vote from respondents with incomes less than $30,000. Trump captured solid majorities in all other income categories. Despite Trump's well-known "education gap," college graduates in the state were just as likely to vote for Trump as noncollege graduates. Trump received 55 percent of the vote from both college and noncollege graduates with Biden winning 43 percent of both groups. Interestingly, this is precisely the opposite of Trump and Biden's relative vote share as recorded in national exit polls (*New York Times* 2020).

Nothing remarkable stands out in how the vote was cast in terms of partisanship and ideology. Comparison with the 2016 South Carolinian exit poll does indicate liberals were more unified in 2020. In 2016, Trump received 13 percent of the liberal vote in South Carolina compared to only 7 percent in 2020. The heightened partisan polarization of 2020 may explain this relative solidarity. This polarization is highlighted when voters are asked what the most important issues were in the election. There was little agreement

Table 7.4 South Carolina Exit Poll Results, 2020

Voter Characteristic/Attitude	Trump	Biden	% of Category
Sex by Race			
White men	75%	23%	28%
White women	71	28	38
Black men	12	85	12
Black women	3	96	14
Age			
18–29	53	43	15
30–44	48	50	20
45–64	57	42	37
65 or older	60	40	27
Income			
< $30,000	38	62	23
$30–49,999	56	42	18
$50–99,999	51	47	31
$100–199,999	64	35	22
Education			
College graduate	55	43	37
No college degree	55	43	63
Party Identification			
Democrat	4	96	30
Republican	95	4	41
Independent	50	46	29
Ideology			
Liberal	7	92	15
Moderate	42	56	38
Conservative	85	14	47
Area Type			
Urban	43	55	14
Suburban	58	40	49
Rural	56	43	37
Vote for President Mainly:			
For your candidate	63	36	72
Against his opponent	41	55	23
Most Important Issue to Your Vote?			
The economy	87	11	36
Coronavirus	10	89	16
Racial inequality	10	88	15
Crime and safety	84	16	14
Which Candidate Quality Mattered Most?			
Is a strong leader	84	15	35
Has good judgment	21	76	23
Cares about people like me	48	52	19
Can unite the country	32	64	17

Source: CNN 2020 Presidential Exit Poll (South Carolina), November 3, 2020, found here: https://www.cnn.com/election/2020/exit-polls/president/south-carolina.

between Republican and Democratic partisans on the most pressing issues. Concerns about coronavirus and racial inequality were foremost on the minds of Biden voters. Close to 90 percent of voters naming these two issues as most important to their vote chose Biden. The law and order vote went decisively to Trump. Eighty-four percent of voters naming crime and safety as the top issue voted for Trump. The economy was the top-named issue among exit-poll respondents and 87 percent of these voters cast a ballot for the incumbent president. South Carolinian Trump voters were also more likely to believe the country needed a strong leader, while Biden scored support among voters wanting a president with good judgment and one that could unite the country.

Table 7.5 presents a regression model predicting the Trump percentage of the vote in the forty-six South Carolinian counties. Four independent variables measuring county economic circumstances, population growth, educational attainment, and racial mix explain an impressive 88 percent of the variation across the counties (adjusted $R^2 = .882$). The strongest effect on Trump's vote percentage was the percent of non-white registered voters. For every one-point increase in this percentage, Trump lost .73 percentage points in his vote share. This one variable dwarfed the others in terms of its impact on the model. The standardized beta coefficient of 1.00 was close to three times larger than the next most important variable, the percent of the county with a bachelor's degree or more. Counties with more college graduates were significantly less supportive of Trump as were counties with higher rates of unemployment. To model the effect of newcomers to the state on Trump's performance, the authors measured the percent of population change in a country from 2010 to 2019. The expectation that such counties would be less Republican was borne out with a negative coefficient; however, it fell short of statistical significance ($p = .112$). Unemployment rates, education levels, and perhaps population change do seem to matter, but these factors pale in

Table 7.5 Correlation Coefficients and Regression Results or County-Level Trump Percentage of Vote in 2020 General Election

Predictor	B	Standard Error	Beta	t-score	Significance Level
Unemployed (%)	−.031	.011	−.211	−2.78	.008
Population change, 2010–2019 (%)	−.001	.001	−.147	−1.62	.112
With bachelor's degree or more (%)	−.005	.001	−.362	−4.96	.000
Registered voters Non-white (%)	−.731	.057	−1.001	−12.73	.000
Constant	1.181	.110		10.74	.000

Note: $N = 46$; adjusted $R^2 = .882$.

comparison to the effect of race. Running the model with the percent of nonwhite registered voters as the sole independent variable explains 76 percent of the variation in county-level support for Trump in 2020. Race clearly matters in South Carolina politics.

Aside from the presidential election, Republicans had quite a good election season. All Republican congressional incumbents won reelection. Two relative newcomers were Republicans William Timmons, congressman from the Fourth District and Ralph Norman of the Fifth District. Representing the northern corner of the state, Timmons replaced retiring Trey Gowdy in 2018 and improved his vote margin by two percentage points in his sophomore election (61.6 to 59.5). Norman also represents Upstate voters and was elected in a 2017 special election following Mick Mulvaney's elevation to Director of the Office of Management and Budget. Norman faced his 2017 Democratic opponent, Archie Parnell, again in the 2018 general election. An investigation by Charleston's *Post and Courier* found that Parnell had been divorced in 1973 and that his then wife had been granted a restraining order "on the ground of physical cruelty" (Lovegrove 2018). Despite calls by the state Democratic Party for him to withdraw, Parnell stayed in the race only to lose with 41.5 percent of the vote. In 2020, Norman's opponent, Moe Brown—former Gamecock wide receiver—did worse than Parnell garnering just shy of 40 percent of the vote.

Lindsey Graham's race for reelection against Jaime Harrison, former chair of the South Carolina Democratic Party, attracted considerable national-level attention. The highly visible Graham was running against a Democratic dream candidate. Harrison had come from humble beginnings in rural Orangeburg, went on to receive a scholarship to Yale University, and subsequently earned a Georgetown J.D. He began his political career in Congressman Jim Clyburn's office and then worked as a prominent lobbyist in Washington, D.C. In 2013, he became the first African American to chair the state Democratic Party. These stellar credentials and the opportunity to unseat Lindsey Graham were irresistible to Democratic donors, which flooded Harrison's campaign with $132 million, which set the record for a U.S. Senate candidate. Graham raised $109 million and was able to outspend Harrison in the past few weeks by $8 million ($33 million compared to Harrison's $25 million). Graham's best day of fundraising came the last day of Amy Coney Barrett's Senate confirmation hearing when he hauled in $5 million (Lovegrove 2020b). A number of polls indicated a tight race leading up to Election Day and at some points even showed Harrison with a two-point advantage (Bustos 2020b). An election-eve poll showed Graham up by six percentage points (Martin 2020). The past two general elections have not been kind to pollsters, and, when the numbers were tallied, Graham won by a decisive 10 percent margin.

The second noteworthy downticket race was between incumbent Democrat Joe Cunningham and Republican Nancy Mace. Cunningham was elected in 2018 as the first Democrat to hold the First District seat in almost four decades. His 2018 opponent was state representative Katie Arrington, who had defeated incumbent Mark Sanford in the primary. A large part of Arrington's primary victor was that she painted as a Trump obstructionist. Cunningham won the general election by 4,000 votes, winning only Charleston County in the five-county Lowcountry district. It is likely that Arrington hitched her wagon too closely to Trump and this hurt her in this midterm election. In particular, Arrington intimated in the primary that she supported Trump's proposal for offshore drilling for oil and natural gas. She spent the remainder of the campaign trying to backtrack on this, which was unpopular in the tourism-dependent coastal district.

Representative Cunningham was as centrist as he could be given that he served a district Trump won by 13 percentage points in 2016, but he was challenged by Mace in 2020. Mace was a state representative and a minor celebrity in the district as she was the first woman to graduate from The Citadel. In a prescient move, Mace had cosponsored a resolution two years earlier advocating a ban on drilling off South Carolina's coast. While she had worked for Trump in the 2016 campaign and remained a supporter, Mace wisely put some distance between herself and the president. In regard to criticism that she was a Trump obstructionist, she wrote on her Facebook page, "I worked for President Trump ... in several states. I support his agenda. But that doesn't mean like a blind sheep I will agree with everything. I represent the Charleston area" (Fears 2018, para. 31). Whether it was her political savvy or Trump's coattails, Mace pulled off an unexpected victory, winning by just short of 6,000 votes. Like the state's U.S. Senate race, the Mace-Cunningham contest attracted substantial national attention and was the most expensive House race in South Carolina history. Mace will have to walk a fine line in office as the First District will likely remain a highly contested seat.[1]

CONCLUSION

Since the initial "First in the South" presidential primary in 1980, South Carolina has consistently played a key role in determining the eventual nominees for both parties. For the GOP, every eventual Republican presidential nominee between 1980 and 2008 won the South Carolina primary. After what turned out to be an anomaly to date, Newt Gingrich's victory in 2012 was an exception to that rule. However, Donald Trump's victories in 2016 and 2020 seem to have restored the Palmetto State's importance in the Republican presidential nomination process. As highlighted previously in this chapter, the state has become increasingly important for Democratic nominees as well. With the exception of 2004, Democratic voters in the state have voted for the eventual nominee since 1988. In both 2016 and 2020, the South Carolinian Democratic Primary proved crucial to "steadying the ship" first for Hillary Clinton and then Joe Biden. Indeed, all evidence suggests that Jim Clyburn's endorsement of Biden and his subsequent win rescued his bid for the nomination and demonstrated his ability to win diverse constituencies.

By the time of the November 2020 general election, Donald Trump easily won the state, as expected, and U.S. Senator Lindsey Graham turned back a challenge from a very well-funded Jami Harrison, the Democratic nominee. Further down the ticket, Republicans managed to not only easily hold onto control of the congressional delegation, but they were also successful in reclaiming the First Congressional District from the Democrats. Given the growth, and increasingly Democratic leanings of Charleston County, this seat will be hotly contested in whatever form the First District might take in 2022 after redistricting takes place.

The 2020 general election further entrenched the power of the Republican Party at the state level. The party won high-profile Senate and House contests and saw all its incumbents elected with safe margins. Republicans added two members to their ranks in the South Carolina House, increasing their majority to 81 members to only 43 for the Democrats. One of the Democratic losses in the South Carolina House was Mandy Powers Norrell. In 2018, Norrell had achieved some visibility as the Democratic candidate for lieutenant governor in 2018 and was considered a bright spot amid generally bleak Democratic prospects. In part, Norrell fell victim to the suburban, and increasingly exurban, growth in Lancaster County. Norrell had also become the source of some controversy in 2019. At the Army-Navy game in 2019, cadets were seen flashing an "OK" hand signal that is sometimes associated with white supremacist groups. After a military investigation though, it was concluded that the cadets were not using the signal as a gesture of white power. Norrell tweeted out a criticism of the cadets initially, but she later removed the tweet and apologized personally to the cadets (Schechter 2019). However, it is likely that this event fired-up the Republican base even further.

The South Carolinian Senate also became more Republican with the loss of three seats by the Democrats. Republican senators now number thirty to the Democrats sixteen, a majority large enough to vote cloture to end debate. One of the Democratic senators that lost reelection was two-time gubernatorial candidate, Vincent Sheheen, who had run unopposed for his Senate seat in 2008, 2012, and 2016. Remarking on Sheheen's defeat, former state Senator Joel Lourie said, "This election was about R versus D, and if you live in a

Republican state, that's not going to bode well for you. I'm fairly confident you had a record number of voters yesterday voting straight ticket. People were not voting against Vincent Sheheen because if you had based your vote on his contributions to the state, he would have won overwhelmingly" (Schechter and John Monk 2020, para. 15).

At the moment, there seems little room for Democratic optimism in the state. Few, if any, high-profile state-level Democrats remain. Overwhelming Republican success in 2020 will also mean that the redistricting process that will occur between now and the next election will likely further entrench GOP incumbents and endanger the scattered pockets of Democratic strength. Yet, South Carolina seems likely to remain a high-growth state for the foreseeable future. Migration to the state's urban and coastal areas continues unabated. Some of the new transplants to the state are retirees and are more likely to vote for Republicans over the coming decade. However, an increasing number of new residents are younger and moving for employment opportunities. As Bullock et al. (2019) demonstrate, younger, more diverse residents to urban and suburban areas in the South over the past two decades have helped to make Democrats competitive again. Evidence for this exists in Joe Cunningham's congressional victory in 2018 and the tightness of his failed reelection bid in 2020. While their hopes certainly seem dim at the moment, long-term demographic trends could, at least, rouse South Carolinian Democrats from their nightmare at some point in the next decade.

NOTE

1. In April 2021, Joe Cunningham announced his intentions to seek the Democratic gubernatorial nomination to challenge Governor Henry McMaster in 2022.

REFERENCES

Alberta, Tim. 2021. "Nikki Haley's Time for Choosing." *Politico Magazine.* 12 February 2021. https://www.politico.com/interactives/2021/magazine-nikki-haleys-choice.

Bass, Jack and Scott Poole. 2009. *The Palmetto State: The Making of Modern South Carolina.* Columbia: University of South Carolina Press.

Black, Earl and Merle Black. 1992. *Vital South: How Presidents Are Elected.* Cambridge: Harvard University Press.

Bohatch, Emily. 2020. "2020 Hopefuls Spend More Than $17.6 Million in SC on Ads ahead of Primary." *The State,* 21 February 2020. https://www.thestate.com/news/politics-government/election/article240509736.html.

Buchanan, Scott E. 2005. "The Dixiecrat Rebellion: Long-Term Partisan Implications in the Deep South." *Politics and Policy* 33: 754–769.

Bullock, Charles S., Susan A. MacManus, Jeremy D. Mayer, and Mark J. Rozell. 2019. *The South and the Transformation of U.S. Politics*. Oxford: Oxford University Press.

Bustos, Joseph. 2020a. "Is South Carolina in Play in the Presidential Election? Here's the Latest Poll." *The State*, 30 September 2020. https://www.thestate.com/article246117830.html.

Bustos, Joseph. 2020b. "Lead Changes in Graham-Harrison SC Senate race, Latest Morning Consult Survey Shows." *The State*, 22 October 2020. https://www.thestate.com/news/politics-government/election/article246629998.html.

Chodas, Nadine. 1993. *Strom Thurmond and the Politics of Southern Change*. Macon: Mercer University Press.

CNN.com. 2016. "2016 South Carolina Presidential Exit Poll. 9 November 2020. https://www.cnn.com/election/2016/results/exit-polls/south-carolina/president.

Davis, Susan. 2019. "Why 2020 Democrats Are Lining Up For Clyburn's 'World Famous' Fish Fry." *National Public Radio*, 14 June 2019. https://www.npr.org/2019/06/14/732330671/why-2020-democrats-are-lining-up-for-clyburns-world-famous-fish-fry.

Del Real, Jose A. 2016. "Trump Picks Up Endorsement from S.C. Lt. Gov. Henry McMaster." *The Washington Post,* 27 January 2016. https://www.washingtonpost.com/news/post-politics/wp/2016/01/27/trump-picks-up-endorsement-from-s-c-lt-gov-henry-mcmaster.

Fears, Darryl. 2018. "For Many Republicans, Trump's Offshore Drilling Plan and Beaches Don't Mix." *Washington Post*, 28 February 2018. https://www.washingtonpost.com/national/health-science/for-some-south-carolina-republicans-trumps-offshore-drilling-plan-and-beaches-dont-mix/2018/02/27/a953dc98-1359-11e8-9065-e55346f6de81_story.html.

FiveThirtyEight.com. 2020. "Latest Polls." 15 October 2020. https://projects.fivethirtyeight.com/polls/president-general/south-carolina/.

Graham, Cole Blease, Jr. and Scott E. Buchanan. 2018. "South Carolina: It's All about the Primary." In *The Future Ain't What It Used to Be: The 2016 Presidential Election in the South*, eds. Branwell DuBose Kapeluck and Scott E. Buchanan, 105–123. Fayetteville: University of Arkansas Press.

Jennings, Scott. 2020. "Election 2020 Exit Polls: Political Pundits Utterly Failed to Predict Donald Trump's Voters," *USA Today*, 7 November 2020. https://www.usatoday.com/story/opinion/2020/11/07/election-2020-exit-polls-trump-minorities-race-women-column/6191966002/.

Key, V.O. 1949 *Southern Politics in State and Nation*. New York: Alfred A. Knopf.

King, Gilbert. 2012. "The Ugliest, Most Contentious Presidential Election Ever." *Smithsonian Magazine,* 7 September. https://www.smithsonianmag.com/history/the-ugliest-most-contentious-presidential-election-ever-28429530.

Koeske, Zak. 2020. "Where Trump Flipped Blue Cotes, and Other Key Takeaways on Election Day in SC," *The State*, 6 November 2020. https://www.thestate.com/news/politics-government/election/article246987642.html.

Lovegrove, Jamie. 2018. "Top South Carolina Candidate Refuses to Quit Congressional Race after Abuse Discovery." (Charleston) *Post and Courier*, 21 May 2018. https://www.postandcourier.com/politics/top-south-carolina-candidate-refuses-to-quit-congressional-race-after/article_a6548188-5d27-11e8-a155-bf21652315cd.html.

Lovegrove, Jamie. 2019. "Jim Clyburn's 'World Famous Fish Fry' Draws Presidential Candidates, Thousands of Voters." (Charleston) *Post and Courier*, 21 June 2019. https://www.postandcourier.com/politics/jim-clyburns-world-famous-fish-fry-draws-presidential-candidates-thousands-of-voters/article_293d13b6-92c5-11e9-9eb7-2bdab5f7476f.html.

Lovegrove, Jamie. 2020a. "Upstate GOP Leaders Plotting to Impact SC Democratic Primary by Boosting Bernie Sanders." (Charleston) *Post and Courier*, 4 February 2020. https://www.postandcourier.com/politics/upstate-gop-leaders-plotting-to-meddle-in-sc-democratic-primary/article_f1e7abd2-4788-11ea-aa9f-33a1d262994c.html.

Lovegrove, Jamie. 2020b. "Graham Outspent Harrison in Crucial Final Weeks of SC's Senate Race." (Charleston) *Post and Courier*, 4 December 2020. https://www.postandcourier.com/politics/graham-outspent-harrison-in-crucial-final-weeks-of-scs-senate-race/article_0c347062-3642-11eb-9110-135506b5ec8c.html.

Martin, Jonathan. 2020. "Lindsey Graham Leads Jaime Harrison in South Carolina Race, Poll Shows," *New York Times*, 3 November 2020. https://www.nytimes.com/2020/10/15/us/politics/south-carolina-polls.html.

McCullough, David. 1993. *Truman*. New York: Simon & Schuster.

McGill, Ralph. 1950. "What Is Jimmy Byrnes Up to Now?" *Saturday Evening Post*, 14 October 1950.

Morris, Roy. 2003. *Fraud of the Century: Rutherford B. Hayes, Samuel Tilden, and the Stolen Election of 1876*. New York: Simon and Schuster.

New York Times. 2020. "National Exit Polls: How Different Groups Voted." *New York Times*, 3 November 2020. https://www.nytimes.com/interactive/2020/11/03/us/elections/exit-polls-president.html.

Oprysko, Caitlin and Marc Caputo. 2020. "Biden Wins Crucial Jim Clyburn Endorsement Ahead of South Carolina Primary." *Politico*, 26 February 2020. https://www.politico.com/news/2020/02/26/jim-clyburn-endorses-joe-biden-117667.

Pramuk, Jacob. 2020. "Biden Holds Small Edge over Sanders in Pivotal South Carolina Primary: NBC News/Marist Poll." *CNBC.com*, 24 February 2020. https://www.cnbc.com/2020/02/24/south-carolina-primary-joe-biden-leads-bernie-sanders-in-nbc-marist-poll.html.

Quinnipiac University Poll. 2020. "South Carolina: 2020 Presidential Election. 6 August 2020. https://poll.qu.edu/south-carolina/release-detail?ReleaseID=3670#States.

Schechter, Maayan. 2019. "SC Lawmaker Apologizes to Military Cadets Over Use of 'OK' Hand Sign. Military.com, 24 December 2019. https://www.military.com/daily-news/2019/12/24/sc-lawmaker-apologizes-military-cadets-over-use-ok-hand-sign.html.

Schechter, Maayan and John Monk. 2020. "SC Sen. Vincent Sheheen Loses Reelection Bid in Stunning Upset Giving GOP More Seats." *The State*, 4

November 2020. https://www.thestate.com/news/politics-government/election/article246961312.html.

Strauss, Daniel. 2020. "'A Chain Reaction': How One endorsement Set Joe Biden's Surge in Motion." *The Guardian*, 4 March 2020. https://www.theguardian.com/us-news/2020/mar/04/joe-biden-jim-clyburn-endorsement-super-tuesday.

U.S. Census Bureau. 2021. "Census QuickFacts." 10 March 2021. https://www.census.gov/quickfacts/SC.

Wilks, Avery and Bryan Brussee. 2020. "Biden Made Gains in SC Cities, Suburbs, but Rural Voters Handed Trump a Big Victory." (Charleston) *Post and Courier*, 5 November 2020. https://www.postandcourier.com/columbia/news/biden-made-gains-in-sc-cities-suburbs-but-rural-voters-handed-trump-a-big-victory/article_4abb4028-1f85-11eb-bb48-5b34333050ee.html.

Yokley, Eli. 2020. "Democratic Primary Voters Flock Back to Biden After South Carolina Victory." MorningConsult.com, 2 March 2020. https://morningconsult.com/2020/03/02/post-south-carolina-poll-joe-biden/.

Part III

ELECTIONS IN THE RIM SOUTH

Chapter 8

Arkansas

Once More with Feeling for Trump

Jay Barth and Janine A. Parry

A politically brutal decade for Arkansas Democrats closed with a victory for Republican Donald Trump, even larger than his landslide 2016 win. In 2016, Trump ran up monster margins in the rural counties of the state (counties historically termed "rural swing" counties to emphasize their political ambidextrousness and their decisive role in the state's politics) that had first defected from the Democrats under Barack Obama (Barth, Parry, and Shields 2009; Parry and Barth 2014; Barth and Parry 2018). Continued rural voting shifts toward Trump outweighed a backlash against the president in more suburbanized areas of central and northwest Arkansas. Preelection polling gave Democrats some hope that suburban dynamics nationally would make the difference in the Second Congressional District race and in some legislative races, but down-ticket success was swamped statewide by continued Republican inroads into rural and exurban areas.

The 2020 presidential campaign showcases another key trend of the decade: the nationalization of the state's politics, a dynamic at odds with the state's history of political and social provincialism. Even as Democrats, not named Clinton, have found presidential elections tough sledding in the state for nearly five decades, Arkansas's Democrats had survived—indeed, thrived—through an ability to uncouple state politics from national patterns. That changed with the introduction of Obama and Trump to the political scene, which finally stitched the politics of Washington, D.C., to those of the smallest hamlets in Arkansas. The result: literally no state in the modern era of electoral politics has shown top-to-bottom shifts as sudden or marked as has Arkansas (Parry 2018).

While the 2020 campaign dynamics and outcomes mirrored the 2016 results, Arkansas's role in the presidential nomination and general election campaigns was less important than four years before. Because of Hillary

Clinton's linkages to the state, Arkansas played a visible role in the presidential campaign of 2016. In 2020, aside from a handful of Arkansas Republican leaders who were loyal Trump supporters and surrogates, Arkansas's role in the presidential campaign was at the margins. However, with a bevy of Arkansas Republicans expressing national ambitions and looking ahead to future presidential campaigns, the state's still maturing GOP dominance is likely to appear on the national electoral stage in 2024 and beyond in the form of those who have thrived in this environment.

THE PRIMARY SEASON

Once again, Arkansas participated in the Super Tuesday primary in early March, meaning the filing period in the state came in early November 2019 before results elsewhere could clear the field. Because Trump avoided meaningful opposition in the primary, all the action was on the Democratic side. This represented a major change in the spring dynamics compared to any cycle since before Barack Obama was elected President.

The most-watched figure for the Democratic nomination in the state was former New York City Mayor Michael Bloomberg. Arkansas's filing deadline coincided with Bloomberg's personal calendar for deciding whether to get in the race, resulting in much drama regarding whether Bloomberg would indeed enter the race. On the final day for filing in the Natural State, he jetted to Little Rock and became the lone presidential candidate to file in person for the Arkansas primary. While Bloomberg claimed he had not yet fully decided on whether to enter the race, the mayor looked very much like a candidate as he shared a barbecue lunch with Little Rock Mayor Frank Scott, Jr., the first elected black mayor in the state's capital city.[1] Continuing the courtship, Bloomberg returned in January to march just behind a popular Mayor Scott in the annual Dr. Martin Luther King, Jr. "Marade" (Moritz, "Michael Bloomberg visits"). In early February, Scott joined a number of other African American mayors around the country in endorsing the New Yorker citing Bloomberg's commitment to economic justice for black Americans as expressed in his Greenwood Initiative along with his attention to "overlooked" southern cities like Little Rock (Herzog 2020).

While Bloomberg had the most visits to the state in the runup to the March primary, several other candidates and surrogates visited Arkansas, divvying up the endorsements of key Democratic leaders. Before he announced his presidential bid, Montana Governor Steve Bullock was the featured Clinton Dinner speaker in the summer of 2018, emphasizing his electability in a red state (Moritz 2018). A year later, Minnesota Senator Amy Klobuchar came to the state during the week leading up to the Clinton Dinner in the summer of 2019 emphasizing her commitment to stronger gun regulation (Moritz,

"Democratic Presidential"). At the dinner itself, Texan Beto O'Rourke was the featured speaker, his first appearance following the mass murder of residents in his hometown of El Paso (Moritz, "O'Rourke Talks"). Earlier that same summer, Vermont Senator Bernie Sanders made an (unwelcome) appearance at the annual corporate stakeholders meeting of Walmart in the megacompany's home region of northwest Arkansas; there, Sanders criticized Walmart's record on worker pay and working conditions (Bhattarai 2019). One candidate with Arkansas ties, Colorado Senator Michael Bennet combined a campaign stop with a visit to the Delta hometown of his wife.

As the crowded field continued to jostle for advantage, Klobuchar returned to the state where she gained the endorsement of Little Rock state House member Tippi McCullough. Pete Buttigieg's college friend Clarke Tucker, the 2018 Second District Democratic Congressional candidate, filed on his behalf in November and then hosted a fundraiser with Buttigieg's husband Chasten a week before the primary (and only days before Buttigieg's departure from the race). Several prominent Democratic legislative leaders endorsed former Vice President Joe Biden and welcomed Dr. Jill Biden to the state in early February and then again just two days before the primary (Field 2020). That same weekend, Massachusetts Senator Elizabeth Warren held a large outdoors rally on the Arkansas River in North Little Rock where she was introduced by state Representative Nicole Clowney of Fayetteville (Lockwood, "At rally").

Bloomberg's massive spending in the state on both television advertisements and approximately twenty campaign staffers appeared likely to deliver him a win (DeMillo 2020). The only public poll in the state just before early voting began in the state in February showed Bloomberg with a slight lead over Biden and Sanders (Brock 2020). In the aftermath of Biden's resounding win in the South Carolina primary though, other moderate candidates left the race and endorsed Biden just before Super Tuesday. This momentum swung the tide toward the former vice president in Arkansas as in other states.

A tossup thus was transformed into a healthy victory in the state for Biden, who gained 40.6 percent of the vote to Bernie Sanders's 22.4 percent, Bloomberg's 16.7 percent, and Warren's 10.3 percent. Geographically, Biden's win was even more impressive as he won pluralities across seventy-four of the state's seventy-five counties (Sanders prevailed in Washington County, the home of the University of Arkansas's main campus). Illustrating the last-second shift in the race, a number of those who ultimately served as Biden delegates to the Democratic National Convention had publicly supported other candidates in the March primary.

Despite the lack of competition on the Republican side, with former Massachusetts Governor William Weld gaining barely 2 percent of the vote to President Trump's 97.1 percent, the majority of Arkansas voters who showed up for the March primary still chose a Republican ballot showing

Table 8.1 Primary Voter Turnout in Arkansas in Presidential Election Years, 1976–2020

Year	Democratic Primary	Republican Primary
1976	525,968	22,797
1980	415,406	8,177
1984	492,321	19,040
1988	497,506	68,305
1992	502,130	52,297
1996	300,389	42,814
2000	246,900	44,573
2004	256,848	38,363
2008 (27% VEP)	315,322	229,665
2012 (16% VEP)	162,647	152,360
2016 (30% VEP)	221,020	410,920
2020 (21% VEP)	229,122	246,044

Source: Arkansas Secretary of State; Voting Eligible Population turnout rates for Arkansas primary elections are available since 2008 at http://www.electproject.org/home/voter-turnout/voter-turnout-data.

Note: Arkansas made an earlier bid to increase its significance in the nominating process in 2008, moving its primary from May to February. Participation levels in the state nearly doubled that of previous years. This also proved significant because it separated voters' national partisan preferences from the overwhelming number of local contests in which Republican candidates had not, to date, appeared or were not competitive. The resulting opportunity for voter targeting undoubtedly played a role in the party's growth.

the emphatic dominance of Republicans in the historically Democratic state. The gap between GOP and Democratic primary participation did close from four years prior, however, as Democratic turnout slightly improved and Republican turnout dropped significantly. Overall participation in the primaries dropped markedly from the 2016 cycle with only 21 percent of the state's eligible voters showing up to vote as compared to 30 percent (see table 8.1).

THE GENERAL ELECTION CAMPAIGN

With Republicans averaging about 60 percent of the popular vote in the state over the previous three elections, Arkansas's outcome in the 2020 presidential contest was never in doubt. As a result, neither major party candidate stepped foot in the state nor made an investment in the state following Super Tuesday. This meant that the national campaign—as played out primarily on cable television and social media—drove the dynamics in the Natural State. In the COVID-impacted election cycle, the primary election action was in the form of yard signs and flags with expressions of support for Trump dominating in rural areas and those in support of Biden dominating in urban areas. Across the state, Arkansas-based individual donors contributed to just over $4 million to the Trump campaign while just under $3 million in contributions were made to the Biden campaign from individual donors. Even larger donations during the cycle were made on the GOP side by two Little Rock–based entities—Stephens

Corporation (securities) and the Mountaire Corporation (poultry)—which contributed $17.0 million and $14.6 million, respectively, to super PACs.[2]

Arkansas Republican elites with future political ambitions clamored to proclaim their support of the incumbent President. Arkansas's junior U.S. Senator Tom Cotton was a featured speaker on the final evening of the Republican National Convention in a speech focused on military and foreign affairs. Trump's former press secretary Sarah Huckabee Sanders, who returned to live in Little Rock after her departure from the White House, made brief remarks at two Trump rallies—one just before the Iowa caucuses and another just before the general election (Gillman 2020; Brantley 2020). Finally, state Attorney General Leslie Rutledge caught flak (including from Governor Asa Hutchinson, a fellow Republican) for her series of social media posts from the final evening of the DNC at the White House because she appeared without a mask ("Leslie Rutledge Posts"). Rutledge also joined a series of lawsuits supporting Trump's position on policy matters but also ultimately joined a lawsuit with other state attorneys general attempting to overturn the election outcome. Tellingly, other Republican elites—led by Governor Hutchinson—chose not to attend the RNC, citing the pandemic as the reason for avoiding the festivities.

The one moment where President Trump's Arkansas juggernaut stumbled was in a poll captured just after his much-criticized appearance at St. John's Episcopal Church across from the White House following the aggressive clearing of peaceful Black Lives Matter protestors (see table 8.2). Even in Arkansas, Trump showed particular weakness during that early summer period with suburban voters (around Little Rock and in Northwest Arkansas) and among younger voters. Trump quickly rebounded, according to later surveys, and his victory in the state was never in doubt after that point ("Poll: Independents dissatisfied").

With the controversial U.S. Senator Cotton facing only a Libertarian challenger (Dale Harrington, Jr., who performed ably in his few public appearances) and three of the state's four GOP members of Congress facing either outmatched opponents (in the Third and Fourth Congressional Districts) or no opponent at all (as was the case for the First District's Rick Crawford), the

Table 8.2 Selected Polls in Arkansas, Presidential Race 2020

Poll and Polling Dates	Trump	Biden	Spread
The Arkansas Poll (University of Arkansas) 10/9-10/1	65	32	33 points
Talk Business/Hendrix College Poll, 10/11-10/13	58	34	24 points
Talk Business/Hendrix College Poll, 6/9-6/10	47	45	2 points

Source: Arkansas Poll results available at tinyurl.com/18jbr6hc. Talk Business/Hendrix College Poll results available at https://talkbusiness.net/. More polling results available from RealClearPolitics at tinyurl.com/hp4dcdsp.

most attention down the ballot came from the Second Congressional District (central Arkansas) and from a series of competitive state legislative races. Veteran Little Rock state senator Joyce Elliott, who had been the Democratic nominee in the 2010 race in the district, showed early fundraising success from inside and outside the state, was praised for her effective television advertisements, and was buoyed by internal and external polling showing her in a tight race with three-term incumbent Second District Congressman French Hill, also of Little Rock. Elliott polled well in Pulaski County, as expected, but, more surprisingly, also showed support in the suburban counties closest to Little Rock ("Poll: Razor Close Race").

Two Democrats running for Republican-held state House seats in Pulaski County likewise were seen as challengers who might break the House GOP's supermajority grip. For their part, Republicans hoped to pick up some of the last Democratic-held seats in the more rural portions of south and east Arkansas. Included in this group were two state senate seats in south Arkansas; victories in one or more would provide Republicans their first supermajority in that chamber in the modern era (Moritz, "State Still").

As elsewhere in the country, these stakes were enough to fan a fight over ballot access in the state. Democrats filed suit in the early summer to include fear of COVID-19 exposure as a qualifying reason to request an absentee ballot. Ultimately, the state's Republican Secretary of State agreed with both the Democrats and Governor Hutchinson, changing the rules and mooting the lawsuit (Lynch 2020). This loosening of access laws led to a dramatic surge of absentee ballots in a number of Arkansas counties. Still, it was no match for the state's reaffirmation of itself as Trump territory.

For weeks following Biden's national win, Trump flags remained flying at homes across the state. Although Governor Hutchinson publicly acknowledged Biden's victory by mid-November, other political elites, including Attorney General Rutledge, steadfastly rejected a Biden presidency (2020). Eventually, on January 6th, despite declarations by both of the state's U.S. Senators that they would not support challenges to the allocation of electoral votes from various states, a number of Arkansans traveled to D.C. for the rally and subsequent attack on the U.S. Capitol. Several Arkansans were arrested in the attack's aftermath, including Richard Barnette of Gravette who infamously was photographed with his feet propped on the desk of Speaker of the House Nancy Pelosi (Feuer 2021).

THE OUTCOME

The fact that Arkansas cast its Electoral College votes for the Republican for a sixth consecutive time—and by the widest margin yet (27 points)—surprised no one (see table 8.3). Turnout among the eligible electorate was up, as elsewhere, its highest level—in Arkansas—since 1992. Still, because the U.S. Senate race also was a foregone conclusion and only one U.S. House contest showed any signs of life, Arkansas's thirty-year record still ranked in the bottom five of the fifty states ("2020 turnout"). Of the voters drawn into the fray, approximately 80,000 more cast ballots for Trump than had in 2016 while Biden's total exceeded Clinton's by about half that.

Particularly telling was yet another uptick in Republican strength among Arkansas's "rural swing counties" in 2020 as compared with 2016 (see Blair 1988). Although these counties for decades swung between Republican and Democratic candidates, often depending on the relative salience of economic as compared with social issues, their movement lately can be characterized as rightward only. Table 8.4 captures this phenomenon for presidential elections since 2008, the year that marks the beginning of

Table 8.3 Results of the 2020 Arkansas Presidential and Congressional Elections

Candidate (Party)	Vote Percentage (2016 Party Vote)	Vote Total (2016 Party Vote)
President		
Donald Trump/Mike Pence (REP)	62.4 (60.6)	760,647 (684, 872)
Joseph R. Biden/Kamala Harris (DEM)	34.8 (33.7)	423,932 (380,494)
Jo Jorgensen/Jeremy "Spike" Cohen (LIB)	1.1 (2.6)	13,133 (29,829)
Kanye West/Michelle Tidball (IND)	0.3 (n/a)	4,099 (n/a)
Howie Hawkins/Angela Walker (GRN)	0.2 (0.8)	2,980 (9,473)
U.S. Senate		
Tom Cotton (REP)*	66.5 (59.8)	793,871 (661,984)
(no candidate) (DEM)	n/a (36.2)	n/a (400,602)
Ricky Dale Harrington, Jr. (LIB)	33.5 (4.0)	399,390 (43,866)
U.S. House of Representatives		
First District		
Rick Crawford (REP)*	100.0 (76.3)	237,596 (183,866)
(no candidate) (DEM)	n/a (n/a)	n/a (n/a)
Second District		
French Hill (REP)*	55.4 (58.3)	184,093 (176,472)
Joyce Elliott (DEM)	44.6 (36.8)	148,410 (111,347)
Third District		
Steve Womack (REP)*	64.3 (64.7)	214,960 (148,717)
Celeste Williams (DEM)	31.8 (32.6)	106,325 (74,952)
Michael J. Kalagias (LIB)	3.9 (2.6)	12,977 (5,899)
Fourth District		
Bruce Westerman (REP)*	69.7 (74.9)	191,617 (182,885)
William H. Hanson (DEM)	27.5 (n/a)	75,750 (n/a)
Frank Gilbert (LIB)	2.8 (25.1)	7,668 (61,274)

Note: * denotes incumbent.
Source: Arkansas Secretary of State.

Arkansas's partisan transformation. Although the table shows a gradual increase in the statewide ratio of Republican to Democrat votes cast, the average for just the twenty-six "swing" counties—disproportionately white and rural—grows at a markedly faster rate. By 2020, the voters of Scott County (fewer than 11,000 people total), for example, preferred Trump over Biden at nearly three times the statewide rate, and more than twice the county's own 2008 rate. Overall, although Trump's statewide margin widened by less than one point, his share in the First and Fourth House Districts—the state's most rural—jumped by four.[3] Conversely, Trump support declined modestly in the state's more populated (and diverse) counties as compared with 2016.

Social/Demographic Factors

The explanation for yet another presidential rout in Arkansas does not lie in the urban-rural divide alone. Drawing upon exit-poll data and the annual Arkansas Poll, we see that the Republican candidate's support both expanded and contracted compared to 2016 in ways that parallel national patterns of nearly every kind (see table 8.5). White voters, for example, who compose more than 80 percent of the Arkansas electorate, overwhelmingly cast their ballots for Donald Trump, as did those identifying as evangelical or born again. Because white women were as likely to support Trump as white men, the six-point gender gap was only about half of the record-setting national average. Even the rebound in turnout by black women as compared with 2016 was not enough to alter Arkansas's continuing rightward march.

Likewise, Arkansans with higher levels of education were less ringing in their endorsement of the incumbent than those with less, but because college attainment remains lower in the state than any place but West Virginia, the influence of those voters in a statewide electorate is diluted. (Of course, it merits note that even among college-educated Arkansans, the Democrat failed to earn a majority.) The same can be observed about the youngest versus the oldest voters, at least for the groups for which we have relatively reliable samples: there is a double-digit deficit in Trump support between retirees/near-retirees and the cohorts below. The magnitude of support provided by older voters, combined with their greater proportion of the electorate, swamps the more divided preferences of all others.

Political Factors

Above all, the Trump presidency seems to have cinched Arkansas's relatively late partisan realignment. Consider as evidence the incumbent president's 63 percent approval rating on the 2020 Arkansas Poll, which was both a 10-point

Table 8.4 Arkansas Realignment (Republican Tilt) by county 2008, 2012, 2016, and 2020

County	08 R/D Ratio	12 R/D Ratio	16 R/D Ratio	20 R/D Ratio
Arkansas	1.6	1.6	2.0	2.4
Ashley	1.8	1.7	2.2	2.6
Baxter	2.0	2.6	3.5	3.4
Benton	2.2	2.4	2.2	1.8
Boone	2.4	3.0	4.2	4.5
Bradley	1.3	1.5	1.6	1.9
Calhoun	**2.1**	**2.2**	**2.4**	**3.4**
Carroll	1.5	1.7	2.0	1.8
Chicot	0.7	0.6	0.7	0.8
Clark	1.1	1.1	1.2	1.3
Clay	**1.4**	**1.9**	**3.2**	**4.2**
Cleburne	2.7	3.3	4.5	5.2
Cleveland	**2.7**	**2.7**	**3.4**	**4.4**
Columbia	1.6	1.6	1.7	2.0
Conway	**1.5**	**1.5**	**1.8**	**2.2**
Craighead	1.7	1.9	2.2	2.1
Crawford	2.8	3.1	3.7	3.8
Crittenden	0.7	0.7	0.8	0.9
Cross	1.7	1.9	2.3	2.8
Dallas	**1.2**	**1.2**	**1.3**	**1.6**
Desha	0.8	0.8	0.9	1.0
Drew	1.5	1.5	1.7	1.8
Faulkner	1.7	2.0	2.0	1.9
Franklin	2.4	2.7	3.7	4.4
Fulton	1.5	2.0	3.3	3.8
Garland	1.7	1.9	2.1	2.1
Grant	**3.2**	**3.3**	**4.2**	**5.4**
Greene	**1.9**	**2.3**	**3.5**	**4.1**
Hempstead	1.5	1.7	1.9	2.1
Hot Spring	**1.7**	**1.9**	**2.6**	**3.0**
Howard	**1.7**	**2.0**	**2.3**	**2.5**
Independence	**2.2**	**2.7**	**3.4**	**4.0**
Izard	**1.8**	**2.3**	**3.6**	**4.5**
Jackson	1.4	1.5	2.1	2.6
Jefferson	0.6	0.5	0.6	0.6
Johnson	**1.6**	**1.8**	**2.5**	**3.0**
Lafayette	**1.5**	**1.5**	**1.7**	**2.1**
Lawrence	**1.6**	**2.0**	**3.2**	**4.2**
Lee	0.6	0.6	0.7	0.9
Lincoln	1.5	1.5	2.0	2.6
Little River	1.9	2.2	2.6	3.0
Logan	2.3	2.5	3.4	4.2
Lonoke	2.9	3.2	3.5	3.4
Madison	1.9	2.0	3.1	3.6
Marion	1.9	2.3	3.7	3.8

(Continued)

Table 8.4 Arkansas Realignment (Republican Tilt) by county 2008, 2012, 2016, and 2020 (Continued)

County	08 R/D Ratio	12 R/D Ratio	16 R/D Ratio	20 R/D Ratio
Miller	2.0	2.4	2.6	2.8
Mississippi	1.0	1.0	1.2	1.6
Monroe	1.1	1.0	1.1	1.3
Montgomery	**2.2**	**2.6**	**3.5**	**4.2**
Nevada	1.4	1.5	1.7	2.0
Newton	2.2	2.5	4.1	4.5
Ouachita	**1.2**	**1.2**	**1.2**	**1.3**
Perry	**2.0**	**2.2**	**2.9**	**3.4**
Phillips	0.5	0.5	0.6	0.7
Pike	**2.5**	**3.3**	**4.6**	**5.5**
Poinsett	**1.8**	**2.1**	**2.9**	**4.2**
Polk	2.8	3.8	5.5	5.6
Pope	2.6	2.9	3.3	3.1
Prairie	**2.1**	**2.4**	**3.1**	**4.3**
Pulaski	0.8	0.8	0.7	0.6
Randolph	**1.5**	**1.8**	**3.2**	**4.4**
Saline	2.4	2.6	2.7	2.5
Scott	**2.7**	**2.9**	**4.5**	**6.1**
Searcy	2.8	3.3	4.9	5.7
Sebastian	2.1	2.2	2.4	2.2
Sevier	2.4	3.0	3.1	3.5
Sharp	1.9	2.4	3.7	4.2
St. Francis	0.7	0.7	0.8	0.9
Stone	**2.2**	**2.8**	**3.4**	**3.9**
Union	1.7	1.7	1.8	1.9
Van Buren	2.0	2.4	3.5	3.8
Washington	1.3	1.4	1.2	1.1
White	**2.9**	**3.5**	**4.1**	**4.0**
Woodruff	0.9	0.9	1.2	1.8
Yell	**1.9**	**2.3**	**3.1**	**4.1**
Statewide Ratio	1.5	1.6	1.8	1.8
RSC Ratio	**2.0**	**2.2**	**3.0**	**3.7**

Note: Bolded counties denote Blair (1988)'s "rural swing counties." RSC = Rural Swing Counties
Source: Data compiled by the authors from the official website of the Arkansas Secretary of State at https://www.sos.arkansas.gov/elections/research/election-results.

jump over 2019 among self-identified "very likely voters" and almost 20 points higher than his rating nationally (Parry 2020, Gallup 2021). Moreover, not only did Arkansas's Republican and Democratic identifiers hit their respective highest (44 percent) and lowest (20 percent) levels since the turn of the twenty-first century, but also only one in six respondents insisted they were truly independent. The persuadable middle—so long a determinant of Arkansas's election outcomes—appears to have hollowed out almost totally. Unsurprisingly, as also seen in table 8.5, there were few partisan defections.

Table 8.5 Poll Results of Arkansas Voters, 2020 (in Percent)

Characteristic	Trump	Biden	Trump '16
Party Identification			
Democrat	8	87	10
Republican	95	4	94
Most Important Problem			
The economy	29	16	na
Education	9	8	na
Healthcare	15	39	na
Drugs	17	7	na
Taxes	9	2	na
Politicians	19	23	na
White Evangelical/Born Again?			
Yes	86	11	65
No	47	50	48
Sex			
Male	66	33	60
Female	60	369	59
White Males	72	27	64
White Females	72	24	67
Racial/Ethnic Identity			
White	72	26	65
Nonwhite	21	74	4
Education			
High school or less	70	26	na
Some college/associate degree	63	34	na
College graduate	53	47	na
Age			
18–29	na	na	56
30–44	55	43	61
45–64	64	33	60
65 or older	71	27	60
Income			
Under $25,000	65	33	45
25,000 = $49,999	61	39	56
$50,000–74,999	62	31	60
Size of Community			
Urban	na	54	42
Suburban	52	46	66
Small town	66	28	65
Rural	72	26	67

Source: The University of Arkansas's Arkansas Poll (October 2020) or AP's VoteCast exit poll. Accessed February 15, 2021, at https://www.nytimes.com/interactive/2020/11/03/us/elections/ap-polls-arkansas.html

With respect to top-of-mind issues for the state's voters, the October Arkansas Poll showed a near tie between healthcare (24 percent) and the economy (23 percent) as the state's most important problem. Although the former was the primary concern of nearly 40 percent of Biden voters, Trump won the support of respondents in nearly every other category. The only other exception was "politicians," newly emergent in 2020 as a top problem to be addressed. The choice of one in five respondents overall, Biden earned the support of a slightly higher percentage of that group.

Turnout

Turnout among registered Arkansas voters, in keeping with the eligible voter record noted earlier, was 67 percent (see table 8.6), the strongest showing in the state since 1992. The distribution however was not uniform. Consider this: about half of the state's total population (see table 8.7) is concentrated into just ten counties. As in elections past, turnout—and vote preference—varied considerably. The booming exurban communities of Saline and Faulkner, for example, not only exceeded the statewide turnout average by four and seven percentage points, respectively, but also showed higher Republican support than in 2016. (Indeed, in White County, the spread was 78 percent to 19 percent.) The comparable increases for Biden as compared with Clinton support in higher-population counties like Pulaski, Benton, and Washington did little to challenge the Trump juggernaut elsewhere. (A significant portion of liberal and/or "never Trump" voters four years earlier had withheld their votes from the Democratic nominee, scattering them instead to a half dozen minor candidates.) Finally, one of the only counties in Arkansas with a sizable black population—Jefferson—not only posted a turnout rate 10 points

Table 8.6 General Election Voter Turnout in Arkansas, 1972–2020

Year	Turnout % (Registered Voters)
1972	69 (g)
1976	71 (g)
1980	77 (g)
1984	76 (g)
1988	69 (p)
1992	72 (p)
1996	65 (p)
2000	59 (p)
2004	64 (p)
2008	65 (p)
2012	67 (p)
2016	65 (p)
2020	67 (p)

Note: Voter turnout figures are based on gubernatorial voting (g) or presidential voting (p) depending on the highest turnout race of the year. After shifting from two- to four-year terms in 1986, Arkansas gubernatorial elections are no longer held in presidential years.

Source: Data compiled from the official website of the Arkansas Secretary of State and from various volumes of *America Votes* (Congressional Quarterly: Washington, D.C.).

Table 8.7 Registered Voter Turnout and Presidential Vote in the Ten Most Populous Arkansas Counties, 2020

County and Population 2019 (2010)	Population Change 2010–2019 (%)	2020 Turnout %	Vote % Republican (2016)	Vote % Democrat (2016)
Pulaski 391,911	2.4	65.6	37.5	60.0
(382,749)		(65.5)	(38.3)	(56.1)
Benton 279,141	26.1	70.8	61.9	35.2
(221,148)		(67.8)	(62.9)	(28.9)
Washington 239,187	17.8	67.4	50.4	46.5
(203,050)		(64.0)	(50.7)	(40.8)
Sebastian 127,827	1.7	64.9	66.2	30.7
(125,740)		(60.9)	(65.3)	(27.6)
Faulkner 126,007	11.3	71.0	63.2	33.7
(113,238)		(64.2)	(61.8)	(30.8)
Saline 122,437	14.3	73.8	69.5	28.2
(107,135)		(70.5)	(68.8)	(25.4)
Craighead 110,332	14.4	66.8	66.4	31.0
(96,443)		(60.4)	(64.4)	(29.6)
Garland 99,386	3.5	67.2	65.8	31.8
(95,999)		(63.1)	(63.9)	(30.2)
White 78,753	2.2	69.0	78.3	19.4
(77,076)		(65.7)	(75.3)	(18.5)
Lonoke 73,309	7.2	61.7	74.6	21.8
(68,382)		(63.1)	(73.7)	(20.9))
Jefferson 66,824	-13.7	57.1	37.8	59.6
(77,456)		(61.5)	(35.7)	(60.9)

Source: Data compiled from the U.S. Bureau of the Census, the Arkansas Economic Development Institute at UALR, and the official website of the Arkansas Secretary of State. Jefferson County—one of Arkansas's few remaining reliably Democratic strongholds—has been among those losing population for decades. Lonoke, new to the top-10 list, has now supplanted it.

lower than the statewide average, but continued to bleed residents, rendering its Democratic majority impotent against the state's Republican juggernaut.

OTHER ELECTIONS

Longtime political analyst John Brummett observed in the fall of 2018 that "Arkansas likes lazy political monopolies" (Brummett 2018). The fact that Democrats in 2020—like Republicans until 2010—again failed even to put forward nominees for several key positions, or to be competitive with the nominees they did, confirms his contention. U.S. Senator Tom Cotton—a first-term Republican wielding both steady approval ratings and a rising profile—was challenged, at first, by Democrat Josh Mahoney. Mahoney, a full-time politician and heir to a gas fortune, had been bested 65-33 in a bid to unseat the incumbent Republican in the state's northwest corner just two years earlier. Undeterred, he declared against Cotton in the spring of 2019. By September, he ran into trouble clarifying his work resumé, and dropped out of the race two hours after the official filing period ended, prohibiting Democrats from naming a replacement (Field and Moritz 2019). It was the first time since the direct election of U.S. Senators under the 17th Amendment in 1913 that the Democratic Party failed to run a candidate (Lockwood, "Libertarian Harrington"). Ricky Dale Harrington, Jr., a Libertarian, consequently became Cotton's only challenger. Running an impressively substantive and energetic campaign against an opponent who refused to engage, the thirty-four-year-old newcomer racked up a third of all votes cast, winning three of the state's counties (Lockwood, "Cotton win"). Still, this figure likely is less a reflection less of the state's appetite for a third party as the approximate ceiling for any non-Republican candidate in Arkansas's coming decades.

Three of the state's four U.S. House races did feature Democratic candidates in 2020, as in 2018, a sign of life perhaps after contesting only one House race in both 2014 and 2016. However, not only were all of the outcomes again double-digit Republican victories, but the one district—the Second—in which national Democrats and their allies invested substantial resources, produced another 55–45 endorsement of the Republican incumbent. With respect to state legislative races, the turnout effort in the Elliott-Hill race likely helped carry one Democratic newcomer over the finish line against a Republican incumbent in west Little Rock neighborhoods (and almost pulled off a second victory in North Little Rock). Otherwise, Republicans ran the table, taking out the remaining rural Democrats and slightly increasing an existing supermajority in the House and gaining one in the Senate. In the House, Republicans now control 78 of 100 seats. They concentrated this power even further during December's seniority-driven committee assignment process. Among the committees they stacked was the one charged with redrawing the state's congressional districts (a panel of statewide elected executives determines state legislative lines) (Moritz, "State house members"). This means Republicans will drive Arkansas's reapportionment and redistricting process—with little Democratic input—for the first time since Reconstruction.

CONCLUSION

The 2020 election—as intense as they come across the nation—was a snoozer in Arkansas. There was almost no engagement by campaigns locally in the presidential race after the primary season, turnout was low compared to the remainder of the nation, and the results in the presidential election in the state were never in doubt. Despite some signs of an anti-Trump backlash in the most urbanized and suburbanized portions of the state, they were overwhelmed by continued positive momentum for Trump's Republican Party in the wide swaths of rural and exurban areas of the state. Democrats knew a statewide win was coming for the president, but they hoped their party would begin a comeback in the state legislature and, possibly, eke out a win in the Second Congressional District. Instead, Trumpism showed its continued potency and overwhelming support from the state's rural regions for both the incumbent and his political movement led to the largest margin in history for Republicans in each legislative body.

Even if 2020 marks Donald J. Trump's last campaign for political office, the results showed Trumpism's power in the state and within the now-dominant Republican Party. That was shown soon after the Inauguration of President Joe Biden as Trump's former Press Secretary Sarah Huckabee Sanders (who had her formative years living in the Arkansas Governor's Mansion) announced her 2022 candidacy for governor with a video heavily focused on her work for Trump and the issues that were the centerpiece for his campaign (Wickline, "Sarah Huckabee Sanders"). Her former boss almost immediately endorsed her candidacy (Jarvis 2021).[4] Sanders's entrance into the race led to the immediate departure of Lieutenant Governor Tim Griffin from the race for an office he had long sought to the state Attorney General's race, showing her momentum (Trump also endorsed his candidacy within weeks); it also threatened the candidacy for Governor of Trump loyalist Leslie Rutledge, the state's term-limited Attorney General (Wickline, "Griffin shifting"). The state legislative session of 2021 also centered on socially conservative, populist issues that were reflective of Trumpist priorities.

At the same time that Trumpism's power was being exhibited, some institutionalists in his party raised concerns about its corrosive effects. State Senator (and former president *pro tem*) Jim Hendren of Sulpher Springs, the nephew of Governor Asa Hutchinson, left the GOP in February 2021 citing "extremism" in both parties but noting the events of January 6th as the tipping point for his remaining a Republican (Wickline, "Hendren to Leave"). Asked to respond to the video announcing his departure from the GOP, Hendren's uncle—Republican Asa Hutchinson—who became consistently critical of former President Trump in a series of national television appearances, praised Hendren and his motives in a press release but affirmed his own confidence that change could come from within the GOP: "I am convinced that for me the best pathway for continued conservative governance is through the GOP" (ibid).

While the battle between Trumpists and institutionalists will move forward in Arkansas in the coming election cycles, it is clear that—for the moment—Trumpists are advantaged. What is even more clear is that the state's Democrats are not part of the conversation at all.

NOTES

1. Lottie Shackelford, Little Rock's first Black candidate to win a citywide Board of Directors seat (in 1980), was elected mayor by the board in 1987 a position she maintained until 1991 (Dumas 2015).
2. Fundraising data reported on OpenSecrets.org.
3. Analysis for all 2012, 2016, and 2020 at the congressional district level made available by the Daily Kos at https://m.dailykos.com/stories/2020/11/19/1163009/-Daily-Kos-Elections-presidential-results-by-congressional-district-for-2020-2016-and-2012.
4. A flurry of additional endorsements followed (Lockwood 2021).

REFERENCES

"2020 Turnout is the Highest in Over a Century," *Washington Post,* November 5, 2021. https://www.washingtonpost.com/graphics/2020/elections/voter-turnout/.

Barth, Jay, Janine A. Parry, and Todd Shields. "Arkansas: He's Not One of (Most of) Us." In *A Paler Shade of Red: The 2008 Presidential Election in the South*, edited by Branwell DuBose Kapeluck, Laurence W. Moreland, and Robert P. Steed. University of Arkansas Press, 2009.

Barth, Jay, and Janine A. Parry. "Arkansas: Trump Is a Natural for the Natural State." In *The Future Ain't What It Used to Be: The 2016 Presidential Election in the South*, edited by Branwell DuBose Kapeluck and Scott E. Buchanan. University of Arkansas Press, 2018.

Bhattarai, Abha. "Walmart Workers Invited a Special Guest to Crash the Company's Annual Meeting: Bernie Sanders." *Washington Post*, May 21, 2019.

Blair, Diane D. *Arkansas Politics and Government: Do the People Rule.* University of Nebraska Press, 1988.

Brantley, Max. "Michael Bloomberg Files in Arkansas, Along with 17 Other Democrats." *Arkansas Times,* November 12, 2019.

Brantley, Max. "Seen in Iowa, Trump and a Wannabe Arkansas Governor." *Arkansas Times*, November 1, 2020.

Brock, Roby. "Poll: Bloomberg Holds Slim Lead Among Logjam in Arkansas Democratic Presidential Primary." *Talk Business & Politics,* February 11, 2020. https://talkbusiness.net/2020/02/poll-bloomberg-holds-slim-lead-among-logjam-in-arkansas-democratic-presidential-primary/.

Brummett, John. "It's about the job, folks," *Northwest Arkansas Democrat Gazette,* October 14, 2018.

DeMillo, Andrew. "Primary Gives Democrats Rare Spotlight in Red Arkansas," *Associated Press*, March 2, 2020.

Dumas, Ernie. "Lottie Lee Holt Shackleford," *Encyclopedia of Arkansas*. https://encyclopediaofarkansas.net/entries/lottie-lee-holt-shackelford-4841/.

Feuer, Alan. "The Man Who Put His Feet Up on a Desk in Pelosi's Office During the Capitol Riot Throws a Tantrum in Court," *New York Times*, March 4, 2021.

Field, Hunter. "Jill Biden Misses One Little Rock Campaign Event but Attends Fundraiser," *Arkansas Democrat-Gazette*, February 7, 2020.

Field, Hunter, and John Moritz. "Josh Mahony drops out of U.S. Senate race," *Northwest Arkansas Democrat Gazette*, November 12, 2019.

Gallup. 2021. "Presidential Approval Ratings—Donald Trump" https://news.gallup.com/poll/203198/presidential-approval-ratings-donald-trump.aspx.

Gillman, Todd. "'They Want to Nullify Your Ballots,' Trump Tells Iowa Rally as Impeachment Trial Comes to a Head," *The Dallas Morning News*, January 30, 2020.

Herzog, Rachel. "Little Rock Mayor Endorses Bloomberg for President," *Arkansas Democrat-Gazette*, February 10, 2020.

Jarvis, Jacob. "Donald Trump Endorses 'Warrior' Sarah Sanders for Arkansas Governor," *Newsweek*, January 26, 2021.

"Leslie Rutledge Posts Photos at RNC Event Without Mask or Social Distancing," *THV11 Digital*, August 28, 2020.

Lockwood, Frank E. "At Rally in North Little Rock, Warren Campaigns for Voters' Support," *Arkansas Democrat-Gazette*, March 1, 2020.

Lockwood, Frank E. "Libertarian Harrington lone foe for Cotton," *Northwest Arkansas Democrat Gazette* October 26, 2020.

Lockwood, Frank E. "Cotton Win Good News, Say Parties of Two Rivals," *Northwest Arkansas Democrat Gazette*, November 7, 2020.

Lockwood, Frank E. "Trump Throws Support Behind 3 Allies in State," *Arkansas Democrat Gazette* March 10, 2021.

Lynch, John. "Absentee Vote Lawsuit Moot, Thurston Says; He Calls Virus Fear Accepted Reason to Skip Going to Polls," *Arkansas Democrat-Gazette*, 7 July 2020.

Moritz, John. "'Soul Searching' Lamented at Arkansas Democratic Party's Clinton Dinner," *Arkansas Democrat*-Gazette, 5 August 2018.

Moritz, John. "Democratic Presidential Candidate Klobuchar in Little Rock, Talks Gun Control," *Arkansas Democrat-Gazette*, August 16 2019.

Moritz, John. "O'Rourke Talks Guns at Clinton Dinner, Other Stops in State," *Arkansas Democrat-Gazette*, August 18 2019.

Moritz, John. "Michael Bloomberg Visits Little Rock for King Day Parade," *Arkansas Democrat-Gazette*, January 21 2020.

Moritz, John. "State Still in Hands of GOP; Democrats Look for House Gains," *Arkansas Democrat-Gazette*, November 4 2020.

Moritz, John. "State House members pick panel seats," *Northwest Arkansas Democrat Gazette*, December 3, 2020.

Parry, Janine A., and Jay Barth. "Arkansas: Another Anti-Obama Aftershock." In *Second Verse, Same as the First: The 2012 Presidential Election in the South*, edited by Scott E. Buchanan and Branwell DuBose Kapeluck. University of Arkansas Press, 2014.

Parry, Janine A. 2018. "From the Bluest of the Blue to the Reddest of the Red? Measuring, Comparing, and Explaining Arkansas's Partisan Earthquake," Public Presentation at the Pryor Center for Arkansas Oral and Visual History, University of Arkansas. https://pryorcenter.uark.edu/event.php?thisEvent=PARRY-Janine-A-20181024-PryorCenterPresents&eventdisplayName=Janine%20Parry%20-%20From%20Blue%20to%20Red:%20Measuring,%20Comparing,%20and%20Explaining%20Arkansas%27s%20Partisan%20Earthquake.

Parry, Janine A. "The Arkansas Poll, 2020. Summary Report," https://fulbright.uark.edu/departments/political-science/partners/arkpoll/2020summaryreport.pdf.

"Poll: Independents Dissatisfied with Trump, Cotton; Biden Competitive in Arkansas," *Talk Business & Politics*, June 14, 2020.

"Poll: Razor Close Race in CD2 Between French Hill, Joyce Elliott," *Talk Business & Politics*, September 13, 2020.

Sollender, Andrew. "Republican Gov. Asa Hutchinson Breaks With Trump, Acknowledges Biden Win," *Forbes*, November 15, 2020.

Wickline, Michael R. "Sarah Huckabee Sanders Launches Bid for Governor," *Arkansas Democrat-Gazette*, January 25, 2021.

Wickline, Michael R. "Griffin Shifting to Make Attorney General Bid, Plans to Exit Governor's Race," *Arkansas Democrat-Gazette*, February 8, 2021.

Wickline, Michael R. "Hendren to Leave GOP, Become Independent," *Arkansas Democrat-Gazette*, February 18, 2021.

Chapter 9

Florida

Kingmaker No More?

Jonathan Knuckey and Aubrey Jewett

The election night call of the battleground state of Florida for the first Florida resident to serve as president provided some early optimism for Republicans that Donald Trump might eke out an unexpected Electoral College majority.[1] Preelection polls had showed, unsurprisingly for the Sunshine State, a close race, although if anything Joe Biden may have had a slight edge.[2] Democrats were buoyed by the large early vote lead that they had banked, with early voting occurring at unprecedented levels against the backdrop of the COVID-19 pandemic, which had hit Florida particularly hard.[3] These short-term forces together with the long-term demographic changes evident in the state seemed to augur well for the Democrats making it three victories out of four in Florida since 2008. However, Trump ultimately carried the state with 51.2 percent of the vote to Biden's 47.9 percent. This marked only the third time since 1992 that the winning candidate received a majority of the popular vote in Florida, the others being George W. Bush in 2004 (52.1 percent) and Barack Obama in 2008 (50.9 percent). Indeed, Trump's 3.3 percent margin of victory was the largest since Bush's 5 percent victory margin in 2004. Despite the loss to Trump, the ability of Biden to rebuild the "blue wall" states in Michigan, Pennsylvania, and Wisconsin, and expand the electoral map by winning Arizona and Georgia, meant that a loss in Florida was not enough to derail his path to a victory in the Electoral College.

    The fact that Trump won Florida but lost the presidential election to Biden also meant that Florida ended its streak of six consecutive elections where the winner of the Sunshine State was also the national winner. Indeed, this was only the third time in the post–World War II period that the winner of Florida failed to become president, Richard Nixon in 1960 and George H. W. Bush in 1992 being the other two. At least Florida could find some solace in the fact that its closest rival for the status of premier bellwether state, Ohio, also voted for the national loser in 2020, the first time it had done so since 1960.

In analyzing prior presidential election results in Florida since 2008, we have argued that the demographics of the state—most notably the growing Hispanic population—have made the Sunshine State a battleground state, although one that was perhaps trending more Democratic (Knuckey 2009; Knuckey and Branz 2013; Knuckey and Jewett 2018). However, as table 9.1 shows, Florida has moved in a more Republican direction relative to the rest of the nation. Indeed, the difference between the Republican vote in Florida and the national share of the vote in 2020 was the largest in all elections shown in table 9.1. One actually has to go back over thirty years to the 1988 presidential election to find a larger difference between the Republican vote in Florida and the nation (+7.5 percent), and this, of course, when Florida was still a solidly Republican state at the presidential level.

This chapter will analyze the 2020 election in Florida and speculate what the result might indicate for future elections and party competition for major statewide office. Can a post-Trump Republican Party continue to assemble the coalition that delivered Florida to Trump in two elections? Will the movement of Hispanics toward Trump mark a permanent shift in voting loyalties, or will it simply be transitory? To what extent can the Democrats continue to build-up large majorities in the major population centers of the state and make inroads among suburban voters? We begin, however, by providing the recent political context of Florida electoral politics.

PARTY REGISTRATION: REPUBLICANS CLOSE THE GAP

Figure 9.1 shows trends in Florida party registration over time. As with most Southern states, Democrats still held a large lead in the 1970s, but Republicans

Table 9.1 Republican Vote in Presidential Elections in Florida and the Nation, 1992–2020

Election	Florida (%)	Nation (%)	Florida More Republican than Nation (%)
1992	40.9	37.5	3.4
1996	42.3	40.7	1.6
2000	48.9	47.9	1.0
2004	52.1	50.7	1.4
2008	48.1	45.6	2.5
2012	49.0	47.2	1.8
2016	48.6	45.9	2.7
2020	51.1	46.8	4.3

Source: Calculated by the authors from *Dave Leip's Atlas of U.S. Presidential Elections*, https://uselectionatlas.org/RESULTS/, retrieved February 1, 2021.

gained ground rapidly during the Reagan Revolution and have continued to close the gap through 2020. Since the implementation of the National Voter Registration Act in 1995 made registration easier, "Other" voters (No Party Affiliation and minor parties) have tripled from 8 percent to more than 27 percent (Jewett 2018, 31). Because of Florida's population growth, the two major parties have still seen gains in the number of registrants during that period, but often declined in percentage terms with Democrats losing a greater share than Republicans. Barack Obama's historic run for president in 2008 helped reverse the trend temporarily with Democrats going from a 2.7 to a 6.1 percentage point lead between 2006 and 2008. However, since then, Republicans have almost achieved parity. Florida's closely divided electorate, combined with a large percentage of unaffiliated voters, helps explain why so many recent statewide elections in Florida have been decided by small margins. In the eleven races for president, governor, or U.S. senator held in Florida since 2008 only one winning candidate got more than 52 percent of the vote.[4]

Florida Democrats were hopeful that President Trump's inconsistent response to the COVID-19 pandemic and the faltering economy would help them gain ground between 2018 and 2020. Instead, by Election Day, Republicans managed to close the registration gap to less than 1 percent (about 134,000 out of 14.4 million)—the smallest margin in Florida history: Democrats 36.7 percent (5.30 million), Republican 35.8 percent (5.17 million), and Other 27.5 percent (3.97 million). The Republican Party of Florida successfully continued door-to-door voter registration outreach in

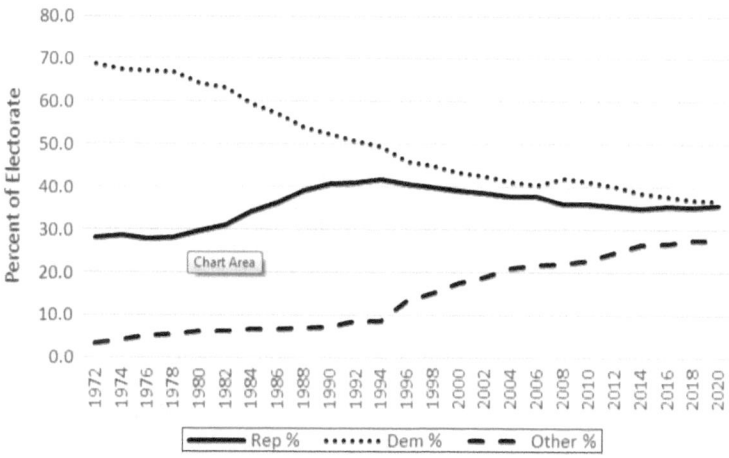

Figure 9.1 Florida Voter Registration, 1972 to 2020. *Source:* Compiled by the authors from Florida Department of State Division of Elections, "Voter Registration - By Party Affiliation," https://www.dos.myflorida.com/elections/data-statistics/voter-registration-statistics/voter-registration-reportsxlsx/voter-registration-by-party-affiliation/by-party-affiliation-archive/, retrieved February 27, 2021.

2020 despite the pandemic, while the Florida Democratic Party refrained from doing so for fear of spreading COVID-19 (Dixon 2020). Republican registration gains, along with key GOP victories in the 2018 midterm, were early signs that Trump might do better in Florida in 2020 than he did in 2016.[5]

2018 MIDTERM ELECTIONS: AFTER RECOUNTS, REPUBLICANS WIN KEY RACES

Florida Democrats were cautiously optimistic that they would do well in 2018 since the president's party often loses seats during the first midterm election and numerous preelection polls showed their candidates with a lead. While Democrats did pick up some legislative and congressional seats and a cabinet position, they lost the high-profile governor and U.S. Senate races after recounts confirmed narrow Republican victories.[6] The Florida gubernatorial race featured Trump-backed white Republican Congressman Ron DeSantis against African American Democratic Tallahassee Mayor Andrew Gillum. The U.S. Senate race pitted three-time incumbent Democrat Bill Nelson against two-time incumbent Republican Governor Rick Scott.

DeSantis was initially an underdog in the GOP primary running behind establishment favorite Agricultural Commissioner Adam Putnam. DeSantis rarely talked about specific Florida policy issues and instead raised his profile without having to raise or spend campaign dollars by appearing on Fox News more than 120 times between December and August frequently defending President Trump (Caputo 2018). Trump repaid the favor with an official endorsement in June and soon after DeSantis overtook Putnam in the polls and won the nomination by 20 points with 56 percent of the vote. Andrew Gillum was an underdog in the Democratic primary. Final preelection polls had Gillum running a distant fourth in a five-person field. However, Gillum was the only black candidate, the most progressive, and youngest and those core Democratic primary constituencies rallied to his side to beat front runner Gwen Graham by 3 points with just 34 percent of the vote.[7] With the victory, Gillum became the first major-party black candidate for governor in Florida.

Race and personal attacks became dominant themes in the campaign starting the day after the primary when DeSantis appeared on Fox News speaking about Gillum and his policies and said "the last thing we need to do is to monkey this up by trying to embrace a socialist agenda" (Jacobs 2018). Gillum and his supporters accused DeSantis of using coded racist language ("monkey") as a "dog whistle" to appeal to white conservative voters and continued making similar charges through Election Day.[8] DeSantis denied the comment had anything to do with race and spent much of the rest of the campaign attacking Gillum as a corrupt failed mayor who oversaw a crime-ridden city whose political leadership was under investigation by the FBI.

Gillum advocated numerous state-specific liberal policy positions, including a $15 minimum wage, expansion of Medicaid, voting rights for felons, minimum $50,000 teacher salaries, and a billion-dollar corporate income tax increase. Bernie Sanders held rallies at college campuses in Central Florida for Gillum to drive turnout among younger voters and progressives. DeSantis largely avoided specific policy positions and ran as a Trump loyalist. President Trump appeared at campaign rallies in conservative areas to boost turnout of the Republican base. The race became widely viewed as a referendum on President Trump with possible national implications. The candidates and their associated political action committees each raised $55 to $60 million (Chokey 2018). Gillum held a small but steady lead in the preelection polls and Democratic turnout in early and mail-in balloting was higher than previous midterm elections. However Republican turnout surged on Election Day, and after a machine recount, DeSantis won the race by about 30,000 votes out of 8 million cast 49.6 percent to 49.2 percent. Exit polls indicate that DeSantis did very well among white men without a college degree (73 percent support) and did better than expected among Hispanic voters (44 percent).

The 2018 U.S. Senate race in Florida set a record as the most expensive Senate race in history with total spending topping $200 million.[9] Term-limited Governor Rick Scott, sixty-five, began attacking incumbent Bill Nelson, seventy-six, with a barrage of advertisements in April. Scott accused Nelson of being a career politician, a liberal who voted the Democratic Party line, ineffective, too old, and out of ideas. Nelson did not begin to respond in earnest until after Labor Day and even then, seemed sluggish by comparison to the aggressive Scott. Nelson stressed his long service and moderate temperament and pledged to keep doing the "right thing" for Florida. Unlike DeSantis, Scott kept Trump somewhat at arm's length for much of the campaign and did make some distinctions on policy. Scott also learned Spanish and made numerous appeals to Hispanic voters. The Senate race ended up even closer than the governor's race and required a manual hand recount. Scott ultimately won by just 10,033 votes out of 8.2 million cast 50.1 percent to 49.9 percent. The race would have been even closer if not for a bad ballot design in Broward County that was estimated to have cost Nelson more than 9,500 votes (Man 2019).[10] Scott, a multimillionaire former healthcare executive, spent a record $64 million of his own money on his campaign, which may have proved decisive (Connolly 2018). Scott's victory helped Republicans maintain control of the U.S. Senate and resulted in both Florida senate seats being held by Republicans for the first time since the Reconstruction era.

In 2018, Republicans also won two statewide cabinet races, Attorney General Ashley Moody, and Chief Financial Officer Jimmy Patronis, and kept control of the Florida House 73–47, Florida Senate 23–17, and congressional delegation 14–13. Democrats did manage to pick up several seats in the legislature and in the congressional delegation. One bright spot for Democrats was the victory by Nikki Fried for Commissioner of Agriculture who won by just 6,000 votes after a hand recount. These gains and wins brought little consolation to most Florida Democrats who had hoped the combination of the moderate Nelson and progressive Gillum would engage both wings of the Democratic party and turn Florida blue.

PRESIDENTIAL NOMINATION CONTEST

In Florida, all the attention was on the Democratic presidential nomination contest in 2020, with Donald Trump facing no serious challenge for the Republican nomination.[11] Scheduled for March 17, Florida's primary took place two weeks after Super Tuesday, the biggest multi-state primary day of the 2020 nomination contest. Of course, Joe Biden's strong showing on Super Tuesday had effectively ended the Democratic nomination contest, with most of Biden's rivals withdrawing from the race and endorsing him over Bernie Sanders.

The two weeks following Super Tuesday coincided with the COVID-19 pandemic dominating the news along with stay-at-home orders. This effectively ended any semblance of traditional campaigning in front of large crowds in the run-up to the primary in Florida, with both the Biden and Sanders campaigns having encouraged early voting. Indeed, on primary election eve, two million voters had already cast ballots in either the Democratic or Republican primary elections (Lemongello, Garza, and Hudak 2020).

Essentially, the 2020 Democratic primary contest in Florida was a replay of four years earlier, when Hillary Clinton routed Sanders. The fact that Florida is a closed primary state deprived Sanders of the participation of Independents, with whom he had demonstrated large support in open primary states. Additionally, the large number of seniors in the state meant that the primary electorate would be skewed toward older voters, again disadvantaging Sanders who appealed more to younger voters. Sanders also ran into controversy during an interview on "60 Minutes" prior to the primary election. In comments about Fidel Castro and the regime in Cuba he said, "It's unfair to simply say everything is bad. When Fidel Castro came to office, you know what he did? He had a massive literacy program. Is that a bad thing? Even though Fidel Castro did it?" (Mazzei 2020). In addition to alienating Cuban Americans in Miami, these remarks along with the "democratic socialist" label Sanders embraced may have also resonated with Hispanic voters in Florida from other Central and South American countries who may have fled from leftist authoritarian regimes such as Nicaragua or Venezuela.

Ultimately, there was little surprise when all media outlets called the Florida primary for Biden as soon as the polls closed. Biden won 62 percent of the vote to just 23 percent for Sanders, carrying every county in the state. Up to that point in the primary contest, it was the third-highest share of the vote for Biden in any state, behind Mississippi (81 percent) and Alabama (63 percent). Despite the primary contest taking place during a lockdown, over 1.7 million votes were cast in the Democratic primary, which was comparable to the 2016 primary. The depth and breadth of Biden's victory can be seen in exit-poll data in table 9.2.

Table 9.2 shows that there were no racial, gender, or education gaps in the Democratic primary electorate, with Biden sweeping men, women, whites, non-whites, noncollege, and college educated by large margins. Only among those aged 18–44 did Sanders enjoy a majority.[12] The exit-poll data also suggest that pragmatism was the key driving force in Florida Democrats deciding on Biden. For example, among self-identified liberals, a natural Sanders constituency, Biden led Sanders by over twenty percentage points, 55 percent to 31 percent. Furthermore, two-thirds of Democrats said that beating Trump was the candidate quality that mattered most. Even among those that said a candidate that agrees with the voter on issues was the most important quality, Biden still led Sanders by over twenty percentage points, 53 percent to 32 percent. Biden also led Sanders, 47 percent to 38 percent among those who supported universal health care, which was Sanders's signature issue as a candidate both in 2016 and 2020. Had the overriding concern of Democrats been issues rather than defeating Trump, Sanders would surely have performed much better among these voters, who constituted a majority of the electorate. But in 2020 that was not the case, with three-quarters of Democratic primary voters (not shown in table 9.2) saying that irrespective of who they had voted for in the primary, Biden had the better chance to defeat Trump in the general election.

GENERAL ELECTION CAMPAIGN

The 2020 presidential general election in Florida saw some major differences and basic similarities to recent top-ticket races. The once-in-a-century COVID-19 pandemic that dragged on for most of the year presented the biggest change and challenge to the candidates, campaigns, voters, and election administration. Despite the pandemic, the candidates still considered Florida one of the most important states due to its twenty-nine electoral votes, history of close elections, and record of voting for the winner six elections in a row. The campaigns again spent more money on television advertising in Florida than any other state: over $257 million by the end of October (Guttman

Table 9.2 Exit Poll Results from Democratic Presidential Primary Election for Selected Demographic Groups and Issue Preferences

	Size of Group (%)	Biden (%)	Sanders (%)
Gender			
Men	41	60	25
Women	59	64	21
Race			
White	49	61	26
Non-white	51	63	20
Age			
18–44	28	39	52
45+	72	71	11
Education			
No college degree	51	63	22
College graduate	49	61	24
Ideology			
Liberal	54	55	31
Moderate/Conservative	46	70	13
Which Quality Most Important?			
Agrees with you on issues	30	53	32
Can beat Trump	66	67	18
A Government Health Care Plan for All Instead of Private Insurance			
Support	55%	47	38
Oppose	33%	75	9

Source: CNN "Florida Primary Polls," https://www.cnn.com/election/2020/primaries-caucuses/entrance-and-exit-polls/florida/democratic, retrieved February 1, 2021.
Note: Percentages for other candidates are not reported.

2021). And the candidates again made Florida one of the most visited states coming thirty-one times for rallies and events, second only to the forty-seven visits made to Pennsylvania (FairVote 2020).

Pandemic-related issues dominated the campaign. President Trump downplayed the seriousness of COVID-19, and associated restrictions like business closures and mask mandates, and promised a vaccine developed in record time. Governor DeSantis, Trump's ally and protégé, largely followed the president's lead as Florida's caseload and death rate skyrocketed in the summer and then declined in the fall. Joe Biden hammered Trump for his inconsistent and ineffective response to the coronavirus in numerous television commercials and promised to get the virus under control and reduce the death rate. Trump advertisements reminded voters of the strong Florida economy before the pandemic and asserted that Trump was best positioned to lead the economic recovery. Michael Bloomberg promised to spend $100 million to defeat Trump in Florida and his super, PAC Independence USA, flooded Sunshine State airwaves with $36 million in additional attack ads (Schwartz 2020).

COVID-19 impacted other aspects of the campaign as well. At first, Trump seemed at a major disadvantage since he had relied heavily on large rallies to gain free news coverage and fire up his base in 2016, and the pandemic took away the rallies for many months in 2020. But by September and October, President Trump resumed his large outdoor rallies bringing thousands of people packed together frequently ignoring social distancing and mask wearing.[13] President Trump himself rarely wore a mask in public. Biden rallies were much smaller, kept people separated or in or near their vehicles, and were quite strict on mask wearing. Biden wore a mask frequently. Both candidates received news coverage from their rallies, but Trump was able to mobilize more voters and generate more enthusiasm (Colombini, Newborn, and Miller 2020).

When President Trump was diagnosed with COVID-19 on October 2 and knocked off the campaign trail, Vice President Pence carried on with two Florida gatherings on October 10: a Latinos for Trump event in Orlando and a rally for Republican seniors at The Villages (Lemongello and Reyes 2020). When Trump recovered and returned to active campaigning on October 12, he returned to Central Florida on the same day for a previously postponed rally in Sanford. Trump's illness affected the second debate, which had been scheduled for October 15th in Miami. Because of Trump's recent diagnosis, the commission announced it would become a virtual debate, but Trump refused to participate in that format and organizers cancelled the debate (Clark 2020).

The pandemic impacted voter mobilization and election administration in Florida as well. The Biden campaign and Florida Democratic Party relied on virtual conversations rather than traditional neighborhood campaigning for fear of spreading COVID-19. To further reduce the risk of COVID-19 transmission, Democrats made a concerted and successful effort to get supporters to vote early by mail. In contrast, the Trump campaign and Republican Party of Florida continued to engage in traditional door-to-door canvassing to register new supporters and to get out the vote (Caputo and Fineout 2020). While Trump actively discouraged followers in most states from voting by mail, he encouraged Sunshine State Republicans to do so, although the mixed messaging sowed confusion (Shalal 2020). These different approaches to campaigning in Florida during the coronavirus era resulted in Republicans reducing the Democratic lead in voter registration, Democrats taking an early lead in vote by mail ballots, but Republicans closing the gap as more of them voted in person early and on Election Day.

Like most states, because of the pandemic, Florida saw a huge increase in the number of people voting early by mail and early in person. However, unlike most other states, Florida was better prepared for this increase (nine million out of eleven million votes were cast early) since Floridians had used these methods in previous elections dating back to the reforms put in place after the controversial 2000 presidential election. Florida law allows any voter to request a mail ballot but requires mail ballots to arrive by 7:00 pm on Election Day to be valid and that mail ballots be tabulated as they arrive. When appropriate equipment and enough trained personnel are in place in every county, and procedures are followed, there is no large backlog in counting ballots or delay in reporting results as happened in numerous other states.[14] Florida received national recognition and praise for holding a smooth election (Spencer 2020).

The campaigns targeted different groups of Florida voters with different messages. Florida seniors supported Trump in 2016. However, several polls found that many Floridians aged 65 and older were disappointed with Trump's response to COVID-19 and might support Biden (Klas 2020). Biden advertisements continually stressed how he would protect the health and safety of seniors. Trump targeted Hispanics by repeatedly attacking Biden as a socialist, which resonated with many Cuban, Venezuelan, Colombian, and Nicaraguan voters in Miami-Dade who fled from socialist or communist countries (Jacobs 2020). Biden pursued Puerto Rican voters by attacking Trump for his tepid response to the devastating hurricane that leveled the island (McCammond 2020). Black voters were targeted by Biden who stressed support for Black Lives Matter and felon voting rights, and attacked Trump as a racist, while Trump mobilized white supporters by stressing support for law and order and accusing Biden of wanting to defund the police (Morgan 2020).

Over the final two months of the campaign, Florida preelection surveys showed a close race with Biden holding a small but steady lead between 1 and 4 percent in most poll aggregation websites. Over the last two weeks, the race tightened with several polls finding Trump inching into the lead. The final RealClear Politics 2020 Florida poll average had Biden up by just .9 percent—well within the margin of error. And the final FiveThirtyEight 2020 forecast had Biden "slightly favored" to win the Sunshine State. Despite the many changes brought on by the pandemic, as Election Day arrived, Florida appeared to be living up to its reputation as one of the most competitive swing states.

RESULTS AND ANALYSIS

Table 9.3 shows that Trump once again carried Florida's 29 Electoral College votes, winning 5,668,731 (51.2 percent) compared to 5,297,045 for Biden

Table 9.3 Results of 2020 Florida Presidential Election

Candidate (Party)	Vote %	Vote Totals
Donald Trump/Mike Pence (Republican)	51.2	5,668,731
Joe Biden/Kamala Harris (Democratic)	47.9	5,297,045
Jo Jorgensen/Spike Cohen (Libertarian)	0.6	70,324
Other candidates and write-ins	0.3	31,356
Total		11,067,456

Source: Florida Department of State Division of Elections, "2020 General Election November 3, 2020. Official Results President of the United States," https://results.elections.myflorida.com/Index.asp?ElectionDate=11/3/2020&DATAMODE= , retrieved, February 1, 2021.

(47.9 percent) and winning 55 of Florida's 67 counties. By Florida's standard of close elections—recent statewide contests being often decided by one percentage point or less—this ended up being a comfortable margin of victory for Trump. Indeed, it was the largest share of the vote and winning percentage margin for any candidate to carry the state since George W. Bush in 2004. Overall, 11 million Floridians turned out to vote, an increase of about 1.5 million voters compared to 2016. Trump received around one million more votes than he did in 2016, a 23 percent increase on total vote from four years earlier, while Biden received around 790,000 more votes than Hillary Clinton in 2016, an increase of 18 percent. The overall turnout based on the voting-eligible population (VEP) was 71.7 percent, an increase of 7 percent compared to 2016. Out of the fifty states plus the District of Colombia, Florida ranked fifteenth in the nation, and the highest of the eleven southern states.[15]

County-Level Analysis

There was largely continuity in the pattern of county-level support in 2020. Compared to 2016, only three counties switched parties, and all were Democratic gains: Duval, which voted for a Democrat for the first time since it supported Jimmy Carter in 1976, Pinellas, and Seminole, the latter voting for a Democrat for the first time since Harry Truman won the county in 1948.[16] How did Trump produce a repeat victory in Florida, and most consequentially increase his share of the vote from 2016? Any analysis of statewide voting in Florida inevitably begins with the seven most populated counties. Table 9.4 shows the vote in these "mega counties," containing almost half of the statewide electorate of Florida. To compare trends in these counties, election results are shown from 2000 through 2020.[17]

The first takeaway from table 9.4 is that Biden carried all seven of the mega counties, the first time that a Democrat had accomplished this feat in the post–World War II period.[18] However, the key point is that Biden's net vote advantage over Trump was 687,855, compared to Clinton's advantage

Table 9.4 Presidential Vote in Florida's "Mega-Counties" in Presidential Elections, 2000–2020

	2000	2004	2008	2012	2016	2020
Miami-Dade	D +7%	D +6%	D +16%	D +24%	D +29%	D +7%
Broward	D +36%	D +35%	D +35%	D +35%	D +35%	D +30%
Palm Beach	D +27%	D +21%	D +23%	D +17%	D +15%	D +13%
Hillsborough	R +3%	R +7%	D +7%	D +7%	D +7%	D +7%
Orange	D +2%	D +0.2%	D +19%	D +19%	D +24%	D +23%
Pinellas	D +4%	R +0.1%	D +8%	D +5%	R +1%	D +0.2%
Duval	R +16%	R +16%	R +2%	R +3%	R +1%	D +4%
Net Democratic Vote Advantage	+331,928	+281,400	+682,524	+707,248	+849,023	+687,855
Percentage of Total Statewide Votes Cast	49.3%	48.8%	48.2%	48.5%	48.2%	47.9%

Source: Compiled by the authors from data from Florida Department of State Division of Elections, https://results.elections.myflorida.com/, retrieved February 1, 2021
Note: Cell entries show the winning party and the percentage point margin of victory.

of 849,023 votes in 2016. This was mostly because of a dramatic vote swing in Miami-Dade, where Biden led Trump by only 7 percent, compared to the 29 percent advantage enjoyed by Clinton in 2016. This was the smallest Democratic percentage vote margin in Miami-Dade since 2004. In terms of raw votes in the county, Trump gained 198,834 on his total in 2016, while Biden was actually down 6,282 votes on Clinton's total, for an incredible net vote swing in Trump's favor of over 200,000 votes. Indeed, this was one of only four counties statewide where Biden received fewer votes than Clinton.[19] Miami-Dade alone was a major part of the story as to how Trump was able to expand his statewide lead compared to 2016.

The second point to note is that Biden failed to increase either his percentage share of the vote and total vote in the two other South Florida Democratic bastions of Broward and Palm Beach. Although Biden carried Broward by a landslide, there was a decline in the Democratic margin of victory of five percentage points. In Palm Beach, the Democratic share of the vote was down two percentage points in 2016. Democratic vote that has been evident since 2000. Indeed, in both counties, the increase in the total vote for Trump exceeded the increase for Biden. Thus, instead of both counties contributing toward and expanded Biden lead, Trump made a net gain of 10,000 votes in these South Florida Democratic strongholds.

Ultimately, the fact that the mega counties provided Biden with a reduced net vote advantage meant that he needed to win approximately 44 percent of the vote in the rest of the state. In the end, Biden fell well short, winning just 40 percent compared to 59 percent for Trump, providing Trump a fairly comfortable statewide winning margin of 3.4 percent.

In order to further understand the county-level vote in Florida, a multiple regression analysis was conducted, regressing the Trump vote on several relevant demographic variables, including the percentage of black population, Hispanic population, college graduate, urban population, population aged 65 old and older, and white evangelical.[20] Three weighted least squares regression models are reported in table 9.5, Model 1 is for the 2016 election, Model 2 for the 2020 election, and Model 3 is for the change in the vote from 2016 to 2020.[21]

Table 9.5 reveals that the demographic determinants of the county-level vote that have structured presidential elections in Florida's past (e.g., see: Conkwright and Knuckey 2018; Knuckey 2004) were once again evident in the 2020 presidential election, with one major and consequential exception: the effect of the percentage Hispanic variable. Counties that are less racially diverse, less urban, have fewer college graduates, have more voters aged 65 and older, and more white evangelicals were more likely to be Trump country. Collectively, these variables explained a large percentage of the variation in Trump's vote in both 2016 and 2020 (adjusted R^2 of 0.887 and

Table 9.5 Regression Analysis of County-Level Presidential Vote in Florida, 2016 and 2020

	Model 1 Trump 2016 % Vote		Model 2 Trump 2020 % Vote		Model 3 Change in Vote 2016–2020 (%)	
	b	beta	b	beta	b	beta
% Black	−0.963*** (0.093)	−0.575	−0.895*** (0.092)	−0.621	0.073*** (0.022)	0.145
% Hispanic	−0.157*** (0.044)	−0.208	0.046 (0.43)	0.072	0.203*** (0.010)	0.906
% College graduates	−0.203* (.113)	−0.098	−0.256** (0.110)	−0.144	−0.072*** (0.027)	−0.117
% Urban	−0.166*** (0.047)	−0.192	−0.201*** (0.046)	−0.270	−0.031*** (0.011)	−0.118
% over 65 years old	0.324*** (0.133)	0.163	0.354*** (0.129)	0.210	0.029 (0.031)	0.049
% white evangelical	0.765*** (0.132)	0.398	0.658*** (0.130)	0.398	−0.102*** (0.031)	−0.177
Constant	69.288*** (7.527)		72.173*** (7.383)		2.799 (1.777)	
Adjusted R^2	0.887		0.851		0.928	

Source: County-level vote taken from Florida Department of State Division of Elections, "Election Results," https://results.elections.myflorida.com/, accessed February 1, 2021. With the exception of percentage white evangelical, all demographic county data are taken from the U.S. Census Bureau "Quick Facts, Florida," retrieved February 1, 2021, https://www.census.gov/quickfacts/FL. Data for percentage white evangelical are taken from Grammich et al. (2012).

Note: Models are all estimated using weighted least squares regression, weighted by total votes cast in each county.

* $p < 0.10$
** $p < 0.05$
*** $p < 0.01$

0.851, respectively). Compared to 2016, the decline in Trump's support was associated with the percentage of college graduates, percentage of urban population, and percentage of white evangelical. Increase in Trump's support was associated with percentage of black and percentage of Hispanic. It is the latter of these racial context variables that was such a change from 2016, with the percentage of Hispanic variable no longer even statistically significant in 2020.

Of course, it is entirely plausible that the failure of the percentage Hispanic variable to attain statistical significance is the result of Miami-Dade, which not only has the largest Hispanic population of any county in Florida, but, as noted earlier, saw the largest pro-Trump movement of votes in the entire state. Thus, a model was estimated excluding Miami-Dade from the analysis, which did result in the percentage Hispanic variable now attaining statistical significance (b = −0.264; p < 0.001).

To further demonstrate just how much of an outlier Miami-Dade was in 2020, table 9.6 presents the top quintile of counties based on Hispanic populations together with the result in each county in 2020 and the change in the vote for Trump. No county with a large Hispanic population came close to the swing evident in Miami-Dade. Indeed, only two other counties saw an increase in Trump's share of the vote that exceeded 5 percent, Osceola (+7 percent) and Hendry (+5 percent). Osceola, with a heavy concentration of Puerto Rican residents, is of interest because Orange County, its neighboring county in Central Florida, only saw a Trump increase of 2 percent. This is suggestive of different dynamics at work among different Hispanic populations. Of course, aggregate data alone cannot conclusively address this question, which will be further explored below in the analysis of exit-poll data, but this analysis suggests that the real story in Florida in 2020 about the Hispanic vote was predominantly a Miami-Dade story.

Exit-Poll Analysis: Demographic and Political Characteristics

Table 9.7 displays the 2020 and 2016 Florida exit-poll results for demographic and political characteristics and helps explain how President Trump was able to increase his margin of victory in Florida from 1 percent to over 3 percent. Compared to 2016, the 2020 Florida electorate was slightly more female, older, slightly more Hispanic, less educated, less religious, more suburban, less urban, more Republican, and less liberal. In 2020, Trump beat Biden among Sunshine State voters who were male, over the age of thirty, white, Cuban, not college graduates, middle-income, Protestant or Catholic, living outside urban areas, Republican, and conservative.[22, 23]

The gender gap remained largely the same in 2020 with men favoring Trump by 6 points compared to women (54–48 percent) and women favoring

Table 9.6 2020 Presidential Election Result in Florida Counties with Largest Hispanic Populations (Top Quintile)

County	Hispanic (%)	Trump (%)	Biden (%)	Change in Trump (%) 2016–20
Miami-Dade	69.4	46.1	53.4	+12
Osceola	55.8	42.6	56.4	+7
Hendry	55.3	61.1	38.1	+5
Hardee	43.6	72.2	27.1	+3
Orange	32.7	37.9	61.0	+2
DeSoto	32.1	65.7	33.6	+3
Broward	31.1	34.8	64.6	+3
Hillsborough	29.7	46.0	52.9	+1
Collier	28.6	62.1	37.4	+0.3
Okeechobee	26.0	71.9	27.5	+3
Monroe	25.3	53.5	45.6	+2
Polk	24.6	56.7	42.3	+1
Palm Beach	23.4	43.3	56.1	+2

Source: County-level vote taken from Florida Department of State Division of Elections, "Election Results," https://results.elections.myflorida.com/, retrieved February 1, 2021. Percentage Hispanic population are taken from the U.S. Census Bureau "Quick Facts, Florida," https://www.census.gov/quickfacts/FL, retrieved February 1, 2021.

Biden by 6 points compared to men (51 to 45 percent). Both candidates did better among both sexes compared to 2016 suggesting that 2016 voters who defected from third-party candidates split evenly by sex in 2020. Neither Trump nor Biden's behavior toward women seemed as salient compared to 2016 when the first female major-party candidate, Hillary Clinton, was on the ticket and Trump's actions and comments were heavily scrutinized.

The Florida electorate skewed much older in 2020 compared to 2016 and this worked to Trump's advantage. Trump did not win senior voters by quite as much in 2020 (by 55 percent compared to 57 percent in 2016) but voters 65 and over made up almost one-third of the Florida electorate compared to just 21 percent four years ago. Thus, Trump won a slightly smaller percent of a much bigger pool. Voters age 30–44 made up slightly less of the electorate in 2020 (20 percent versus 23 percent four years previously) but Trump improved his performance considerably by winning 50 percent of their vote compared to just 39 percent in 2016. There had been much speculation and some preelection polling that suggested Trump might do worse among Florida seniors due to their concerns about his handling of the COVID-19 pandemic (Lush 2020). In the end, Trump still won the senior vote by a comfortable margin (as well as the middle-aged vote from 45–64) and offset small losses among older voters with improved performance among those aged 44 and younger.

Table 9.7 Florida Presidential Exit Poll Results: Demographic and Political Characteristics

	2020			2016		
Category	Electorate	Biden	Trump	Electorate	Clinton	Trump
Gender						
Men	45	45	54	47	43	52
Women	55	51	48	53	50	46
Age						
18–29	14	60	38	17	54	36
30–44	20	48	50	23	54	39
45–64	34	45	54	38	43	56
65+	32	45	55	21	40	57
Race						
White (not Latino)	62	37	62	62	32	64
Black	14	89	10	14	84	8
Hispanic	19	53	46	18	62	35
Race and Gender						
White men	28	34	65	29	28	67
White women	35	40	60	33	36	60
African American men	6	85	13	6	81	10
African American women	9	91	7	8	87	6
Latino men	10	52	46	8	60	36
Latino women	10	53	45	10	63	34
Ethnicity						
Cuban	6	42	56	6	41	54
Puerto Rican	5	69	31	NA	NA	NA
Education by Race						
White, college degree	24	43	57	35	35	62
White, no college degree	39	34	66	27	30	66
Non-white, college degree	12	66	31	18	69	24
Non-white, no college degree	25	67	32	20	71	24
LGBT						
Yes	6	83	15	N/A	N/A	N/A
No	94	46	53	N/A	N/A	N/A
Religion						
Protestant or other Christian	42	41	58	49	38	60
Catholic	27	41	59	25	44	54
Jewish	4	62	38	4	n/a	n/a
Another religion	7	58	40	6	64	34
No religion	20	67	31	17	58	32
Geography (Urbanism)						
Urban	41	55	44	46	53	41
Suburban	50	44	55	45	43	53

(Continued)

Table 9.7 Florida Presidential Exit Poll Results: Demographic and Political Characteristics (Continued)

Category	2020			2016		
	Electorate	Biden	Trump	Electorate	Clinton	Trump
Rural	9	38	61	9	36	61
Party						
Democrats	30	94	5	32	90	8
Republicans	38	7	93	33	8	89
Independents	32	54	43	34	43	47
Ideology						
Liberal	19	83	16	25	81	14
Moderate	42	59	40	38	51	43
Conservative	39	16	83	36	17	79
Timing of Vote Decision						
Within the last week	4	50	45	11	38	55
Before that	93	49	50	88	49	48

Source: CNN "Florida Exit Poll, President, 2020," https://www.cnn.com/election/2020/exit-polls/president/florida, retrieved, February 27, 2021.

Florida housed a very racially and ethnically diverse 2020 electorate: 62 percent white, 14 percent black, and 19 percent Hispanic (up one percentage point from 2016). Trump won white voters with 62 percent and Biden won black voters with 89 percent. Compared to 2016, Trump did 2 percent worse among white voters, but 2 percent better among black voters. Trump's greatest improvement came from Hispanics. Although Biden won 53 percent of the Hispanic vote, Trump improved by a whopping 11 percentage points over his 2016 performance (46 percent to 35 percent). Trump won a majority (56 percent) of the Cuban vote as he had in 2016 and pulled in 31 percent of the fast-growing Puerto Rican vote. Trump's performance with Hispanic voters largely explains his larger margin of victory in 2020. Trump's attacks on Biden as a socialist, numerous rallies courting Hispanics, and continued ground game during the pandemic were strikingly successful (Sesin 2020).

Trump did somewhat worse among white men in 2020 compared to 2016 (down to 65 from 67 percent) but the same with white women (60 percent in both cycles). However, Trump did better among black males (increasing to 13 from 10 percent) and much better with Hispanic males and females (10 and 11 percentage points higher, hitting 46 and 45 percent, respectively). Looking at education and race, Trump still relied heavily on whites without a college degree (winning 66 percent both times and making up 39 percent of the electorate in 2020, a 12-point jump from 2016). Trump's support among the 24 percent of whites with college degrees dropped by five percentage points to 57 percent, but he made up for that with a seven or eight percentage point increase in support from people of color with or without college degrees (collectively making up about 37 percent of the electorate).

Florida LGBT voters, 6 percent of the electorate, supported Biden in large numbers (83 to 6 percent) but Trump won the much larger pool of straight voters 53 to 46 percent. Trump won Christian voters by almost 60 percent (a slight drop for Protestants but an improvement among Catholics compared to four years ago). Those with no religion (up 3 percentage points from 2016 to 20 percent of the electorate) supported Biden by a large margin of 67 to 31 percent. There was little change from 2016 in support based on population density although voters were about five percentage points more suburban and less urban. Trump won suburban and rural voters with 55 and 61 percent, respectively and Biden won urban voters with 55 percent.

Biden did better among Florida Democrats and Independents with 94 and 54 percent support, respectively (compared to 90 and 43 percent in 2016). But Florida Republicans made up a larger share of the electorate in 2020 than they had in 2016 (38 versus 33 percent) and supported Trump at higher levels than four years ago (93 percent versus 89). Ideology tells a similar story. Compared to 2016, Biden did better among liberals (83 to 81 percent) and much better among moderates (59 percent to 51 percent), but Trump did 4 points better among conservatives (83 percent support) and conservative turnout was 3 points higher in 2020 (39 percent of the electorate). Compared to 2016, Trump did much worse among voters who made up their mind in the last week. He won that group with 55 percent four years previously when they made up 11 percent of voters and were largely responsible for his 1 percent victory. Trump only got 45 percent of late deciders in 2020, but they only constituted 4 percent of the electorate. After four years, Trump was no longer an unknown quantity, most Floridians had strong feelings about him well before Election Day, and he eked out a win over Biden with early deciders (50 to 49 percent).

Exit-Poll Analysis: Issues and Candidate Characteristics

Table 9.8 displays the Florida 2020 exit-poll results for issues and candidate characteristics. The most important issue for Florida voters was the economy mentioned by 38 percent. These voters overwhelmingly went for Trump 87 to 13 percent. Fifty-two percent felt the condition of the nation's economy was excellent or good and 82 percent of them voted for Trump. Fifty-two percent also felt Trump would handle the economy better than Biden and a whopping 96 percent of that group voted for Trump.

The COVID-19 pandemic was named the most important issue by 18 percent of Florida voters and 88 percent of this cohort voted for Biden. Fifty-two percent of Floridians thought that efforts to contain COVID-19 were going well and 88 percent of that group voted for Trump. Fifty percent of voters felt Biden would handle the pandemic better than Trump (who got 45 percent) and 93 percent of that group supported Biden. While COVID-19 turned life upside down and was the dominant news story for much of 2020, more Floridians were concerned about the economy than about the pandemic and Florida's economic recovery in the months preceding the election helped Trump beat Biden in Florida (Sasso 2020).

Racial equality was named the most important issue by 13 percent of Floridians and 86 percent of that group voted for Biden. Sixty-nine percent felt racism was an important problem in the United States and 62 percent of that cohort supported Biden. Ten percent of Florida voters named crime and safety as the most important issue and 88 percent of them voted for Trump. These splits reflect the differing points of view among Floridians about the death of George Floyd and the widespread protests in support of Black Lives Matter. Some voters were more concerned with racial justice while others were more concerned about the violent protests that occurred in some cities and states.

Strong leadership was the number one candidate quality among Floridians (named by 36 percent) and 84 percent of people looking for a strong leader voted for Trump. The other three candidate qualities all favored Biden. People looking for good judgment (22 percent), empathy (19 percent), or a uniter (18 percent) supported Biden with 62, 65, and 75 percent, respectively.

Favorability was evenly split between the candidates with Biden at 48 percent and Trump at 49 percent (and both candidates had a 49 percent unfavorable rating). Not surprisingly, vote support tracked with favorability at a high level (96 percent for Trump and 94 percent for Biden). Temperament was also evenly split with 48 percent saying Trump had the temperament to serve effectively and 50 percent saying the same about Biden. The percentage of candidate support based on temperament was also in the mid-1990s for both candidates. Sixty-eight percent said that their vote was mainly a vote for their candidate and 60 percent of these voters chose Trump. Conversely 25 percent said their vote was mainly a vote against a candidate and 70 percent of that group voted for Biden to register their dislike of Trump.

Fifty-two percent of Florida voters approved of the way Trump handled his job as president and 93 percent of that group supported Trump. While President Trump struggled with approval ratings in Florida public opinion surveys during his four years in office, these results show the only approval that really matters to an incumbent running for reelection is winning the majority of those who turn out.[24] Finally, 86 percent of Florida voters felt very or somewhat confident that votes in Florida would be counted accurately

Table 9.8 Florida 2020 Presidential Exit Poll Results: Issues and Candidate Characteristics

Category	Electorate	Biden	Trump
Which issue mattered most in deciding how you voted for president?			
Racial inequality	13	86	12
Corona virus pandemic	18	88	10
The economy	38	13	87
Crime and safety	10	12	88
Health care policy	13	83	16
Do you think the condition of the nation's economy is:			
Excellent or good	52	18	82
Not so good or poor	46	82	16
Who would better handle the economy?			
Joe Biden	45	98	1
Donald Trump	52	4	96
U.S. efforts to contain the corona virus are going:			
Well	52	12	88
Badly	46	89	9
Who would better handle the coronavirus pandemic?			
Joe Biden	50	93	5
Donald Trump	45	1	98
Is racism in the United States:			
Most important or one of the many important problems	69	62	36
A minor problem or not a problem at all	29	14	86
Which candidate quality mattered most in voting decision?			
Can unite the country	18	75	24
Is a strong leader	36	16	84
Cares about people like me	19	65	34
Has good judgment	22	62	36
Is your opinion of Joe Biden:			
Favorable	48	94	5
Unfavorable	49	4	94
Is your opinion of Donald Trump:			
Favorable	49	4	96
Unfavorable	49	93	5
Does Trump have the temperament to serve effectively as president?			
Yes	48	4	96
No	50	92	7
Does Biden have the temperament to serve effectively as president?			
Yes	50	93	5
No	48	4	95
Was your vote for president mainly:			
For your candidate	68	39	60
Against your candidate	25	70	29

(Continued)

Table 9.8 Florida 2020 Presidential Exit Poll Results: Issues and Candidate Characteristics *(Continued)*

Category	Electorate	Biden	Trump
How do you feel about the way Trump is handling his job as president?			
Approve	52	6	93
Disapprove	47	94	5
How confident are you that votes in your state will be counted accurately?			
Very or somewhat confident	86	48	51
Not very or not at all confident	12	44	54

Source: CNN "Florida Exit Poll, President, 2020," https://www.cnn.com/election/2020/exit-polls/president/florida, retrieved, February 27, 2021.

and Trump won that group by a slight margin (51 to 48 percent). While President Trump regularly criticized mail voting and state voting systems in most states, in August, he specifically tweeted that Florida's voting system was "Safe and Secure, Tried and True," which may have installed more confidence among his supporters in the Sunshine State at the time of the election (Kilgore, 2020).

DOWN-BALLOT RACES

With no major statewide contest below the presidency in 2020, the focus of down-ballot races was on the U.S. House of Representatives. The Republicans went into the election holding fourteen seats compared to thirteen for the Democrats. Table 9.9 shows Republicans increased that margin to 16 to 11 by regaining the two Miami districts lost to the Democrats in the 2018 midterm elections, the 26th and 27th Districts, which is suggestive of a Trump coattail effect in South Florida. Indeed, just as labeling the Biden/Harris ticket as "socialist" may have been responsible for the large movement of votes toward Trump in the presidential election, that same charge against Debbie Mucarsel-Powell and Donna Shalala may have been a key factor in unseating both Democratic U.S. House incumbents (Mutnick 2020). With respect to the remaining congressional districts, all incumbents were easily re-elected, with only Democrat Charlie Crist held to below 55 percent of the vote in the St. Petersburg-based Thirteenth district. Additionally, the Republicans easily held three open seats, where incumbents had retired.

With respect to the Florida state legislature, there was also disappointment for the Democrats because despite the hope of building on their 2018 gains, the party lost seats in both the state House and state Senate. In the state

House, the Republicans increased their majority, winning 78 seats compared to 42 seats for the Democrats, with three incumbent Democrats defeated.[25] In the state Senate, the Republicans unseated a Democratic incumbent in a Miami-based district to increase their majority, taking twenty-four seats to sixteen for the Democrats.[26]

If congressional and state legislative races offered little to cheer Florida Democrats, the party could take some satisfaction that Constitutional Amendment 2, which sought to incrementally raise the hourly minimum wage to $15 by 2026, easily passed by 61 percent to 39 percent.[27] There were thirty-two counties that voted in favor of the amendment, including all seven mega-counties, where support was no lower than 60 percent. Interestingly, despite the pro-Republican swing evident in Miami-Dade, the county backed the amendment by 71 percent. Indeed, this was the third-highest level of support for the amendment behind Broward and Osceola counties. Thus, while the label of "socialism" in the abstract may have been used to siphon off support to the Republicans among many voters in Miami-Dade, evidently there was no reluctance in embracing a specific policy like a minimum wage proposal that many Republicans might consider an exemplar of socialism.

CONCLUSIONS: BATTLEGROUND STATE OR REPUBLICAN ADVANTAGE?

In our analysis of Florida in the 2016 election, we noted that long-term demographic change was increasing the racial and ethnic diversity of Florida and would make it difficult for the Republicans to keep winning with an "Old South" strategy. Specifically, we viewed Trump's victory in 2016 "as representing the high-water mark of a Republican electoral coalition in Florida that essentially relies on securing landslide support among whites to win elections" (Knuckey and Jewett 2018, 172). Trump's 2020 victory suggests this observation was correct. The Hispanic share of the electorate was larger, and Trump won less of the white vote, but still won the state by a larger margin by gaining vote share among blacks and especially Hispanics.

Florida offers much fodder for both parties to contemplate in the aftermath of the 2020 presidential election. Had Democrats been told that Biden would win all seven of the most populous counties in Florida, including being the first Democrat to carry Duval county in almost a quarter of a century, the party would have been bullish about its prospects of carrying the state. What they would not have anticipated was a huge vote shift toward Trump in Miami-Dade County. Together with Trump's base among whites in rural and exurban counties, Trump was able to win Florida for a second successive

Table 9.9 Results of 2020 Florida U.S. House of Representatives Elections

	Republican Vote (%)	Change in Republican Vote (%) 2018–20	Winning Candidate & Outcome
First District	64.6	−2.5	Matt Gaetz*, Republican hold
Second District	97.9	n/aª	Neal Dunn*, Republican hold
Third District	57.1	−0.5	Kat Cammack, Republican hold
Fourth District	61.1	-4.1	John Rutherford*, Republican hold
Fifth District	34.9	+1.7	Al Lawson*, Democratic hold
Sixth District	60.6	+4.3	Michael Waltz*, Republican hold
Seventh District	43.2	+1.1	Stephanie Murphy*, Democratic hold
Eight District	61.4	+0.9	Bill Posey*, Republican hold
Ninth District	44.0	+2.0	Darren Soto*, Democratic hold
Tenth District	36.4	n/aᵇ	Val Demings*, Democratic hold
Eleventh District	66.7	+1.6	Daniel Webster*, Republican hold
Twelfth District	62.9	+4.8	Gus Bilirakis*, Republican hold
Thirteenth District	47.0	+4.6	Charlie Crist*, Democratic hold
Fourteenth District	39.7	n/aᵇ	Kathy Castor*, Democratic hold
Fifteenth District	55.4	+2.4	Scott Franklin, Republican hold
Sixteenth District	55.5	+0.9	Vern Buchanan*, Republican hold
Seventeenth District	64.6	+2.3	Greg Steube*, Republican hold
Eighteenth District	56.3	+2.0	Brian Mast*, Republican hold
Nineteenth District	61.3	−1.0	Byron Donalds, Republican hold
Twentieth District	21.3	n/aᵇ	Alcee Hastings*, Democratic hold
Twenty-First District	39.1	n/aᵇ	Lois Frankel*, Democratic hold
Twenty-Second District	41.4	+3.4	Ted Deutch*, Democratic hold
Twenty-Third District	41.8	+5.8	Debbie Wasserman Schultz*, Democratic hold
Twenty-Fourth District	20.4	n/aᵇ	Frederica Wilson*, Democratic hold
Twenty-Fifth District	Uncontested	n/a	Mario Diaz-Balart*, Republican hold
Twenty-Sixth District	51.7	+2.4	Carlos Gimenez, Republican gain
Twenty-Seventh District	51.4	+5.6	Maria Elvira Salazar, Republican gain

Source: Florida Department of State Division of Elections, "2020 General Election November 3, 2020, Official Results United States Representative," https://results.elections.myflorida.com/Index.asp?ElectionDate=11/3/2020&DATAMODE=, retrieved, February 1, 2021.
ª No Democratic challenger in 2020
ᵇ No Republican challenger in 2018
* Incumbent

election by a comfortable margin, at least by Florida's standards. Moreover, this stymied any progress the Democrats were hoping to make in down-ballot races where they actually lost seats.

Of course, predicting the future from a single election is difficult. The key question for the Republicans, is whether the Trump coalition that delivered in 2020 is transferable to other Republicans running statewide? Specifically, will the gains among black and Hispanic voters be durable, or are these defections simply attributable to transitory forces in 2020? It may be that Trump's dominant personality was the driving factor and cannot be easily duplicated by other candidates. It may be that accusations of "socialism" in future elections may not sway Hispanics in large numbers. It may simply be that the unprecedented pandemic created conditions for a 2020 election that will never be duplicated. In the long term, the Republican Party in Florida faces the same predicament that it does nationally: in order to win, it must figure out a way to continue attracting more minority voters as the state and the nation become more diverse.

Despite Florida's racial diversity, however, winning major statewide elections in Florida has been a challenge for the Democratic Party. Indeed, while Democrats have frequently been competitive in statewide elections, only four Democrats have won statewide since 2000: Barack Obama in the 2008 and 2012 presidential elections, Bill Nelson in the 2000, 2006, and 2012 U.S. Senate elections, Alex Sink for Chief Financial Officer in 2006, and most recently Nikki Fried for Commissioner of Agriculture in 2018. The problem for Democrats in statewide elections is that by routinely winning less than 40 percent of the white vote, there is little margin of error for vote defections from its base. Even though Biden increased the white share of the vote from 2016 to 37 percent, that proved insufficient given the loss of support among Hispanics. If Democrats cannot figure out how to appeal to more white Florida voters, or regain traditional levels of support from Florida black and Hispanic voters, then Florida Democrats will rarely win statewide elections.

Once considered the nation's premier battleground state in presidential elections, does the 2020 result suggest that Florida is no longer a swing state? Commenting on the election, Republican state representative Blaise Ingoglia observed that "it's time to start thinking about taking Florida out of the toss-up column. We're red" (Dixon, Fineout, and Caputo 2021). Given that Trump won Florida by a little over 3 percent, it would be difficult to see how Florida would be considered anything other than a battleground state in 2024. The Democrats have a solid electoral base, and as noted, demographic change fueled by racial diversity and generational replacement will likely continue. It would be folly for any Democrat to concede Florida, even though the 2020 election proved that it was no longer a kingmaker on the path to 270 Electoral College votes.

Solid Republican control of the state legislature and governor's office has allowed them to adopt policies that enhance their chances of winning elections. For example, in 2018, Floridians approved Amendment 4 to restore voting rights to felons who completed all terms of their sentence. The state legislature, supported by Governor Ron DeSantis, sought to undermine the spirit of the amendment by passing a law requiring ex-felons pay all restitution, fees, and fines associated with the case before restoration. Critics saw the shadow of the Jim Crow South being cast across Florida, equating this measure to poll taxes that had once been used as a means of disfranchisement (Totenberg 2020). Ultimately the federal courts disagreed and allowed the legislation to stand. Consequently, only a fraction of Florida felons regained their rights and were able to vote in 2020 (Kam 2020). Since blacks are disproportionately in the felon population and estimates are that over one million felons are blocked from voting in Florida, conventional wisdom holds that this may have cost Democratic votes. Furthermore, Governor Ron DeSantis proposed legislation to make mail-in voting more difficult and restrict access to ballot drop boxes. Since Democrats were more likely to use mail voting in 2020, they might be hurt in future elections should this idea become law. DeSantis indicated his motives were to strengthen election security and faith in the electoral process, even though there has been no evidence to suggest widespread voter fraud in Florida in 2020 and Governor DeSantis himself bragged about how smoothly the 2020 election was handled in the state (Stracqualursi 2021).[28]

Voting rights will certainly be at the forefront of Florida politics ahead of the 2022 midterm and 2024 presidential elections. The 2022 midterm elections should receive national interest as DeSantis seeks reelection as governor and Marco Rubio to his U.S. Senate seat. Both might be considered possible contenders for the Republican presidential nomination in 2024.[29] A diverse field of Democratic contenders are considering a run for governor or U.S. Senate in 2022, including Congressional Representatives Val Demings (who was a House impeachment manager and on Biden's list for Vice President), Stephanie Murphy (centrist member of the Problems Solvers caucus), and Charlie Crist (a former Republican governor who switched parties); former member of the U.S. House Gwen Graham (an unsuccessful candidate for the Democratic gubernatorial nomination in 2018); and State Representative Anna Eskamani (an Iranian-American who would be the most progressive choice).

Looking ahead to 2024, in addition to DeSantis and Rubio, Florida's other U.S. Senator Rick Scott might also seek the Republican presidential nomination. Of course, looming over the 2024 nomination is one other "Florida Man": Trump himself. Indeed, if Trump chooses to run for president again, it is almost certain that none of these three would run against him. Florida has evidently emerged as the Trump family's new center of operations, with Trump relocating from New York to his Mar-a-Lago resort, with Ivanka

Trump and husband Jared Kushner having bought property in Miami, and Donald Trump, Jr. reportedly looking to follow suit (Bennett 2021). There was even speculation of Ivanka Trump challenging Rubio in the Republican primary for U.S. Senate, although Trump herself ended that speculation saying she would not be a candidate (Haberman 2021).

For some time, Florida has been the exemplar of a state that might represent the future of the South's electoral and party politics. When Trump acts like a political demagogue, establishes a cult of personality, and appeals to racial animus, he embodies the old politics of the South. When he enlarges the GOP base of support in Florida by attracting more black and Hispanic voters, he represents the new. This interaction between past and present will likely continue to shape the dynamics of electoral politics in the Sunshine State for the foreseeable future.

NOTES

1. Trump changed his voter registration from New York to his Mar-a-Largo resort in Palm Beach (Choi 2020).

2. The poll aggregator website Five Thirty Eight had Biden leading in its final average of polls, 49.1 percent to 46.6 percent for Trump, https://projects.fivethirtyeight.com/polls/president-general/florida/, retrieved November 3, 2020.

3. For example, in July, 2020, Florida had recorded more COVID-19 cases than many other nations (Yan and Watts 2020).

4. Democratic Senator Bill Nelson won reelection with 55.2 percent in 2012. The average for the victor in the other ten races was just 49.9 percent of the vote.

5. Trump won Florida in 2016 by about 113,000 votes and the Democratic registration edge in 2016 was more than 327,000. By 2020, the Democratic registration edge had declined by 214,000 people.

6. For a more detailed look at the 2018 midterm elections in Florida, see MacManus et al. (2019, 139–169).

7. Gwen Graham is a moderate former member of the U.S. House of Representatives and daughter of Florida icon Bob Graham: a three-term U.S. senator and two-term governor.

8. In late October at the final debate, Gillum said: "I'm not calling Mr. DeSantis a racist, I'm simply saying the racists believe he's a racist" (Rodriguez and Donato 2020).

9. This record was short lived as five senate races in 2020 went on to break that mark Georgia, North Carolina, South Carolina, Iowa, and Arizona.

10. Directions for the multi-page, multi-column, multi-lingual ballot were put in the first column rather than across the top of the ballot and the U.S. senate race then appeared below the instructions in the first column at the bottom left of the page. Many voters missed the contest and began voting with the governor's race which was the first one listed at the top of the second column. Since Broward County is the largest reliably

Democratic county in the state it hurt Nelson more than Scott. Legislators changed election law in the aftermath to ensure that this ballot design would not be used again.

11. Trump received 93.8 percent of the vote in the Republican primary election. Data are taken from Florida Department of State Division of Elections, "March 17, 2020 Primary Election

Republican Primary Official Results, President of the United States," https://results.elections.myflorida.com/Index.asp?ElectionDate=3/17/2020&DATAMODE=, retrieved February 14, 2021.

12. The exit poll's sample size was too small to reliably calculate percentages based on a further disaggregation of those under the age of 45.

13. Trump and Pence held seventeen Florida rallies during the general election while Biden and Harris hosted fourteen.

14. In 2018, Broward County did not have the resources to count all their mail ballots early and fell way behind in counting and reporting results. In addition, in 2018, Palm Beach County had older equipment that was incapable of conducing multiple required recounts in a timely fashion. The Supervisor of Elections was replaced in each of those counties and these issues were addressed. The problems in 2018 prodded all sixty-seven local Supervisors of Elections to be better prepared for 2020.

15. Turnout data are taken from United States Elections Project, "2020 November General Election Turnout Rates," http://www.electproject.org/2020g, retrieved February 1, 2021.

16. Seminole county's realignment toward the Democrats was foreshadowed in that both Bill Nelson and Andrew Gillum had carried the county in the 2018 midterm elections.

17. Data from each election are taken from Florida Department of State Division of Elections, "Election Results," https://results.elections.myflorida.com/, retrieved February 1, 2021.

18. In addition to the seven mega-counties, the only other counties carried by Biden were: Alachua, Gadsden, Leon, Osceola, and Seminole.

19. Biden's total vote was down by very small margins compared to Hillary Clinton in 2016 in Baker (seventy-five votes less), Calhoun (thirty-two votes less), and Lafayette (eight votes less) counties.

20. Trump's county-level vote percentage are taken from Florida Secretary of State Elections Division, "Election Results," https://results.elections.myflorida.com/. With the exception of percentage white evangelical, all demographic county data are taken from the U.S. Census Bureau "Quick Facts, Florida," retrieved 1 Feb, 2021, https://www.census.gov/quickfacts/FL. The percentage of white evangelical data are taken from Grammich et al. (2012).

21. Weighted least squares regression was preferred to ordinary least squares regression because of the large variation in county population sizes.

22. Though not shown in the table, 64 percent of Florida voters did not have college degrees and they broke for Trump by 53–47 percent. Biden won college-educated voters (36 percent of the electorate) by 51–48 percent.

23. The exit poll did not report income in 2020 but the AP Votecast did. Among voters making $50,000 to $100,000 (36 percent of the electorate), Trump won 50–48

percent over Biden. Biden won among the 38 percent of Floridians making less than $50,000 (53–45 percent) and among the 26 percent making over $100,000 (51–47 percent).

24. Based on fifteen polls tracked by Real Clear Politics, Trump never exceeded 48 percent approval in Florida in the three years before the 2020 election. https://www.realclearpolitics.com/epolls/approval_rating/president/fl/president_trump_job_approval_in_florida-6287.html, retrieved, February 27, 2021.

25. These were state House districts 69th (St. Petersburg), 84th (Fort Pierce), and 103rd (Pembroke Pines).

26. To win Senate District 37, Republican operatives recruited an independent "shadow candidate" who did not live in the district, did not campaign, and had no interest in winning. This "shadow candidate" shared the same last name as the Democratic incumbent Senator Rodriguez. Republican affiliated outside groups then spent several $100,000 on mailers touting the supposed liberal policy positions of the independent Rodriguez to appeal to progressive voters who otherwise might vote for the Democratic Rodriguez. The "phantom candidate" received more than 6,000 votes and the Republican challenger won the race after a hand recount by just thirty-four votes. The Miami-Dade State Attorney is investigating (Martin 2020).

27. Florida Department of State Division of Elections "November 3, 2020 General Election, Official Results, Constitutional Amendment," https://results.elections.myflorida.com/Index.asp?ElectionDate=11/3/2020&DATAMODE=, retrieved, February 1, 2021.

28. The success of Amendment 4 in 2018 might have also been a motivating factor in Amendment 4 in 2020, which would have required that any future constitutional amendment be approved twice by voters, by the 60 percent threshold in both instances, to be adopted. This amendment was, however, defeated by 52.5 percent to 47.5 percent, Florida Department of State Division of Elections "November 3, 2020 General Election, Official Results, Constitutional Amendment," https://results.elections.myflorida.com/Index.asp?ElectionDate=11/3/2020&DATAMODE= , retrieved, February 1, 2021.

29. Indeed, at the Conservative Political Action Conference straw poll held in Orlando in February 2021, DeSantis was the top choice for presidential candidate if Trump does not run again.

REFERENCES

Bennett, Kate. 2021. "Trump plots future – and revenge – from sunny Florida links," *CNN*, February 25, 2021, https://www.cnn.com/2021/02/25/politics/donald-trump-plans-family/index.html.

Caputo, Marc, 2018, "How Ron DeSantis won the Fox News primary," *Politico*, August 29, 2020, https://www.politico.com/story/2018/08/29/ron-desantis-fox-news-florida-governor-primary-800706.

Caputo, Marc and Gary Fineout, 2020, "'Something's in the water': Florida Republicans see surge in voter registration," *Politico*, September 24, 2020, https://www.politico.com/news/2020/09/24/florida-republicans-voter-registration-surge-420936.

Choi, Matthew. 2019. "Trump, a symbol of New York, is officially a Floridian now," *Politico*, October 31, 2019, https://www.politico.com/news/2019/10/31/trump-florida-residence-063564.

Clark, Dartunorro, 2020, "Presidential Debate in Miami canceled after Trump refused to participate virtually," *NBC News*, October 9, 2020, https://www.nbcnews.com/politics/2020-election/presidential-debate-miami-canceled-after-trump-refuses-participate-virtually-n1242790.

Colombini, Stephanie, Steve Newborn, and Daylina Miller. 2020. "Tampa Appearances By Trump, Biden Ara A Contrast In Views, And Crowds," *WUSF Public Media*, October, 29, 2020, https://wusfnews.wusf.usf.edu/politics-issues/2020-10-29/tampa-appearances-by-trump-biden-are-a-contrast-in-crowds-views.

Conkwright, Ethan, and Jonathan Knuckey. 2018. "Partisan Change in Florida: A County-Level Analysis of Presidential Voting, 2000–2016." Paper presented at the annual meeting of the Southwestern Social Science Association, Orlando, FL, October 10–13, 2018.

Connolly, Griffin, 2018, "Rick Scott spend record $64 million of his own money in the Florida senate race," *Roll Call*, December 10, 2010, https://www.rollcall.com/2018/12/10/rick-scott-spent-record-64-million-of-his-own-money-in-florida-senate-race/.

Dixon, Matt, 2020, "Florida Republicans cut Democrats' registration edge to historic lows," *Politico*, October 15, 2020, https://www.politico.com/states/florida/story/2020/10/15/florida-republicans-cut-democrats-registration-edge-to-historic-low-1325644.

Dixon, Matt, Gary Fineout, and Marc Caputo. 2020. "'This is Trump country': Florida is a swing state no more," *Politico*, November 4, 2020, https://www.politico.com/states/florida/story/2020/11/04/this-is-trump-country-florida-is-a-battleground-no-more-1333745.

FairVote, 2020, "2020 Presidential candidate general election events tracker," *National Popular Vote*, November 3, 2020, https://docs.google.com/spreadsheets/d/1oR_x3wGpFi1wO2V0BNMV529s_V-AgGH7tKd66DD7rrM/edit#gid=2025398596.

Grammich, Clifford, Kirk Hadaway, Richard Houseal, Dale E. Jones, Alexei Krindatch, Richie Stanley and Richard H. Taylor (principal investigators). 2012. *Longitudinal Religious Congregations and Membership File*, 1980–2010 (County Level).

Guttman, Agnieszka. 2021. "TV advertising spending during presidential campaign in the U.S. 2020, by state," *Statista*, January 14, 2021, https://www.statista.com/statistics/1182139/tv-advertising-spending-presidential-campaign-by-state-united-states/.

Haberman, Maggie. 2021. "Ivanka Trump will not run against Marco Rubio for one of Florida's Senate seats," *New York Times*, February 18, 2021, https://www.nytimes.com/2021/02/18/us/ivanka-trump-florida-senate.html.

Jacobs, Ben. 2020. "Why 'Socialism' Killed Democrats in Florida," *New York Magazine*, November 17, 2020, https://nymag.com/intelligencer/2020/11/republican-socialism-attacks-haunt-democrats-in-florida.html.

Jacobs, Julia, 2018, DeSantis Warns Florida Not to 'Monkey This Up' and Many Hear a Racist Dog Whistle," *New York Times*, August 29, 2018, https://www.nytimes.com/2018/08/29/us/politics/desantis-monkey-up-gillum.html.

Jewett, Aubrey, 2018, *A Concise Introduction to Florida Politics.* Thousand Oaks, CA: Sage CQ Press.

Kam, Dara.2020. "Fraction of Florida felons will be able to vote in November," *News4Jax*, September 28, 2020, https://www.news4jax.com/news/local/2020/09/28/fraction-of-florida-felons-will-be-able-to-vote-in-november/.

Kilgore, Ed. 2020. "Trump says voting by mail is Satanic – except in Florida, where it's Angellic," *New York Magazine*, August 4, 2020, https://nymag.com/intelligencer/2020/08/trump-vote-by-mail-corrupts-the-election-except-in-florida.html.

Klas, Mary Ellen. 2020. "Florida's senior vote shifting from Trump to Biden, polls show. But is it really?" *Tampa Bay Times*, October 10, 2020, https://www.tampabay.com/news/florida-politics/elections/2020/10/12/floridas-senior-vote-shifting-from-trump-to-biden-polls-show-but-is-it-really/.

Knuckey Jonathan. 2004. "The Structure of Party Competition in the South: The Case of Florida." *American Review of Politics* 25, Spring: 41–65.

Knuckey, Jonathan. 2009. "Florida: Obama Gives GOP the 'Blues.'" In *The 2008 Presidential Election in the South: A Paler Shade of Red*, edited by Branwell DuBose Kapeluck, Laurence W. Moreland and Robert P. Steed, 137–159. Westport, CT: Praeger.

Knuckey, Jonathan, and Tyler Branz. 2013. "Florida: Sí, Se Puede!" *In Second Verse Same as the First: The 2012 Presidential Election in the South*, edited by Scott E. Buchanan and Branwell DuBose Kapeluck, 143–170. Fayetteville, AR: University of Arkansas Press.

Knuckey, Jonathan and Aubrey Jewett. 2019. "Old South Electoral Strategy Trumps the Newest Southern Politics." In *The Future Ain't What It Used to Be: The 2016 Presidential Election in the South*, edited by Branwell DuBose Kapeluck and Scott E. Buchanan, 147–173. Fayetteville, AR: University of Arkansas Press.

Lemongello, Steven and Cristobal Reyes. 2020. "Pence campaigns in Central Florida, with Trump to follow on Monday," *Orlando Sentinel*, October 11, 2020, https://www.orlandosentinel.com/politics/2020-election/os-ne-2020-mike-pence-campaign-saturday-20201010-xamxnvbzo5ealnkled7qh4q53y-story.html.

Lemongello, Steven, Lisa Maria Garza, and Stephen Hudak. 2020. "Florida's presidential primary still set for Tuesday as Ohio Gov. orders postponement amid coronavirus worries," *Orlando Sentinel*, March 16, 2020, https://www.orlandosentinel.com/coronavirus/os-ne-florida-primary-preview-20200316-ikdgmb3lofcjjfebgm65ez2mma-story.html.

Lush, Tamara, 2020, "A senior warning sign for Trump: 'Go Biden' cry at sprawling retirement community The Villages," *USA Today*, October 10, 2020, https://www.usatoday.com/story/news/politics/elections/2020/10/10/trump-loss-support-reflected-the-villages-retirement-community/5954176002/.

MacManus, Susan A., Aubrey Jewett, David J. Bonanza, and Thomas R. Dye. 2019. *Politics in Florida*, 5th edition. Tallahassee, FL: John Scott Daly Institute of Government.

Man, Anthony, 2019, "Bad ballot design in Broward County cost Bill Nelson 9,658 votes in the ultra-tight loss to Rick Scott," *South Florida Sun Sentinel*, July 12, 2019, https://www.sun-sentinel.com/news/politics/fl-ne-bill-nelson-rick-scott-broward-ballot-design-20190711-deqpxqouwrggtgps6jmqdoezw4-story.html.

McCammond, Alexi. 2020. "Biden campaign turns focus to Puerto Rican voters," *Axios*, September 15, 2020, https://www.axios.com/joe-biden-florida-puerto-rican-voters-2020-election-3981a51a-7104-4a0e-b8fb-a884d9dad325.html.

Martin, Annie. 2020. "Mysterious NPA candidate in South Florida Senate race under investigation," *Orlando Sentinel*, December 19, 2020, https://www.orlandosentinel.com/politics/os-ne-npa-candidate-investigation-20201216-4ut3dzzzq5cebjuzt6aeqlvxde-story.html.

Mazzei, Patricia. 2020. "Sanders's Comments on Fidel Castro Provoke Anger in Florida," *New York Times*, February 24, 2020, https://www.nytimes.com/2020/02/24/us/bernie-sanders-fidel-castro-florida.html.

Morgan, Issac. 2020. "'A culture of Black reticence and Black hypersensitivity': Race and police reforms take center state in election," *Florida Phoenix*, October 20, 2020, https://www.floridaphoenix.com/2020/10/20/a-culture-of-black-reticence-and-black-hypersensitivity-race-and-police-reforms-take-center-stage-in-election/.

Mutnik, Ally. 2020. "The biggest surprises of the 2020 Democratic House debacle," *Politico*, November 11, 2020, https://www.politico.com/news/2020/11/11/2020-election-surprises-democratic-house-436190.

Rodriguez, Lissette and Christopher Donato, 2018, "I'm simply saying the racists believe he's a racist: Florida governor's debate gets heated," *ABC News*, October 24, 2018, https://abcnews.go.com/Politics/im-simply-racists-racist-florida-governors-debate-heated/story?id=58718754.

Sasso, Michael. 2020. "In Must-Win Florida, An Economic Rebound Gives Trump a Shot," *Bloomberg*, October 23, 2020, https://www.bloombergquint.com/onweb/in-must-win-florida-an-economic-rebound-gives-trump-a-shot.

Schwartz, Brian. 2020. "Mike Bloomberg takes big losses after spending over $100 million in Florida, Ohio and Texas," *CNBC*, November 4, 2020, https://www.cnbc.com/2020/11/04/bloomberg-sees-losses-after-spending-over-100-million-in-florida-ohio-texas.html.

Sesin, Carmen. 2020. "Trump cultivated the Hispanic vote in Florida, and it paid off," *NBC News*, November 4, 2020, https://www.nbcnews.com/news/Hispanic/trump-cultivated-Hispanic-vote-florida-it-paid-n1246226.

Shalal, Andrea. 2020. "Trump sows confusion with tweet urging 'vote by mail' in Florida," *Reuters*, August 4, 2020, https://www.reuters.com/article/us-usa-election-trump/trump-sows-confusion-with-tweet-urging-vote-by-mail-in-florida-idUSKCN2502KU.

Spencer, Terry. 2020. "Yes, it's true—Florida ran a smooth election," *Associated Press*, November 4, 2020, https://apnews.com/article/election-2020-joe-biden-donald-trump-pennsylvania-florida-a3f6319cd9d447e094b6c92755ef1067.

Stracqualursi, Veronica. 2021. "Florida GOP Gov. DeSantis proposes voting restriction bills for state lawmakers to pass this session," *CNN*, February 19, 2021, https://www.cnn.com/2021/02/19/politics/desantis-florida-election-proposals/index.html.

Totenberg, Nina. 2020. "Supreme court deals major blow to felons' right to vote in Florida," *National Public Radio*, July 17, 2020, https://www.npr.org/2020/07/17/892105780/supreme-court-deals-major-blow-to-ex-felons-right-to-vote-in-florida.

Yan, Holly and Amanda Watts. 2020. "Florida has more Covid-19 than most countries in the world. These stats show how serious the problem is," *CNN*, July 13, 2020, https://www.cnn.com/2020/07/13/health/florida-coronavirus-cases-comparisons/index.html.

Chapter 10

Kentucky 2020
Bluegrass, Red State
Joel Turner, Scott Lasley, and Jeffrey P. Kash

Although Kentucky's status as a southern state is questioned by some outside observers, recent research into voters' perceptions demonstrates that Kentucky has clearly earned its Southern identity (Binnix et. al 2018; Turner et. al. 2020). In part, Kentucky's identity crisis is exemplified by its position in Civil War politics. Kentucky was one of four slave-dependent states that officially remained in the Union. However, like Missouri, Kentucky was represented by a star (the thirteenth and central) on both the Union flag and the Confederate Battle flag. The Confederacy recognized the provisional Confederate Government of Kentucky established by Confederate sympathizers and admitted the state into the Confederacy in December 1861. These early political conflicts clouded the perceptions of Kentucky as a southern state.

As was the case with its overtly Southern neighbors, race relations across the Commonwealth have a tumultuous history. Racially motivated violence was a common occurrence. While the state was under the political control of conservative Democrats, Kentucky rejected the 13th Amendment and did not ratify it until more than one hundred years after the conclusion of the Civil War. A Confederate general proposed a monument to former Confederacy President Jefferson Davis that was ultimately completed in 1924, with the obelisk celebrating the former president of the Confederate States rising 350 feet in rural Todd County in Southern Kentucky. Within a few years after the dedication of the Jefferson Monument, the Kentucky legislature reaffirmed its Southern bona fides by making "My Old Kentucky Home" the state song. These post–Civil War activities solidified Kentucky's regional identity as Southern.

Like many of its Southern neighbors, Kentucky is currently undergoing a deep introspection regarding the institutional legacies of current and past racial politics. The highest-profile example of this involves the killing of Breonna Taylor in Louisville in early 2020. This tragedy, which will be discussed in greater detail later, involved the killing of an unarmed black woman during a controversial police raid of an apartment. The incident resulted in protests, investigations, and ultimately an indictment of a police officer, which further enhanced racial tensions. In a less-serious but high-profile process, the history and necessity of Confederate Monuments were also debated. In some instances, the monuments were removed, such as the removal of a Jefferson Davis monument located in the Kentucky Capitol Building in Frankfort (Bailey 2020). Additionally, institutions of higher learning across the state are in the process of reviewing the history behind the names of campus buildings potentially changing them to strike a balance between paying homage to the past while recognizing the need to make some changes to address transgressions.

Ultimately, the case for Kentucky to be classified as a Southern state is twofold. First, a clear majority of Kentuckians identify as being Southern. As the research of Binnix et al. (2018) and Turner et. al. (2020) demonstrated, nearly two-thirds of Kentuckians identify as Southern. Additionally, respondents across a variety of socio-demographic categories identify as "Southern," and residents in seven of the nine economic regions of Kentucky were statistically likely to self-identify as "Southern." The second argument supporting Kentucky's identification as a Southern state is that electoral outcomes closely mirror those of their Southern neighbors. The evolution of Kentucky politics looks a lot like those of Tennessee, as opposed to a more deeply Southern state such as Alabama. Like Tennessee, the Commonwealth was never as monolithically Democratic as Alabama and, as a result, the transition to being a Republican stronghold was ultimately not as abrupt.

THE ROAD TO RED

Like many Southern states, Republican success in Kentucky first occurred at the federal level. At the senatorial level, Kentucky has only elected two Democratic senators since 1956, as compared to six Republicans. Currently two of the nation's most visible, if not most powerful, U.S. Senators are Kentucky Republicans, the recently reelected minority leader Mitch McConnell and Rand Paul. At the presidential level, evidence of a willingness to support Republican candidates came early, as Kentuckians threw their support behind William McKinley in 1896 and Calvin Coolidge and Herbert Hoover in 1924 and 1928, respectively. The more consistent Kentucky pattern of supporting Republicans emerged in 1956 with the candidacy of

Dwight D. Eisenhower, with Kentucky voters demonstrating a propensity to support Republican presidential candidates since that election.

Republican presidential coattails have also played a role in Kentucky politics, as Dwight D. Eisenhower's strong showing in his reelection bid helped Thurston Morton defeat Democratic incumbent Earle Clements, while John Sherman Cooper dispatched former governor Lawrence Wetherby in a special election to fill the seat of Alben Barkley, who had passed away earlier in 1956. Cooper went on to win reelection in 1960 and 1966 before retiring. He was replaced by Democrat Walter (Dee) Huddleston who defeated former Republican Governor Louie B. Nunn in 1972. Huddleston served two terms before being famously upset by then Jefferson County Judge-Executive Mitch McConnell. McConnell's victory would ultimately help usher in unprecedented Republican success in the state.

After, his initial election in 1956, Thurston Morton would serve two terms in the Senate. Fellow Republican Marlow Cook was elected in 1968. However, Cook encountered far less success in the Senate, as he only served one term before being defeated by popular Democratic governor Wendell Ford, who was easily re-elected three times following his initial victory. Ford's retirement in 1998 set the stage for a contest between two athletes turned politicians and sitting U.S. representatives. Hall of Fame pitcher Jim Bunning narrowly defeated fellow congressman and former University of Kentucky basketball player Scotty Baesler. Bunning was reelected in 2004, and his retirement in 2010 set the stage for the emergence of Rand Paul and the rise of the Tea Party in Kentucky.

The history regarding the composition of Kentucky's U.S. House delegation is consistent with Senate outcomes in that an electoral surprise ultimately helped pave the way for Republican domination. Democrats enjoyed a congressional majority in the six-member delegation until the passing of William Natcher in the spring of 1994. Natcher, whose funeral service attracted numerous dignitaries from the Democratic Party, was a staple of Kentucky's U.S. House delegation, having represented Kentucky's Second District for over forty years. In the subsequent special election, Republican religious bookstore owner Ron Lewis upset state Senator Joe Prather to even the House delegation at three Republicans and three Democrats. Lewis's election was rightly seen by pundits as a precursor to the Republican Revolution that occurred that fall in the general election. When former Democrat turned Republican Ed Whitfield was elected to Congress from Kentucky's First District, it gave the Republicans a majority in the House delegation that it has not relinquished. In addition to both U.S. senators, Republicans currently hold five out of Kentucky's six House seats. John Yarmuth is the lone Democratic exception, currently representing the Third Congressional District located in Louisville, Kentucky's most populous city and by far the most prominent urban area in the state (table 10.1).

As expected, presidential results in the state generally mirror those of other federal races. Jimmy Carter in 1980 is the last Democratic presidential candidate to win a higher share of the two-party vote in Kentucky than they did nationally. While Ronald Reagan (1984) and George H. W. Bush (1988 and 1992) just narrowly outperformed their national performance, the gap steadily increased during the 1990s and 2000s. Mitt Romney (2012) and Donald Trump (2016 and 2020) exceeded the national vote share by double digits. Trump's 2016 Kentucky vote share surpassed his national share by almost 17 percent. Over the past quarter-century, the Commonwealth made the transition from barely blue to reliably red.

The emergence of Republican domination in Kentucky state and local elections took longer. After Democratic domination during the twentieth century, the Kentucky Senate was the first institution to fall for Kentucky Democrats. Republicans secured their first-ever state majority in the senate in 1999, although notably this did not occur at the ballot box but when two Democratic state senators switched their party affiliations. In addition to ratcheting up the animosity between parties in the state, the party switchers gave Republicans a 20–18 majority, which they have slowly expanded ever since, including maintaining at least a two-thirds majority in the chamber since 2015.

The road to Republican success in the Kentucky House and governorship has been a bit bumpier. Republicans have won just two gubernatorial elections since 1970. Congressman Ernie Fletcher defeated Attorney General Ben Chandler to win in 2003, while businessman and Tea Party favorite Matt Bevin won in 2015. Unfortunately for Republicans, self-inflicted mistakes

Table 10.1 Counties with Largest Relative Democratic Trend, 1996–2020

County	Relative to State Trend
Fayette	−23.94
Jefferson	−18.32
Oldham	−15.58
Kenton	−13.42
Warren	−12.70
Campbell	−12.40
Boone	−9.82
Woodford	−9.78
Jessamine	−7.27
Hardin	−4.89

Note: Calculated: (Change in County-Level Republican Two-Party Vote Share from 1996–2020 − (Change in State Level Republican Two-Party Vote Share from 1996–2020).

Example: Oldham County saw a decline in Republican Two-Party Vote Share of −1.85 percent, while the increase in statewide two-party vote share was 13.73 percent. Calculation: −1.85 percent − 13.73 percent = −15.58 percent.

derailed the reelection efforts of both Fletcher and Bevin. In the case of Fletcher, he was indicted on misdemeanor charges that he illegally rewarded his political supporters with state jobs. This resulted in Fletcher issuing blanket pardons and ultimately taking a plea deal for himself that required him to admit that he had acted "inappropriately" (Alford 2006). Even though he avoided both jail time and resignation, the scandal completely derailed his term. Fletcher's struggles not only led to the election of Democrat Steve Beshear in 2007 but also helped slow the Republican takeover of the state House of Representatives until 2016. Ultimately, the political dam that was holding back the Republican majority finally gave way and the Republicans now hold a three to one majority in the House.

The only jewel left in the Democratic crown at the state level is the governorship. Once again, gubernatorial success for the Democrats came as the result of missteps by a sitting Republican governor. Matt Bevin, a Republican who was elected governor in 2015, was plagued by both an ongoing teacher pension crisis and the abrasive manner in which he often chose to conduct himself (Loftus 2018). Andy Beshear, the son of former Governor Steve Beshear, was able to benefit from the missteps of Governor Matt Bevin to eke out a 5,189-vote victory in 2019. Unlike his father, however, the younger Beshear's reelection was a longshot, as the state mood at the time was more anti-Bevin than anti-Republican, clearly illustrated by the fact that the other five statewide offices were held by Republicans (Kolb, 2020).

While the aggregate shift to the Republican Party is significant, the shifting vote patterns within the state are notable. Several of these trends merit special attention. First, Republican strongholds continue to be Republican strongholds. For example, south central Kentucky, which includes the geopolitical area referred to as the "Old 5th," has been and continues to be overwhelmingly Republican. Bob Dole received 60 percent of the two-party vote in 23 of Kentucky's 120 counties in 1996. Trump carried at least 75 percent of the two-party vote in twenty of those twenty-three counties in both of his races.

Second, old Democratic strongholds are now overwhelmingly Republican. Out of the twenty-three counties where Dole won less than 40 percent of the two-party vote, Trump won all of them in 2020 including at least 70 percent of the votes in 20 of them. These include areas of traditional Democratic strength in the Appalachian Mountain region of Eastern Kentucky as well as the Jackson Purchase area, which consists of the eight most western counties in the state. The overwhelming nature of this transition is driven by the fact that not too long ago the counties of the Jackson Purchase were referred to as the "Gibraltar of Democracy" due to Democratic strength in the region. That is no longer the case.

Third, the most heavily populated counties are now the strongest Democratic counties in the state. Jefferson County (Louisville, by far the largest city and most urban area in the Commonwealth) and Fayette County (Lexington and the home of the University of Kentucky) are the only two counties in the state to go Democrat in each of the last two presidential, senatorial, and gubernatorial elections. The decline of Republican fortunes in Fayette County has been the most precipitous. Despite losing the state, George H. W. Bush carried the county in 1992 by 3 percent. By contrast, Fayette County was where Trump performed worst, underperforming Bush's total by 5 percent and underperforming his statewide total by 24 percent. These trends in populated areas prove interesting because they highlight how voters in these areas differ from the majority of the state.

Finally, in addition to the two most populated counties, there is at least anecdotal evidence that Republicans are seeing some slippage in the wealthier, better educated, and faster growing counties. This includes Oldham (the wealthiest), the Northern Kentucky counties (Kenton, Campbell, Boone) that serve as suburbs to Cincinnati, Scott County (just north of Lexington), and Warren County, which is located an hour from Nashville. This slippage is occurring at multiple electoral levels (figure 10.1).

For instance, although Trump won the state handily, he did not run as well in these specific areas as he did across the state. Also, in the last gubernatorial election, the Democratic candidate won Warren, Campbell, Kenton, and Scott counties, and only narrowly lost in Oldham County. Essentially, although these counties are still considered Republican, they are far less Republican

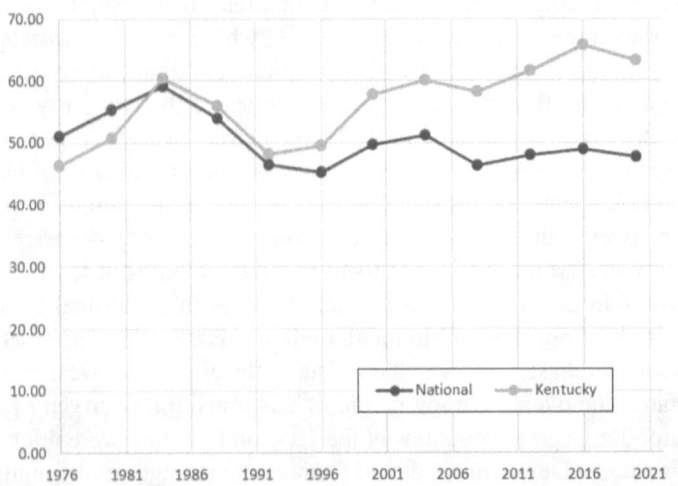

Figure 10.1 **Republican Party Share of Two-Party Vote 1976–2020.** *Source:* Data compiled by the authors from Dave Leip's Atlas of U.S. Presidential Elections (https://uselectionatlas.org/). Last accessed March 5, 2021.

than the rest of the state. The question generated by this weakening of support is whether it will lead to changes in Democratic electoral fortunes in the future.

THE UNDERCARD IS THE MAIN EVENT

The 2020 election continued the trend where Kentucky is largely ignored by the major parties in presidential primary and general elections. It has now been twenty years since a major party candidate came to Kentucky to campaign in the general election. The fact that Kentucky's primary date is the third Tuesday in May generally means that primary contests are resolved by the time Kentucky's voters head to the polls. Democratic primaries in 2008 and 2016 were still close enough by the time May rolled around to encourage long shot candidates Hillary Clinton and Bernie Sanders to visit the state, but the 2020 primary barely registered a blip. In Kentucky, the main event has proven to be far less interesting than the undercard of congressional and statewide elections. The 2020 election was no different. While President Donald Trump coasted to a predictable and resounding victory, his impact on the U.S. Senate race featuring Senate Majority Leader Mitch McConnell running for a seventh term and Republican efforts to build on their majority in the Generally Assembly is worth exploring.

Donald Trump won 62 percent of the vote in Kentucky, running about 15 percent above his national average. He won all but two counties (Jefferson and Fayette), including winning at least 80 percent of the vote in 31 of 120 counties. Kentucky was also one of the very first states to be called nationally for the president. However, as impressive as these numbers are, they do represent a small decline from 2016. Trump saw a drop in his two-party vote share in almost two-thirds of the counties and a 2.6 percent dip statewide. Still, Trump's largely dominating evening translated to big success for Republicans across the state. Senator Mitch McConnell defeated challenger Amy McGrath by 19.5 percent, despite McGrath spending $90 million in her efforts to topple him. Republicans also managed to pick up 14 seats in the Kentucky House giving them 75 out of 100 seats. These results reveal the growing importance of national issues and political orientation in Kentucky state politics.

Demographically and politically, Kentucky is a home run for Donald Trump. Kentucky is less diverse than the nation, and over half of exit poll participants considered themselves to be evangelicals. Kentucky voters are also about 10 percent more likely to self-identify as Republicans and as conservatives than the national average. Trump not only benefited from a friendly playing field but also enjoyed enthusiastic support from his voting base. Over 85 percent of Trump voters in Kentucky were voting for Donald Trump rather than against Joe Biden, while only 42 percent of Biden voters were voting for Biden rather than against Trump. Additionally, "Trump Trains" and pop-up Trump Stores were common sights across the state. Just as in 2016, local parties found it difficult to keep Trump material in stock, and Trump-supporting capitalists made sure to fill in that gap.

In addition to both demographics and the political leanings of voters, the issues that dominated the election in the Commonwealth also largely favored former President Trump. AP VoteCast (Associated Press 2020) data from Kentucky provides a snapshot into what issues were salient for voters. Specifically, the economy (31 percent) and the coronavirus pandemic (39 percent) topped Kentuckian's lists of the most important issues facing the country. President Trump did particularly well among voters who identified economy as the most pressing national issues, as nine out of ten of these voters supported President Trump's policies. The former president's handling of the coronavirus pandemic hurt his performance in Kentucky, but not to the same extent it did in other parts of the country. Among those who viewed the pandemic as the most important issue, Biden outperformed Trump but the difference was much more modest when compared to national numbers as well as when compared to the difference between Trump and Biden on the economy in Kentucky. Overall, just 56 percent of those who identified the coronavirus pandemic as the number one issue preferred Biden over Trump.

While the presidential election in Kentucky generally stayed off the national radar, the eyes of the nation were on Louisville for much of the late spring and early summer due to protests following the death of twenty-six-year-old black woman, Breonna Taylor at the hands of Louisville Metro Police.[1] Although Taylor was shot and killed in March, protests did not begin in earnest until the 911 audio of the events was released in late May. Protests continued in Louisville on and off throughout the summer, occasionally turning violent and essentially shutting down the downtown area of the city during the peak of the protests. The initial wave of protests was largely intertwined with protests of George Floyd's death in Minnesota, but Taylor's death received more explicit attention as the summer wore on. When, in September, the grand jury returned indictments for just one of the officers involved in the shooting for wonton endangerment and no officers were charged for the death of Taylor, outrage sparked protests across the country. Kentucky Attorney General Daniel Cameron, a protégé of Senator Mitch McConnell, emerged as the face of the grand jury investigation. Cameron had previously made a splash speaking at the Republican National Convention and is seen as a possible heir to McConnell's seat after the senator retires.

An October Ipsos (2020) poll provides some interesting perspectives on the fallout and effects of a summer of discontent. What this data illustrates is a citizenry that is largely conflicted on this entire situation. Kentuckians were largely split on Cameron's handling of the grand jury proceedings, with 39 percent of respondents indicating that they believed that he handled things well and 38 percent indicating that he had not handled things well. This is compounded by the fact that, even in the wake of the grand jury's decision, a majority of respondents supported continued investigations into the death of Taylor as well as legislative steps, such as ending the practice of no-knock warrants. However, even in the face of Taylor's controversial death and subsequent support for police reform, respondents still tended to view the protests in a negative light because they believed these protests endangered the lives of police officers. In fact, AP VoteCast (Associated Press, 2020) exit-poll results show that almost two-thirds of respondents disapproved of protests against police violence in the Commonwealth. Not surprisingly, Trump had a five to one advantage among those voters expressing disapproval of the protest. This suggests that, if anything, the protests strengthened Trump's hand in Kentucky as they played nicely into the role he had cast himself into as the "law and order" president.

As expected, Kentucky voters express broad support for many of Donald Trump's policy positions. Economically, roughly two-thirds of survey respondents favored increasing tariffs on imports and reducing regulation on business. Additionally, Trump's positioning of himself as a friend to the coal industry helped him tremendously, particularly in the Eastern part of the state. On several social issues, Trump's positions also sat well with many in this conservative-leaning state. Specifically, respondents were largely supportive of Trump's advocacy for building a wall along the U.S.-Mexican border, as well as his pro-life, and pro-gun positions. Also, in what may come as a surprise to some, Trump held substantive advantages over Biden on a variety of personal characteristics. Overall, voters in the Commonwealth perceived Trump to be more honest, a stronger leader, more empathetic, and more likely to stand up for what he believes in. Essentially, Trump's "say what people are really thinking" approach, which rubbed voters the wrong way in some places worked well for him in Kentucky.

Overall, Donald Trump's easy victory in Kentucky is not particularly surprising. What is more interesting, however, is the intertwined fate between Donald Trump and Senate Majority Leader Mitch McConnell as McConnell was running for his seventh term in the U.S. Senate. In the twenty years following his upset victory over Walter (Dee) Huddleston in 1984, McConnell gained influence in Washington, broadened his support in Kentucky, and built the Republican Party in the Commonwealth. Following his easiest reelection victory over Lois Combs Weinberg in 2002, McConnell was elected as the Majority Whip in the Senate. This followed his role in helping engineer the aforementioned Republican takeover of the Kentucky Senate by helping persuade two Democrats to switch parties. It was shortly after this time that he found himself in the sights of political opponents from the Left and the Right.

Senator McConnell ran almost twelve percentage points worse in his 2008 reelection race against businessman Bruce Lunsford than he had in 2002. Two years later, he saw Secretary of State Trey Grayson, his chosen candidate to replace retiring Senator Jim Bunning, defeated handily by anti-establishment Tea Party candidate Rand Paul. Following Paul's general election victory in November 2010, McConnell and Paul were able to carve out a working political relationship that has proven to be beneficial for both. The payoff for McConnell came in 2014 when Senator Paul endorsed him for reelection over Tea Party businessman Matt Bevin. With the help of an aggressive campaign and the public support of Paul, McConnell was able to inoculate himself from Bevin's primary challenge. He then dispatched Secretary of State Allison Lundergan Grimes easily in November to win a sixth term to the Senate. The 2014 Senate elections also helped him realize a long-time goal to serve as the majority leader for Senate Republicans.

The survival skills on display as McConnell pushed back both a spirited Tea Party primary challenge on the right and a well-funded general election challenge from the left prepared him well to navigate his relationship with Donald Trump. Despite stark contrasts in both style and background, McConnell was able to forge a working relationship with Trump. This relationship laid the groundwork for some of Trump's most substantive successes as a president including the 2017 Tax Cut and Jobs Act. McConnell and Trump also forged a symbiotic relationship to make a long-lasting impact on the federal judiciary, particularly on the Courts of Appeals and the Supreme Court. McConnell's decision to not move forward on Barack Obama's appointment of Merrick Garland to the Court paid significant political dividends in terms of both generating goodwill among more ardent conservatives and cementing McConnell's legacy with regard to helping shape the Court for years to come.

Another dynamic that helped foster the relationship between McConnell and Trump was Trump's appointment of Elaine Chao, Senator McConnell's wife, as Secretary of the Department of Transportation. This was Chao's second time serving in a presidential cabinet, as she previously served as Secretary of the Department of Labor under then President George W. Bush. Reporting on the appointment of Chao indicated that Senator McConnell played a key role in securing the appointment for Secretary Chao. According to Jane Mayer (2020 of *The New Yorker*:

> Mitch McConnell was very important in getting Elaine Chao that job. As soon as Trump was elected, Mitch McConnell was on the phone reaching out to the people in the Trump administration saying, Elaine Chao would like to be the secretary of transportation. And, lo and behold, she got the job.

Chao's appointment as transportation secretary was beneficial to all sides. From McConnell's perspective, the move placed Kentucky in a very favorable spot as it relates to receiving one of the thousands of grants handed out annually by the Department of Transportation. From Trump's perspective, having Chao as part of his Cabinet certainly gave it the gravitas it needed, as many consider Chao to have been one of his most qualified and accomplished appointees. It also provided Trump with one of his most loyal Cabinet officials, with Chao remaining in her position until the bitter end of the Trump administration. It is clear that the mutual benefits promoted a better working relationship between the majority leader and the president.

Perhaps as much as any politician, McConnell has been able to set aside personal feelings to achieve political goals and he was certainly successful in doing so with Trump. McConnell's cultivation of a relationship with Trump strengthened his standing with anti-establishment Republicans, making it easier to maintain political coalitions in the Senate. These dividends also played out electorally. In the AP VoteCast (Associated Press, 2020) survey, only 13 percent of respondents felt that McConnell did not provide enough support for Trump, while 50 percent indicated that it was the right amount. The only token opposition that emerged to challenge McConnell is the Republican primary and he cruised to victory with over 80 percent of the vote.

In the general election, McConnell faced former Navy fighter pilot Amy McGrath. McGrath had lost a close contest in 2018 to incumbent U.S. Representative Andy Barr in Kentucky's Sixth District, which includes Kentucky's second-largest city, Lexington. McGrath was a favorite among national Democrats and ultimately raised almost $90 million to challenge McConnell. While typically underwater in favorability and approval ratings (Jones 2020), he also trailed McGrath in voter perceptions of honesty and caring about average people in a preelection Mason-Dixon poll (Roberts, 2020).

None of this ultimately mattered. As was the case in 2014, McConnell's perceived vulnerability was a mirage. McGrath escaped a surprisingly difficult primary challenge from Louisville-based state legislator Charles Booker and never found her footing for the general election. Much of McGrath's damage was self-inflicted, but McConnell and his campaign team were able to magnify her early mistakes to coast to an easy November victory. McConnell posted the second-largest winning margin of his seven Senate victories and defeated McGrath by 19.5 percentage points. As he did in 2014, he won 117 of the 120 counties across the state. In addition to losses in Jefferson County (Louisville) and Fayette County (Lexington), McConnell lost Franklin County, which is the home of the state capital Frankfort.

The Trump factor has also played some role in reshaping the Kentucky House of Representatives. Republicans were able to pick up seventeen seats in 2016 to win majority control of the House for the first time in almost one hundred years. After losing three seats in the 2018 midterm and special elections, Republicans rebounded in 2020 by winning an additional fourteen seats propelling them to a supermajority in the House with seventy-five out of one hundred seats. Republican domination at all levels of Kentucky politics suggests that the nationalization of Kentucky politics is almost complete. With just a couple of exceptions in the Eastern part of the state, rural Democrats are extinct. The legislature now has just a single Democrat representing a district west of Interstate 65, which runs from Louisville to Nashville. Patti Minter, a liberal history professor, represents the Twentieth District in Bowling Green that is the home of Western Kentucky University. Commentators in the state have joked that Minter would have to drive at least two hours to find a colleague in the Kentucky House of Representatives that shares her political beliefs. Odds are that once redistricting is completed following the 2020 Census, she will have a significantly less friendly district to run in.

If there was a surprise in the 2020 results in Kentucky, it was the strength of Republicans in suburban areas. This illustrates both the strength of Trump and the Republican Party overall in the Commonwealth, as this pattern is vastly different than the suburban trends we saw nationwide. Republicans in Louisville, Lexington, and Northern Kentucky who appeared to be at risk heading into the general election all survived and many won with comfortable margins. Public reaction to the protests and unrest in Louisville played to the advantage of Republicans in these suburban districts. Most notably, Ken Fleming regained his Forty-Eighth District House seat in northeast Jefferson County. Absent redistricting, the odds are some of the Republican successes in suburban districts are a one-election reprieve. Redistricting will be a wild card. Republicans will control the redistricting process for state House districts for the first time in history. This will provide them an opportunity to bolster the electoral fortunes of vulnerable candidates for 2022. The ultimate question is how much flexibility they will find to reconfigure friendlier districts in these areas.

Another interesting emergence in the aftermath of the 2020 campaign is Senate Bill 228, which is currently making its way through the Kentucky Senate (Storm, 2021; Williams 2021). This bill would dramatically alter how potential vacancies in the U.S. Senate are filled. Current law allows the sitting governor to choose whomever he or she wants to fill the seat. The purpose of this new legislation is to change that process. Instead of the governor having total freedom to choose a replacement, that duty would fall to the executive committee of the party of the vacant Senate seat. The committee would choose three nominees from which the governor would then be compelled to choose. Critics of the legislation have charged that this is solely being discussed so that McConnell could have an exit strategy if necessary, in the face of a Democratic governor. Supporters argue that, while McConnell indeed supports the legislation, the discussion began following the assault of Rand Paul by Rene Boucher, which led to Senator Paul having to undergo multiple surgeries. The legislation is currently under consideration during the shorter thirty-day legislative session and is not guaranteed to pass, but it is certainly an interesting development.

CONCLUSION

As American politics becomes increasingly nationalized, interstate distinctiveness is decreasing. The urban/rural divide plays a much larger role in defining American politics than regional differences. Kentucky is no different, it is simply more rural than most states, which means the short- to mid-term prospects continue to be very favorable for Republicans. They hold supermajorities in both chambers of the General Assembly and almost all major elected offices in the state. They also boast a deep bench of potential candidates to run for governor and U.S. senator in the future. Treasurer Alison Ball, Agriculture Commissioner Ryan Quarles, and Attorney General Daniel Cameron head a strong list of potential candidates for higher office. Of course, there are never enough chairs available when playing political musical chairs.

As is often the case when one party dominates state politics, meaningful debates occur within parties rather than between them. This used to be the case in Kentucky where much of the political intrigue centered on factions within the Democratic Party. It is now the Republicans' turn. Although they avoid direct engagement in the factional fight, Kentucky's U.S. senators clearly represent the two factions that will struggle for control of Kentucky politics in the upcoming decade. While Mitch McConnell is the quintessential member of the establishment, Rand Paul's victory in 2010 legitimized Tea Party and anti-establishment candidates. In many ways, Trump's base expanded the Tea Party base by integrating with anti-establishment Christian conservatives. Variations of this divide within the Kentucky Republican Party have played out over the past ten years and have been exposed once again following the Capitol riots and Trump's second impeachment trial. Establishment Republicans continue to hold a firm grasp on the state party organization, but several county organizations have vented their displeasure at Senator McConnell's perceived betrayal of former President Trump. This has led to a handful of county organizations voting to censure McConnell and calling on him to resign. While unlikely to faze Senator McConnell, there is a real and meaningful philosophical split in the party that is brewing and will play out over the near future.

While the immediate future of the Kentucky Democratic Party is bleak, they will be able to play in the suburban districts over the next decade. Their path to success in these districts will be determined largely by the behavior of the national parties and the outcome of upcoming redistricting. The one glimmer of hope for Kentucky Democrats is long-term demographic change in the state. Democratic candidates are performing better in counties that are growing the fastest in the Commonwealth. This includes the Golden Triangle, which connects Louisville, Lexington, and Northern Kentucky suburbs of Cincinnati and the Interstate 65 corridor running from Louisville to Bowling Green. Oldham County, located just east of Jefferson County and the wealthiest county in Kentucky, was long among the most Republican of Kentucky counties but has seen Democrats increasing vote share in recent elections. The same holds true for Warren County, located on Interstate 65, in Southern Kentucky. Warren County has seen steady growth and is starting to trend less Republican relative to the rest of the state. Warren County was the fifth-best county in the state for Joe Biden. Unfortunately for Democrats, he still received less than 42 percent of the two-party vote in November. Ultimately, this is not much consolation for Kentucky Democrats as there will be plenty of time for both parties to adapt and evolve. In the end, perhaps the most consequential question will be just exactly how long the Republican Party will remain the party of Trump.

NOTE

1. For thorough coverage of the killing of Breonna Taylor, see the *Louisville Courier Journal* from the spring and summer of 2020, especially the work of Tessa Duvall and Phillip Bailey.

REFERENCES

Alford, Roger (2006). "Deal Struck to End Case Against Fletcher – Governor Must Now Try to Rebuild His Reputation." *The Kentucky Post.*
Associated Press (2020). "AP VoteCast: Kentucky Voters Mixed on State of Nation." https://apnews.com/article/joe-biden-donald-trump-virus-outbreak-health-kentucky-b1a6cad5ec392701bab6688214e38200.
Bailey, Phillip (2020). "Sins of Our Past: After 84 Years, Jefferson Davis Statue Removed From Kentucky Capitol." *Louisville Courier Journal.*
Binnix, Erika, Joel Turner, Scott Lasley, and Jeffrey P. Kash (2019). "The Great Divide: The Political Implications of Southern Regional Identification in Kentucky." *The Commonwealth Review of Political Science.*
Jones, Matt and Chris Tomlin (2020). *Mitch Please: How Mitch McConnell Sold Out Kentucky (and America, Too).* Simon and Schuster.
Kolb, Chris (2020). "Kentucky's Democratic Party Should Disband. It Has No Soul to Search or Vision to Offer." *Louisville Courier Journal.*

Loftus, Tom (2018). "Bevin Attacks Teachers Union, Says Adults Need to Behave on Social Media." *Louisville Courier Journal.*

Mayer, Jane (2020). "How Mitch McConnell Became Donald Trump's Enabler-in-Chief." *The New Yorker.*

Newall, Mallory and Sara Machi (2020). "Kentuckians Give AG Cameron Mixed Reviews Over Breonna Taylor Case." https://www.ipsos.com/en-us/news-polls/spectrumnetworks-statepolling-KY.

Roberts, Brandon (2020). "Mason-Dixon Poll Shows Kentucky Strongly Supports Trump." https://spectrumnews1.com/ky/lexington/news/2020/10/23/mason-dixon-poll-for-kentucky.

Storm, Nick (2021). "Mitch McConnell Working With Kentucky Legislature on Senate Exit Strategy." *The Intercept.*

Turner, Joel, Scott Lasley, Jeffrey P. Kash, and Scott Buchanan (2020). "The Political Implications of Southern Regional Identification in Kentucky, Missouri, and West Virginia." Presented at The Citadel Symposium on Southern Politics, Charleston, SC.

Williams, Chris (2021). "Kentucky Lawmakers Debate Changing How to Replace U.S. Senators Who Don't Finish Their Term." https://www.whas11.com/article/news/politics/kentucky-lawmakers-debate-how-replace-us-senators-unfinished-term/417-13f2f104-6c43-4826-a3bc-f25910930cdc.

Chapter 11

North Carolina
Even More Deeply Divided in 2020
J. Michael Bitzer

North Carolina's recent political environment can best be described in two distinct periods: before and after 2008. From the mid-1980s up to 2004's presidential election, North Carolina's modern political environment settled into a fairly reliable pattern, with Republicans winning the majority of federal contests, while at the same time Democrats securing the state-wide executive offices and controlling the state legislature (Prysby 2009; Bitzer 2021). This was the usual pattern in North Carolinian politics due to the presence of a large swath of ticket-splitting voters (Fleer 1994, 162–163; Kazee 1998) and the paradox of Tar Heel politics (Luebke 1998; Christensen 2008). For example, 2004's election saw Republican presidential incumbent George W. Bush win the state by twelve percentage points, while in the same election, Democratic incumbent governor Mike Easley won his reelection bid by twelve percentage points (Prysby 2007, 163).

However, 2008 marked a significant shift in the state's politics. While generally retaining its red federal and blue state dynamic, North Carolinian elections have become much more intense and competitive. The key reasons to this increased intensity and competitiveness were the after-effects of the 2008 and 2010 elections, which appear to have nationalized and polarized North Carolinian voters into their respective partisan camps. In 2008, Barack Obama shifted the normally Republican-safe presidential state into a half-point victory for the Democrats, breaking the Republican presidential streak of winning the Tar Heel state since 1980. The 2008 election also saw Democrats pick up one of the state's U.S. Senate seats, when Kay Hagan defeated incumbent Republican Elizabeth Dole by a larger margin than Obama secured. That same election saw history made in the state, with Beverly Perdue elected the first female governor in North Carolina's history.

Democrats swept the state's top three contests, something the party had not accomplished since 1960.

Yet the political pendulum swung back to the Republicans with the 2010 elections, fueled by the Tea Party insurgency within the Republican Party and the party's capture of the state legislature that controlled redistricting. Since these two elections, North Carolina's politics appear to retain their red federal and blue state dynamics, but state-wide elections with a margin of victory greater than five percentage points are now considered landslides. Some recent elections have provided variations to the "red-blue competitive" hues, but the post-2008 and 2010 competitive dynamics have continued to entrench themselves into the state's political landscape.

The 2012 election saw not just the Republicans reclaim the presidential contest by a two-point margin of victory, but also captured the governorship by an eleven-point margin . In 2014's mid-term, the U.S. Senate seat, acquired six years prior by the Democrats, flipped back to Republican control by one-and-a-half points. The 2016 election saw North Carolina resume its trademark federal red with Republicans holding the presidential and U.S. Senate contests, while Democrats brought about the first defeat of a sitting incumbent governor vying for a second term. In the state's 2018 blue-moon election (with no major state-wide contest), the national Democratic wave did not materialize, although the state witnessed a significant issue of electoral fraud in the Ninth Congressional contest (Gardner 2019). Most recently, the 2020 election played again to the same song that has been the historic tune of North Carolina's politics: red federal and blue state. The dynamics of North Carolina's politics continue to the reflect the paradox that many observers contend is the hallmark of Tar Heel politics (Luebke 1998; Christensen 2008), from the late twentieth century into the first two decades of the new millennium.

This chapter analyzes the 2020 election cycle in North Carolina, which made history for its turnout among registered voters and the election of an African American as the state's number two executive officer. Beyond the electoral contests themselves, this chapter focuses on the turnout and demographic dynamics that have contributed to North Carolina's intensely competitive and divided politics. Even in the midst of a pandemic, North Carolina's voters were mobilized and energized up and down the ballot for a host of competitive elections.

THE MARCH PRIMARY

Held on Super Tuesday, North Carolina's 2020 presidential primary on March 3rd saw fifteen Democrats on the ballot, while on the Republican primary ballot, there was only token opposition to President Donald Trump and U.S. Senator Thom Tillis. Trump secured 93.5 percent of the vote, while Tillis garnered 78 percent for his renomination.[1] On the Democratic side, the major question for Super Tuesday's contests focused on whether former Vice President Joe Biden could revive his campaign with a win in South Carolina after disappointing finishes in Iowa (fourth), New Hampshire (fifth), and Nevada (a distant second). Following U.S. Representative Jim Clyburn's critical endorsement in the South Carolina primary, Biden's campaign got a significant boost three days before Super Tuesday's contests, especially in North Carolina. One can look at the voting methods and results in the Tar Heel state to see the potential dynamics of how important the South Carolina win was for Biden.

North Carolina's voters have three primary methods for casting ballots: absentee by mail, which begins forty-five days before the election, with the last ballots mailed out a week prior to Election Day; absentee one-stop, which is "early in-person voting" that started February 13th and ended Saturday prior to the Tuesday, March 3rd election; and Election Day voting. With South Carolina's February 29th primary held the same day as North Carolina's last day of absentee one-stop voting, the voting methods give a sense of the boost that Biden got after his Palmetto State victory. As noted in table 11.1, among the absentee by mail ballots (which constituted only one percent of the total votes cast), Bernie Sanders received 27 percent to Biden's 25 percent. Among the absentee one-stop (38 percent of total ballots cast),

Table 11.1   2020 North Carolina Democratic Primary Election Results by Vote Methods and Primary Electorate Composition of Voters Casting Ballots by Party Registration and Race

Results:	Absentee by Mail	Absentee One-Stop	Election Day	Total
Biden	25	28	52	43
Sanders	27	24	24	24
Bloomberg	14	18	10	13
Warren	16	12	9	11
Buttigieg	9	8	0	3
All others	9	10	4	6
Voting Method Composition:				
Registered Democrats	68	72	70	71
Registered Unaffiliated	31	27	30	29
White	73	58	57	57
Black/African American	13	33	34	33

Note: Numbers are percentages.
Source: Data from Voter Registration and Vote History files from the NC State Board of Elections website https://www.ncsbe.gov/results-data

Biden led with 28 percent to Sanders's 24. However, on Super Tuesday, with 60 percent of the primary's ballots cast that day, Biden won 52 percent to Sanders's 24. While registered Democrats made up seven-out-of-ten primary voters, the primary saw a diverse electorate, with one-third of Democratic primary voters being African-American and 57 percent White. Biden walked away from North Carolina's primary with 43 percent of the vote and 68 of the state's 110 delegates.

Both parties saw spirited primary nomination contests down the ballot. The Democratic Party's U.S. Senate nomination battle pitted former one-term state senator Cal Cunningham against three-term state senator Erica Smith, along with three other candidates. Cunningham was the consensus candidate from Washington, aided by Chuck Shumer's fundraising operation. Smith sought to appeal to the party's more liberal wing with progressive stances on health care and the Green New Deal, but in the end, Cunningham secured 56 percent of the Democratic primary vote to Smith's 35 percent. In the Republican primary, the contests for both governor and lieutenant governor were contested. Sitting Republican Lieutenant Governor Dan Forest defeated state senator Holly Grange with 89 percent. Forest would challenge incumbent Democratic governor Roy Cooper in the general election. Nine Republicans vied for lieutenant governor, with first-time candidate Mark Robinson, an African American grass-roots activist, securing the Republican nomination over more well-known Republicans, including state superintendent of public instruction Mark Johnson and former U.S. Representative Renee Ellmers. Six candidates vied for the Democratic lieutenant governor nomination, which was secured by Yvonne Lewis Holley, an African American state senator. Holley secured 27 percent of the primary vote, below the thirty-percent threshold, but the second-place candidate, fellow state senator Terry Van Duyn, chose not to call for a runoff. The Robinson-Holley contest would make history in the state by being the first African American to be elected lieutenant governor.

The state's major congressional nomination battle was in the western Eleventh Congressional District, an open-seat contest due to the appointment of former U.S. Representative Mark Meadows as the White House Chief of Staff. The Republican-leaning district saw a crowded GOP field with twelve candidates. Ultimately, Republicans Lynda Bennett and Madison Cawthorn finished first and second, respectively, but Bennett failed to secure the needed 30 percent threshold to avoid a second, runoff primary election. During the primary, Bennett had the backing of both the White House and Meadows, with supportive tweets from President Donald Trump. Cawthorn, who would turn twenty-five years old during the fall campaign, also positioned himself as a Trump supporter. In the June 23 runoff, Cawthorn won the nomination with 65.8 percent of the vote over Bennett, where only 12 percent of the district's eligible voters showed up to cast ballots. Out of five Democratic candidates, Moe Davis, a former prosecutor of the Guantanamo military commissions, secured his party's nomination with 47 percent to face Cawthorn. Cawthorn would come under scrutiny for embellishments of his campaign narrative, and the campaign became one of the most negative races in the state, drawing more than five million dollars between the two candidates (Chemtob 2020).

The other closely watched congressional districts were the redrawn Second and Sixth Districts. Following a state court ruling in September 2019 that struck down state legislative districts as violating the state constitution's "free and fair elections" clause as partisan gerrymanders (Sonmez and Barnes 2019) and a subsequent ruling that intimated that the congressional districts were also suspect (Ax 2019), the state legislature redrew the congressional districts, specifically moving the second and sixth into urban areas. Once formerly safe Republican districts, the Second District shifted into Wake County, home to the state's capital of Raleigh, while the Sixth District shifted into Guilford County, home to Greensboro, and neighboring Forsyth County, home to Winston-Salem. Both became districts where Hillary Clinton would have won with 60 percent of the 2016 vote.[2] Ultimately, two female Democratic candidates with previous campaign experience won their party's nomination: Kathy Manning, who had run previously for the Thirteenth Congressional District, won the Sixth District nomination, while Deborah Ross, who had been the Democrat's 2016 U.S. Senate candidate, secured the Second District's nomination.

THE PRESIDENTIAL ELECTION

Once again, North Carolina was seen as a competitive battleground state, with the top-three contests—presidential, U.S. Senate, and governor's races—drawing national attention. At the presidential level, the state was seen as a critical state for Trump to keep in his electoral win column than necessarily for Biden. Since Reagan's elections, Republican presidential candidates built their electoral campaigns around a Southern strategy of a solidly red presidential region (Black and Black 1992, 2003). But cracks in the Republican solid presidential South became evident in 2008 (Kapeluck, Moreland, and Steed 2009). As Virginia has trended more Democratic over the past few elections (McGlennon 2014), Republican resources and time were spent in the battleground states of Florida (a traditional competitive state) and North Carolina, new to the competitive status since 2008, along with the surprising state of Georgia. One measure of this interest in keeping North Carolina red were the ten trips by Trump, and eight by Mike Pence, to the state during the general campaign season, even during the COVID-19 pandemic.³ By comparison, Biden made three trips and Kamala Harris made five stops to the state. Granted, the fewer Democratic trips to the state was reflective of the Biden's campaign of taking into consideration the pandemic and limiting public events.

Another indicator of Republican interest in North Carolina was the selection of Charlotte for the Republican National Convention (Seipel 2018). But in the midst of the pandemic, Trump and the RNC threatened to pull the convention when the state did not agree to the president's plans to have a full convention crowd without state-required public health measures in place (Haberman 2020). Attention quickly shifted to where the RNC would hold their proceedings, with Jacksonville, Florida, being named the new site just three months before the convention (Morrill, Funk, and Murphy 2020). However, the pandemic forced the cancellation of the Jacksonville venue (Haberman, Mazzei, and Karni 2020), and Charlotte hosted a shortened meeting to formally renominate Trump, with most of the convention's other activities occurring in Washington, D.C., and virtually.

A significant example of resources committed to North Carolina was the amount of spending done by both candidates and their campaigns. According to the Center for Responsive Politics, the Biden campaign spent over $20 million in North Carolina, with the Trump campaign devoting $16.2 million.⁴ Biden's largest share (41 percent) was spent in the state's capital region of Raleigh-Durham-Chapel Hill, with another 20 percent in the Charlotte-Gastonia-Rock Hill area. Along with the state's Triad region of Greensboro-Winston-Salem-High Point (10 percent) and the Norfolk-Virginia Beach-Newport News region (13 percent), Biden spent nearly 85 percent of his total in those four regions. In comparison, Trump's spending was slightly more diffused: 22 percent in the Charlotte area, 19 percent in Raleigh, 15 percent in Norfolk, 14 percent in Greensboro, and the remaining 30 percent spread across the rest of the state. Among all candidates and PACs in the 2020 cycle, North Carolina saw over $168 million contributed, with 49.8 percent going to Democrats and 48.3 percent going to Republicans.

Throughout the fall campaign, public opinion polls in North Carolina indicated a highly competitive contest. Between May and November, the widest lead that Biden held was less than 5 percentage points, while Trump would only see a one-percentage point lead in the early summer. Trump would never break 50 percent in the polls, while Biden would manage a high of 52 percent.⁵ In the end, the final RealClearPolitics average for North Carolina showed Trump at 47.8 to Biden's 47.6, a statistical dead-heat. Ultimately Trump bested his polling average by 2 points, winning the state with 49.93 percent of the total vote, while Biden added one point to his polling average in the final results. Trump secured North Carolina's 15 electoral votes by the closest margin of any state he won, with a two-party vote margin of 1.3 percent.

The presidential election results yielded interesting patterns across the state. One notable pattern was the difference in results by vote methods. As shown later in this chapter, North Carolina's voters' use of different methods has changed over time as well as which political party utilizes these vote methods. Table 11.2 demonstrates the presidential two-party vote results and the clear differences between how North Carolina partisans utilized the three vote methods. Biden's 72 percent among absentee by mail votes showed that Democratic voters used that method amidst the COVID-19 pandemic. For Republican voters, their preference was voting on Election Day, where Trump won with two-thirds of that vote method. It was among the early in-person (absentee one-stop) voting method that Republicans generally garnered a slight advantage in "winning" that method, with the exception of Democratic Roy Cooper tying Republican Dan Forest in the governor's race. It is also notable that the top-three ballot races tended to see similar results in the evenly-divided races, with the Democratic governor performing best in the three vote methods.

Other aspects of North Carolina's politics are variations on different national narratives, one of which is the urban versus rural divide, with the suburbs being battleground areas for both parties. In order to capture these "regions," a classification system utilized the Office of Management and Budget's 2020 Memo regarding the state's Metropolitan Statistical Areas (MSAs). Urban counties were based on the MSAs' principal cities, while the other counties within the various MSA were designated as suburban, with the remaining counties considered rural.[6] In classifying North Carolina's one-hundred counties, nineteen are urban counties with principal cities, thirty-one are suburban, and the remaining fifty are rural. Table 11.3 provides the total

Table 11.2 2020 North Carolina General Election Two-Party Results by Vote Methods for President, U.S. Senate, and Governor

Election	Candidates	Absentee by Mail Results	Absentee One-Stop Results	Election Day Results	Total Results
Presidential	Trump	28	53	67	51
	Biden	72	47	33	49
U.S. Senate	Tillis	30	53	66	51
	Cunningham	70	47	34	49
Governor	Cooper	75	50	38	52
	Forest	25	50	62	48

Source: Data from the NC State Board of Elections website https://www.ncsbe.gov/results-data

Table 11.3 Trump and Biden Two-Party Vote Totals and Percentages within North Carolina Regions

	Trump 2020	Biden 2020
Urban Counties	1,183,790 (40%)	1,759,764 (60%)
Suburban Counties	942,040 (64%)	521,833 (36%)
Rural Counties	632,946 (61%)	402,706 (39%)
State	2,758,776 (51%)	2,684,303 (49%)

Source: North Carolina State Board of Elections website https://www.ncsbe.gov/results-data.

two-party votes (and percentages) received by Trump and Biden in each of the three regions.

While the overall state two-party vote reflects a closely divided environment of 51–49, the three regions reflect lop-sided dynamics. Biden won urban counties with 60 percent of the vote, while Trump won suburban and rural counties with 64 and 61 percent, respectively. Thus, North Carolina's "regional" divide could be considered "urban versus everyone else."

One can take a deeper look at this urban/rest-of-the-state divide through precinct results, especially by dividing urban counties into two distinct areas: the central cities and the "urban suburbs," which are outside of the central city's limits but inside the urban county. When evaluated within this four-region aspect, a unique dynamic is very evident, as shown by the percentage of votes for Trump and Biden in table 11.4.

In comparing these percentages to the same dynamics in 2016, the central city precincts were even more Democratic (Clinton received 68 percent of the vote). In 2016, the urban suburbs were a 50–50 split between Trump

Table 11.4 Trump and Biden Two-Party Vote Percentages within North Carolina's Four Regions

	Trump	Biden	Tillis	Cunningham	Forest	Cooper
Central Cities	30	70	31	69	27	73
Urban Suburbs	54	46	55	45	51	49
Surrounding Suburban Counties	64	36	64	36	61	39
Rural Counties	61	39	60	40	58	42
State	51	49	51	49	48	52

Note: Numbers reflect two-party vote percentages. Calculated by the author.
Source: Data from Voter Registration and Precinct Results files from the NC State Board of Elections website https://www.ncsbe.gov/results-data

and Clinton, yet Trump managed a 54-46 win in 2020. Biden also managed a two-percentage-point increase over Clinton's performance in surrounding suburban counties and held the same as Clinton in rural county precincts.

One other analysis of precinct election data can illuminate the state's political divide based on geography. In this analysis, individual precincts were categorized into different groups: precincts with results that saw one political party receive more than 60 percent of the vote; precincts with 55-59 percent for one party; and precincts with 50-54 percent. Out of the nearly 2,700 precincts across the state, 40 percent of the precincts went for Trump by 60 percent or more, with another 30 percent going for Biden by 60 percent or more. Among the 55-59 percent precincts, 8.5 percent went for Trump, with 7 percent for Biden. In total, more than 85 percent of the state's precincts saw results for one candidate at 55 percent or greater, with a little over 6 percent of the "competitive" precincts going for Biden and 7 percent going for Trump. This political geography of few competitive precincts, while seven-out-of-ten precincts went heavily for one party, demonstrates the dynamic of lop-sided regions combining to make a competitive state.

U.S. SENATE AND HOUSE ELECTIONS

The U.S. Senate contest between incumbent Republican Thom Tillis and Democrat Cal Cunningham was one of the nation's most-watched races, with some considering the contest to be a deciding race as to which political party would control the upper chamber of Congress. It would also be considered one of the most expensive U.S. Senate races in 2020's general election, barring the two runoff races in Georgia. According to Federal Election Commission (FEC) data, Cunningham raised and spent $52.5 million, while Tillis raised and spent over $26 million. However, the bulk of the money came from outside groups, notably from political action committees aligned with Senate Republican Leader Mitch McConnell and Democratic Leader Chuck Schumer. Nearly $215 million in independent expenditures was spent on the race, with 80 percent of it opposing a candidate.

Polling showed Cunningham leading throughout the general campaign, with a 10-point margin at the end of July. However, by the middle of October, Cunningham's lead had shrunk to within the margins of error for many polls. This was likely due to news that broke at the beginning of October for both campaigns, with one news story impacting the race much more than the other.

After Tillis attended the September 26 White House announcement of Trump's U.S. Supreme Court nominee Amy Coney Barrett (where he was wearing a mask), the Republican senator tested positive for the coronavirus on Friday, October 2, and isolated himself from the campaign trail (Murphy

2020). Later that same night, Cunningham's campaign acknowledged that the candidate had "sent text messages of a sexual nature to a woman who was not his wife," and subsequently that Cunningham did have an intimate relationship with a California public relations strategist. Following the revelation, Cunningham chose not to campaign in-person, instead doing video campaign events and generally avoiding the press. Polls at the time indicated that a small minority believed that the extramarital affairs were important: an ABC News/Washington Post survey on October 20 showed only 26 percent said the affair was "very" or "extremely" important, while 50 percent said it was "not so" important. But the revelation in the last month of the campaign, in what was considered an extremely tight race, was thought to have done some damage to the Democratic candidate.

By November 3, the polling average ended with Cunningham with 47.6 to Tillis's 45 percent, a statistical dead-heat. The final result demonstrated the tightness of the election, with Tillis winning 48.7 percent to Cunningham's 46.9 percent; as was the case in the presidential race, it was another 51–49 two-party split. As noted in table 11.2, Cunningham's vote was consistent with Biden's vote in both absentee one-stop and Election Day results, while running two points behind Biden among absentee by mail vote results. But within the state's four regions, differences between Biden's and Cunningham's performances are apparent (see table 11.4). Biden ran ahead of Cunningham in both the central cities and the urban suburbs. While they both received the same percentage in surrounding suburban counties, Cunningham edged Biden's performance by one point in rural counties.

Following a 2019 state court decision that partisan gerrymandering violated the state constitution's "free and fair elections" and the equal protection clauses (Baier and Tiberii 2019), the North Carolinian General Assembly redrew the congressional district maps. Among the state's thirteen congressional districts, one served as the most closely watched at the national level, while two one-seat races were considered as likely Democratic gains and two others were potential competitive races. National attention was focused on the Eleventh Congressional District, centered in the western mountains of the state. The race between Republican Madison Cawthorn and Democrat Moe Davis became an intensely polarized contest. Cawthorn garnered national attention among Republican candidates, seen as a potential GOP counter to the Democrat's Alexandria Ocasio-Cortez. Cawthorn's national profile increased as a primetime speaker at the virtual RNC, but with the attention came accusations of racism, sexual misconduct, and ties to white supremacy. One instance involved a car accident that left him paralyzed in a wheelchair at eighteen years old. Cawthorn had claimed the accident was the reason for not being able to attend the Naval Academy when, in fact, he had been denied admission prior to the accident. Another was a public letter, signed by more than 150 former Patrick Henry College schoolmates of Cawthorn's, that called into question his character and allegations of sexual misconduct during his one semester attending the conservative Christian institution (Fiedler 2020). Cawthorn and his campaign hit back at the accusations, seeking to energize the base as Democratic energy in the GOP-leaning district intensified as well. Davis also had to defend himself regarding "aggressive, sometimes profane tweets" that the candidate had sent prior to his campaign (Chemtob 2020). In the end, both parties' "bases" were highly energized: in a district that saw a 77 percent registered voter turnout rate (2 points higher than the state's rate), 81 percent of registered Republicans and 79 percent of registered Democrats in the eleventh voted, while 73 percent of registered unaffiliated voters cast ballots. Cawthorn won the election with 54.5 percent of the vote against Davis and two other candidates, matching Trump's performance in the district at 55 percent.[7]

In the open-seat districts considered potential Democratic flips, the alignment of presidential voting and congressional candidate voting again showed a close relationship. In the reconfigured Second Congressional District, Democrat Deborah Ross secured 63 percent of the vote, in line with Biden's 64 percent in the district as well. In the redrawn Sixth Congressional District, Democrat Kathy Manning won with 62 percent of the vote, also matching Biden's performance. In two other Republican-held districts that generated national interest, both the eighth and ninth saw Democratic candidates

Table 11.5   North Carolina 2020 U.S. House Election Results, for Republican Presidential and Congressional Candidates

District	Trump %	GOP Congressional Candidate %	Outcome
1	45.3	45.8	Democratic incumbent reelected
2	34.0	34.8	Open seat; Democratic elected from previous Republican-held
3	60.9	63.3	Republican incumbent reelected
4	32.2	32.6	Democratic incumbent reelected
5	67.4	66.9	Republican incumbent reelected
6	37.2	37.7	Open seat; Democratic elected from previous Republican-held
7	58.1	60.3	Republican incumbent reelected
8	52.5	53.2	Republican incumbent reelected
9	53.4	55.6	Republican incumbent reelected
10	67.7	68.9	Republican incumbent reelected
11	55.4	54.5	Open seat; Republican-held
12	28.5	no GOP candidate	Democratic incumbent reelected
13	67.1	68.2	Republican incumbent reelected

Source: North Carolina State Board of Elections website https://www.ncsbe.gov/results-data.

break into "competitive," but ultimately, unsuccessful attempts to defeat Republican incumbents. Republican Richard Hudson of the eighth won with 53 percent of the vote against former North Carolina's associate justice Patricia Timmons-Goodson, while Republican Dan Bishop won with 56 percent of the vote against Democratic newcomer Cynthia Wallace. Both Hudson's and Bishop's performances mirrored Trump's performance in the state, as shown in table 11.5.

With the exception of the Twelfth Congressional District that had no Republican candidate opposing Democratic incumbent Alma Adams, each district's Trump vote and the GOP congressional candidate's vote percentages were very close, indicating a nationalization effect of presidential and congressional voting patterns (Hopkins 2018).

STATE ELECTIONS

As one of the few states in the nation that holds a gubernatorial race in presidential election years, North Carolina's race for governor would highlight the top of the ticket in terms of competitive races. In 2016, Democrat Roy Cooper defeated incumbent Republican Pat McCrory by a little more than 10,000 votes, marking both one of the closest elections to that point in the state and the first time a sitting NC governor had been defeated in an election bid.[8] When Cooper defeated McCrory in 2016, Republican lieutenant governor Dan Forest was seen as the leading candidate to challenge Cooper in 2020. A staunch social conservative who was elected in his first run for public office as the state's lieutenant governor in 2012, Forest campaigned on reopening the state and challenging the Cooper's decisions regarding the COVID-19 pandemic.

Like the presidential and U.S. Senate contests, the governor's race attracted significant amounts of money. Cooper ultimately raised and spent more than $40 million, compared to Forest's $11 million. Polling for the race showed Cooper with a consistent double-digit lead throughout the campaign, while Forest never peaked above 44 percent. One important polling aspect that remained consistent throughout the campaign was Cooper's job approval numbers, which were generally in the mid-to-upper fifties. This approval rating may have been related to Cooper's response to the coronavirus pandemic. In a September SurveyUSA Poll conducted for WRAL-TV in Raleigh, 58 percent of North Carolinians approved or strongly approved of the governor's COVID-19 response.[9] While most analysts believed the gubernatorial race was a Democratic-leaning contest, in the end, the results came close to being in line with the other top two races, though Cooper garnered 51.5 percent of the vote (the two-party vote was Cooper 52 to Forest 48).

Along with the governor's office, North Carolina elects nine other executive officers, collectively known as the Council of State offices. In the historic contest of two African American candidates for lieutenant governor, Republican Mark Robinson, in his first campaign, defeated Democratic state senator Yvonne Lewis Holley 51.6 to 48.4 percent. Democrats held on to their control of the attorney general, auditor, and secretary of state, while Republican incumbents won as commissioner of agriculture and treasurer. Three offices were open-seat elections, with Republicans sweeping the commissioner of insurance, commissioner of labor, and superintendent of public instruction. In tallying all Council of State state-wide votes, Republicans garnered 51 percent of the total votes to Democrats' 49 percent.

North Carolina also elects justices and judges in partisan elections. Before the election, Democrats controlled the state's supreme court, holding six seats to one Republican. Following the departure of Republican Chief Justice Mark Martin, Democrat Cheri Beasley was appointed by Governor Cooper as the first African American woman to serve as chief justice, by-passing the senior associate justice Paul Newby, the lone Republican on the court (Doran 2019). Newby subsequently challenged Beasley, and the contest ended being the closest election in modern North Carolina history, with Newby beating Beasley by only 401 votes out of over 5.3 million cast. Republicans also defeated Democrats to capture two associate justice seats on the high court, bringing the court to a 4–3 Democratic control.

While not garnering the attention that the top of the ticket ballot races generated, the battle for the North Carolina General Assembly was intensely fought, with control of the redistricting process in 2021 being the major prize for whoever controlled the legislature. One critical aspect of the 2020 election was the 2019 redistricting that brought about new legislative district lines for several counties in both chambers, following a state court decision striking down the maps as partisan gerrymanders. Republicans controlled 65 seats going into the election in the 120-member state house, with 29 out of 50 seats in the state senate. Several of the redrawn districts were in urban and suburban counties, with Democrats hopeful to capture at least one of the chambers, and thus have a seat at the redistricting table. In the end, however, Democrats were only able to pick up one seat in the Senate, while losing a net total of four house seats. Republicans failed to regain their supermajorities, as they had in the early 2010s, and thus were deprived of the necessary votes to override gubernatorial vetoes (table 11.6).

Table 11.6 2004–2020 North Carolina Presidential General Elections, Percentage of Total Ballots Cast by Vote Methods

	2004	2008	2012	2016	2020
Total Ballots Cast	3,551,675	4,354,052	4,540,583	4,769,640	5,545,847
Registered Voter Turnout	64	69.5	68.3	69	75.4
% by Absentee by Mail	0	5	5	4	18
% by Absentee OneStop	31	56	56	60	65
% by Election Day	67	38	38	33	16

	Registered Democrats	Registered Unaffiliated	Registered Republicans	All other parties	State Total
Turnout Rate	75	70	81	63	75
Absentee by Mail	23	20	11	16	18
Absentee One-Stop	65	62	69	58	65
Election Day	12	17	19	25	16

Note: Remaining vote method percentages include provisional/transfers.
Source: Data from Voter Registration and Vote History files from the NC State Board of Elections website https://www.ncsbe.gov/results-data.

DEMOGRAPHIC DYNAMICS AND TURNOUT RATES

Since 2008's election, North Carolina has averaged a registered voter turnout rate of 69 percent in presidential election years. Between 2008 and 2016, North Carolina generally added 200,000 more voters casting ballots than the previous presidential election, with expectations that in 2020, that typical increase would be exceeded. But with the interest and enthusiasm generated, even in the midst of a pandemic, over 775,000 more voters participated in 2020 from 2016's 4.7 million. The 5.5 million registered voters casting a ballot in 2020 represented a turnout rate of 75 percent. The last time such a jump in actual voters occurred was between 2004's 3.5 million and 2008's 4.3 million.

With North Carolina State Board of Elections' data for both voter registration and voter history, analysis can demonstrate who participated in the election by several factors. Among party registrations, North Carolina's total pool of 7.3 million registered voters was 36 percent registered Democrats, 33 percent registered unaffiliated voters, and 30 percent registered Republicans, with the remainder being party registrations among Libertarian, Green, and Constitution parties. Among the three major party registration, Republicans had the highest turnout rate at 81 percent, while Democrats were even with the state's rate at 75 percent, and unaffiliated voters were at 70 percent. This created an electorate that was 36 percent Democratic, 33 percent Republican, and 31 percent unaffiliated. Not surprisingly, the North Carolina exit-polls showed that 97 percent of self-identified Democrats voted for Biden, with 96 percent of self-identified Republicans voting for Trump. Among those North Carolina's voters who indicated they were "independent," Biden won 50-46.[10]

Racial dynamics have always played a critical role in North Carolina's politics (Prysby 2008, 67). White non-Hispanic/Latino turnout was 79 percent, followed by black/African American non-Hispanic/Latino turnout at 68 percent, an increase over previous elections but still below the state's turnout rate. All other non-Hispanic races[11] had an average turnout rate of 72 percent. With a registered voter pool that was 63 percent white, 20 percent black, and 13 percent all other races (all non-Hispanic), North Carolina's 2020 electorate was 66 percent white non-Hispanic, 19 percent black non-Hispanic, and 13 percent all other non-Hispanic races. Hispanic/Latino voters, who constituted three percent of the voter pool, had a turnout rate of only 59 percent, making them 2 percent of the overall electorate. According to North Carolina exit polls, White voters voted for Trump two-to-one over Biden (66–33), while black voters went once again overwhelming for Biden, with 92 percent of the vote. Among Latino voters, Biden won 57–42 over Trump.

Turnout among generational cohorts demonstrated an electorate that skewed older. The mean age of North Carolina's voters was fifty, two years older than the voter pool. Voters in the Boomer generation (those 56 and 74 in 2020) had a turnout rate of 86 percent, and were 34 percent of the electorate. Generation X (aged 50–55) had a turnout rate of 79 percent and constituted 27 percent of the electorate, followed by the Silent Generation (aged 75 and above).[12] These oldest voters had a turnout rate of 79 percent, but made up only 9 percent of the electorate. The youngest voters, Millennials (aged 24–39) and Generation Z (aged 18–23), had turnout rates of 62 percent each, but combined were 31 percent of the electorate (Millennials at 23 percent and Gen Z at 8 percent). Exit-poll data indicated that voters under the age of 45 went for Biden with 56 percent of the vote, while Trump secured older voters' support: those 45–64 went for Trump with 52 percent, and those 65 and older went 59 percent for the Republican presidential candidate.

COVID-19 AND VOTING

Like many states across the nation, North Carolina confronted the COVID-19 pandemic in the midst of conducting a general election. In past presidential elections, the majority of votes came from the state's voting method known as absentee one-stop, or in-person early voting. As indicated in table 11.7, following the 2008 presidential election, the majority of ballots cast came from absentee one-stop and has increased as a percentage of the total votes cast since 2012's election.

Between 2008 and 2016, absentee by mail voting had been about 5 percent of the ballots cast. However, with the concerns about COVID-19, North Carolina experienced a huge surge in requests for mail-in ballots. In past elections, between 200,000 and 250,000 requests for mail-in ballots were made, with typically 200,000 being returned and accepted. The 2020 general election saw 1.1 million requests for absentee by mail ballots submitted, with 1 million mail-in ballots returned and accepted, accounting for 18 percent of the total ballots cast. Of those, 44 percent came from registered Democrats, a third from registered unaffiliated voters, and only 21 percent from registered Republicans. As shown in table 11.7, this marked a significant shift from the past pattern of Republicans dominating absentee-by-mail voting in North Carolina. The 2020 dynamic did align with polls indicating that Democrats preferred voting by mail over Republicans, due to repeated criticisms by Trump against mail-in voting.[13]

Conversely, registered Republican voters increased their percentage of absentee one-stop (AOS) voting to its highest level since 2004, with both Republicans and Democrats split at 35 percent each of the total AOS

Table 11.7 2004–2020 North Carolina Presidential General Elections, Vote Methods by Party Registration Percentages

Vote Method	Party Registration	2004	2008	2012	2016	2020
Absentee by Mail						
	Democrats	43	28	29	31	44
	Unaffiliated	15	18	21	28	34
	Republicans	42	54	50	40	21
Absentee OneStop (In-Person Early)						
	Democrats	49	54	49	42	35
	Unaffiliated	14	18	20	26	29
	Republicans	37	28	30	32	35
Election Day (In-Person)						
	Democrats	47	41	39	35	27
	Unaffiliated	16	21	25	30	33
	Republicans	37	37	35	35	39
Total Ballots Cast						
	Democrats	48	48	45	39	36
	Unaffiliated	15	19	22	27	31
	Republicans	37	33	33	33	33

Source: Data from Voter Registration and Vote History files from the NC State Board of Elections website https://www.ncsbe.gov/results-data.

Table 11.8 2020 North Carolina General Election, Party Registration Turnout Rates and Vote Method Distribution (Percentages)

	Registered Democrats	Registered Unaffiliated	Registered Republicans	All other parties	State Total
Turnout Rate	75	70	81	63	75
Absentee by Mail	23	20	11	16	18
Absentee One-Stop	65	62	69	58	65
Election Day	12	17	19	25	16

Source: Data from Voter Registration and Vote History files from the NC State Board of Elections website https://www.ncsbe.gov/results-data.

ballots cast. It was among Election Day voting that Republican registration held the advantage, with 38 percent of the ballots cast coming from GOP voters and only 27 percent from registered Democrats. Ultimately, registered Republicans won the turnout rate among the three major registration groups, with 81 percent of GOP registered voters casting a ballot. Registered Democrats matched the state's turnout rate at 75 percent, while seven out of ten unaffiliated voters participated. This trend of partisan voters having a higher turnout rate than unaffiliated voters has been evident in the state for some time. Table 11.8 documents the vote methods used within each party registration.

CONCLUSION

In the mid-twentieth century, noted Southern politics scholar V.O. Key (1950) described the state as being a "progressive plutocracy," dominated by the Democratic Party, which constantly had a reliable Republican minority always present. Between Key's observations to the end of the twentieth century, North Carolina witnessed a political realignment, much like the rest of the South. But the state did not move as Republican as other southern states. This was due to the adaptability of North Carolina Democrats to fend off growing the rising tide of Republicanism (Prysby 1995, 2002). At the beginning of the twenty-first century, Paul Luebke (1998) described Tar Heel politics as a battle between modernizers and traditionalists in the state's political and economic factions. A decade later, Christopher Cooper and Gibbs Knotts (2008) noted the tension between progressives and traditionalists in the state, which often resulted in the political competitiveness of the late twentieth century. Rob Christensen (2008), long-time political reporter for the Raleigh *News & Observer*, contended that the state's politics were a "paradox" where neither political party or ideology could rest easily. Political scientist Tom Eamon (2014) contended that conflicts over race, the strengthening and polarization of two-party politics, the fierce competitiveness of elections, and the impact of individual politicians shape the state's political environment.

During the first two decades of the twenty-first century, North Carolina has undergone a distinctive change in its politics, but general patterns and trends have continued from its late twentieth century dynamics (Bitzer and Prysby 2018). The state continued its pattern of federal red to state blue electoral contests into the 2020 elections, albeit by narrower margins and slightly different patterns. At the federal level, Trump's and Tillis's victories demonstrated the state-wide red nature, albeit that both saw closer margins of victory than they previously had. In terms of the blue dynamics for the Council of State offices, Republicans made progress, winning six offices to the Democrats' four in 2020. But the biggest prize of the state-wide executive offices remained elusive for Republicans, with Democrats retaining the chief executive office. Among the congressional contests, Democrats picked up two seat courtesy of redrawn districts, bringing the delegation from a 10–3 Republican majority to an 8–5 GOP majority. And while Democrats celebrated their gubernatorial win and two U.S. House seat pick-ups, their state legislative and supreme court results proved a disappointment, with the Republicans continuing their majority control of the general assembly and rebalancing the state's highest court.

North Carolina's dynamics reflect many of the national narratives regarding American politics. The urban-rural divide is alive in the Tar Heel state, and 2020's elections indicate an intensification of that split. While different conceptualizations of "suburbs" exist, it is best to think of two separate suburbia in North Carolina: the urban suburbs and the surrounding suburban counties (sometimes known as "exurbs"). While the national discussion is that the suburbs are the battleground locations in many states, North Carolina's most competitive areas are the urban suburbs, while the surrounding suburban counties are the state's most Republican areas.

In terms of North Carolina's electorate, the influence of older voters is still very apparent, even though the registered voter pool is skewing more toward younger voters. The racial and ethnic characteristics of the electorate indicated a slightly more white electorate in 2020 than the voter pool as a whole. In the end, turnout remains the key to winning in North Carolina. With the apparent nationalization of Tar Heel voter behavior, winning North Carolina elections means energizing and mobilizing voters. And with 2020's record turnout, it is apparent that the fight will continue, albeit within close margins, in a deeply divided and competitive North Carolina.

NOTES

1. Election returns from the North Carolina State Board of Elections website (https://er.ncsbe.gov/), accessed February 22, 2021.

2. Data on presidential results within congressional districts from: https://docs.google.com/spreadsheets/d/1PqnWZUImDYMBzl7eHCVB7gluCWKyexC4EUxD2qwhGxg/edit#gid=1191354284. Accessed February 22, 2021.

3. Trips made by the presidential and vice-presidential candidates from https://www.chicagotribune.com/politics/ct-viz-presidential-campaign-trail-tracker-20200917-edspdit2incbfnopchjaelp3uu-htmlstory.html Accessed Feb. 17, 2021.

4. Data regarding candidate fundraising from https://www.opensecrets.org/states/pres.php?cycle=2020&state=NC. Accessed Feb. 17, 2021.

5. https://www.realclearpolitics.com/epolls/2020/president/nc/north_carolina_trump_vs_biden-6744.html. Accessed Feb. 18, 2021.

6. https://www.census.gov/programs-surveys/metro-micro/about/omb-bulletins.html. Accessed February 1, 2021.

7. Data on presidential performances in congressional districts can be found at https://www.dailykos.com/stories/2012/11/19/1163009/-Daily-Kos-Elections-presidential-results-by-congressional-district-for-the-2012-2008-elections. Accessed February 21, 2021.

8. North Carolina's governors only gained the opportunity to run for a second consecutive term with a constitutional amendment passed in 1977. Since then, those governors who sought reelection had been reelected up to McCrory's 2016 defeat. The only governor after the amendment who decided not to seek reelection was Democrat Beverly Perdue in 2012.

9. https://wwwcache.wral.com/asset/news/state/nccapitol/2020/09/14/19286159/PollPrint-DMID1-5o6uj4sqc.pdf. Accessed February 22, 2021.

10. https://www.cnn.com/election/2020/exit-polls/president/north-carolina. Accessed February 24, 2021.

11. Asian, American Indian, Native Hawaiian/Pacific Islander, multi-racial, other races, and unknown/unreported.

12. Generation cohorts defined by the Pew Research Center: https://www.pewresearch.org/fact-tank/2019/01/17/where-millennials-end-and-generation-z-begins/. Accessed February 22, 2021.

13. A September 28, 2020, poll by Meredith College found that North Carolina Republican voters were half as likely to prefer voting by mail as Democratic or Unaffiliated voters. https://www.meredith.edu/news/meredith-poll-provides-snapshot-of-n.c.-voter-opinions-as-election-2020-app. Accessed February 20, 2021.

REFERENCES

Aldridge, Bailey. 2020. "Voters Weigh Tillis' Support for Trump, Cunningham Sexting in Tight Senate Race: Poll." *The Raleigh News & Observer*, October 20, 2020.

Ax, Joseph. 2019. "North Carolina's Congressional Map is Illegal Republican Gerrymander, Court Rules." *Associated Press*, October 28, 2019.

Baier, Elizabeth and Jeff Tiberii. 2019. "NC Judges Throw Out Current Congressional Map." *WUNC*, October 29, 2019.

Bitzer, J. Michael and Charles Prysby. 2018. "North Carolina: Up and Down the Tar Heel Political Roller Coaster." In *The Future Ain't What It Used to Be: The 2016 Presidential Election in the South*, edited by Branwell DuBose Kapeluck and Scott E. Buchanan. Fayetteville, AR: University of Arkansas Press.

Bitzer, J. Michael. Forthcoming. "North Carolina: A Deeply Divided Partisan State." In *The New Politics of the Old South: An Introduction to Southern Politics*, edited by Charles S. Bullock and Mark J. Rozell, ed. Seventh Edition. Boulder, CO: Rowman & Littlefield.

Black, Earl and Merle Black. 1992. *The Vital South: How Presidents are Elected*. Cambridge, MA: Harvard University Press.

Black, Earl and Merle Black. 2003. *The Rise of Southern Republicans*. Cambridge, MA: Harvard University Press.

Chemob, Danielle. 2020. "How GOP Star Madison Cawthorn Polarized the Battle for Asheville's Seat in Congress." *The Charlotte Observer*, October 31, 2020.

Christensen, Rob. 2008. *The Paradox of Tar Heel Politics: The Personalities, Elections, and Events That Shaped Modern North Carolina*. Chapel Hill, NC: University of North Carolina Press.

Cooper, Christopher A. and H. Gibbs Knotts. 2008. "Introduction: Traditionalism and Progressivism in North Carolina." In *The New Politics of North Carolina*, edited by Christopher A. Cooper and H. Gibbs Knotts. Chapel Hill, NC: University of North Carolina Press.

Doran, Will. 2019. "Cheri Beasley will become the first black woman to be chief justice of the NC Supreme Court." *The Raleigh News & Observer*, February 12, 2019.

Eamon, Tom. 2014. *The Making of a Southern Democracy: North Carolina Politics from Kerr Scott to Pat McCrory*. Chapel Hill, NC: University of North Carolina Press.

Fiedler, Tom. 2020. "Attack by Madison Cawthorn's Schoolmates Goes Viral." *Blue Ridge Public Radio*, October 23, 2020.

Fleer, Jack D. 1994. *North Carolina Government and Politics*. Lincoln, NE: University of Nebraska Press.

Gardner, Amy. 2019. "N.C. Board Declares a New Election in Contested Race after the GOP Candidate Admitted He Was Mistaken in his Testimony." *The Washington Post*, February 21, 2019.

Haberman, Maggie. 2020. "Trump Threatens to Pull Republican National Convention From North Carolina." *New York Times*, May 25, 2020.

Haberman, Maggie, Patricia Mazzei and Annie Karni. 2020. "Trump Abruptly Cancels Republican Convention in Florida: 'It's Not the Right Time.'" *New York Times*, July 23, 2020.

Hopkins, Daniel J. 2018. *The Increasingly United States: How and Why American Political Behavior Nationalized*. Chicago: University of Chicago Press.

Kapeluck, Branwell DuBose, Laurence W. Moreland, and Robert P. Steed. 2009. *A Paler Shade of Red: The 2008 Presidential Election in the South*. Fayetteville, AR: University of Arkansas Press.

Kazee, Thomas A. 1998. "North Carolina: Conservatism, Traditionalism, and the GOP." In *The New Politics of the Old South: An Introduction to Southern Politics*. Boulder, CO: Rowman & Littlefield.

Key, V.O. 1950. *Southern Politics in State and Nation.* New York: Knopf.

Luebke, Paul. 1998. *Tar Heel Politics 2000.* Chapel Hill, NC: University of North Carolina Press.

McGlennon, John J. 2014. "Virginia: Obama's Unexpected Firewall." In *Second Verse, Same as the First: The 2012 Presidential Election in the South,* edited by Scott E. Buchanan and Branwell DuBose Kapeluck. Fayetteville, AR: University of Arkansas Press.

Morrill, Jim, Tim Funk, and Kate Murphy. 2020. "RNC Convention will head to Jacksonville after 1 day in Charlotte." *The Charlotte Observer,* June 11, 2020.

Murphy, Brian. 2020. "Sen. Thom Tillis announces he has coronavirus; NC challenger Cunningham tests negative." *The Raleigh News & Observer,* October 2, 2020.

Prysby, Charles. 1995. "North Carolina: Emerging Two-Party Politics." In *Southern State Party Organizations and Activists,* edited by Charles D. Hadley and Lewis Bowman. Westport, CT: Praeger.

Prysby, Charles. 2002. "North Carolina: Continued Two-Party Competition." In *The 2000 Presidential Election in the South,* edited by Robert P. Steed and Laurence W. Moreland. Westport, CT: Praeger.

Prysby, Charles. 2007. "North Carolina: Two-Party Competition Continues into the Twenty-first Century." In *The New Politics of the Old South: An Introduction to Southern Politics,* edited by Charles S. Bullock III and Mark Rozell. Third Edition. Boulder, CO: Rowman & Littlefield.

Prysby, Charles. 2008. "The Reshaping of the Political Party System in North Carolina." In *The New Politics of North Carolina,* edited by Christopher A. Cooper and H. Gibbs Knotts. Chapel Hill, NC: University of North Carolina Press.

Prysby, Charles. 2009. "North Carolina: Change and Continuity in 2008." In *A Paler Shade of Red: The 2008 Presidential Election in the South,* edited by Branwell DuBose Kapeluck, Laurence W. Moreland, and Robert P. Steed. Fayetteville, AR: University of Arkansas Press.

Seipel, Arnie. 2018. "Republicans to Hold 2020 Convention in Charlotte, N.C." *National Public Radio News,* July 20, 2018.

Slodysko, Brian and Gary D. Robertson. 2020. "Cal Cunningham Affair Included July Encounter in NC, New Texts and Interviews Show." *The Raleigh News & Observer,* October 6, 2020.

Sonmez, Felicia and Robert Barnes. 2019. "North Carolina Court Rules Partisan State Legislative Districts Unconstitutional." *Washington Post,* September 3, 2019.

Chapter 12

Tennessee

Trump Territory, Again

Vaughn May

Approximately thirty minutes south of downtown Nashville on Interstate 65, sits Ramsey Solutions, a glistening forty-seven-acre, six-story business campus that headquarters the hugely popular "Dave Ramsey Show," as well as office space for hundreds of employees. Ramsey, a middle Tennessee native, built an enormous empire offering "God and Grandma's" advice on money matters, an enterprise that has assisted millions of persons in taking control of their finances and achieving fiscal solvency. Ramsey also seamlessly integrates a large dose of inspirational thinking into his money advice: a devout Christian, he signs off each radio broadcast with the line, "Remember, there's ultimately only one way to financial peace, and that's to walk daily with the Prince of Peace, Christ Jesus."

Before the construction of Ramsey Solutions was completed in 2019, a large sign reading "Pray with Us as We Grow" greeted travelers driving through Tennessee. That motto—testifying to the twin pillars of Christian piety and economic growth—likewise serves as a descriptor of the state's political culture, a culture that has propelled the Republican Party to electoral heights that were unimaginable two decades ago. State party data paint a depressing picture for Democrats: of the eleven states of the old Confederacy, Tennessee, Alabama, and Arkansas lead the pack in terms of GOP party affiliation of state residents (Jones 2019). McKee (2019) has confirmed this as well: his application of David's Index indicates that only Alabama outranks Tennessee in terms of Republican Party strength.

On November 3, 2020, Donald Trump's victory was called minutes after the polls closed in the state. The political intrigue and accompanying media attention surrounding the outcomes in the neighboring states of North Carolina and Georgia were entirely missing. That Trump won Tennessee's eleven electoral votes is unsurprising. The fact that Trump's vote margins in Tennessee outpaced every other southern state except those in Alabama and Arkansas, however, deserves deeper reflection, especially given that this trajectory was not predictable two decades ago. This chapter examines the changing political context that led to Trump's two landslide victories.

A HISTORY OF POLITICAL DIVERSITY

Historically, the electoral results from Tennessee's track more with the Rim South, but a relatively new phenomenon is the state's political tendencies tracking more with the Deep South. Tennessee has been labeled a "somewhat reluctant southern state" (Lyons, Scheb, and Stair 2001, 17) and an "emergent" state (Woodard 2006, 17) conceptually distinct from its more traditionalistic neighbors on a wide variety of political and cultural metrics. Significantly higher levels of black voting registration (McKee 2019, 73) denoted a state with a more moderate racial history, at least in comparison to the rest of the region.

The political diversity and electoral competition on display in the three grand divisions of the state is the predominant theme of most historical analyses. In his seminal work, *Southern Politics in State and Nation*, V. O. Key (1949) noted various "coalitions and combinations that struggle for control of the state," which were grounded in vast geographical and historical differences among the state's sub-regions (59). In the broadest of outlines, East Tennessee was the home of Mountain Republicanism, while Democratic power brokers dominated Middle and West Tennessee. Within the Democratic Party, scholars pointed to factional fights between E. H. Crump's political machine in Memphis and anti-Crump forces scattered across the state (Brodsky 1998, 168). Crump cut a fearsome figure in Tennessee politics, skillfully using his political patronage to dominate both gubernatorial and legislative elections (Bass and Devries 1977, 289). Tennessee Republicans could take solace in their control of two eastern congressional districts as well as their role in fostering moderately competitive national elections. GOP strength was at least formidable enough that Key (1949) could label Tennessee as one of only three states in the South where Republicans "approximate the reality of a political party" (277).

In the five decades spanning 1950 to 2000, loyal voters of both parties could locate role models to celebrate. Tennessee Democrats proudly watched political luminaries such as Estes Kefauver, Senator Al Gore, Sr., Governor Frank Clement, Senator Jim Sasser, and Senator Al Gore Jr. became sought-after voices on the national scene. Republicans could take pride in their own politicos, including "the Great Conciliator" Howard Baker Jr., who won a Senate seat in 1966 and set the table for a talented group of conservatives who would emerge in the decades to follow. Governor (and Senator) Lamar Alexander, Senator Bill Frist, and Senator Fred Thompson were among those who would become national media personalities and subjects of endless speculation about possible presidential runs.

That Tennesseans were open to the appeals of both parties is most evident at the gubernatorial level. From 1979 to 2019, the parties leapfrogged one another in power, with all five governors serving eight-year stints. If any patterns held among these state executives—Republican Lamar Alexander (1979–1986), Democrat Ned McWherter (1987–1995), Republican Don Sundquist (1995–2003), Democrat Phil Bredesen (2003–2011), and Republican Bill Haslam (2011–2019)—it was that all of the winning candidates promised competent government, exhibited a pragmatic style once in office, and eventually earned the contempt of the ideological wings of their respective parties (May 2018). This trend was finally disrupted in 2019 when Republican businessman Bill Lee was inaugurated as the fiftieth governor of the state.

Competition was evident at the presidential level as well. In the century stretching from 1900 to 2000, Democratic candidates won a plurality or majority in fifteen contests, while Republicans won a plurality or majority in eleven elections. Tennessee was often the electoral outlier in the era of the "Solid South." It held the distinction of being the first state from the former Confederacy since Reconstruction to vote for a Republican—Warren Harding—in 1920, and it was only one of four states that voted for Herbert Hoover in 1928. Thomas Dewey received almost 40 percent of Tennessee's votes in 1944, recording the highest percentage of any state in the old Confederacy (Key 1949, 278). Dwight Eisenhower's victories in 1952 and 1956 further signaled that the GOP could expand its power beyond the East and capture swaths of the state's growing middle class (Nelson 2013, 187).

Beginning in 1952, Tennessee's electoral vote would be in the Republican column in thirteen of the next seventeen presidential elections. Tennesseans gave the Democratic candidate a majority or plurality of their vote four times: for Lyndon Johnson in 1964 (55.5 percent), Jimmy Carter in 1976 (55.9 percent), Bill Clinton in 1992 (47.08 percent), and again in 1996 (48 percent). Although the GOP emerged as the preferred presidential brand during the second half of the twentieth century, a southerner at the top of the ticket offered hope for the Democratic standard-bearer, a pattern that held until 2000.

The Volunteer State, then, has offered widespread opportunity for aspirational politicians of all ideological stripes. In a 2018 *New York Times* article, Al Gore Jr. noted the partisan push and pull of the state's history, labeling Tennessee's political culture as "resilient" and open to any party that promised "a common-sense approach to governing well" (Martin 2018). Ironically, it was Al Gore's last run for office that would signal the beginning of a new political era. The skillful GOP fusion of free-market economics and evangelical social concerns proved to be an electorally potent combination, and twenty-first-century Democrats statewide struggled mightily to compete in statewide elections, no matter how well they promised to govern.

2000–2020: TAXES AND TRADITIONALISM

Whether free-market libertarianism and cultural traditionalism can be fused into a workable political philosophy is subject to robust academic discussion. Practically, however, the debate appears settled on Election Day in the South. M. V. Hood et al., for instance, found evangelicalism to be one of the chief drivers behind the anti-tax Tea Party movement in the region, concluding that the Tea Party was "the religiously and fiscally conservative vanguard of the Republican Party" (Hood, Kidd, and Morris 2015, 16). In Tennessee, the fusion of these energies has powered the GOP to significant heights. Locals might call it "The Dave Ramsey effect."

The tax revolts at the turn of the century were the defining moments in modern Tennessee politics. In addition to framing future iterations of an income tax as political poison, the protests had two other impacts: they launched the careers of several conservative firebrands and showcased the power of alternative media—particularly talk radio—in challenging establishment narratives. One of those new media personalities was the colorful and popular conservative radio show host Phil Valentine, whose book *Tax Revolt* chronicles the intense battles between the pro- and anti-tax forces. Valentine emerged as one of the leading voices against the resurrection of the income tax and a major player in its eventual defeat. His book often takes on a Manichean tone; he notes of the anti-tax forces that "like a determined goal line defense, these ordinary men, women, and children, rose up on numerous occasions, against insurmountable odds, to beat back those trying to push an unconstitutional income tax into the endzone," a description that the establishment wings of both state parties would find objectionable (Valentine 2005, xii). It is also clear that Valentine accurately diagnosed the stirrings of a significant grassroots uprising that the establishment missed.

The tax revolt story begins on an unusual note. In 1999, Republican Governor Don Sundquist surprised many political observers by proposing a state income tax to address state budgetary woes. His announcement, which was a reversal of previous campaign promises, all but guaranteed that tax reform would become *the* dominant issue in General Assembly debates. Few, however, could have predicted what was to follow. The legislative sessions from 2000 to 2002 were the most intense in the state's modern political history, drawing national attention for a number of dramatic moments, including confrontations between anti-tax protestors and state troopers in riot gear. Local talk radio hosts maintained a relentless focus on the daily legislative maneuvering of both factions and each pressure-packed vote, a context that apparently caused some legislators to collapse from the stress of the proceedings (Valentine 2005, 74).

The ultimate defeat of the income tax in May of 2002 was close—the tax failed by only four votes in the House—but the political fallout heralded a culture that would make the income tax proposals the "third rail" of politics in the state (Valentine 2005, 224). Little-known anti-tax legislators like Marsha Blackburn and Diane Black would use these battles as springboards to successful careers in Congress. Dave Ramsey, who had been known almost exclusively for financial stewardship on his afternoon show, began to attract the admiration of the right's national political infrastructure. Notably, both Ramsey's and Valentine's radio work during this era earned them the "Heroes of the Taxpayer" award from Grover Norquist's advocacy group (Valentine 2005).

The other unassailable energy present on Election Day is connected to the state's fervent religious traditions. The Volunteer State serves as the historic headquarters to a number of religious denominations, and politicians from a variety of ideological traditions have been comfortable discussing their faith walks on the stump. More recent data confirms the centrality of faith issues to the electorate. Utilizing a number of measures connected to religious attendance, prayer frequency, belief in God, and self-assessment of the importance of religion, scholars at the *Pew Research Center* found that Tennessee ranked third in its measure of religiosity, only behind Alabama and Mississippi (Lipka and Wormald 2016). Another *Pew* monograph (2014) ranked Tennessee first in the percentage of the population that identifies as evangelical.

The rapid "Republicanization" of evangelical Protestants has placed the state GOP in an enviable position and guaranteed the prominence of culture war battles for the foreseeable future (Schwadel 2017). Recent legislative sessions have featured robust tussles over legislation with keenly Christian overtones, including debates over the Bible as the official book of Tennessee, as well as fierce debates over the constitutional boundaries of religious liberty legislation (May 2018, 202–3). One of the first bills to pass in the 2020 General Assembly session was a hotly contested piece of legislation that allowed adoption agencies to decline child placement "if doing so would violate the agency's written religious or moral convictions or policies" (Allison 2020a).

Over the past decade, the most clarifying single moment illustrating the power of fusionism involved the 2014 state ballot results. Amendment 1, a measure that furnished legislators more flexibility to regulate abortion rights, passed with 53 percent of the vote, despite pro-Amendment 1 forces being outspent considerably (Wadhwani 2014). The other high-profile amendment on the ballot—Amendment 3, which codified in the state constitution that the state legislature cannot enact an income tax—passed easily with two-thirds support. The passage of both amendments affirmed that the twin engines of cultural conservatism and libertarian economics were ascendant politically.

2016: TRUMP TRIUMPHS

By the time the 2016 presidential election came into focus, the GOP had a seismic advantage. The night of November 7, 2000, laid to rest the theory that a southerner at the top of the ticket could deliver Tennessee's electoral votes to the Democrats. Native son Al Gore Jr.'s defeat—he lost to George W. Bush by a margin of about four percentage points or a little more than 80,000 votes—reset Democratic aspirations in Tennessee. The tight margins on display in the 2000 presidential race—the last time Tennessee could plausibly be labeled a battleground state—would not be repeated in subsequent elections. Both George W. Bush and John McCain bested the respective opponents with almost 57 percent of the state's votes, and that margin grew even larger in 2012, as Romney won a staggering 59.48 percent of Tennessee voters.

The only question remaining concerned which Republican would seize the nomination. Several moments hinted at the nascent power of candidates who were willing to wage war against the GOP establishment. In the 2014 Senate primary, Senator Lamar Alexander had struggled against a weak challenger, and the 2015 and 2016 Tennessee General Assembly sessions showcased the growing nationalization of American politics and the attendant problems that would create for state Democrats. The GOP's conservative supermajority in the state legislature made it clear that it would not collaborate on any policy that had the slightest connection to the Obama administration, even if the initiative had significant support from the GOP establishment. The battle over healthcare coverage is instructive. In November 2014, secure from his landslide victory, Republican Governor Bill Governor Halsam introduced "Insure Tennessee"—a policy designed to furnish coverage for Tennesseans who did not qualify for TennCare or who were unable to purchase insurance through the Affordable Care Act—and called for a special session of the General Assembly to debate its merits.

In significant ways, the debate over Insure Tennessee mirrored the income tax debates over a decade earlier: a newly elected conservative with political currency to spend proposed a contentious policy that would rely on significant bipartisan support for its passage (May 2018, 205). The denouement in this case, however, was far less dramatic. Insure Tennessee went down to a resounding defeat, killed by two Senate committees, never even making it to the floor of the Senate and House of Representatives for deliberation (Plazas 2015). It was a thorough defeat that highlighted an important political reality for any Republican running in the state: not only was the Democratic brand badly damaged in the Volunteer State, establishment Republicans considered "too bipartisan" would also be considered suspect by a large contingent of Tennessee's voters.

Enter Trump. The 2016 Republican primary results were incontrovertible: Trump won comfortably with almost 39 percent of the vote, followed by Cruz with 24.7 percent, and Rubio with 21.2 percent. Observers looking to tease out major differences in the grand divisions in the state would search in vain: Trump won every county in both East and West Tennessee and lost only in one Middle Tennessee county to Rubio by a slim margin. Trump's popularity was extraordinarily broad. Shattering the myth that he had little appeal beyond working-class whites, Trump won a plurality of primary voters in virtually every income and age category. Additionally, he won a plurality of women (38 percent), men (43 percent), high school graduates (51 percent), college graduates (36 percent), Republicans (40 percent), independents (40 percent), evangelicals (41 percent), and non-evangelicals (37 percent) (CNN Politics 2016). The general election was similarly undramatic, as fears over cultural conservatives abandoning Trump never materialized. Trump cruised to victory with 61.1 percent of the state's vote compared to Clinton's 34.9 percent. Twenty years after Bill Clinton won the state with a near-majority and captured large sections of West and Middle Tennessee, Hillary Clinton lost 92 of 95 counties to Donald Trump in a landslide. Indeed, Clinton registered the worst loss for a Democratic presidential nominee since George McGovern's woeful performance in 1972.

2018 SENATE RACE: "TRUMPISM" OUTLASTS TRUMP

Would "Trumpism" have any staying power in Tennessee? When Republican Senator Bob Corker announced his retirement, the subsequent 2018 Senate race between Seventh District Republican Congresswoman Marsha Blackburn and former Democratic Governor Phil Bredesen offered an interesting test case of the respective power of both parties. Blackburn had cut her political teeth fighting against the state income tax almost two decades earlier, a fact that she emphasized repeatedly in her advertising. Her opening campaign salvo featured the declaration: "I'm a hardcore, card-carrying Tennessee conservative. I'm politically incorrect, and proud of it," as well as prominent attacks on abortion, gun control, and government spending. That Blackburn had hitched her electoral fortunes to Trump was also clear. She referenced her support for both the president's immigration ban and his southern border wall, and embraced Trump's culture war fights, including the need to stand for the Star-Spangled Banner (Why I'm Running 2018). Trump returned the favor, visiting three times and holding raucous rallies that featured Blackburn center stage.

Under normal circumstances, most pundits would have treated this as a GOP slam-dunk, but the race was complicated by two factors. First, the outgoing Republican Senator was, at best, an uneasy ally to the president. Trump had considered Corker for prominent roles in his administration, including Secretary of State, but the relationship soured over a number of policy areas. Corker had expressed enormous frustration over the fiscal implications of the White House's 2017 tax reform bill, and although eventually voting for it, he described it as "one of the worst votes I made" (Bryan 2018). As chair of the Senate Foreign Relations Committee, he quarreled forcefully with Trump on a number of issues, including Russian election interference and the partial shutdown of the federal government. These public fights earned him the White House moniker "Liddle Bob Corker," to which the senator responded in kind, comparing the White House "to an adult daycare center" (Ebert and Allison 2019). Trump supporters took their cues: at a Nashville rally for Blackburn, the president's introduction of Corker drew loud boos (Sanchez 2018).

Second, Bredesen was no Democratic sacrificial lamb. A savvy, popular two-term former governor, Bredesen was the only Democratic candidate who had won a statewide race in over a decade, and his experience and pragmatism made him a dream candidate. Some pundits announced Bredesen's run as a "game changer" while the Cook Political Report had the race listed as a "tossup" state less than two months before the election (Duffy 2018). Bredesen was measured in his rhetoric, stressing his bipartisan bona fides, and indicating on numerous occasions that he would work with Trump on solutions benefiting Tennessee. He likewise attempted to steer clear of any contaminating events with national Democratic officials, with the exception of a New York fundraiser hosted by Michael Bloomberg (Ebert 2018).

Ultimately, the thoroughly nationalized tone of the race would sink Bredesen. Trump referred to him as "a total tool of Chuck Schumer and of course the MS-13 lover, Nancy Pelosi," (Wanser 2018), hyperbolic charges that the former governor nonetheless struggled to ward off. The Judge Kavanaugh hearings did Bredesen no favors either: he initially declined to indicate whether he would support the embattled judged and praised Christine Blasey Ford as a "heroine," but eventually decided that the allegations "didn't rise to the level of disqualifying him" thus drawing ire from the left (Garrison 2018).

On Election Night 2018, Blackburn significantly outperformed the polls, ultimately winning by almost 11 percent and ending the most expensive election in Tennessee history. A well-liked former governor who had won every county in the state a little over a decade earlier was reduced to winning three counties—the same counties that Hillary Clinton won in 2016. Democrats once again found themselves in the political wilderness.

Historian Jon Meacham posited that the 2018 Senate election was indicative of a deep philosophical divide between establishment Republicans like Corker and Alexander and Trump, supporting firebrands like Blackburn (Boucher, Ebert, and Buie 2017). Although Meacham's point is certainly exaggerated in a policy sense, it is evident that Blackburn's political tone and visual cues have taken on a Trumpian style. At the president's impeachment hearing, Blackburn was criticized by Democrats for leaving the chamber for an interview with *Fox News* and later for reading Kimberly Strassel's *Resistance at All Costs* during the proceedings. Blackburn also branded at least one of the witnesses with a derogatory nickname, tweeting "Vindictive Vindman" during Lieutenant Colonel Alexander Vindman's testimony (Timms 2020). The quiet, behind-the-scenes negotiating style exhibited by former Tennessee Senators like Howard Baker Jr. appears to be a relic of the past.

2020 DEMOCRATIC PRIMARY

Tennessee held its primary on March 3, three days after Joe Biden's astonishing political resurrection in South Carolina. During the primary season, various candidates had lodged scattered appearances across the state, with both Amy Klobuchar and Pete Buttigieg attempting to carve out space in the center with appeals to Independents and disaffected Republicans. Both, however, dropped out after disappointing performances in South Carolina. Joe Biden was largely absent in Tennessee. Jill Biden served as a stand-in for her husband in Memphis, but Joe Biden had not appeared in the state in over a year, and his campaign spent a paltry 200,000 dollars on campaign communications (Allison and Ebert 2020). Mike Bloomberg emerged as the wildcard candidate and the potential alternative to Sanders. Bloomberg vastly outspent the other candidates combined in Tennessee, visited the state several times, peeled off a few establishment endorsements, and held some of the more memorable campaign events of the season (Ebert 2020). Bloomberg's rallies were often Trump-esque: ornate, raucous, and occasionally interrupted by counter-protestors. At a Chattanooga event, one rally-goer ascended the stage and proclaimed "that is not democracy ... that is a plutocracy!" a theme echoed elsewhere by angry progressives (Jackson 2020).

By 8:30 pm, Central Standard Time on election night, Biden emerged as the convincing winner, garnering almost 42 percent of the vote, and netting victories in ninety-one of ninety-five of Tennessee's counties. According to CNN exit polls, Biden won a plurality of primary voters in most demographic and ideological categories, including women (44 percent), men (38 percent), moderates (57 percent), conservatives (33 percent), college graduates (35 percent), and those with no college degrees (47 percent). Statewide, Sanders finished a respectable second with 25 percent and performed especially well with voters aged 18–44 (47 percent). Bloomberg finished third with approximately 15 percent of the vote. The rest of the field featured a dozen candidates who split the remaining 17.9 percent of the votes cast (CNN Exit Polls, 2020).

Table 12.1 data suggests that the heralded and historic "grand divisions" of Tennessee were not pronounced in the 2020 Democratic primary. In East Tennessee, Biden carried thirty-one of thirty-three counties, almost reaching the 39 percent mark to Sanders's 28 percent and Bloomberg's 15 percent. Sanders did eke out victories over Biden only in two rural counties and ran exceptionally well in Knox County, home of the University of Tennessee's flagship campus, losing only by 163 votes. Bloomberg was consistently in third place, although he did outpace Sanders in two East Tennessee counties. Middle Tennessee voter preferences were a near carbon copy of the East: Biden won nearly 39 percent of the vote, Sanders placed second, winning 26.2 percent of the vote, while Bloomberg earned approximately 14.5 percent of the vote. Again, Sanders earned narrow victories in two counties, and Bloomberg eclipsed Sanders for second place in a handful of locations.

West Tennessee offered even better news for the frontrunner. Biden captured a slight majority of voters, with Sanders edging Bloomberg for second place (19.4–17.5 percent). It was a disappointing showing for Sanders, who carried no counties in the region and fell to third place in seven of the twenty-one of counties in West Tennessee. What explains Sanders's

Table 12.1 Tennessee Democratic Primary Results, 2020

	Biden	Sanders	Bloomberg	Others (n = 12)
Total Votes	215,390	129,168	79,789	91,903
% Statewide	41.7	25	15.4	17.9
% East TN	38.6	28	15	18.4
% Middle TN	38.8	26.2	14.5	20.5
% West TN	50.5	19.4	17.5	12.6

Source: "2020 Primary Results" CNN Politics, https://www.cnn.com/election/2020/primaries-caucuses/state/tennessee

under-performance in the West? Racial demographics likely have something to do with it. CNN exit polls indicated that although Biden won a plurality of white voters statewide (37 percent) he maintained an even larger edge with African American voters (57 percent). West Tennessee is the smallest region in terms of the number of counties, but it is also home to thirteen of the twenty largest black populations in the state. Sanders's struggles attracting African American votes have been documented elsewhere, including negative perceptions of his largely white campaign infrastructure and his inability to connect on criminal justice issues (Harris 2020). In her endorsement of Biden, African American state legislator and chair of Senate Democratic Caucus, Raumesh Akbari was likely speaking for many of her Shelby County constituents when she noted that Sanders "seems to be someone who wants to tear it all down" (Allison 2020b). On the Democratic side, the establishment wing of the party had triumphed.

2020 GENERAL ELECTION

The general election season featured no intrigue or surprise. If the Tennessee election were a murder mystery, the killer left fingerprints, DNA, and three signed affidavits at the scene testifying to his guilt. While national media flocked to the competitive races in Georgia, North Carolina, and Florida, the Republican machine in Tennessee quietly rolled on.

Table 12.2 compares the 2016 and 2020 general elections. Trump's statewide percentage dipped slightly—from 61.1 percent to 60.7 percent, but it was still a resounding victory by any definition. Democrats searching for a silver lining might note that Biden outpaced Clinton in the state's three grand divisions and improved on her total by over 273 thousand votes, but it was the third presidential election in a row in which the Democratic standard-bearer failed to register 40 percent.

Table 12.2 Tennessee Presidential Election Results, 2016–2020

	2016		2020	
	Trump	*Clinton*	*Trump*	*Biden*
Total Votes	1,522,925	867,695	1,852,475	1,143,711
% Statewide	61.1	34.9	60.7	37.4
% East TN	73	27	70	30
% Middle TN	63	37	60	40
% West TN	50.5	49.5	50.19	49.81

Source: "2016 Tennessee Results," *CNN Politics*, https://www.cnn.com/election/2016/results/states/tennessee; "2020 Tennessee Results," *CNN Politics*, https://www.cnn.com/election/2020/results/state/tennessee.

Trump won landslide majorities in both East Tennessee and Middle Tennessee counties and eked out a victory in West Tennessee counties. The latter appears to be the only region of the state that is in play for both parties, a reality that highlights Memphis's disproportionate influence. In the 2020 election, for instance, almost 40 percent of the voters in West Tennessee resided in Memphis's Shelby County. Statewide, Biden snagged just three counties, the same three that Clinton carried in 2016. These included Nashville's Davidson County and the only two counties in the state with a majority African American population—Shelby County and Haywood County.

It's been proposed that the political destiny of Southern Democrats is tied to urban density (Thompson 2019).

Table 12.3 lists the seven most populated counties in Tennessee, home to both the state's biggest media markets as well as populations of 200,000 or greater. These counties also represent approximately one-half of the state's voters in any given presidential election. Interestingly, none of these counties has flipped parties in two decades. Shelby and Davidson counties are Democratic fortresses, but the next five largest counties have voted Republican in six straight presidential elections, and in only two instances was the election even reasonably close (Montgomery County in 2000 and 2008). The good news for Democrats is that the Republican vote margin shrunk in all five GOP-leaning counties in 2020, leading to a 7 percent advantage for Biden in Tennessee's most populated areas. The bad news

Table 12.3 Partisan Advantage in Tennessee's Most Populated Counties in Presidential General Elections, 2000–2020

	2000	2004	2008	2012	2016	2020
Winning party and percentage-point margin of victory						
County						
Shelby	D+14	D+16	D+27	D+26	D+28	D+30
Davidson	D+17	D+10	D+21	D+19	D+26	D+32
Knox	R+17	R+25	R+23	R+29	R+24	R+15
Hamilton	R+12	R+16	R+12	R+15	R+17	R+10
Rutherford	R+10	R+24	R+19	R+25	R+26	R+15
Williamson	R+35	R+45	R+39	R+47	R+36	R+26
Montgomery	R+2	R+17	R+8	R+10	R+19	R+13
Totals for seven counties						
Share (%) of Statewide 2-Party Vote	47%	47%	48%	48%	47%	47%
Party advantage	Dem +1.8%	GOP +4.2%	Dem +3.7%	GOP +.3%	Dem +1.4%	Dem +7%

Source: CNN Politics, https://www.cnn.com/election/2020/results/state/tennessee; Tennessee Secretary of State, https://sos.tn.gov/elections/results.

is that none of the GOP-leaning counties appear poised to move into the blue column in 2024. Democrats wanting to transform the state will need to continue to expand their appeal beyond two urban enclaves, a task that will likely require multiple electoral cycles.

Down ticket in 2020, Republicans held serve. Trump-supported Senate candidate Bill Hagerty breezed to election over Democrat Marquita Bradshaw (62–35 percent) in the wake of Lamar Alexander's retirement, and the GOP easily retained seven of the state's nine congressional seats. Indeed, no House incumbent of either party received less than 66 percent of the vote. At the state legislative level, Democrats flipped one Senate seat in suburban Nashville, but still trailed badly 27-6. In the state House, the GOP retained an enormous forty-seven-seat advantage (73-26) in the ninety-nine-seat body.

CONCLUSION

At the height of Tennessee's 2018 Senate election, the nationalization of politics took on celebrity overtones. Country superstar and Tennessee resident Taylor Swift Instagrammed her tens of millions of followers, offering a ringing—and unsolicited—endorsement of Democratic candidate Phil Bredesen. The endorsement received a counter tweet from President Trump, and a great deal of media buzz, with national pundits pontificating about registration spikes and the potential power of progressive young voters. In discussing high-profile endorsements, journalist Phillip Bump (2018) noted that "it's the sort of race where a small turn of a dial can have outsize effect."

Blackburn, though, had a prominent endorsement of her own. In a message to Tennessee voters, Dave Ramsey noted Blackburn's "family values," her "voice of common sense," and their shared battles against the income tax in Tennessee (Dave Ramsey 2018).[1] Although neither message was likely to dislodge partisans nor to create significant political swings, Ramsey's endorsement was far more tethered to Tennessee's dominant political culture. Blackburn's comfortable victory over Bredesen was another indicator that the political ethos exhibited by Ramsey on his radio show—a powerful fusion of traditionalism and libertarianism—reigns supreme in the Volunteer State.

Historically, Tennessee's balanced ideological landscape and energized two-party system made for exciting election nights. That era is over. In 2020, Donald Trump won the state a second time in a race that was not remotely competitive. Trump—and those Republicans who mirror his style and substance—is poised to be kingmakers for the foreseeable future.

NOTE

1. Dave Ramsey's national profile in the right's media ecosphere continues to rise. In addition to regular appearances on *Fox Business*, he was featured prominently on Ben Shapiro's "Sunday Special" Podcast in 2019.

REFERENCES

Allison, Natalie. 2020a. "First Up in Tennessee Senate: Bill Allowing Adoption Agencies to Deny Same-Sex Couples." *The Tennessean*, January 13, 2020. https://www.tennessean.com/story/news/politics/2020/01/13/same-sex-adoption-bill adoption-agencies-tennessee/4455059002/.

Allison, Natalie. 2020b. "It's Time for Tennessee Democrats to Pick a Candidate. They're Facing a Divide Over Bernie Sanders." *The Tennessean*, March 2, 2020. https://www.tennessean.com/story/news/politics/2020/02/27/tennessee-democrats-face-divide-over-bernie-sanders-impact-downballot/4858261002/.

Allison, Natalie, and Joel Ebert. 2020. "Joe Biden Wins Tennessee's Democratic Primary." *The Tennessean*, March 3, 2020. https://www.tennessean.com/story/news/politics/2020/03/03/tennessee-democratic-presidential-primary-results-bloomberg-biden-sanders/4904852002/.

Bass, Jack, and Walter Devries. 1977. *The Transformation of Southern Politics*. New York: Basic Books.

Boucher, Dave, Joel Ebert, and Jordan Buie. 2017. "Analysis: Shifting Political Winds Forecast Trouble for Tennessee's Establishment Republicans." *The Tennessean*, October 7, 2017. https://www.tennessean.com/story/news/2017/10/08/analysis-shifting-political-winds-forecast-trouble-tennessee-establishment-republicans/736931001/.

Brodsky, David. 1998. "Tennessee: Genuine Two-Party Politics." In *The New Politics of the Old South*, edited by Charles S. Bullock and Mark Rozell, 167–84. Lanham: Rowman and Littlefield Publishers.

Bryan, Bob. 2018. "Top Republican Senator Says Voting for GOP Taw Law Could Be One of the Worst Votes I've Made." *Business Insider*, April 12, 2018. https://www.businessinsider.in/top-republican-senator-says-voting-for-the-gop-tax-law-could-be-one-of-the-worst-votes-ivemade/articleshow/63721821.cms?mobile=no.

Bump, Phillip. 2018. "Why Taylor Swift's Activism Has a Better Chance that Kanye West's." *The Washington Post*, October 8, 2018. https://www.washingtonpost.com/politics/2018/10/08/why-taylor-swifts-political activism-has-better-chance-success-than-kanye-wests/.

CNN Politics. 2016. "Tennessee Exit Polls." *CNN Politics*, March 1, 2016. https://www.cnn.com/election/2016/primaries/polls/tn/Rep.

CNN Politics. 2020. "Tennessee Exit Polls." *CNN Politics*. March 4, 2020. https://www.cnn.com/election/2020/primaries-caucuses/entrance-and-exit-polls/tennessee/democratic.

Dave Ramsey Endorses Marsha Blackburn; Marsha Blackburn for Senate. YouTube Video, 1:11, October 12, 2018. https://www.youtube.com/watch?v=xWsSW1LmIBE.

Duffy, Jennifer. 2018. "September Senate Overview: Three Rating Changes." *Cook Political Report*, September 21, 2018. https://cookpolitical.com/analysis/senate/senate-overview/september-senate-overview-three-ratings-changes.

Ebert, Joel. 2018. "Blackburn, Bredesen, Deliver Closing Arguments to Voters With Election Day Looming." *The Tennessean*, November 2, 2018. https://www.tennessean.com/story/news/politics/tn-elections/2018/11/02/marsha-blackburn-phil-bredesen-tennessee-senate/1808769002/.

Ebert, Joel. 2020. "Joe Biden Barely Campaigned in Tennessee. He Still Won Big." *The Tennessean*, March 4, 2020. https://www.tennessean.com/story/news/politics/2020/03/04/super-tuesday-primary-results-tennessee-joe-biden-bernie-sanders/4946530002/.

Ebert, Joel, and Natalie Allison. 2019. "Bob Corker Leaves Office With Legacy of Bipartisanship, Rocky Relationship with Trump." *The Tennessean*, January 2, 2019. https://www.tennessean.com/story/news/politics/2019/01/02/bob-corker-retires-donald-trump-twitter-marsha-blackburn/2424389002/.

Garrison, Joey. 2018. "Bredesen, Explaining Party Break on Kavanaugh, Says Evidence Didn't Rise to the Level of Disqualifying." *The Tennessean*, October 7, 2018. https://www.tennessean.com/story/news/politics/tn-elections/2018/10/07/tennessee-elections-bredesen-kavanaugh-allegations-not-disqualifying/1551730002/.

Harris, Adam. 2020. "Bernie Sanders Reached Out to Black Voters. Why Didn't It Work?" *The Atlantic*, March 10, 2020. https://www.theatlantic.com/politics/archive/2020/03/bernie-sanders-black-voters/607789/.

Hood, M. V., Quentin Kidd, and Irwin Morris. 2015. "Tea Leaves and Southern Politics: Explaining Tea Party Support in the Region." *Social Science Quarterly* 96, no. 4: 923–940.

Jackson, Daniel. 2020. "Bloomberg Woos Voters in Gateway to Deep South Ahead of Super Tuesday." *Courthouse News Service*, February 12, 2020. https://www.courthousenews.com/bloomberg-woos-voters-in-gateway-to-deep-south-ahead-of-super-tuesday/.

Jones, Jeffrey. 2019. "Democratic States Exceed Republican States by Four in 2018." *Gallup*, February 22, 2019. https://news.gallup.com/poll/247025/democratic-states-exceed-republican-states-four-2018.aspx.

Key, V.O. 1949. *Southern Politics in State and Nation*. New York: Alfred A. Knopf.

Lipka, Michael, and Benjamin Wormald. 2016. "How Religious us Your State?" *Pew Research Center*, February, 29, 2016. https://www.pewresearch.org/fact-tank/2016/02/29/how-religious-is-your-state/?state=alabama.

Lyons, William, John Scheb, and Billy Stair. 2001. *Government and Politics in Tennessee*. Knoxville: University of Tennessee Press.

Martin, Jonathan. 2018. "A Changing Tennessee Weighs a Moderate or Conservative for Senate." *New York Times*, October 24, 2018. https://www.nytimes.com/2018/10/24/us/politics/tennessee-senate-phil-bredesen-marsha-blackburn.html.

May, Vaughn. 2018. "From Crump to Trump." In *The Future Ain't What It Used to Be: The 2016 Presidential Election in the South*, edited by Branwell Dubose Kapeluck and Scott Buchanan, 195–205. Fayetteville: University of Arkansas Press.

McKee, Seth. 2019. *The Dynamics of Southern Politics*. Thousand Oaks: CQ Press.

Nelson, Michael. 2013. "Tennessee: From Bluish to Reddish to Red." In *The New Politics of the Old South*, edited by Charles Bullock, Mark Rozell, and Patrick Cotter, 181–231. Lanham: Rowman and Littlefield Publishers.

Pew Research Center. 2014. "Evangelical Protestants." *Pew Research Center*. https://www.pewforum.org/religious-landscape-study/religious-tradition/evangelical-protestant/.

Plazas, David. 2015. "Governor: Call New Special Session on Insure Tennessee." *The Tennessean*, April 19, 2015. https://www.tennessean.com/story/opinion/editorials/2015/04/18/call-special-session-insure-tennessee/25967287/.

Sanchez, Luis. 2018. "Trump's Mention of Corker Draw Boos at Tennessee Rally." *The Hill*, May 5, 2018. https://thehill.com/homenews/administration/389813-trumps-mention-of-corker-draws-boos-at-tennessee-rally.

Schwadel, Philip. 2017. "The 'Republicanization' of Evangelical Protestants in the United States: An Examination of the Sources of Political Realignment." *Social Science Research* 62: 238–254.

Thompson, Derek. 2019. "How Democrats Conquered the City." *The Atlantic*, September 13, 2019. https://www.theatlantic.com/ideas/archive/2019/09/brief-history-how-democrats-conquered-city/597955/.

Timms, Mariah. 2020. "'Marsha' Trends as Nation Notices Sen. Blackburn Reading a Book, Tweeting During Impeachment Arguments." *The Tennessean*, January 23, 2020. https://www.tennessean.com/story/news/local/2020/01/23/marsha-blackburn-senator-reading-book-tweeting-impeachment-vindman-patrotic-trending/4559676002/.

Valentine, Phil. 2005. *Tax Revolt: The Rebellion Against an Overbearing, Bloated, Arrogant, and Abusive Government*. Nashville: Nelson Current.

Wadhwani, Anita. 2014. "Tennessee Amendment 1 Abortion Measure Passes." *The Tennessean*, November 4, 2014. https://www.tennessean.com/story/news/politics/2014/11/04/amendment-takes-early-lead/18493787/.

Wasner, Brooke. 2018. "Bredesen Campaign Releases Statement in Response to President's Comments at Nashville Rally." *Brentwood Homepage*, May 30, 2018. https://www.williamsonhomepage.com/brentwood/bredesen-campaign-releases-statement-in-response-to-president-s-comments-at-nashville-rally/article_280e12f5-bdbc-530a-87af-e390c968d86d.html.

Why I'm Running; Marsha Blackburn for Senate. YouTube video, 2:43. October 5, 2017. https://www.youtube.com/watch?v=wxSPO4V7FYI.

Woodard, David. 2006. *The New Southern Politics*. Boulder: Lynne Rienner Publishers.

Chapter 13

Texas

Partisan Changes Finally Afoot

Seth C. McKee

In *Southern Politics in State and Nation*, V. O. Key (1949, 254) had this to say about Texas: "The Lone Star State is concerned about money and how to make it, about oil and sulfur and gas, about cattle and dust storms and irrigation, about cotton and banking and Mexicans." Seventy years hence and all these things still concern Texans but not to the extent that they once did. Texas is the colossus of the South, and it continues to grow in ways that threaten current Republican electoral dominance. In 1950, Texas had twenty-one congressional districts. In 2021, the Lone Star State had thirty-six, which amounts to more than one of every four (26 percent) U.S. representatives in the eleven ex-Confederate states' House delegation (36 out of 138). Key may not have anticipated the 1960s civil rights movement (Black and Black 1987) that peaked right around the time of his passing in October 1963, but he was correct to expect that urbanization would alter the balance of power in southern politics. Nevertheless, population growth has meandered a peculiar political path in the Lone Star State. In mid-twentieth century, the rise of Texas's megacities initially fostered presidential Republicanism (Bartley and Graham 1975). In the decades since, the locus of the GOP's power is now firmly entrenched in the Lone Star State's least populated rural and heretofore Democratic counties where Anglo Texans now supply huge Republican vote margins (Hood and McKee 2022; Myers 2013). In contrast, Texas's once-Republican cities, especially the most populous among them, are increasingly shifting in favor of a revived Democratic opposition.

This chapter chronicles recent developments in Texas party politics. In line with previous editions of this volume, the emphasis is placed on presidential elections and rightfully so, because in an age of nationalization (Hopkins 2018; Jacobson and Carson 2020), the dynamics at the top of the ticket set the course for all contests below. A brief recap of Texas politics since the time of Key (1949) is offered and then the bulk of the chapter focuses on electoral patterns from 1998 to 2020. The evidence suggests that Texas Republicans are gradually loosening their firm grip on electoral politics. As recent scholarship has demonstrated (see Bullock 2021; Bullock et al. 2019; Morris 2021), southern Republicans are facing serious problems at the ballot box in those settings where there is considerable population growth and with it demographic change. As much as any southern state, Texas takes a place near the head of the pack with regard to population growth and the demographic changes accompanying it. Indeed, since the surprising presidential victory of Republican Donald Trump in 2016, election data reflect how a growing and changing Texas electorate is finally yielding tangible gains for what was until the past decade a politically hapless Democratic Party.

TEXAS REPUBLICANISM

In the insurgent Dixiecrat campaign of 1948, Strom Thurmond carried four southern states' electoral votes but was least formidable against Democratic President Truman in Texas. Four years later, when war hero Dwight Eisenhower led the GOP's first breakthrough in southern presidential politics since 1876, Texas was one of four southern states to back the Republican presidential nominee and then did so again in 1956. Figure 13.1 shows the two-party percentage of the Republican popular vote cast in Texas and the entire South from 1952 to 2020. When Eisenhower twice carried the Lone Star State in the 1950s, he won majorities in all of Texas's "Big Six" counties: Bexar (San Antonio), Dallas (Dallas), El Paso (El Paso), Harris

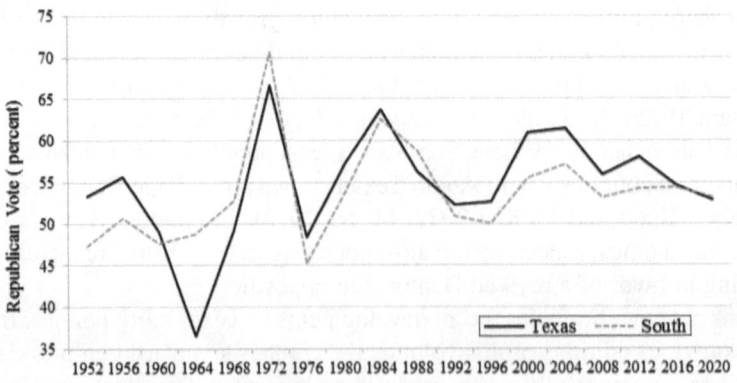

Figure 13.1 The Republican Presidential Vote in Texas and the South, 1952–2020. *Source:* Data compiled by the author from Dave Leip's Atlas of U.S. Presidential Elections (https://uselectionatlas.org/). Last accessed February 28, 2021.

(Houston), Tarrant (Fort Worth), and Travis (Austin). Thus, the early success of the southern GOP registered strongest in Texas's largest metropolitan centers where a growing and upwardly mobile Anglo (non-Latino white) middle-class electorate embraced the Republican Party for being more concerned with making money and keeping more of it, whereas southern Democrats remained united and perhaps fixated in their opposition to an emerging but still nascent black civil rights movement.

There is little question that Republican advancement in Texas was very much of a top-down nature, with electoral success most pronounced and manifesting earliest in presidential politics (Aistrup 1996). Nevertheless, the outsized presence and influence of Texan and Democrat Lyndon B. Johnson had the effect of placing GOP presidential victories on hold throughout the 1960s when he offered a huge assist to John F. Kennedy as his running mate in 1960. After JFK's assassination, Johnson easily won Texas as President in 1964, and then managed to hold the state for his Vice President Hubert Humphrey in 1968. Like the rest of the southern states, Texas contributed to Republican President Richard Nixon's landslide win over his liberal Democratic challenger and South Dakota Senator George McGovern in 1972. Former Georgia Governor Jimmy Carter's victory over Republican President Gerald Ford in 1976 was the last time Texans favored a Democrat at the top of their tickets. In 1980, except for Travis County, with the culturally liberal capital city of Austin as its hub, Republican Ronald Reagan beat Carter in the remaining Texas Big Six counties mentioned earlier, and then carried all six in his blowout win over Democrat Walter Mondale in 1984. After 1976, Texas along with three Deep South states (Alabama, Mississippi, and South Carolina) are Dixie's only four to stay wholly within the presidentially Republican fold through 2020.

As the GOP secured its dominance at the presidential level, the intra-party feud taking place within the Texas Democratic Party eventually created an opening for the Republican Party to ascend to hegemonic status in state and local elections. Since the middle of the twentieth century, the conservative/ establishment wing (culturally and economically) of the Texas Democratic Party typically controlled the party's electoral apparatus (Green 1979).[1] But as a growing share of lower-class and minority voters grew the ranks of the Texas Democratic coalition after the 1960s civil rights era, more and more conservative Democrats exited their ancestral party in favor of the rather moribund Republican opposition (Davidson 1990). This sorting process took decades to complete, but by the late 1990s, the vast majority of Anglo Texans had aligned with the GOP and in numbers great enough to defeat Democrats in all statewide elections. In fact, no Democrat has held a U.S. Senate seat in Texas since Lloyd Bentsen vacated his office in 1993 to serve as Treasury Secretary in the Clinton administration. Bentsen's successor in the special contest to replace him was Republican Kay Bailey Hutchison. In Texas's nine statewide (nonjudicial) elective offices, the last victorious Democrats date back to 1994.[2] Only Republicans have won these positions in every election taking place after 1994.

Outside of statewide contests for state (e.g., governor) and federal office (president and senator), Republican growth in district-based positions has been relatively slower, especially in U.S. House elections. Table 13.1 shows the number of Republicans comprising the 150-member Texas House, the thirty-one-member Texas Senate, and the U.S. House delegation from 1998 to 2020. Over this timespan the Texas U.S. House delegation went from thirty members (1998–2000) to thirty (from 2002 to 2010) to thirty-six (2012 to 2020), while the size of the Texas Legislature was constant. For all three offices, once the GOP captured a majority of seats the party has not relinquished control. Republicans gained a majority of Texas Senate seats in 1996, a Texas House majority in 2002, and finally the majority of congressional districts in 2004. Since Republicans held the governorship, and the state senate, after winning majority control of the state house in 2002, this enabled the GOP to pursue its widely known and ruthlessly successful power grab in U.S. House contests by enacting a 2004 "re-redistricting" of congressional boundaries, which produced the first Republican majority since Reconstruction (Bickerstaff 2007; McKee and Shaw 2005; McKee, Teigen, and Turgeon 2006). But for a dispassionate political observer, it is hard to bestow sympathy upon Texas Democrats because, thanks to a highly effective Democratic gerrymander engineered by Congressman Martin Frost for the 1992 elections, this map was principally responsible for delaying the GOP takeover that took more than a decade to materialize (see Barone and Ujifusa 1993; Black and Black 2002).[3]

There are several factors to note in table 13.1. First, in the two nationally favorable back-to-back Democratic election cycles of 2006 and 2008, the number of Republicans declined in the Texas Legislature and U.S. House. Indeed, the reduction of Republican Texas state representatives to seventy-six put the GOP Texas House majority at a bare minimum in 2008. However, two years later in the tea party-fueled 2010 Republican wave elections, Texas Republicans peaked with respect to their presence in the U.S. House and Texas Legislature. This GOP high-water mark in district-based Republican officeholding is revealing of the most recent electoral dynamics in the Lone Star State. By dint of their holding majorities in all three of these offices, for the past decade and a half, Texas Republicans have crafted districts that have successfully mitigated the Democratic electoral threat. Despite these efforts, ten years since the apex of Republican representation in Texas's district-based offices, the GOP majority has declined ten percentage points, from 67.1 percent in 2010 to 57.1 percent in 2020.

Table 13.1 Texas Republicans in District-Based Elections, 1998–2020

Republicans	1998	2000	2002	2004	2006	2008	2010	2012	2014	2016	2018	2020
House	72	72	88	87	81	76	101	95	98	95	83	83
Senate	16	16	19	19	20	19	19	19	20	20	19	18
U.S. House	13	13	15	21	19	20	23	24	25	25	23	23
Total	101	101	122	127	120	115	143	138	143	140	125	124
N	211	211	213	213	213	213	213	217	217	217	217	217
Rep (percent)	47.9	47.9	57.3	59.6	56.3	54.0	67.1	63.6	65.9	64.5	57.6	57.1

Notes: Data compiled by the author from various volumes of *The Almanac of American Politics* for 1998–2018 and also data on state legislative partisan composition for 2018 and 2020 from the *National Conference of State Legislatures* (https://www.ncsl.org/). Through reapportionment, the Texas U.S. House delegation was 30 until 2002 when it increased to 32 and then increased again to 36 in 2012. The size of the Texas House and Texas Senate has remained constant over this timespan with 31 Texas Senate districts and 150 Texas House districts.

The last two elections in 2018 and 2020 are telling for the new, if only brief (redistricting will occur for the 2022 elections), partisan equilibrium in these contests. The notable drop in GOP officeholders in 2018 reflected the general weakness of Republicans representing districts that were located in what once were the party's stronghold: urban and suburban areas with substantial white electorates. In the Texas House, Republicans shed a dozen seats in 2018 (Chang and Walsh 2018) and did not recoup their losses in 2020.[4] In perhaps the two most salient cases in 2018, Congressional Districts 7 and 32, two longtime Republican incumbents lost in 100 percent urban districts and their Democratic challengers were reelected in 2020 in these racially diverse constituencies with plurality Anglo electorates that are trending Democratic.[5] Since 2014, the overall number of Texas Republicans holding district-based offices has declined, and therefore the GOP should be thankful to once again (barring legal interference) use redistricting in 2022 as a means to stanch Democratic gains.

TEXAS STATEWIDE ELECTIONS SINCE 1998

Table 13.2 splits statewide elections for governor, senator, and president into two periods, 1998 to 2008 and 2010 to 2020. Splitting the election data this way is equal with respect to the number of contests for each office, ten contests in the earlier and later period; three for governor, four for senator, and three for president. The table shows the two-party Republican percentage of the vote cast by Texans in these offices. Additionally, the table displays the total GOP votes cast across the three offices for each period and the sum of the two-party vote total as well. Finally, the last column presents the percentage and percent difference in the Republican vote cast for each office for 2010–2020 versus 1998–2008. Comparing the second decade of elections to the first, the number of Republican votes increased by over 28 percent.

Table 13.2 Waning Texas Republicanism in Statewide Elections

Republican Vote (percent)	1998–2008	2010–2020	Change: 2010–2020 – 1998–2008
Governor	62 (3)	58 (3)	−4 points, −6.5 percent
Senator	60 (4)	56 (4)	−4 points, −6.7 percent
President	59 (3)	55 (3)	−4 points, −6.8 percent
Republican Votes	33,283,641	42,860,665	
Total Votes	55,305,152	76,521,099	
All Offices	60	56	−4 points, −6.7 percent

Notes: Data compiled by the author from *Dave Leip's Atlas of U.S. Presidential Elections* (https://uselectionatlas.org/). Number of elections is displayed in parentheses.

Similarly, the total vote increased by over 38 percent. The expanding Texas electorate is showing clear indications of a Democratic shift.

There is a striking, consistent, and perhaps surprising pattern revealed in the data presented in table 13.2. Texas Republican strength in these statewide elections clearly peaked from 1998 to 2008. Also, in both decades the Texas GOP is most dominant in gubernatorial elections, followed by senatorial contests, and actually weakest/most competitive in presidential races. The most important finding is that, regardless of the office, in the later decade, the GOP percentage of the two-party vote has declined by 4 points, which amounts to more than a 6 percent drop in Republican voting. To be sure, Texas Republicans retain the upper hand in these statewide contests, but the past ten years highlight an across-the-board reduction in GOP support and conversely the nontrivial uptick in Democratic voting in these most politically powerful offices. From 1998 to 2008, Texas Republicans benefited from landslide-level support, averaging 60 percent of the two-party vote in elections for governor, senator, and president. In the past ten years (2010–2020), including the unusually auspicious 2010 midterm elections for the GOP, Texas Republicans find themselves in a much more electorally competitive environment in which they now average 56 percent of the major party vote in the aforementioned contests.[6]

THE TEXAS GOP IN THE TRUMP ERA

Thus far, Texas politics has been examined in isolation, but in a book on southern politics, it is prudent to place the Lone Star State in its regional context. Table 13.3 does this. Data on the Republican share of the major party vote for the past three presidential contests (2012, 2016, and 2020) are shown for all eleven ex-Confederate states and also for the South-wide total. In addition, there is a column that provides the percentage difference in the GOP presidential vote between 2020 and 2012. The last column presents the percent change in the population of each state and the South, from 2012 to 2019. By covering the past three presidential elections, it is possible to discern any actual patterns in Republican voting. Additionally, population change is shown in order to emphasize the point that southern presidential Republicanism is generally negatively associated with rapidly growing electorates.

In the 2012 presidential election, there were three states in which the Republican nominee Mitt Romney won at least 60 percent of the vote (Arkansas, Alabama, and Tennessee). Texas falls in the next tier of states with its GOP presidential vote in the high fifty percentile range (58 percent), right below Louisiana (58.7 percent Republican) and therefore ranking it the

Table 13.3 Texas in a Changing South: Republican Presidential Vote and Population Growth

State	2012 Presidential Vote (R %)	2016 Presidential Vote (R %)	2020 Presidential Vote (R %)	2020–2012 Change in Presidential Vote (%)	Population Change 2012 to 2019 (%)
Alabama	61.2	64.4	62.9	1.7	2.1
Arkansas	62.2	64.3	64.2	2.1	2.7
Florida	49.6	50.6	51.7	2.1	12.4
Georgia	54.0	52.7	49.9	-4.1	8.2
Louisiana	58.7	60.2	59.5	0.7	1.6
Mississippi	55.8	59.1	58.4	2.6	-0.1
North Carolina	51.0	51.9	50.7	-0.3	8.7
South Carolina	55.3	57.5	55.9	0.6	10.2
Tennessee	60.4	63.6	61.8	1.5	6.7
Texas	58.0	54.7	52.8	-5.2	13.0
Virginia	48.0	47.2	44.8	-3.2	5.2
South	54.3	54.4	53.2	-1.1	9.1

Notes: Presidential data compiled by the author for Dave Leip's Atlas of U.S. Presidential Elections (https://uselectionatlas.org/). Population data compiled by the author from the Missouri Census Data Center (https://mcdc.missouri.edu/). Population change is based on the percentage difference in the ending population estimate for 2018–2019 versus the starting population estimate for 2011–2012.

fifth most presidentially Republican southern state in the 2012 cycle. In the aggregate, the GOP percentage of the South's 2012 presidential vote was 54.3 percent, and hence the Lone Star State was considerably more Republican than the regional percentage. Four years later, in the 2016 presidential contest Texas's Republican share of the vote declined 3.3 points, which made the Lone Star State the seventh most presidentially Republican in Dixie. Now, Republican presidential voting in Texas (54.7 percent) nearly matched the regional percentage of 54.4 percent Republican in the 2016 election.

In 2020, Texas was again the seventh most presidentially Republican southern state, but with President Trump losing support and ultimately this election, his share of the Texas vote dropped to 52.8 percent. Referring back to figure 13.1, for the first time since 1988, in 2020, the South-wide percentage of the Republican presidential vote (53.2 percent) was higher than the GOP vote share registered in the Lone Star State. Furthermore, comparing the difference in the Republican presidential vote in 2020 versus 2012, the reduction in the GOP percentage of the vote is greatest in Texas, with a decline of 5.2 points. Three other states registered a decline in the Republican presidential vote between 2020 and 2012 (Georgia, Virginia, and North Carolina), including the only two that the Democrat Joe Biden won in 2020 (Georgia and Virginia). The last column of the table shows that from 2012 to 2019, among the southern states, Texas experienced the highest rate of population change, with a 13 percent growth rate. A simple bivariate correlation of the 2020 Republican presidential vote in the southern states and the South with the corresponding population change (2012–2019) for the same observations results in a Pearson correlation coefficient of $-.539$ ($p = .07$, two-tailed). In other words, it is generally the case that the more rapidly growing southern states are those exhibiting lower support for the Republican nominee/President Trump in the 2020 election.

With the general pattern established that Texas is no longer one of the most presidentially Republican states in the South, returning to an analysis confined to the Lone Star State further illuminates some interesting dynamics. Before proceeding further though, it is worth reflecting again on the sheer size and growth of the Texas population. In the United States, only California has a larger population than Texas, but these days more people are migrating to the Lone Star State than to the Golden State. In the 1980s, California experienced impressive population growth, and reapportionment rewarded the state with a whopping seven additional seats for the 1992 U.S. House elections, which brought the Golden State delegation to fifty-two members. Since the 1990 decennial census, California has only added one additional seat through reapportionment and is actually projected to lose one of its fifty-three total congressional districts following the completion of the 2020 reapportionment. Texas went from thirty congressional districts in the 1990 reapportionment to its current total of thirty-six House seats, by gaining four in the 2010 reapportionment. The latest projection has the Lone Star State receiving three more House seats once the 2020 reapportionment is finalized.[7]

In the first section of this chapter, it was noted that Texas Republicanism took hold in the state's most populous cities and those counties that encompassed them. From the 1950s through the 1980s, it made sense to talk about these so-called Big Six counties where most of the population of Houston, Dallas, San Antonio, Fort Worth, Austin, and El Paso resided. In the first two decades of the twenty-first century, because of such impressive population growth, Texas has twelve counties in which at least half a million people live. These twelve counties and the major cities (noted in parentheses) that are primarily encompassed within them are presented in table 13.4. These counties are referred to as the "Big 12," admittedly a loose reference to the major collegiate athletic conference that has the flagship University of Texas as one of its, ahem, ten total members. Texas's twelve most populous counties actually contain more than 63 percent of the state population.[8] These dozen counties are highlighted because, among the eleven southern states, Texas is one of the most geographically polarized in electoral politics (see Hood and McKee 2022; Myers 2013). Specifically, Texas urban voters are heavily Democratic, whereas Texas rural voters are markedly more Republican. In recent years, this geographic partisan polarization in voter preferences has widened.

In addition to listing the twelve most populous Texas counties, table 13.4 also shows their percent population change spanning 2012 to 2019; the percentage non-white population in these counties; the Republican share of the two-party presidential vote in 2016 and 2020; and the difference in the GOP presidential vote between these two elections (2020 versus 2016). Data on the remaining 242 Texas counties are displayed as a point of comparison, and likewise for the entire state in the last row of the table. Population change in the Big 12 counties exceeds double digits in all but three (Dallas, Hidalgo, and El Paso), and averages 15.6 percent compared to 8.9 percent for the remainder of Texas.

With respect to the percentage of non-white (non-Anglo) residents, it is 64 percent in the Big 12 versus 47 percent in the 242 other Texas counties. Put differently, on average, the Big 12 contain majority-minority populations, whereas the rest of Texas is still majority Anglo (non-Latino white). In the 2016 presidential election, 45 percent of the Big 12 vote went to Republican Donald Trump. By comparison, in 2016, Trump almost garnered 70 percent of the vote in Texas's other 242 counties. In 2020, the Republican share of the presidential vote declined slightly in both the Big 12 and the rest of Texas. Because Trump performed relatively worse in the Big 12 vis-à-vis Texas's remaining counties, a 24.4 percentage point Republican

Table 13.4 The Big 12: Population Growth, Race, and the Republican Vote in Texas Presidential Elections

County (City)	Population Change 2012–2019	Non-White (%)	2016 President (R %)	2020 President (R %)	Change %: (2020–2016 Vote)
Harris (Houston)	12.7	70.4	43.5	43.3	-0.3
Dallas (Dallas)	9.4	70.9	36.3	33.9	-2.4
Tarrant (Fort Worth)	13.7	53.3	54.5	49.9	-4.6
Bexar (San Antonio)	14.1	72.3	42.9	40.8	-2.2
Travis (Austin)	19.9	51.0	29.2	27.0	-2.2
Collin (DFW)	27.0	43.0	58.8	52.2	-6.6
Hidalgo (Edinburg, McAllen)	9.2	93.9	29.0	41.4	+12.3
El Paso (El Paso)	2.4	88.0	27.3	32.1	+4.8
Denton (DFW)	29.4	40.8	60.6	54.1	-6.5
Fort Bend (Houston)	33.6	66.9	46.5	44.6	-1.9
Montgomery (Houston)	28.7	34.0	76.6	72.2	-4.4
Williamson (Austin)	33.5	40.6	55.2	49.3	-5.9
All 12 Counties	15.6	64.2	45.2	43.4	-1.9
Remaining 242 Counties	8.9	47.4	69.6	68.7	-1.0
Texas	13.0	58.0	54.7	52.8	-1.9

Notes: Data compiled by the author. See the note under the previous table for computation of population growth and data source. Percentage non-white is calculated from the 2015 to 2019 American Community Survey five-year estimate. Presidential vote data are from *Dave Leip's Atlas of U.S. Presidential Elections* (https://uselectionatlas.org/). The major city (or cities) in the county is noted in parentheses. DFW stands for Dallas-Fort Worth. The change calculations are more precise than the single decimal point shown in the table since the data were not rounded prior to computing the vote difference for 2020 versus 2016.

presidential advantage in the 242 least populated Texas counties in 2016, actually increased to 25.3 percentage points in 2020.

One curious pattern evident in the data from the table is with respect to Trump's improved 2020 performance among the Latino electorate in Texas. This development is palpable, even with the county-level data shown in table 13.4. For instance, Hidalgo and El Paso counties have by far the largest percentage of Latino residents among the Big 12 counties (92 percent and 83 percent Latino, respectively), and they are the only two among the Big 12 where Trump performed better in 2020. In fact, in most of the heavily Latino counties at or near the Mexico border, the vote shifted notably in favor of Trump. Between 2016 and 2020, eight of these Texas counties flipped from Democratic to Republican in the presidential election.[9] In contrast, three counties went from Republican to Democratic between 2016 and 2020; two bordered either side of Travis County (Williamson to the north and Hays to the south) and the other was Tarrant County (Fort Worth).

If the counties that flipped in favor of Trump and Biden in 2020 are viewed similar to the zero-sum nature of the Electoral College, and hence each is treated as winner-take-all, then the gains made by Biden in the counties that flipped to his party are much more substantial than the much less populated counties that switched in favor of Trump. For instance, compared to the 2016 election, Trump netted 8,878 votes in the eight counties that he turned in 2020. By comparison, in 2020, Biden netted 208,802 votes in the three substantially more urban and populated counties that went from Republican to Democratic.[10] Finally, it is difficult to view the Latino shift toward Trump as anything more than an embrace of this president, rather than a long-term move in favor of the Republican Party. If this assessment is accurate, then the pronounced movement of Latinos in south Texas to Trump in 2020 is ephemeral and certainly not a development that Lone Star State Republicans should or can, bank upon in future elections. Instead, what should be of greater concern to the Texas GOP is the decline in support among urban Anglos, since the Anglo electorate has always been the foundation of contemporary Republican dominance in the Lone Star State. This issue is addressed in the next section.

THE RURAL-URBAN ANGLO DIVIDE IN TEXAS POLITICS

An insightful way to document the growing rural-urban divide in the Anglo vote in Texas is with the use of exit poll data. It has already been determined that during the Trump era, the percentage of the Republican presidential vote in Texas has declined. This development is not confined to presidential elections and that is easily inferred from the data presented in table 13.2, even though the latter period started with the 2010 midterm elections. With exit-poll data on Texas, Anglo voters can be partitioned into rural/small-town (ST) or urban. Rural/ST voters are those who reside in rural communities or cities with under 50,000 inhabitants. Urban voters are those who live in suburban communities or cities with over 50,000 residents. Table 13.5 makes comparisons of the Republican percentage of the two-party vote cast by rural/ST and urban Anglo Texans in statewide races for governor, senator, and president, which took place before and during the Trump presidency. All of the data are from Texas exit polls and not from the subset of Texans in the national exit polls for these listed years.[11]

For each type of election in table 13.5, there is at least one contest that occurred before Trump won the White House in 2016 and at least one contest that occurred during his presidential tenure. The last name of the Republican candidate is shown in parentheses next to the year of each contest. The overall percentage of the GOP vote cast by Anglos is displayed ("All") and then it is shown for rural/ST and urban Anglos. With the exception of the two races for governor in 2014 and 2018, the rural-urban difference in the Republican vote is notably higher during the Trump years than prior. In summing up the GOP votes before Trump, the rural-urban Republican disparity amounts to almost 12 percentage points. In contrast, with Trump as president, the aggregation of the Republican vote across these three offices results in a rural-urban divide that has increased to sixteen percentage points.

Table 13.5 The Anglo Republican Vote for Statewide Offices before and During Trump Era

White Voters	All	Rural/ST	Urban	Rural-Urban Difference
Governor				
2014 (Abbott)	74.4	83.5	73.3	10.1
2018 (Abbott)	75.2	83.7	73.5	10.2
Senator				
2014 (Cornyn)	77.3	85.2	76.4	8.8
2018 (Cruz)	69.7	81.9	67.4	14.5
2020 (Cornyn)	69.1	83.8	67.6	16.2
President				
2008 (McCain)	74.1	87.0	71.5	15.5
2016–20 (Trump)	68.9	84.7	67.2	17.5
Pre-Trump	75.2	85.5	73.8	11.7
Trump Era	69.6	83.9	67.9	16.0

Notes: Data computed by the author from Texas exit polls. "ST" means small town (less than 50,000 residents). "Urban" combines cities (over 50,000 residents) and suburban communities. Data are limited to non-Latino white voters. The Rural-Urban differences are more precise than rounding to the first decimal place and subtracting, and that accounts for why this difference appears incorrect in the first row for the 2014 gubernatorial election.

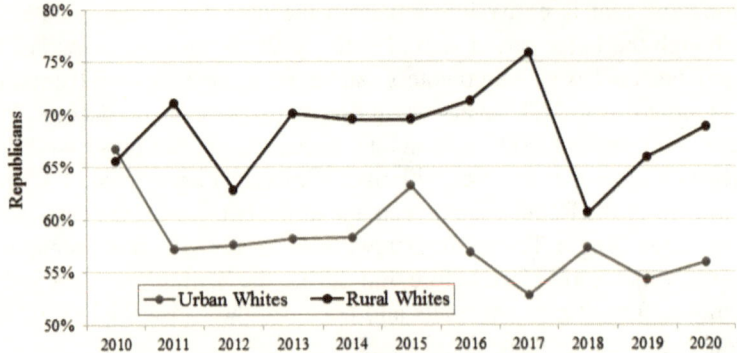

Figure 13.2 Republican Affiliation of Anglo Texans, 2010–2020. *Source:* Data compiled by author from the University of Texas/Texas Tribune Poll (https://www.texastribune.org/series/ut-tt-polls/). Last accessed February 28, 2021.

Not surprisingly, the considerable rural-urban Anglo division in Texas elections, as demonstrated in table 13.5, also materializes with regard to party affiliation. Figure 13.2 presents the percentage of rural and urban Anglo Texans who affiliate with the GOP, from 2010 to 2020 based on data from the University of Texas/Texas Tribune Polls. Independents who lean toward the GOP are classified as Republicans. There are several things to note from the figure. First, the percentage of urban Republicans was only higher (but certainly within the sampling margin of error) at the start of the time series in 2010. Second, after 2010, the share of urban Republicans only exceeds 60 percent one more time, when it is 63 percent in 2015. By comparison, the percentage of rural Republicans never drops below 60 percent. There would appear to be sampling variability that is reflected in the substantial variation in the percentage of GOP identifiers from one year to the next. For instance, in 2017, the rural-urban GOP identification gap amounts to a twenty-three-percentage-point chasm. A year later in 2018, there is marked convergence with the rural-urban Republican affiliation difference narrowing to four percentage points. Nevertheless, after this midterm, which was considerably harsh to President Trump's Republican Party (Jacobson 2019), the rural-urban GOP identification disparity increases to 12 points in 2019 and then to 13 points in 2020.

CONCLUSION

If there were no faithless electors in 2016, then the Republican Donald Trump would have amassed 306 votes in the Electoral College and Democrat Hillary Clinton would have received the remaining 232.[12] Although again in 2020, the political handicappers did a lousy job of prognosticating the outcomes in elections for president and Congress, no one expected President Trump to turn a single state in his favor, and he did not. The question was, how many states would Democrat Joe Biden gain over Hillary Clinton? So, remarkably, given Texas's total number of electoral votes (38), if the Lone Star State was the only one to flip Democratic in 2020 and no electors strayed from their pledges to the major party nominees, then Joe Biden would have prevailed with a bare majority of 270 Electoral College votes. Of course, Texas did not go blue in 2020. Nevertheless, as documented in this chapter, the recent movement away from the GOP in Texas presidential elections is notable and furthermore, not isolated to this office. For the past decade, Texas Republicans have been ceding ground to the Democratic opposition all down the ballot, both in terms of their share of the major party vote and with respect to election outcomes in district-based contests.

It is too early to determine whether the Trump years uniquely contributed to the electoral slippage endured by the Texas GOP. Yet, one thing is certain, Trump's presidency did not wear well for the Republican Party in Texas. To be sure, rural Anglos stayed stalwart in their support of Trump and the GOP more generally, and interestingly, there was a short-term Trump effect that boosted south Texas Latino support for the president in 2020 (Campo-Flores and Findell 2020). But conversely, Texas's already remarkable geographic polarization in partisan voting has only widened over the past several election cycles and the primary reason for this is the decline in Republican voting exhibited by urban Anglos. Among the southern states, Texas is the only one that is majority-minority, containing a 42 percent non-Latino white (Anglo) population (lowest in the South). Texas has the proportionally smallest African American population at 12 percent and the largest Latino population at 39 percent.

To the casual observer, for years, Texas has appeared primed to favor Democrats in statewide contests for any office because of the demographic composition of its electorate. Those who understand Texas politics know that the GOP retains several advantages despite truly inhospitable demographic trends. For one, the most Republican and largest component (though declining) of the Texas electorate is Anglo voters and they are consistently more participatory than African Americans and Latinos (Hood and McKee 2017). Second, in percentage terms, the most Democratic group in the country, African Americans, constitute the smallest share of the Texas electorate among the three major racial/ethnic populations. Finally, as demonstrated in 2020, Texas Latinos are a highly variable group with regard to their partisan voting behavior. Hence, in spite of President Trump's demeaning language toward immigrants, dating back to the speech kicking off his White House run in 2015, in 2020 Latino Texans closest to the Mexico border shifted strongly in his favor.

All things considered, the extant and immediate Republican advantage in Texas politics still makes it more likely for ambitious politicians to run under the GOP label. Nevertheless, the future would appear to favor Democratic gains. High population growth now translates into greater Democratic support (Bullock et al. 2019; Bullock 2021; Morris 2021), and Texas is at the forefront of southern states that are growing at a rapid clip. No other state in the region can boast of the number of cities Texas can claim with such large populations, and these electorates possess political attitudes/opinions and demographic characteristics that translate into a large and growing Democratic vote that the more rural and Republican countryside cannot keep pace with. In sum, if the current electoral dynamics in Texas persist, and urban Anglos do not make an about-face back to the GOP, then the ingredients for a majority Democratic coalition are present, and this account will have appropriately served as a harbinger of the changing party politics clearly underway in the Lone Star State.

NOTES

1. One high-profile exception to the Texas Democratic establishment was Senator Ralph Yarborough, a true liberal who served from 1957 (won a special election) to 1970 and in 1964 defeated his Republican challenger George H.W. Bush.

2. Currently, these nine statewide offices, which mostly have four-year terms and are up for election in midterm years, include: governor, lieutenant governor, attorney general, comptroller of public accounts, commissioner of the general land office, commissioner of agriculture, and three railroad commissioner offices that have six-year terms and hold staggered elections so one seat is up every two years.

3. Because of a court ruling, substantial changes were made to thirteen Texas congressional districts for the 1996 elections (McKee 2010), but this did not wipe away the underlying Democratic gerrymander established in 1992. In the 2002 redistricting, an incumbent protection plan was implemented since Democrats did not lose their Texas House majority until after the 2002 elections. Nevertheless, the two U.S. House seats added through reapportionment were drawn for Republicans to win (and they did).

4. Of the dozen Texas House districts that flipped to the Democrats in 2018, six were located in the greater Dallas area: District 65 (Denton County), and Districts 102, 105, 113, 114, and 115 (all in Dallas County). Four Democratic gains were in the Austin/Central Texas area: District 45 (Blanco and Hays counties); District 47 (Travis County/Austin); and Districts 52 and 136 (Williamson County/Round Rock). And two more Democratic districts were netted on the western side of greater Houston/Harris County (Districts 132 and 135). The winners and losers in these contests are documented by Pollock, Anchondo, and Waller (2018).

5. In the 2018 midterm, Democratic attorney Lizzie Fletcher defeated Republican Congressman John Culberson (first elected in 2000) in the Houston-based Texas

District 7, while former NFL linebacker (and Baylor Bear) and Democrat Colin Allred defeated Republican Congressman Pete Sessions (first elected in 1996) in Dallas-based Texas District 32. Interestingly, when Republican Congressman Bill Flores retired from Texas District 17 in 2020, Republican Pete Sessions won the open seat, which is located south of Dallas and hence contained a Republican-leaning electorate Sessions had never represented in Congress.

6. In the 2018 Texas Senate election, former Democratic Congressman Beto O'Rourke (Texas District 16 in El Paso) gave Republican Senator Ted Cruz a serious challenge. The two-party vote went 51.3 percent to 48.7 percent in favor of the Republican Cruz. At the time of the election, Senator Cruz was not a very popular incumbent, and it was widely thought that this close call for a Texas Republican was a unique case. Based on the evidence presented in table 13.2, it is now apparent that the Texas GOP is generally losing support in recent statewide elections.

7. These 2020 reapportionment projections come from the following report compiled by Election Data Services and available at this link: https://www.electiondataservices.com/wp-content/uploads/2020/12/NR_Appor20wTableMaps.pdf.

8. Population and demographic data in table 13.4 were compiled by the author from the 2015–2019 American Community Survey five-year estimates.

9. The eight counties that went from Democratic to Republican in 2020 were: Frio, Jim Wells, Kenedy, Kleberg, La Salle, Reeves, Val Verde (borders Mexico), and Zapata (borders Mexico).

10. In the eight counties that flipped to the Republican Trump in 2020, the average Anglo percentage was 16.5 and the average Latino percentage was 80.2. In the three counties that switched in favor of the Democrat Biden in 2020, the average Anglo percentage was 49.7 and the average Latino percentage was 28.7.

11. Unfortunately, there was no 2012 Texas exit poll and that is why only the data for the 2008 presidential election are displayed in the table.

12. In actuality, two Texas Republican electors in 2016 did not cast their votes for Trump, and five Democratic electors (one in Hawaii and four in Washington) did not vote for Clinton.

REFERENCES

Aistrup, Joseph A. 1996. *The Southern Strategy Revisited: Republican Top-Down Advancement in the South*. Lexington: University Press of Kentucky.

Barone, Michael, and Grant Ujifusa. 1993. *The Almanac of American Politics 1994*. Washington, DC: National Journal.

Bartley, Numan V., and Hugh D. Graham. 1975. *Southern Politics and the Second Reconstruction*. Baltimore: Johns Hopkins University Press.

Bickerstaff, Steve. 2007. *Lines in the Sand: Congressional Redistricting in Texas and the Downfall of Tom DeLay*. Austin: University of Texas Press.

Black, Earl, and Merle Black. 1987. *Politics and Society in the South*. Cambridge: Harvard University Press.

Black, Earl, and Merle Black. 2002. *The Rise of Southern Republicans*. Cambridge, MA: Harvard University Press.

Bullock, Charles S., III. 2021. "Growth Versus Stagnation and a New Realignment." In *The New Politics of the Old South*, eds. Charles S. Bullock III and Mark J. Rozell. Lanham, MD: Rowman & Littlefield.

Bullock, Charles S., III, Susan A. MacManus, Jeremy D. Mayer, and Mark J. Rozell. 2019. *The South and the Transformation of U.S. Politics*. New York: Oxford University Press.

Campo-Flores, Arian, and Elizabeth Findell. 2020. "Latino Voters Move Toward Trump." *Wall Street Journal*, November 6, A6.

Chang, Julie, and Sean Collins Walsh. 2018. "GOP Loses 12 Seats in Texas House, 2 in the Senate." *Austin American-Statesman*, November 7. https://www.statesman.com/news/20181107/gop-loses-12-seats-in-texas-house-2-in-senate.

Davidson, Chandler. 1990. *Race and Class in Texas Politics*. Princeton: Princeton University Press.

Green, George Norris. 1979. *The Establishment in Texas Politics: The Primitive Years, 1938–1957*. Norman: University of Oklahoma Press.

Hood, M. V., III, and Seth C. McKee 2017. "Texas: Big Red Rides On," in *The New Politics of the Old South*, eds. Charles S. Bullock III and Mark J. Rozell. Lanham, MD: Rowman & Littlefield.

Hood, M. V., III, and Seth C. McKee. 2022. *An Untold Story: Rural Republican Realignment in the Modern South*. Columbia: University of South Carolina Press.

Hopkins, Daniel J. 2018. *The Increasingly Nationalized United States: How and Why American Political Behavior Nationalized*. Chicago: University of Chicago Press.

Jacobson, Gary C., and Jamie L. Carson. 2020. *The Politics of Congressional Elections*. Lanham, MD: Rowman & Littlefield.

Key, V. O., Jr. 1949. *Southern Politics in State and Nation*. New York: Alfred A. Knopf.

McKee, Seth C. 2010. *Republican Ascendancy in Southern U.S. House Elections*. New York: Routledge.

McKee, Seth C., and Daron R. Shaw. 2005. "Redistricting in Texas: Institutionalizing Republican Ascendancy." In *Redistricting in the New Millennium*, ed. Peter F. Galderisi. Lanham, MD: Lexington Books.

McKee, Seth C., Jeremy M. Teigen, and Mathieu Turgeon. 2006. "The Partisan Impact of Congressional Redistricting: The Case of Texas, 2001–2003." *Social Science Quarterly* 87(2): 308–317.

Morris, Irwin L. 2021. *Movers and Stayers: The Partisan Transformation of 21st Century Southern Politics*. New York: Oxford University Press.

Myers, Adam. 2013. "Secular Geographical Polarization in the American South: The Case of Texas, 1996–2010." *Electoral Studies* 32: 38–62.

Pollock, Cassandra, Carlos Anchondo, and Allyson R. Waller. 2018. "Democratic Women Lead Biggest Shift in Texas House since 2010 Midterms." *Texas Tribune*, November 6. https://www.texastribune.org/2018/11/06/texas-midterm-election-results-texas-house-races/.

Chapter 14

Virginia

Trump Accelerates the Bluing of the Commonwealth

John J. McGlennon

Few states have had political histories as stable as Virginia. Over the course of the twentieth century, the Commonwealth divided its Presidential support into two mirror images. From 1900 to 1948, the Electoral Votes of the Old Dominion were awarded to Democratic Presidential candidates in every case but one, 1928. From 1952 to 2000, the Republican Presidential candidate won the vote every time but one, 1964. As the twenty-first century has moved through its first two decades, the GOP streak has come to an end, and the Democrats have now won four straight contests.

Democratic success has resulted from a transformed electorate driven by three factors: the explosion of metropolitan (and especially suburban) communities, diversification of the electorate along racial and ethnic lines, and the mobilization of previously underrepresented groups (McGlennon 2018). These factors have interacted to move the state at every level in a more liberal and more Democratic direction. What once was the epitome of Southern Conservatism has emerged as the first state in the region to abolish the death penalty and legalize marijuana (Gabriel 2021). Massive resistance to integration in the 1950s gave way to expungement of Confederate iconography in 2020. Adoption of an anti-gay marriage constitutional amendment fifteen years ago contrasts with rejection of a "right to work" constitutional amendment by voters in 2016 (Jamieson 2016).

The 2020 election produced a decisive victory for Democrat Joseph R. Biden, Jr., as he finished ahead of Donald J. Trump by a margin of 10.1 percent. Biden's edge was the largest for either party in any Presidential election since 1988. His 2,413,568 votes represented the highest number of votes for a presidential candidate (and second only to U.S. Senator Mark Warner's

2020 re-election total in all elections). In contrast, Trump's tally placed him eighth among all statewide candidates. After three elections as a battleground, Virginia has moved solidly into the Democratic column.

VIRGINIA POLITICS IN THE TWENTY-FIRST CENTURY

The transition of Virginia over the past two decades reflected the broader impact of polarization, realignment, and mobilization. Although Bill Clinton made the presidential race in Virginia close in his two successful national runs, the 2000 election outcome generated a sharp division in the electorate. The U.S. Supreme Court decision, *Bush v. Gore*, may have ended the counting of votes, but it appeared to harden partisan feelings in Virginia and elsewhere. Although John Kerry's 2004 candidacy improved only slightly on Al Gore's Virginia performance in 2000, it was accomplished with a surge of suburban support.

Bush won the state by virtually the same margin in both elections, but he depended on a more robust turnout of rural Republican voters to offset Kerry's suburbanites. The social conservatism that drew the rural electorate to the GOP seemed to have the opposite effect among voters in the rapidly growing metro areas. Fairfax County, the largest jurisdiction in the Commonwealth and home to one of every eight state residents, gave a Democrat the majority for the first time in forty years. Albemarle joined in switching sides, and other suburban counties saw traditional GOP margins shrink. Disaffection with the Bush Administration's policy in Iraq combined with the promotion of traditional values to alienate suburban voters from the GOP.

History was made in 2008 with the election of Barack Obama as the nation's first African American president, and Virginians made clear that they wanted to be part of that moment. The Obama candidacy, though, also accelerated the growth of the urban/rural divide nationally and in the Commonwealth. While Obama became the first Democrat to carry Virginia in a presidential race since Lyndon Johnson in 1964, he lost reliably Democratic cities and counties in rural Southside and Southwest Virginia. Those rural and small-town votes were more than offset by massive mobilization and suburban realignment (McGlennon 2009).

Buchanan County, a "coal county" in the far southwest of the state bordering on West Virginia, gave strong support to Gore's 2000 campaign. Though Gore lost West Virginia over his support for strict environmental laws that were seen as a threat to coal mining and his support for gun control, Buchanan County retained its historic Democratic preference. Bush's traditional social agenda, directed toward rural voters in particular, narrowed the Democratic edge in 2004, but Kerry retained a clear edge. In 2008, though,

Buchanan joined a wide swath of Appalachian counties in Virginia and a number of other states in defecting to John McCain, even as McCain was losing badly nationally.

Obama's positions on climate, energy, guns, and other issues, along with the lack of connection to rural, lower-income, less-educated white voters, began a massive shift toward the Republicans. In his reelection contest, Obama lost a quarter of his 2008 margin. With the nomination of Hillary Clinton in 2016, the desertion of Democrats seemed nearly total. Yet Buchanan's Democratic vote dropped even more in 2020. This one county shifted from giving Gore 58 percent to delivering a mere 16 percent to Joe Biden, even as Biden was sweeping the state. In all these contests, participation remained fairly stable in an area that has not grown in recent decades. From 2000, when 9,856 votes were cast to 2020, when 9,953 voted, Buchanan's stable turnout represented a declining share of the statewide vote and a growing part of the GOP constituency.

Obama's candidacy may not have resonated among rural white voters, but it energized black voters and the young and old in university areas. Cities like Norfolk, Richmond, and Newport News saw a surge of black voters to the polls in support of Obama. College towns produced sharp increases in both turnout and the Democratic share of the vote. Despite little increase in population, the numbers of voters rose. From Montgomery County (Virginia Tech) to Harrisonburg (James Madison University) to Charlottesville (University of Virginia), to Williamsburg (College of William & Mary), the growth of Democratic support reflected the combination of student registration and voting, and the shift of college-educated voters toward Democrats.

The impacts of population growth, polarization, realignment, and mobilization all were in motion when Trump rode the escalator down to the lobby of his building to declare his presidential candidacy in 2015. However, the impact of Trump on politics in Virginia was palpable and served as a predictor of the four-year Trump era. Virginia became "the Canary in the Coal Mine" (McGlennon and Deel 2018).

DONALD TRUMP TRANSFORMS VIRGINIA

The election of Donald Trump stunned the world. His victory, with fewer popular votes than his Democratic opponent, Hillary Clinton, pierced the "Blue Wall" of Midwestern states that many believed would ensure Clinton's election. One place that did not succumb to Trump's appeal was Virginia. Though Clinton's margin was thinner than Obama's first term win in the state, she beat his second term margin, winning by 5.3 percent. The heavily suburban, highly educated, affluent electorate was notably disinclined to support a candidate heavy on anti-government rhetoric (McGlennon 2019). Clinton's decisive win over Vermont Senator Bernie Sanders in the Democratic primary that year also served as testament to Clinton's appeal to suburban women, who comprised a large share of the electorate.

THE 2017 ELECTIONS FOR GOVERNOR AND HOUSE OF DELEGATES

Trump's campaign and his Presidential administration drew strong criticism and opposition within the state, and sent an early message about Trump's ability to generate passionate opposition. As one of two states that hold statewide elections for Governor in the odd-numbered year following the Presidential election, Virginia offered an early test of Trump's ability to grow his support in office. Democrats nominated the state's lieutenant governor, a pediatric neurologist named Ralph Northam. Northam, having sown up most of the establishment and organizational party leaders at an early stage, prompted the state's attorney general, Mark Herring, to opt for a reelection campaign over seeking a promotion. A late entrant into the party's primary, former Congressman Tom Perriello, challenged Northam from the left, pushing him to more liberal positions. Nonetheless, Northam comfortably won the nomination.

Among Republicans, the party leadership hoped that Edward Gillespie, former Chair of the Republican National Committee, could use his near-upset of Mark Warner in the 2014 Senate election as a springboard to the open governorship. Gillespie was pushed to the right by a challenge from Corey Stewart, the Chairman of the Board of Supervisors of Prince William County, a large suburban Northern Virginia jurisdiction. Stewart first came to public attention as an outspoken critic of undocumented immigrants, and had just come off of a stint as a chair of Trump's statewide campaign. Gillespie barely held off Stewart, and adopted the harsh anti-immigrant tone of the primary challenger to energize his party base.

In the general election campaign, Northam took on a more aggressive posture toward Trump and his administration, despite concern among cautious party leaders that he needed a moderate profile. Northam's instincts proved accurate, as he won by a 9-point margin, while his running mates for lieutenant governor and attorney general both claimed victory. While these wins were impressive, it was the state's legislative elections that stunned the state and nation.

During these statewide election years, Virginia voters also select all one hundred members of the House of Delegates for two-year terms. In the other odd-year cycle, the Delegates all stand for election again, and the forty-member Senate is elected to four-year terms. In 2017, the elections were being held under lines drawn by a Republican House majority, a narrow Democratic majority in the Senate and a Republican governor. While the two chambers' majority parties agreed to leave the redistricting plans for the other house alone, in the Senate, the governor indicated that he would not prevent the Democrats from developing a plan but would veto any map that he did not feel gave a fair shot to the GOP. By the 2015 elections, the GOP emerged with an edge in the Senate.

In the House of Delegates, as the 2017 election approached, the GOP's unchecked district plan had produced a 66–34 advantage. Political observers assumed that the gerrymandered districts would prevent Democrats from any realistic prospect of victory for a couple of decades. That advantage had been built on reliably Republican rural and suburban areas, but those suburbs were changing. Democrats noticed that Clinton's victory in 2016 had extended to seventeenth House district currently held by GOP Delegates. Democrats targeted those districts, hoping that over two election cycles they might get to the point where they could challenge for control of the chamber. What happened was beyond their most optimistic expectations. On election night, both parties watched as Republican district after district flipped to the Democrats, sometimes to candidates who had run with little expectation of winning. By the end of the night, Democrats had won fifteen of the seventeen seats. Republicans had won fifty seats, Democrats held forty-nine, and one was headed to a recount, with a single-digit lead. After a court hearing that came down to whether or not to count a single ballot, the recount court declared a tie vote, which was resolved by drawing a name out of a bowl. The Republican incumbent's name was drawn and the party had a 51–49 margin in the House.

The election for governor and House generated enormous activism on the Democratic side, a surge in voter participation, and a mountain of small-dollar donations to candidates up and down the Democratic ballot. The new delegates included several African Americans, twelve new women, the first openly transgender state legislator, two Latinas, an Asian American woman, a Democratic Socialist, and a former television anchor motivated by the issue of gun control after his fiancé was shot to death on air while covering a story. With the Democrats on the verge of control, newly elected Governor Northam was able to convince a handful of Republicans in the General Assembly to support Medicaid expansion to bring the state more fully under Obamacare.

THE MIDTERM CONGRESSIONAL ELECTIONS OF 2018

The 2017 elections in Virginia may have sent an early message of resistance to Trump, but Virginia was not about to be left out of the midterm Congressional election story. With a U.S. Senate seat on the ballot and a

7–4 GOP advantage among the eleven House of Representatives seats, the Commonwealth emerged as a top target in the battle for Congressional control. Senator Tim Kaine may have lost as the vice presidential nominee on Hillary Clinton's ticket, but they had comfortably carried his home state. Democrats targeted four seats that they felt offered opportunities for defeating Republican House members. Four women emerged from the nomination process in the Second, Fifth, Seventh, and Tenth Congressional Districts for the Democrats, who contested all House districts.

One Republican, Representative Tom Garrett, unexpectedly upset the Fifth District race when he resigned, acknowledging a struggle with alcoholism amid a scandal over using his Congressional staff as personal servants (Isenstadt and Bresnahan 2018). Garrett was replaced as the party nominee by Denver Riggleman, a wealthy distiller and "Bigfoot" erotic fiction devotee. In a district which seemed just out of reach for Democrats following Perriello's one term (2009–2011), the party got new energy to challenge for the open seat. In the end, it remained in Republican hands.

The GOP nominee for the Senate, unsuccessful 2017 Governor candidate Corey Stewart, managed to upset party favorite Delegate Nick Freitas, and promised a "vicious, ruthless" campaign against Kaine (Wise 2017). His decisive loss in the race led Stewart to withdraw from electoral politics (Inside NOVA 2019). As in 2017, turnout in 2018 statewide dramatically exceeded the previous comparable election, in 2014, by a wide margin, part of a surge nationwide that brought midterm participation to the highest level since World War II.

In the end, three Democratic women ousted Republican incumbents Scott Taylor, David Brat, and Barbara Comstock. While state senator Jennifer Wexton defeated Comstock in a district that had supported Hillary Clinton by 40,000 votes, Wexton's vote was 5 percent higher than Clinton's share two years earlier. Both Elaine Luria, a Navy veteran who beat freshman Representative Scott Taylor, and Abigail Spanberger carried districts won by Trump in 2016. Spanberger's defeat of David Brat was notable as Brat had gotten national attention for upsetting U.S. House Majority Leader Eric Cantor in the GOP primary in 2014. Both Luria and Spanberger, a former CIA analyst, focused on their national security credentials and managed to balance appeal to progressives with moderate stances designed to attract suburbanites turned off by Trump's first two years.

THE GENERAL ASSEMBLY ELECTIONS OF 2019

Through the course of the twenty-first century, Democrats had systematically come to dominate most sectors of elective office in Virginia. From 2006 to

2018, Democrats won every race for the U.S. Senate, with Jim Webb upsetting Senator and prospective presidential candidate George Allen in 2006. Mark Warner won a landslide in 2008 and hung on to the seat in the national 2014 GOP sweep. Tim Kaine succeeded Webb in 2012, then coasted to reelection in 2018. Democrats won the governorship in four of the five elections, and have not lost a statewide constitutional office since 2009. Starting in 2008, the party won three straight presidential contests in the Old Dominion. By 2018, the party won a majority of the U.S. House delegation. By 2019, only the General Assembly remained in Republican control.

As discussed earlier, the districting plan adopted in 2011 for the state Senate produced a "fair fight" map, which allowed Republicans to hold a narrow edge for most of the decade. On the other hand, the House of Delegates plan was an artful gerrymander, drawn to concentrate minority voters in heavily black districts and giving most districts a solid but not overwhelming Republican cast. The first few elections under this plan achieved the desired results: an overwhelming GOP majority. However, the plan assumed a continued party advantage in suburbs of Northern Virginia, Richmond, and Hampton Roads, and in 2017, the suburban rejection of Donald Trump took its toll.

With the House divided by the narrowest of margins, 51–49, and Republican performance collapsing everywhere but the declining rural counties, a Democratic majority seemed unstoppable in 2019. Then the Democrats gained a lock on the majority they sought: a federal court ruling that a dozen House districts had been drawn in ways that unconstitutionally packed black voters in order to limit their influence in state government. The result was a court-ordered redistricting plan that significantly weakened Republican incumbents in a number of districts, including those held by the Speaker of the House and the architect of the original, unconstitutional plan.

In November 2019, Democrats won fifty-five of the one hundred seats, leaving no Republicans in Northern Virginia districts, ousting Chris Jones, the original mapper, and producing another set of new minority representatives. The district that had been tied in 2017 saw a rematch in 2019, but this time the Democrat won by 17 percent. In the Senate, Democrats needed to net two seats, and they hoped to do better, with the first Senate election of the Trump era and the experience of the House Democrats. As it happened, they had to be satisfied with the bare majority achieved with a net gain of two seats, but completion of a "trifecta" of party control of both chambers and the governorship.

As the 2020 Presidential election approached, Virginia's parties were in very different places. Democrats had not lost a statewide election in a decade, had gained majorities in the House of Representatives delegation, won control of both chambers of the General Assembly, and used their new state government control to extend the opportunity to vote more broadly. Democrats were contesting virtually every office on the ballot while Republicans were building firewalls, concentrating on just enough contests to hold on to one chamber of the legislature. Democratic activists sent tens of thousands of small donations to their candidates while the GOP continued to rely on large donations by interest groups. As 2020 began, Democrats finally were able to focus on the candidates seeking their nomination for president, confident that they would have the upper hand in November.

THE 2020 ELECTION: THE NOMINATION

The crowded field of Democrats seeking the party's presidential nomination offered someone for everyone, it seemed. Former Vice President Joe Biden and Vermont Senator Bernie Sanders both had contingents of supporters from the beginning, though both faced challenges as well. Many Democrats wondered if Biden would be able to maintain a "front runner" image by the time the Virginia primary arrived as part of Super Tuesday on March 3. Sanders had performed poorly against Hillary Clinton in the 2016 contest, with support largely limited to college towns and the populist voters of Southwest Virginia, Clinton's weak spot in her otherwise overwhelming victory.

A range of other candidates eagerly worked to position themselves to pick up the pieces, should either stumble. Senators Cory Booker, Kamala Harris, Amy Klobuchar, and Elizabeth Warren all had niche support that they hoped to grow if they managed to bottle lightning in one of the first four primaries. South Bend, Indiana, Mayor Pete Buttigieg, former Secretary of Housing and Urban Development Julian Castro, former Congressman Beto O'Rourke and wealthy entrepreneur Tom Steyer never seemed to catch on. But former New York City Mayor Michael Bloomberg, who had invested heavily in several of the Virginia elections of the preceding years, presented himself as a centrist with the resources needed to beat President Trump.

The early stages of the national nominating process produced an unsettled outcome: a tie between Sanders and Buttigieg in Iowa, followed by a narrow Sanders win in New Hampshire, not nearly as convincing as his 2016 win over Clinton in his neighboring state. Senator Klobuchar's better-than-expected performance injected energy, while Senator Warren's fifth-place finish was a stunning setback in a state that also neighbored her own. Biden finished poorly in both states, but clung to the notion that these overwhelmingly rural white states did not reflect the Democratic constituency, and that he would surely improve in the next contests.

Biden did finish second in Nevada, but lagged far behind Sanders, and increasingly, it looked as if the Vermont socialist was building momentum.

That prospect appeared to galvanize both moderate Democrats and African Americans, who worried that Trump could easily paint Sanders as too extreme for the Presidency. In one of the clearest examples of "king-making" in modern nomination politics, long-time South Carolina Congressman James Clyburn endorsed Biden in the state's party-run primary (held the Saturday before Super Tuesday). With overwhelming support from his fellow black voters and from suburbanites, Clyburn guided Biden to a convincing win in the Palmetto State.

Almost immediately, Democrats united behind Biden as the most acceptable candidate to both stop Sanders and to beat Trump. One after another, Biden's competitors dropped their bids and endorsed President Obama's vice president. On Tuesday, Virginia joined nine other states in backing Biden. In short order, Biden began to wrap up the nomination, winning every primary and losing only three caucus states as the contest ground on for months.

The dramatic shift in Virginia voter preferences shows up in a survey conducted by the Wason Center at Christopher Newport University over a period from February 3 to 24 (Wason Center 2020), leaving the field roughly ten days before the primary. The 561 "likely voters" in the Democratic primary narrowly preferred Biden (22 percent), with Sanders at 17 percent and Bloomberg (13 percent) not far behind in a fragmented field. While the overwhelming majority of primary voters (82 percent) said they would support the eventual nominee, among the uncertain, the vast majority feared the candidate would be "too liberal" rather than "too moderate."

Other polling provided further insight into the Virginia primary electorate's calculations. A Monmouth University survey conducted February 13–16 (Murphy 2020) found the 400 likely voters divided closely, with Bloomberg (22 percent), Sanders (22 percent) and Biden (18 percent) effectively tied, and only one in four of these voters firm in their candidate choice. Fully 52 percent of the voters said there was a high or moderate possibility that they would change their votes before primary day. Monmouth posed hypothetical two-person tests between Sanders and several of the more moderate candidates, demonstrating the fluidity of the electorate, but also the fundamental strength of Biden, should he emerge as the alternative to Sanders.

In hypothetical one-on-one contests against Buttigieg and Klobuchar, Sanders held a statistically insignificant 2 percent and 3 percent advantage, respectively. However, Bloomberg bested Sanders 47–41 percent, as he won among White voters by a 50–39 split, as Sanders won among Black voters, 49–43 percent. Biden, though, bested Sanders by a wide 51–38 margin, built on strong support from Whites (49–40), and overwhelming Black support (63–27). Even at a time when the Biden campaign seemed on the verge of collapse, its potential to unify Democrats was evident in this poll. Biden's strength among women also put him at an advantage in an electorate likely to skew heavily female. While the former vice president led Sanders among men (48–42 percent), he dominated among women by a 54–35 percent margin. Bloomberg, who faced criticism of his treatment of women (Kranish, 2020), trailed Sanders among female voters in the match-up, while winning among men.

The ink on the South Carolina primary results had not even dried as pollsters rushed into Super Tuesday states, including Virginia, and in four polls conducted in the two days immediately following the Saturday vote, Biden sported margins ranging from 14 to 20 points. Sanders's vote stayed fairly constant, but over a period of hours, candidates exited the race and their voters shifted to Biden. Those who remained in the race were left in the dust in Virginia and most other states.

The Virginia primary concluded just as the state was about to join much of the nation in shutting down in response to the coronavirus pandemic. With state election law in the process of revision, polling places all over the state opened as usual. Although 2020 would prove to be a year in which Virginians flocked to absentee in person or mail ballots, in the primary, the total number of votes cast by means other than in person on Primary Day inside polling locations was 5 percent. The unsettled nature of the nomination apparently caused many voters to delay their choice until the last moment. Turnout was record-setting, with 1,334,671 votes, shattering the 2008 primary record vote of 986,203.

Biden won a majority of the vote (53.3 percent), while Sanders trailed him by 30 percent. Warren was the only other candidate to reach double digits, and Bloomberg fell just short of 10 percent. Of the state's 130 cities and counties, only three failed to deliver at least a plurality win for Biden: the cities of Charlottesville and Harrisonburg, and Floyd County. The first two, the homes of the University of Virginia and James Madison University respectively, reflected Sanders's general stronger base among students. Floyd can best be described as an anti-establishment, bluegrass-loving, pottery-making counter-cultural haven.

Though Biden led most polls prior to the primary, his performance was better. He did particularly well among African American voters but also outpaced his challengers among suburban and rural constituencies. Overall, the day was a national success for Biden, as he won six Southern states, a Border state, two New England primaries and Senator Klobuchar's home state of Minnesota. Sanders was the only other candidate to come away from this first Super Tuesday with any wins, in the California, Colorado, Utah, and Vermont primaries.

Biden's candidacy had wide appeal to Virginia Democrats, and the large turnout, broad regional and demographic support suggested that he would fit well with the state's electorate in November. Though Sanders (and for a shorter time, Warren) continued their candidacies, Biden was not to be denied. Most of his rivals had rallied to his support in the days preceding March 3, and his campaign had the opportunity to start looking past the nomination to the general election.

Though Trump had attracted a handful of challengers, none of whom were able to attract much traction, he was unopposed in Virginia's primary. With only one candidate qualifying for the ballot, the primary was cancelled and Trump won all of the state delegates to the national convention.

CONGRESSIONAL NOMINATIONS

While Virginia's presidential primary occurred just before the COVID-19 pandemic shutdown, local elections and primaries for U.S. Senate and House of Representatives were scheduled for later in the spring. As concern about the spread of the virus grew, Governor Northam and the General Assembly reacted with a deluge of permanent and temporary changes to balloting. The governor pushed back the dates for both the May city and town elections and the June federal primaries by the two weeks permitted under his emergency powers. The legislature provided for easier access to mail ballots, "no-excuse" absentee-in-person (early) voting, reductions in signature requirements and other revisions.

The federal legislative elections offered a full card, as Senator Mark Warner stood for his third term, while Republicans targeted the three seats they had lost in 2018 and Democrats renewed their challenges to the remaining four Republican members, especially in the Fifth Congressional District.

Although Warner had barely survived the GOP wave election of 2014, his prospects in 2020 seemed bright enough to discourage politically experienced opponents. A small field of challengers produced a nominee in Daniel Gade, a disability and veterans affairs activists and professor of practice in public administration at American University. The other notable primary resulted in the renomination of former one-term (2017–2019) Congressman Scott Taylor in the Second District, setting up a rematch with freshman Democratic Representative Elaine Luria, who had defeated him in 2018.

Three other notable GOP nominations were settled in conventions, carried out in improvised procedures to address limitations required by the pandemic. In the Seventh District, Republicans settled a hotly contested battle by nominating Delegate Nick Freitas on the third ballot with 56 percent of the votes, defeating his fellow delegate, John McGuire. Freitas, well connected to national GOP donors, had been upset in the 2018 Senate primary, where he had been the party favorite to stop Corey Stewart. More damagingly, Freitas had nearly forfeited his safely Republican seat in the House of Delegates by failing to properly complete paperwork required to be placed on the

November ballot in 2019. He would need to spend several hundred thousand dollars waging a write-in campaign to hold his seat. In this campaign, he once again failed to get all his required paperwork in to the state Department of Elections, and had to receive an exception from the state board (Mattingly 2020).

By far, the most significant Republican contest came in the Fifth District, as social conservatives organized around Bob Good, a Campbell County Supervisor and development officer at Liberty University, in challenging Representative Denver Riggleman for renomination. Riggleman, a libertarian Republican, had alienated GOP activists by officiating at a single-sex wedding of a former campaign volunteer, and by insufficiently conservative positions. In a controversial decision, the district's GOP committee opted for a convention over a primary, and then made the convention site a church in Good's home area (Portnoy 2020).

Good's nomination encouraged Democrats' hopes of winning the Fifth District, which was competitive but usually just out of reach for the party's nominees. In an expensive and hotly contested primary, Cameron Webb, a physician and attorney, swept to an overwhelming win in the primary, and attracted the attention of national Democrats who saw some opportunity in an unexpectedly open seat contest once again.

THE GENERAL ELECTION

From the beginning, Virginia's presidential election outcome seemed fairly settled. In the Wason Center survey in February, voters expressed a preference for "Someone Else" over Donald Trump by a 59–38 percent margin. The fact that Hillary Clinton had improved on Barack Obama's 2012 Virginia margin, and the three subsequent years of Democratic success demonstrated that Trump would not find fertile territory here. The presidential election largely bypassed the Old Dominion, other than the occasional fund-raising effort. The pandemic sharply limited in-person events, so it was difficult to compare travel schedules. Virtual gatherings were often national in scale, and Virginians did see some television advertising. Most of the latter tended to be in media markets directed to or located in North Carolina, a more competitive state, part of a Biden campaign decision to advertise nationally given the geographic spread and cost of single market advertising, or the Trump campaign's periodic advertising in the Washington metropolitan market so that Trump could see his ads while he watched television in the White House.

Moving on from the primary, Joe Biden maintained a polling average advantage through Election Day. The lead started in the mid-single digits, and by November had climbed to just over a double-digit advantage (see table 14.1). The state's accommodation to voting in a pandemic was thoroughly embraced by the state's voters. With the opening of "no-excuse absentee-in-person voting" in mid-September and the distribution of mail ballots around the same time, the vote count grew day by day, assuring a record turnout by November 3. More than twenty Virginia surveys were reported in the political website, *FiveThirtyEIght.Com*, between February 24 and November 2. Every single one showed Biden with a lead, and in almost every one, the lead was over ten points (FiveThirtyEight 2020).

A *Washington Post* survey from October 23, which awarded Biden an 11 point lead statewide, gave Trump poor marks on his handling of the coronavirus pandemic, a stark comparison to the praise the survey contained for Governor Ralph Northam. The governor enjoyed a 56-38 percent approval/disapproval rating, a dramatic improvement from the low point of his administration during revelations of racist photographs in his medical school yearbook, which brought his rating down to a net approval of −3 percent (Schneider et.al. 2020). Trump's October rating was 41-57, a net −16 points.

Table 14.1 Virginia General Election Polls, March–November

Date	Pollster	Biden	Trump	Biden Margin
March 3	Hampton University	45	38	+7
April 14	VA Commonwealth University	51	41	+10
May 19	Roanoke College	51	39	+12
July 28	Morning Consult	52	42	+10
July 30	VA Commonwealth University	50	39	+11
August 26	Roanoke College	53	39	+14
September 15	VA Commonwealth University	53	39	+14
September 24	Christopher Newport Univ.	48	43	+5
October 3	Survey Monkey	58	40	+18
October 15	Roanoke College	53	38	+15
October 15	Civiqs	55	42	+13
October 19	Cygnal	51	42	+9
October 20	Survey Monkey	55	43	+12
October 22	Washington Post/GMU	52	41	+11
October 28	Christopher Newport Univ.	53	41	+12
October 29	VA Commonwealth University	51	39	+12
October 30	Swayable	55	44	+11
October 31	Roanoke College	54	43	+11
November 1	Data for Progress	54	43	+11
November 2	Survey Monkey	57	41	+16
November 2	Swayable	56	41	+15

Source: "Who's Ahead in Virginia?" *FiveThirtyEight.com* https://projects.fivethirtyeight.com/polls/president-general/virginia/

The Results

To the surprise of few, Virginia delivered its thirteen electoral votes to Joe Biden, with the results clear before Election Day was over. As state law permitted the counting of mail ballots before Election Day, and in-person votes having been fed into scanners consistently throughout the early voting period, only a small number of mail ballots postmarked by 7 pm on November 3, but arriving prior to noon on Friday, November 6 were still outstanding.

Biden's victory was substantial, as he finished 10.1 percent ahead of Trump, almost doubling Clinton's margin of 2016, and exceeding both of Obama's winning margins. Exit polls and locality election results demonstrate the basis of Virginia's move out of the set of competitive states.

Exit-Poll Results

Exit polling continues to create greater challenges. As more voters express reticence to respond to surveys, fewer votes are actually cast at traditional polling places on Election Day, and voters carry mobile phones based in area codes that may have little connection to their current states of residence, getting surveys completed requires persistence, patience, and luck. But with a decisive outcome that is consistently reflected, the exit polls of Virginia in 2020 can provide at least a fairly reliable indicator of the groups that supported each candidate and the share of the electorate represented by each.

The polling demonstrated the bases of support for each candidate, and why Biden emerged with such a clear win. Each candidate carried their own fellow partisans, but Biden's net win was about eleven points greater among Democrats than Trump's margin among self-identified Republicans. Independents and other party members gave Biden a 19 percent advantage. Biden won liberals by a larger margin than Trump won conservatives, but the latter were a larger group of voters. Still, Biden's 34 percent edge among moderates allowed him a comfortable edge (table 14.2).

Though there was a gender gap, Biden won both men (+1) and women (+13). Whites supported Trump (+8) but Biden won blacks (+79), Latinos (+25), Asian voters (+22) and others (+7). With minorities comprising 33 percent of the Virginia electorate, these margins more than offset Trump's edge with non-Hispanic whites. Biden's strength with women extended to white women, a group that narrowly favored him (+1). That edge was explained by his success among white women college graduates, who gave him a wide margin (+17). Although Trump did win among white men, his performance among white men who did not graduate from college (+37) versus +3 among white male college graduates explains the ex-president's claim that "I love the poorly educated (Nelson 2016)."

Table 14.2 Virginia Exit Poll Results

Demographic	Share of vote (%)	Biden	Trump	Biden Margin
Race				
White non-Hispanic	67	45	53	−8
Black	18	89	10	+79
Latino	7	61	36	+25
Asian	4	60	38	+22
Other	3	50	43	+7
Gender				
Male	49	49	48	+1
Female	51	61	38	23
Income				
Under $50,000	33	60	39	+21
Over $50,000	67	48	51	−3
Marital Status				
Married	57	51	48	+3
Not Married	43	64	34	+30
Age				
18–29	20	62	33	+29
30–44	24	59	39	+20
45–64	38	52	47	+5
65+	18	45	54	−9
Education by race				
White/College degree	33	52	45	+7
White/no degree	34	38	62	−24
Non-white/College degree	10	75	24	+51
Non-white/No degree	23	76	22	+54
PartyID				
Democratic	36	96	4	+92
Republican	34	9	90	−81
Independent	30	57	38	+19
Ideology				
Liberal	24	94	5	+89
Moderate	40	66	32	+34
Conservative	36	16	83	−67
Community Type				
Urban	24	64	34	+30
Suburban	60	53	45	+8
Rural	16	46	52	−6

Source: "Exit Polls: Virginia." CNN.com. https://www.cnn.com/election/2020/exit-polls/president/virginia.

Biden won every age group but the oldest in Virginia, but did especially well among 18–29-year-olds (+29). Trump's win among the roughly equal number of sixty-five-year-olds and above (+9) was much more modest. Trump scored a massive advantage among white evangelical Christians

(+61), but lost all other voters, a group three times larger (+39) (Washington Post, 2020).

Finally, in the urban (+30) and suburban (+8) areas, Biden prevailed, while in rural areas, Trump won (+6). Given that three-fifths of the voters live in suburbs, which had not long ago been reliably Republican territory, Biden's success here was both part of a continuing growth of Democratic dominance and a barrier to GOP prospects (see table 14.2). The exit poll also demonstrated sharp divisions over questions of the personal characteristics of the candidates, the trade-off between containing the coronavirus and reopening the economy, and what issues were most important to the voters.

Those who identified the economy (34 percent) or crime and safety (10 percent) as their prime issues in deciding how to vote favored Trump overwhelmingly, but they were offset by those who identified racial inequality, the pandemic, or health care, who strongly favored Biden. Though voters who prioritized handling the economy voted overwhelmingly for Trump, the incumbent had lost his advantage on confidence in leadership on this issue overall, as Biden outscored him 51–46 percent. With Biden holding a commanding lead over Trump in terms of the confidence of voters to handle the pandemic (57–39 percent), Trump offered Virginians little to attract their votes.

Breaking Down the Vote by Locality and Region

Donald Trump's total share of the vote in Virginia actually declined between 2016 and 2020, dropping from 44.4 to 44.0, while Joe Biden improved on Hillary Clinton's share of the vote by nearly 4.4 percent. Votes for minor party, independent and write-in votes fell from nearly 6 percent to less than 2 percent. While the distribution of the vote increased slightly for Biden, it followed the pattern that emerged over the past several elections. That growing Democratic trend in the state simply expanded over the course of the four years.

Clinton's comfortable 2016 margin was built despite winning only five of the state's eleven Congressional districts. Her victory in the Fourth District was a swing toward the Democrats, but not really surprising, as court-ordered redistricting had changed the partisan and racial balance of the district significantly for this election year. The wide margin in the Tenth District was somewhat more surprising, and an indication of suburban discomfort with the Trump style. As discussed earlier, this district became a prime target for Democratic pick-up in 2018. Of course, Democrats also gained the second and seventh House seats in 2018, and these districts moved from Trump to Biden in 2020, as they reelected Congresswomen Luria and Spanberger. Biden's 7–4 Congressional district margin showed the partisan polarization so evident in contemporary American politics, as the presidential and Congressional outcomes in all districts were consistent. The narrowing margins in both the First and Fifth Districts gave Democrats some optimism for future gains, especially as redistricting would be likely to add more suburban voters to both, reducing the impact of the rural vote. Only the Shenandoah Valley-based sixth and the Southwestern Virginia ninth seem to be safe for the GOP, should current trends continue.

A glance at a map of Virginia's election returns would show a sea of red across the western two-thirds of the state, with only the occasional dot of blue. Cities like Roanoke, Danville, and Lynchburg, each with substantial black populations and more numerous college graduates, along with Montgomery County, home to the Town of Blacksburg and Virginia Tech, Radford (Radford University), Lexington (Washington & Lee, Virginia Military Institute) and Prince Edward County (Longwood University and Hampden-Sydney College) are surrounded by rural, largely white communities with fewer college graduates and high levels of evangelical Christians. But acres do not vote, and a small and declining portion of the state's population live here. The northern and eastern cities and suburbs drive Virginia's population and economy to a high level of education, affluence, and diversity. It is here that the Democrats have built and expanded their majorities over the past two decades.

In twentieth-century Virginia, Democrats won by stitching together a triangle of support in NOVA, especially the localities of Alexandria and Arlington, and Fairfax (where the goal was to keep close to the GOP rather than winning), Hampton Roads, where a large African American and blue-collar population voted Democratic, and the Southwest, where union mine and factory workers backed them. Their inability to crack the rapidly expanding, largely white suburban vote consigned them to defeat for much of the last thirty years of the century.

Biden's win was based on increased turnout and staggering margins in central cities, and competitiveness then dominance in diversifying suburbs more than offsetting the party's collapse among white rural voters. Biden built on both turnout and share of vote in Norfolk, Richmond, Portsmouth, and Petersburg, but the suburban areas continued their decisive role in delivering the state to the Democrats. Fairfax County accounted for 600,000 of the 4.5 million votes cast in the election, and Biden drew 69.9 percent, a 5.5 percent improvement over Clinton's county landslide.

Suburbs like the Richmond-area Henrico County, Prince William, and Loudoun in NOVA and Albemarle (Charlottesville-adjacent) all saw turnout grow along with Democratic margins. Suburbs that had been on the knife's edge in 2016, like Chesterfield County (Richmond), Virginia Beach and Chesapeake (Hampton Roads), and Stafford (NOVA) all flipped from Trump to Biden. Outer suburbs that remained heavily white and Republican saw Trump margins drop.

As states certified their results, Virginia's new status as a Democratic state solidified. Like Colorado, Virginia represented the new model of highly educated, racially/ethnically diverse suburban-heavy electorate.

U.S. SENATE AND HOUSE RACES

The straight-ticket voting of the modern era was on full display in the races for seats in the U.S. Senate and House of Representatives, as the same party prevailed for both president and representative in each district. All three Democratic women completing their first terms won reelection, and in the Second and Seventh Districts, Biden managed to flip the districts from Trump. The Fifth District was close, but with Trump prevailing, Republican Bob Good managed to win by a slightly smaller margin. Incumbents prevailed elsewhere comfortably. Senator Mark Warner won his third term by a margin of 12 percent, slightly outpolling Biden's margin, and easily exceeding his nail-biter win in 2014, while falling far short of his initial 2–1 win in 2008.

The 2020 Election also saw the adoption of a constitutional amendment on redistricting reform. With population shifting from rural to metro areas and remapping assigned to a "citizens committee," it seems likely that the main impacts will be to reinforce the underlying trends of the past several years.

MOVING FORWARD: VIRGINIA IN 2021 AND BEYOND

With the 2020 election now behind us, questions of how the political system in the United States, the South, and Virginia have been affected are already on us. Virginia's practice of holding its statewide elections for Constitutional office (Governor, Lieutenant Governor, and Attorney General) as well as the entire House of Delegates in the year following the presidential contest provides another test of the new Democratic majority. Will the removal of Donald Trump from the scene alter the patterns of activism and partisan realignment that have been evident over the past four years? Will the Democratic majority in the General Assembly find support among the electorate for a more progressive agenda for the Commonwealth?

As the 2021 races began to take shape, the impact of race and sex scandals seemed to have the potential to disrupt Democratic candidacies but not necessarily party ascendancy. Governor Northam will be ending his electoral career due to Virginia's unique ban on consecutive reelection.[1] However, Governor Northram leaves with a unified Democratic government, a litany of progressive legislation, and strong approval among the state's voters, despite the legacy of the 2019 scandal, which shaped the races for state office.

The normal pattern of succession to the Executive Mansion has run through the offices of Lieutenant Governor and Attorney General, and Democrats held both offices. But both Justin Fairfax, the Lieutenant Governor, and Mark Herring, the two-term Attorney General, were casualties of the Northam scandal. Northam's initial clumsy handling of the yearbook photo discovery led to widespread calls for his resignation, including from the state's two U.S. Senators and Herring. Fairfax, who would succeed Northam should he resign, did not join the calls. However, the prospect of the Lieutenant Governor ascending to the office led two women to come forward with allegations of sexual assault from his college days and an event at the 2004 Democratic National Convention. The sexual assault allegations against Fairfax, still in legal limbo as of this writing, had almost certainly derailed his hopes of winning the governorship. With five candidates in the race, former Governor Terry McAuliffe emerged as the favorite, having raised more money than all of his intra-party competitors combined, while Fairfax struggled. By the end of 2020, McAuliffe had raised more than $5.7 million, with former delegate Jennifer Carroll Foy raising $1.9 million, and Senator Jennifer McClellan had gathered $1.1 million. Fairfax lagged far behind at $200,000, while Delegate Lee Carter had not raised any funds.

Attorney General Herring's call for Northam's resignation became stunningly hollow in the days following the Northam revelations, as he acknowledged that he had also appeared in blackface, as a sophomore at the University of Virginia, where he and friends impersonated rap singers at a party. With all three statewide officials suddenly compromised, Democrats worried that the uncertain paths to succession might open the door to a Republican becoming the ultimate beneficiary of a chain of resignations.

Although Herring continued to prepare for a run for governor and actually became the first announced candidate, he did not find much support and dropped back to a reelection campaign. His change in plans did not dissuade Delegate Jerrauld "Jay" Jones from his announced campaign for the chief legal post, which drew unexpected support from Governor Northam in early March. Though Herring seemed the prohibitive favorite for renomination, his failure to develop significant support in the race for governor suggested his own blackface incident might make him vulnerable even in a re-election contest.

The fate of the Republican Party also remains in question. Can a party whose base has moved farther and farther to the right and receded to the declining portions of the state's electorate find ways to attract suburban voters? Early in 2021, the evidence is starting to emerge. In its 2021 session, the General Assembly majority approved legalization of marijuana and abolition of the death penalty, becoming the first Southern state to do either, let alone both. Democratic legislative leaders and the governor argued that they were fulfilling the promises made when they were elected, and at least according to the Wason Poll conducted in February, the Governor retained popular approval with 54 percent of Virginians. Voters also judged Virginia as being headed in the right direction by a 47–41 percent split, and in a generic House of Delegates ballot, Democrats led the GOP by a 49–37 point margin (Wason 2021).

Democrats were largely united in the state and federal delegations, strongly supporting President Biden's early program and supporting efforts to impeach and convict Donald Trump for his role in refusing to acknowledge the outcome of the presidential election and in inciting his supporters in attempting to interfere with the Congressional counting of the Electoral College votes.

Among Republicans, all four members of the House delegation voted to challenge at least one of the certified state results. None voted for impeachment. The state GOP engaged in a bitter dispute over how to nominate their candidate for Governor. One leading candidate, Senator Amanda Chase of Chesterfield County, who had traveled to Washington for the January 6 Trump rally that led to the attack on the Capitol, praised the violent attackers as "patriots," which led to her censure by the Senate. Chase had already been stripped of her committee assignments by the GOP caucus over her misuse of state property and of the state police and for attempting to carry a firearm into the General Assembly. After initially suggesting that she would run as an independent candidate for governor if the state party did not use a primary nomination method, she later changed her mind and began a campaign to win the party's nod in a convention. But fights over the rules of such a convention threatened to prevent agreement, even as the poll cited earlier showed her as the leading candidate for the GOP nomination, albeit with only 17 percent of the vote.

Unless the Republicans can find a way to once again reach out to more moderate voters, they do not appear to be on a road to recovery. With a Democratic Party largely supported by state voters, the Bluing of Virginia appears to be a continuing trend.

NOTE

1. Since the 1830 Constitution, Virginia governors may not succeed themselves. Governors may run after sitting out a term, though only two governors have accomplished this feat since 1830.

REFERENCES

Gabriel, Trip. "Virginia, Shifting Left Fast, Moves Closer to Abolishing Death Penalty." *The New York Times*, February 4, 2021. https://www.nytimes.com/2021/02/04/us/politics/virginia-death-penalty-northam.html?searchResultPosition=2.

Isenstadt, Alex, and John Bresnahan. "Garrett to Quit Congress Amid Servant Scandal, Alcoholism." *Politico.* May 28, 2018. https://www.politico.com/story/2018/05/28/garrett-to-quits-congress-amid-servant-scandal-alcoholism-610033.

Jamieson, Dave. "Unions Defeat Right-To-Work Amendment in Virginia." *Huffington Post.* November 8, 2016. https://www.huffpost.com/entry/right-to-work-amendment-virginia_n_581ca561e4b0d9ce6fbb5241.

Kranish, Michael. "MikeBloomberg for years has battled women's allegations of profane sexist comments." *Washington Post.* February 15, 2020. https://www.washingtonpost.com/graphics/2020/politics/michael-bloomberg-women/.

Mattingly, Justin. "Freitas wins GOP nomination to take on Spanberger in 7th District." *Richmond Times-Dispatch.* July 18, 2020. https://richmond.com/news/virginia/freitas-wins-gop-nomination-to-take-on-spanberger-in-7th-district/article_4fbc1958-c050-5c39-b10d-e8ee0240afec.html.

McGlennon, John. "Virginia: The Old Dominion Stands Out in Blue ." In *A Paler Shade of Red: The 2008 Presidential Election in the South,* edited by Branwell Dubose Kapeluck, Laurence W. Moreland, and Robert P. Steed. Fayetteville: University of Arkansas Press. 2009.

McGlennon, John. "Virginia: The New Math of the Old Dominion." In *The Future Ain't What It Used to Be: The 2016 Presidential Election in the South,* edited by Branwell DuBose Kapeluck and Scott E. Buchanan. Fayetteville: University of Arkansas Press. 2018.

McGlennon, John and Jakob Deel. "Canary in the Coalfields: What Virginia's 2017 Election Can Tell Us About the 2018 National Midterm Elections." Presented at the Citadel Symposium on Southern Politics Charleston, South Carolina, March 1–2, 2018.

Murray, Patrick. "Virginia: Only 1 in $ Voters Firm About Choice." *Monmouth University Poll.* February 18, 2020. https://www.monmouth.edu/polling-institute/documents/monmouthpoll_va_021820.pdf/.

Nelson, Libby. "The Strangest Line from Donald Trump's Victory Speech: 'I Love the Poorly Educated.'" *Vox,* February 24, 2016. https://www.vox.com/2016/2/24/11107788/donald-trump-poorly-educated.

Portnoy, Jenna. "Drive-Through Convention Will Decide GOP Nominee for Congress in Central Va." *Washington Post.* June 11, 2020. https://www.washingtonpost.com/local/virginia-politics/drive-through-convention-will-decide-gop-nominee-for-congress-in-central-va/2020/06/10/c444f066-a9a0-11ea-9063-e69bd6520940_story.html.

Schneider, Gregory, Laura Vozzella, Emily Guskin and Alauna Safarpour. "Post-Schar Poll: Majority of Virginia Voters Approve of Northam's Job Performance." *Washington Post.* October 23, 2020. https://www.washingtonpost.com/local/virginia-politics/northam-job-approval-poll/2020/10/22/1e6e7bc8-13c5-11eb-ad6f-36c93e6e94fb_story.html.

Schneider, Gregory, Laura Vozzella, Emily Guskin and Alauna Safarpour. "Corey Stewart Leaving Politics, Won't Seek Re-Election." *Inside NOVA.* January 8, 2019. https://www.insidenova.com/news/election/corey-stewart-leaving-politics-wont-seek-re-election/article_3937c120-ff0f-11e8-bd1d-f775a929527e.html.

Schneider, Gregory, Laura Vozzella, Emily Guskin and Alauna Safarpour. "All-Time Top Vote Getter—1996 to Present." *Virginia Department of Elections.* Accessed February 13, 2021. https://www.elections.virginia.gov/resultsreports/election-results/.

Schneider, Gregory, Laura Vozzella, Emily Guskin and Alauna Safarpour. "Election Poll results and analysis from Virginia." *Washington Post.* November 12, 2020. https://www.washingtonpost.com/elections/interactive/2020/exit-polls/virginia-exit-polls/.

Schneider, Gregory, Laura Vozzella, Emily Guskin and Alauna Safarpour. "Poll: Biden leads Virginia's Super Tuesday field at 22%; in striking rage are Sanders at 17%, Bloomberg at 13%." *Wason Center Press Release, Christopher Newport University,* February 28, 2020. https://cnu.edu/wasoncenter/surveys/archive/2020-02-28.html.

Schneider, Gregory, Laura Vozzella, Emily Guskin and Alauna Safarpour. "Virginia Primaries—February 2021." *Wason Center, Christopher Newport University,* February 19, 2021. https://cnu.edu/wasoncenter/surveys/archive/2021-02-19.html.

Wise, Scott. "Corey Steward Promises 'Vicious, Ruthless' Race against Tim Kaine." *6News Richmond.* July 13, 2017. https://www.wtvr.com/2017/07/13/corey-stewart-senate/.

Wise, Scott. "Who's Ahead in Virginia?" *FiveThirtyEight.Com.* Accessed February 20, 2021. https://projects.fivethirtyeight.com/polls/president-general/virginia/.

Chapter 15

Five Southern States That Could Change American Politics

H. Gibbs Knotts

The South continues to be the most reliably Republican region of the country. According to the 2020 exit polls, Donald Trump won 53 percent of the vote in the South, compared to 51 percent in the Midwest and a paltry 41 percent in both the East and West regions (CNN 2020). In fact, Republicans have dominated twenty-first-century southern presidential politics. There have been sixty-six southern state presidential contests in six election cycles between 2000 and 2020. Republicans won fifty-eight of sixty-six of these elections, an astounding 88 percent victory rate. Republicans won all six twenty-first-century elections in Alabama, Arkansas, Louisiana, Mississippi, South Carolina, Tennessee, and Texas. Of the eight Democratic victories during this time period, the most occurred in Virginia with Democratic wins in 2008, 2012, 2016, and 2020. Democrats also won Florida in 2008 and 2012 as well North Carolina in 2008 and Georgia in 2020.

Despite this high level of Republican success, there is hope for Democrats. A closer look at recent election results shows five states (Florida, Georgia, North Carolina, Texas, and Virginia) that hold the best prospects for Democrats and have the potential to reshape the national political landscape. Virginia has clearly moved into the Democratic column, and recent trends indicate that Florida, Georgia, North Carolina, and Texas are increasingly competitive. It is also important to note that these five states have the highest population totals in the region. Taken together, they represent 111 Electoral College votes, an impressive 69 percent of the votes in the South. Moreover, sweeping these states would give a candidate 41 percent of the total votes needed to get to the winning number of 270 Electoral College votes. If a future Democratic presidential candidate were to hold Virginia and Georgia and add Florida, North Carolina, or Texas, they would almost certainly have a lock on the presidency.

In this final chapter, we will take a closer look at what separates these five states from other states in the region, focusing specifically on race, education, and the economic makeup. Indeed, a number of encouraging signs exist for Democrats, including strong support among younger voters and evidence that Democrats thrive in high voter turnout elections. Finally, we will highlight other states that may be positioned to join this group of five competitive states.

THE GOP TAKEOVER OF THE SOUTH

Race has always been, and continues to be, a driving force in southern politics (Key 1949; Lamis 1984; McKee 2018). The Civil War was fought over slavery, and the primary objective of the Jim Crow era was maintaining racial segregation. One-party control by Democrats helped maintain racial order, and the white primary blocked African Americans from participating in the political system (Key 1949). Race was also the key component of Richard Nixon's "Southern Strategy," helping shift socially conservative white voters from the Democratic to the Republican Party in the 1960s and 1970s (Phillips 1969). As Angie Maxwell and Todd Shields (2019) argue, the "long southern strategy" extended for decades and went beyond just racial appeals. Specifically, the GOP embraced anti-feminism and the Christian Right to gradually take control of the region (Maxwell and Shields 2019).

The Republican transformation of the South was also driven by the suburbanization of the region (Black and Black 1987; Black and Black 2002). The sunbelt suburbs supported Republican presidential candidates as early as the 1950s. White southerners fled cities to maintain racial segregation (Kruse 2005), and in-migration from Republican parts of the country also shaped southern suburbs (Black and Black 1987). This new mix of suburban voters reshaped the southern political landscape and launched the careers of GOP leaders such as Newt Gingrich and Dick Armey in the 1980s. The penultimate event was Gingrich and Armey's successful effort to nationalize the 1994 congressional elections by creating specific legislative priorities known as the "Contract with America." The strategy was successful, and the Republican Party ended four decades of Democratic control of the U.S. House of Representatives.

Figure 15.1 displays the percentage of Republicans of the southern congressional delegation over the past forty years. While Democrats held majorities in the 1980s and early 1990s, Republicans took control in 1994 and have dominated southern politics since this time. In the 2020 cycle, Democrats had a net increase of one U.S. Senate seat. Democrats gained two U.S. Senate seats in 2020 when Jon Ossoff and Raphael Warnock won runoff elections in

Figure 15.1 Republican Congressional Success in the South. *Source:* Data compiled by the author from The Almanac of American Politics, various years.

Georgia. However, Democrats lost a seat in 2020 when former Auburn football coach, Tommy Tuberville defeated Democrat Doug Jones in Alabama.[1] In the U.S. House, there was no net change in partisan control of the southern delegation. Democrats picked up two seats in North Carolina and one seat in Georgia but lost two seats in Florida and 1 seat in South Carolina.

Ironically, the factors that drove the GOP to dominate southern politics could lead to a reshuffling of the South's political dynamics. The region's growing racial diversity, particularly the return of African Americans to the South, could propel Democrats to victory (Frey 2004). Likewise, the suburban areas that drove the region toward the GOP in earlier decades could lead the charge back to Democrats in future contests. While these dynamics were in play before the Trump presidency, they certainly accelerated during his time in office. As Ron Brownstein observed, "Like a film spooling backward, Republicans are retreating along the same suburban pathways they had followed to establish their first durable beachheads in the region" (Brownstein 2020). GOP pollster Whit Ayres concurred, "Republicans are trading gains in smaller slower-growing counties for [loses in] larger faster-growing suburban counties" (Brownstein 2020).

MOVING BEYOND BLACK AND WHITE

Even in the contemporary era, the racial fault lines of Southern politics continue. The majority of white voters support Republican candidates while the majority of black, Latinx, and Asian voters support Democrats. According to national exit polls, 58 percent of whites voted for Trump in 2020, while 87 percent of blacks voted for Biden (CNN 2020). Biden also won 65 percent of Latinx voters and 61 percent of Asian voters (CNN 2020).

The connection between race and voting is more complicated when examining the influence of racial context on aggregate election outcomes. Given the strong support for Democrats among African Americans, it would make sense that Democratic candidates would win in states with a higher proportion of black voters. However, research on "racial threat" has shown that support for a conservative candidate increases in communities with a greater proportion of African Americans (Key 1949). This occurs because "larger black populations cause whites to feel threatened by potential inter-racial competition over social, economic, and political resources" (Avery and Fine 2012, 392).

As a first step, figure 15.2 shows the relationship between the vote percentage for Biden and the percentage black in the southern states. Despite the fact that the vast majority of African Americans supported Biden, there is no discernable pattern in figure 15.2 ($r = -0.12$), NS (not significant), and considerable variation in support for Biden across the five states with a black population over 25 percent (Alabama, Georgia, Louisiana, Mississippi, and South Carolina). Likewise, support for Biden varied considerably across the six states with percent black populations under 25 percent (Arkansas, Florida, North Carolina, Tennessee, Texas, and Virginia).

While race can be a strong predictor of individual voting behavior, figure 15.2 demonstrates that the racial makeup of a geographic region does not

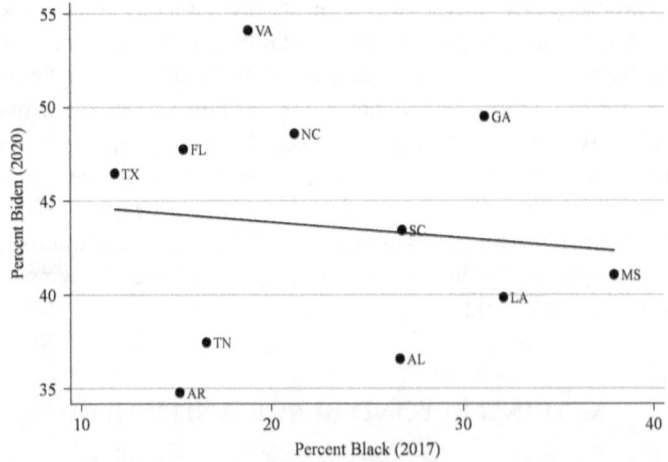

Figure 15.2 Percent Black and Support for Biden in the Southern States. *Source:* Data compiled by the author from U.S. Census Quick Facts (https://www.census.gov/quickfacts) and New York Times Election Results (https://www.nytimes.com/interactive/2020/11/03/us/elections/results-president.html). Last accessed February 28, 2021.

always correlate with support for a particular political party. As the racial threat hypothesis predicts, some of the strongest support for Republican candidates among whites can be found in states with higher percentages of black voters.

It is also critical to recognize that racial dynamics extend beyond simply black and white. Most notably, Latino voters have become an increasingly important factor in southern politics. Between 2000 and 2019, the Latino population grew by 26 percent in the South, the highest rate of growth for any region (Noe-Bustamante, Lopez, and Krogstad 2020). Moreover, Texas has the second-highest percentage of Latino of all states at 39 percent, and Florida has the sixth-highest percentage at 26 percent (U.S. Census 2020).

A prime example of the region's growing diversity can be seen in Gwinnett County, Georgia. This Atlanta suburb was a bedrock Republican county in the 1980s and 1990s and helped propel the state's GOP takeover in the late 1990s and early 2000s. Gwinnett also has a very large population, with nearly one million residents and boasts considerable racial and ethnic diversity. According to the U.S. Census (2020), the county's population breakdown is 54 percent white, 30 percent black, 22 percent Latino, and 13 percent Asian. Biden ran up big numbers in 2020, winning 58 percent of the vote while Trump won just 40 percent (NBC News 2020). This pattern repeated itself in suburban counties across the country (Frey 2020b).

To get a better sense of the effect of racial diversity on southern politics, a more holistic measure of state-level diversity developed by the National Equity Atlas (2020) is used. This diversity score is a measure of six major racial/ethnic groups (white, black, Latino, Asian or Pacific Islander, Native American, and Mixed/other race) within each state, and a maximum score of 1.79 would occur if each of the six racial/ethnic groups were represented evenly in the state (National Equity Atlas 2020).

Figure 15.3 shows the relationship between the percentage of the vote for Biden and the diversity score in each of the southern states. As you can see, there is a strong positive correlation between a state's diversity and its support for Biden ($r = 0.84$, $p \leq .01$). Take note of the five states in the top right of figure 15.3: Florida, Georgia, North Carolina, Texas, and Virginia. These states represent the best prospects for Democrats and have a mix of racial and ethnic diversity that makes putting together a winning political coalition possible. As *Scalawag* reporter Michael Cooper (2000) noted, "A multiracial democracy in the South is within sight," at least in these particular southern states.

Note there are six states where Trump performed very well: Alabama, Arkansas, Louisiana, Mississippi, South Carolina, and Tennessee. Each of these states had much lower diversity scores but they are certainly not monolithic in their racial makeup. In four of the states (Alabama, Louisiana,

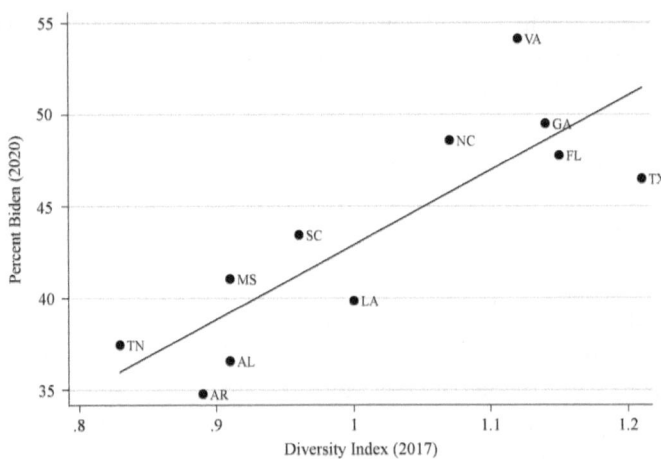

Figure 15.3 State Diversity and Support for Biden in the Southern States. *Source:* Data compiled by the author from National Equity Atlas (https://nationalequityatlas.org/indicators/Diversity_index) and New York Times Election Results (https://www.nytimes.com/interactive/2020/11/03/us/elections/results-president.html). Last accessed February 28, 2021.

Mississippi, and South Carolina) the black populations are well over 20 percent, providing a potential base of non-white voters for Democratic success. However, these states are among the most ideologically conservative, and as political reporter Ed Kilgore has argued, "conservative economic and cultural patterns have inhibited the growth of a progressive white voting bloc" (Kilgore 2020). In Arkansas and Tennessee, the percentage of black population is much lower at 16 percent and 17 percent, respectively. In the case of Tennessee, Kilgore (2020) noted "there aren't enough minority voters to serve as a party base," and much the same could be said for Arkansas.

THE BATTLE FOR COLLEGE-EDUCATED VOTERS

College-educated voters—particularly college-educated whites—were a big focus during the 2020 presidential election. This demographic group had become a mainstay of Republican support, especially in the South, but President Trump's inflammatory rhetoric and erratic style alienated many of these voters (Frey 2020a). According to national exit polls, Biden won 55 percent of college graduates, up slightly from the 52 percent won by Hillary Clinton in 2016 (CNN 2016; CNN 2020). Differences in voting patterns between college and noncollege graduates become even starker when broken down by race. Biden won 51 percent of white voters with a college degree (compared to 45 percent for Clinton in 2016), but 70 percent of voters of color with a college degree and 72 percent of voters of color without a college degree (CNN 2016; CNN 2020). Trump dominated with white noncollege voters, winning 67 percent in 2020 (CNN 2020).

These national trends also played out across the South in 2020. Southerners are often stereotyped as being less educated, and a few southern states are among the least educated in the United States. For example, the percent of college graduates in Louisiana (23 percent), Arkansas (22 percent), and Mississippi (21 percent) is among the lowest in the United States (U.S. Census 2020). However, there is considerable variation in education levels across the South. Virginia ranks sixth with 38 percent of adults with a bachelor's degree (U.S. Census 2020). There is also a middle tier of southern states that includes Florida at thirtieth (29 percent), Texas at twenty-ninth (29 percent), North Carolina at twenty-fifth (30 percent), and Georgia at twenty-fourth (30 percent) (U.S. Census 2020).

Figure 15.4 shows the relationship between percent Biden and each state's percent college graduate. There is a strong positive correlation between these two variables ($r = 0.83$, $p \leq .01$). Virginia is the region's leader in educational attainment and has the highest percentage for Biden in 2020. It is also important to note the next four states on the education score: Florida, North Carolina, Georgia, and Texas. These states tightly bunched together are also the states that hold the best prospects for Democrats. Five states appear in the bottom left quadrant of figure 15.4: Alabama, Arkansas, Louisiana, Mississippi, and Tennessee. These states have the lowest levels

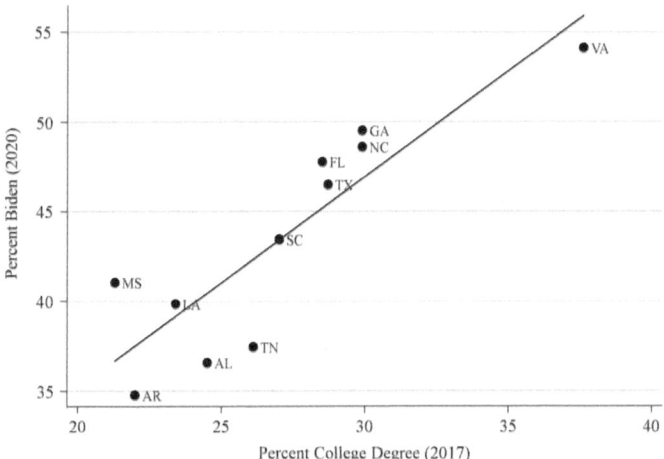

Figure 15.4 Percent College and Support for Biden in the Southern States. *Source:* Data compiled by the author from U.S. Census Quick Facts (https://www.census.gov/quickfacts) and New York Times Election Results (https://www.nytimes.com/interactive/2020/11/03/us/elections/results-president.html). Last accessed February 28, 2021.

of educational attainment and the least support for Biden. South Carolina appears in the middle between these two groups.

THE NEW ECONOMY AND SOUTHERN POLITICS

The economy always plays an important role in national elections (Tufte 1978), and during much of the Trump administration, economic conditions favored the incumbent president. Unemployment rates were historically low, and the stock market soared to record highs. Of course, economic conditions deteriorated with the onset of the pandemic in spring 2020. It is also important to note that Trump's economic policies veered away from traditional Republican mantras of free trade and reduced deficit spending. At times, Trump's economic populism and focus on renegotiating trade deals had more in common with Bernie Sanders than with mainstream Republicans. According to the national exit polls, voters were split over how they rated the nation's economy. Of the 49 percent who said the economy was excellent or good, Trump won 78 percent (CNN 2020). Of the 50 percent who rated the economy as not good or poor, Biden won 80 percent (CNN 2020).

While economic conditions are important, it is also worthwhile to consider a state's economic makeup. It makes sense that Biden would do better in states with certain types of industries, particularly places with high technology and service-based economies. Moreover, the South has considerable economic diversity. The region is no longer dominated by agriculture or textiles, and is now home to technology hubs like the Research Triangle in North Carolina. Southern governors have also lured a number of international firms to the region by using tax incentives and the promise of a low-cost and right-to-work labor force. In South Carolina alone, the state has recruited major manufacturing plants for Boeing, BMW, and Volvo.

To better understand how the economic makeup of southern states affected voting trends, a measure of the "new economy" is utilized, which was created by the Information Technology & Innovation Foundation (ITIF). The new economy index consisted of twenty-five indicators in five categories: knowledge jobs, globalization, economic dynamism, the digital economy, and innovation capacity. It is important to note that there is considerable diversity in the new economy index across southern states. Virginia was ranked sixth, Texas fourteenth, Georgia sixteenth, North Carolina nineteenth, and Florida twenty-second, nationally. The remaining southern states were near the bottom. Mississippi had the lowest new economy score and was ranked fiftieth.

Figure 15.5 shows the strong positive relationship between each southern state's new economy index and support for Biden ($r = 0.85, p \leq .01$). Virginia once again sticks out. The state has the highest new economy score as well

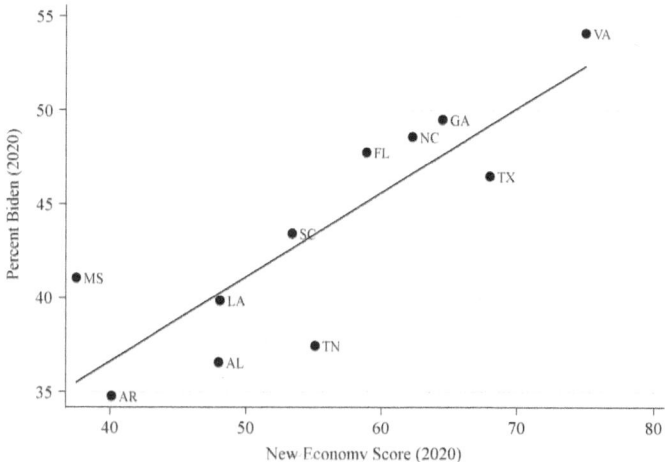

Figure 15.5 New Economy Score and Support for Biden in the Southern States. *Source:* Data compiled by the author from The Information Technology & Innovation Foundation (https://itif.org/publications/2020/10/19/2020-state-new-economy-index) and New York Times Election Results (https://www.nytimes.com/interactive/2020/11/03/us/elections/results-president.html). Last accessed February 28, 2021.

as the highest percent for Biden. That same cluster of four states (Georgia, Florida, and North Carolina, and Texas) are also grouped closely together and are clearly separated from the other states in figure 15.5. As before, South Carolina occupies a middle crowd, located between Georgia, Florida, North Carolina, and Texas and the states in the bottom left quadrant.

OTHER POSITIVE SIGNS FOR DEMOCRATS

There are a number of other positive signs for Democrats in the South. First, there is evidence that younger voters support Democrats at higher rates. At the national level, 60 percent of voters in the 18–29 years old category supported Biden (CNN 2020), and though we do not have exit polling in all southern states, this trend appeared to hold throughout the South. In Virginia, support for Biden from the 18–29 years old group was 62 percent, and even in the ruby-red state of Alabama, 54 percent of voters in this age group supported Biden (CNN 2020). This is an impressive feat considering that Biden lost Alabama by over twenty-five percentage points.

Another positive sign for Democrats is how well they perform in high turnout elections. Though we need to examine the impact of voter turnout on election outcomes in more detail, preliminary evidence from the 2020 presidential contest indicates that increased turnout helps Democratic candidates.

Figure 15.6 shows the strong relationship between voter turnout in southern states and support for Biden ($r = 0.84$, $p \leq .01$). Turnout was the highest in four states (Virginia, North Carolina, Florida, and Georgia). Texas was an outlier, with just over 60 percent voter turnout in 2020. States with the lowest support for Biden also had the lowest turnout. These results should be viewed with some caution, since turnout is typically higher in close elections, and the contests in North Carolina, Florida, and Georgia were particularly close.

There are also many groups working to increase voter turnout and build grassroots support for Democratic candidates across the region. Two noteworthy examples are Mississippi Votes and Engage Miami, and these types of organizations can help shape future election results in the South (Hagenah 2020). Of course, turnout will be stymied with continued efforts to restrict voting in many southern states. In general, southern states have some of the most restrictive voting rules (Li, Pomante, and Schraufnagel 2018) and efforts to purge voter rolls, increase voter ID laws, and eliminate polling locations have been shown to more negatively affect minority voters (Johnson 2020).

Southern cities also provide fertile ground for Democrats. As cities continue to grow, urban voters will make up a greater percentage of the statewide electorate. Moreover, cities can be important places for the development of future Democratic politicians. Many southern cities are governed by Democratic mayors who are likely to one day run for statewide office. Steve Benjamin, the longtime mayor of Columbia, South Carolina, is often mentioned as a potential gubernatorial candidate in the Palmetto State. Likewise,

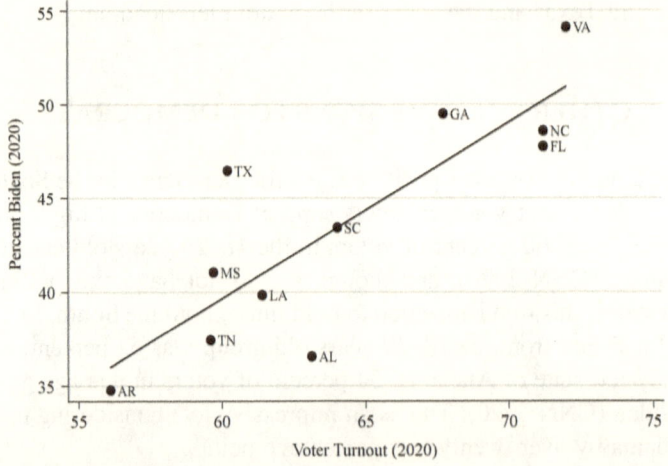

Figure 15.6 Voter Turnout and Support for Biden in the Southern States. *Source:* Data compiled by the author from United States Elections Project (http://www.electproject.org/2020g) and New York Times Election Results (https://www.nytimes.com/interactive/2020/11/03/us/elections/results-president.html). Last accessed February 28, 2021.

newly elected mayor of Montgomery, Alabama, Steven Reed has the potential to bring together a new coalition of Alabama voters if he decides to run for statewide office one day.

CONCLUSION

While Republicans continue to dominate southern politics, the future is bright for southern Democrats. The region's growing diversity helped propel Biden to victories in Virginia and Georgia and has the potential to move Florida, North Carolina, and Texas to the Democratic column. Predictions about future demographic shifts, particularly declines in the percent white and increases in percent Latinx and percent Asian (Vespa, Medina, and Armstrong 2020) all point to a bright future for Democrats. There is also clear evidence that Democrats will continue to benefit from the shift of college-educated voters away from the GOP, and the continued growth in the percentage of college educated (Ryan and Bauman 2016) will bode well for Democrats in future elections. And finally, as the region's economy continues to evolve, the growth of high-tech industries will also drive support to Democratic candidates.

The best hope for Democrats rests in five key states: Georgia, Florida, North Carolina, Texas, and Virginia. Virginia is already safely in the Democratic column, and the recent successes in Georgia will ensure that the Peach State is a true battleground. Florida, North Carolina, and Texas are the next in line, and if current trends continue, will continue to be battlegrounds. Even South Carolina is a state to watch.

NOTE

1. With the resignation of Jeff Sessions to become U.S. Attorney General in 2017, Doug Jones was elected in a special election in 2017 to complete the remainder of that term ending in 2020.

REFERENCES

Avery, James M., and Jeffrey A. Fine. 2012. "Racial Composition, White Racial Attitudes, and Black Representation: Testing the Racial Threat Hypothesis in the United States Senate." *Political Behavior* 34(3): 391–410.

Black, Earl, and Merle Black. 1987. *Politics and Society in the South*. Cambridge, Massachusetts: Harvard University Press.

Black, Earl, and Merle Black. 2002. *The Rise of Southern Republicans*. Cambridge, MA: Harvard University Press.

Brownstein, Ronald. 2020. "Why the Southeast is up for grabs in the 2020 election," *CNN*, October 6, 2020. https://www.cnn.com/2020/10/06/politics/southeast-swing-states-2020/index.html.

Cooper, Michael. 2020. "What it will take for progressives to win the South in November," *Scalawag*, June 8, 2020. https://scalawagmagazine.org/2020/06/georgia-alabama-election-preview/.

CNN. 2016. "Exit Polls." https://www.cnn.com/election/2016/results/exit-polls.

CNN. 2020. "Exit Polls." https://www.cnn.com/election/2020/exit-polls/president/national-results.

Frey, William H. 2004. "The New Great Migration: Black Americans' Return to the South, 1965–2000." Brookings, May 1, 2004. https://www.brookings.edu/research/the-new-great-migration-black-americans-return-to-the-south-1965-2000/.

Frey, William H. 2020a. "Exit Polls Show Both Familiar and New Voting Blocs Sealed Biden's Win." Brookings, November 12, 2020. https://www.brookings.edu/research/2020-exit-polls-show-a-scrambling-of-democrats-and-republicans-traditional-bases/.

Frey, William H. 2020b. "Biden's Victory Came From the Suburbs." *Brookings*, November 13, 2020. https://www.brookings.edu/research/bidens-victory-came-from-the-suburbs/.

Hagenah, Iliana. 2020. "Democrats Eventually Won Black Youth Voters, But Will They Keep Them?" *Scalawag*, December 10, 2020. https://scalawagmagazine.org/2020/12/mississippi-florida-black-youth-vote/.

Information Technology & Innovation Foundation. 2020. "The 2020 State New Economy Index," October 19, 2020. https://itif.org/publications/2020/10/19/2020-state-new-economy-index.

Johnson, Theodore R. 2020. "The New Voter Suppression." Brennan Center for Justice, January 16, 2020. https://www.brennancenter.org/our-work/research-reports/new-voter-suppression.

Key, V.O. 1949. *Southern Politics in State and Nation*. New York: Alfred A. Knopf.

Kilgore, Ed. 2020. "Will 2020 Be Jimmy Carter's Revenge?" *New York Magazine*, October 15, 2020. https://nymag.com/intelligencer/2020/10/will-2020-election-in-the-south-be-jimmy-carters-revenge.html.

Kruse, Kevin M. 2005. *White Flight: Atlanta and the Making of Modern Conservatism*. Princeton, NJ: Princeton University Press.

Lamis, Alexander. 1984. *The Two-Party South*. New York: Oxford University Press.

Li, Quan, Michael J. Pomante II, and Scot Schraufnagel. 2018. "Cost of Voting in American States." *Election Law Journal* 17(3): 234–247.

Maxwell, Angie, and Todd Shields. 2019. *The Long Southern Strategy: How Chasing White Voters in the South Changed American Politics*. New York: Oxford University Press.

McKee, Seth C. 2018. *The Dynamics of Southern Politics: Causes and Consequences*. Thousand Oaks, CA: CQ Press.

National Equity Atlas. 2020. "Diversity Index: Racial and Cultural Diversity Create Thinking and Prosperous Communities." https://nationalequityatlas.org/indicators/Diversity_index#/.

NBC News, 2020. "Georgia Presidential Election Results 2020." https://www.nbcnews.com/politics/2020-elections/georgia-president-results.

New York Times. 2020. "Presidential Election Results." https://www.nytimes.com/interactive/2020/11/03/us/elections/results-president.html.

Noe-Bustamante, Luis, Mark Hugo Lopez, and Manuel Krogstad. 2020. "U.S. Hispanic Population Surpassed 60 Million in 2019, But Growth Has Slowed." *Pew Research Center*, July 7, 2020. https://www.pewresearch.org/fact-tank/2020/07/07/u-s-hispanic-population-surpassed-60-million-in-2019-but-growth-has-slowed/.

Phillips, Kevin. 1969. *The Emerging Republican Majority*. New Rochelle, NY: Arlington House.

Ryan, Camille L., and Kurt Bauman. 2016. "Educational Attainment in the United States: 2015." U.S. Census Bureau, March 2020. https://www.census.gov/content/dam/Census/library/publications/2016/demo/p20-578.pdf.

Tufte, Edward R. 1980. *Political Control of the Economy*. Princeton, NJ: Princeton University Press.

United States Elections Project. 2020. "2020 November General Election Turnout Rates." http://www.electproject.org/2020g.

U.S. Census. 2020. "Quick Facts." https://www.census.gov/quickfacts/fact/table/US/PST045219.

Vespa, Jonathan, Lauren Medina, and David M. Armstrong. 2020. "Demographic Turning Points for the United States: Population Projections for 2020 to 2060." *U.S. Census Bureau*, March 2020. https://www.census.gov/content/dam/Census/library/publications/2020/demo/p25-1144.pdf.

Index

Note: *Italic* page number refer to figures and tables; Page numbers followed by "n" denote endnotes.

Abraham, Ralph, 106, 107
Abrams, Stacey, 3, 82, 91, 92, 118
absentee-by-mail voting, 33, 225, 229, 232, 238
absentee-in-person (early) voting, 238, 288–89
absentee one-stop voting, 238
ACA. *See* Affordable Care Act (ACA)
Adams, Alma, 234
Affordable Care Act (ACA), 24, 25, 250
Akbari, Raumesh, 255
Alabama: ADC in selecting state executive committee, 55; Biden, radio program, 67; Biden's win on Super Tuesday, 56; campaign messages, 60; changes of Trump vote, county level, 2016 to 2020, *67*; college education, 65, *65*; constitutional amendments, 61; convention, 2020, 54; democratic vote, county characteristics, *65*; democrats, 55–56; determinants of Trump vote, county level, *66*; federal election results, *63*; fundraising success, 56; GOP runoff, 59; House of Representatives, 57; immigration policies, 53; influence, Trump Administration, 53–54; insurrection, fallout, 70; March primary election, 59; March to Save America rally, 69; national trends, 66; one-party competition, 70; partisan and racial voting patterns, 66; partisan-based voting, 70; policy preferences, 59–60; presidential preferences, 63–64; presidential voting, 64; racially aligned partisan voting, 64; Republicans, 54–55; runoff election results, 60–61; Senate, 57–59; statewide elections, 61; support for Trump's legal options, 68; Tuberville's residency and financial scandal, 59–60; "Tuberville + Trump 2020," 60; voter turnout, 61
Alexander, Lamar, 247, 250, 257
Allen, George, 285
Anderson, Reuben, 118
anti-feminism, 302
anti-gay marriage constitutional amendment, 279
Arkansas: COVID-19 exposure, 160; Democratic National Convention,

315

157; general election campaign, 158–60; general election voter turnout, 1972–2020, *166*; outcome, 160–67; political factors, 162–66; poll results of voters, 2020, *165*; primary season, 156–58; primary voter turnout in 1976–2020, *158*; realignment by county 2008, 2012, 2016, and 2020, *163–64*; registered voter turnout and presidential vote, 2020, *167*; Republican National Convention, 159; results of 2020 presidential and congressional elections, *161*; selected polls in 2020, 159; social/demographic factors, 162; Trumpism's power, 169; turnout, 166–67; U.S. House races, 168
Armey, Dick, 302
Arrington, Katie, 146

Baesler, Scotty, 209
Baker, Howard Jr., 246, 253
Baker, Tod, 3
Barbour, Haley, 113, 118
Barkley, Alben, 209
Barnette, Richard, 160
Barr, Andy, 217
Barrett, Amy Coney, 145, 231
"Battle for the soul of America," 115. *See also* Mississippi
Beasley, Cheri, 235
Bennet, Michael, 157
Bennett, Lynda, 226
Bentsen, Lloyd, 263
Beshear, Andy, 211
Beshear, Steve, 211
Bevin, Matt, 210, 211, 216
Biden, Joe: Alabama, 55–56, 63–67, 70; Arkansas, 157–62, 165–66, 169; five Southern states, 304–11; Florida, 173, 178–83, 185, 187–95, 197–98; Georgia, 77–86, 89, 91; Kentucky 2020, 214–15, 220; Louisiana, 95, 97–99, 101, 103–7, 108n4; Mississippi, 115–17, 120, 122–24; nomination process, 33–34, 37–44, 46–48; North Carolina, 225–33, 237–38; South Carolina, 135–44, 147; Southern Electorate, 2020, 7–8, 12, 14–27; Tennessee, 253–56; Texas, 269, 272, 275; Virginia, 279, 281, 286–88, 290–94, 296, 298
"Big 12," 270
Big Six counties, 270
Binnix, Erika, 208
biracial coalition, 111, 131
Bishop, Dan, 234
Black, Diane, 249
Blackburn, Marsha, 249, 251–53, 257
Black Lives Matter movement, 27, 159, 182, 192
Bloomberg, Michael, 38, 56, 115, 156, 180, 252, 286–88
Booker, Charles, 217
Booker, Cory, 112, 118, 286
Boucher, Rene, 219
Bourdeaux, Carolyn, 90
Bradshaw, Marquita, 257
Brat, David, 284
Bredesen, Phil, 247, 251–52
Briggs, Eddie, 120
Brooks, Mo, 57, 69, 70
Brownstein, Ron, 303
Brummett, John, 167
Bryant, Phil, 112, 113, 118, 119
Buchanan, Scott E., 4, 41, 280, 281
Bullock, Charles S. III., 2, 148
Bullock, Steve, 156
Bump, Phillip, 257
Bunning, Jim, 209, 216
Bush, George W., 77, 173, 183, 216, 223, 250
Bush v. Gore, 280
Buttigieg, Pete, 253, 286, 287
Byrne, Bradley, 57–58, 58, 59, 60, 68

Cagle, Casey, 85
Cameron, Daniel, 214
campaign issues, 23–27; abortion rights, 26; attitudes on various, *24*; climate

change, 25–26; criminal justice issues, 26–27; financial situations, 25; health care, 25; Medicare for All (MFA) proposal, 25; racism, 27
Carl, Jerry, 57
Carter, Jimmy, 77, 111, 131, 183, 210, 247, 263
Carter, Lee, 297
Cassidy, Bill, 107
Castro, Fidel, 178
Cawthorn, Madison, 226, 232, 233
Chandler, Ben, 210
Chao, Elaine, 216, 217
Chase, Amanda, 298
Christensen, Rob, 240
civil rights movement, 1960s, 261, 263
Civil Rights museums, Mississippi, 115
Clark, Eric, 119
Clement, Frank, 246
Clements, Earle, 209
Clinton, Bill, 247, 251
Clinton, Hillary, 8, 35, 46, 66, 79–83, 104, 105, 108, 113, 137, 138, 140, 142, 147, 155, 156, 161, 166, 178, 183, 185, 188, 189, 213, 231, 247, 251, 253, 255, 256, 263, 274, 275, 277, 280–84, 286, 290, 292, 294, 295, 306
Clowney, Nicole, 157
Clyburn, James, 43, 134, 135, 137, 287
Clyburn, Jim, 147
Cochran, Thad, 111, 112, 117, 125
Commonwealth, 1, 207–8, 210, 212, 214–15, 218, 220, 279–80, 284, 296
Comstock, Barbara, 284
Conservatism, 64, 250, 279–80
"Contract with America," 302
Cook, Marlow, 209
Cook Political Report, 7–8, 252
Coolidge, Calvin, 208
Cooper, Christopher, 240
Cooper, John Sherman, 209
Cooper, Michael, 305
Cooper, Roy, 226, 229, 234, 235
Corker, Bob, 251–53

Cotton, Tom, 167–68
COVID-19 pandemic, 1, 17–21, 59, 289; accommodation to voting in Virginia, 291; Arkansas, 160; attitudes on COVID-related items, *19;* "COVID voters," 18; government policy priorities, 20–21; impact on nomination process, 37; Louisiana, 105; North Carolina, 238; opinion on masks, 21; related issues in Florida, 178, 180–81, 191–92; state-level COVID impacts, 20; Trump on, 17–18
Crist, Charlie, 194
Crump, E. H., 245
Cunningham, Cal, 148, 148n1, 226, 231

Davis, Jefferson, 207
Davis, Moe, 227, 232
Dawson, Katon, 142
DC Madam Scandal, 97
Democratic National Convention, 2020, 115, 130, 157, 159, 297
DeSantis, Ron, 176–77, 180, 198
Dewey, Thomas, 247
Dixiecrats, 130
Dole, Bob, 211
Dole, Elizabeth, 223
Duncan, Geoff, 91
DuPree, Johnny, 126
Duyn, Terry Van, 226
Dye, Brad, 120

Eamon, Tom, 240
early in-person voting, 23, 33, 83, 225
Easley, Mike, 223
Eastland, James, 111
education gap, 15–16
Edwards, John Bel, 97, 106, 132
Eisenhower, Dwight D., 95, 130, 209, 247, 262
Elliott, Joyce, 160
Ellmers, Renee, 226
Engage Miami, 310
Espy, Mike, 112, 113, 115–18, 123–26

Fairfax, Justin, 297
Flaggs, George Jr., 126
Fleming, Ken, 218
Fletcher, Ernie, 210, 211
Florida: county-level analysis and results, 183–87; COVID-19 pandemic related issues, 178, 180–81, 191–92; down-ballot races, 194–95; exit-poll: demographic and political characteristics, 187–91; exit-poll: issues and candidate characteristics, 191–94; exit poll results, Democratic Presidential Primary election, 179, *180*; gender gap, 188–89; general election campaign, 179–82; midterm elections, 2018, 176–78; party registration, 174–75; preelection surveys, 182; presidential election result in counties with largest Hispanic populations, 2020, *188*; presidential exit poll results: demographic and political characteristics, *189*, *190*; presidential exit poll results: issues and candidate characteristics, 2020, *193–94*; presidential nomination contest, 178–79; presidential vote in "mega-counties" in presidential elections, 2000–2020, *184*; prior election results since 2008, 174; race and personal attacks, 176–77; racial equality, 192; regression analysis of county-level presidential vote, 2016 and 2020, *186*; Republican control of state legislature and governor's office, 197–98; Republican vote in presidential elections,1992–2020, *174*; results of 2020 Florida U.S. House of Representatives elections, *196*; results of 2020 presidential election and analysis, 182–94, *183*; U.S. Senate race, 2018, 176–78; voter registration, 1972 to 2020, *175*; voting early by mail and early in person, 181–82; voting rights, 198
Floyd, George, 27, 192, 214, 288
FNVA. *See* Fox News Voter Analysis (FNVA) survey
Ford, Christine Blasey, 252
Ford, Gerald, 263
Ford, Wendell, 209
Forest, Dan, 226, 234
Fox News Voter Analysis (FNVA) survey, 8–10, 16, 18, 20, 23, 28n1
Foy, Jennifer Carroll, 297
Frazier, Hillman, 114
Freitas, Nick, 289
Fried, Nikki, 177, 197
Frist, Bill, 247
Frost, Martin, 264

Gardner, Daniel, 116
Garland, Merrick, 216
Garrett, Tom, 284
gender gap, 15, 105, 188–89, 292
Georgia: absentee votes, 85; ad slots, 87–88; ballots cast on election day, 83–84; black vote, 78–79; candidate support by age, *82*; challenges to election, 84–86; competitive status, 82, 91; democratic challengers, 87; demographics and partisan implications, 77–84; exit poll data, Trump support, *80*; factors, erosion of Republican support, 78; factors for Democratic win, 91; generational replacement, 81; Loeffler attacks on Warnock, 87; minority vote, 82–83; National Pool exit poll, 79; other elections, 89–90; performances of Biden, Clinton, and Warnock, *81*; person-to-person campaigning, 88; Raffensperger, attacks on, 91; relative GOP success, 90; runoffs, 86–89; shifts in composition of electorate, 82; size of democratic loss or win by numbers of votes, *78*; slippage in white support, 79;

support for democrats by ethnic group, 79; touch screens, 84; Trump and Kemp, 85–86; Trump's loss, 86–89; urban centers, 80
"Gibraltar of Democracy," 211
Gillespie, Edward, 282
Gillum, Andrew, 176–77
Gingrich, Newt, 302
Giuliani, Rudy, 69, 85
Goldwater, Barry, 77, 130, 131
Gore, Al Jr., 246, 247, 250, 280
Gowdy, Trey, 145
Graham, Cole Blease, Jr., 41
Graham, Lindsay, 85, 112, 141, 145, 147
Grange, Holly, 226
Grayson, Trey, 216
Green New Deal, 116, 226
Griffin, Tim, 169
Gunn, Philip, 114

Hagan, Kay, 223
Hagerty, Bill, 257
Halsam, Bill, 250
Harding, Warren, 247
Harrington, Ricky Dale Jr., 168
Harris, Kamala, 55, 82, 86, 107, 112, 116, 122, 228, 276, 286
Harrison, Jaime, 141, 145, 147
Haslam, Bill, 247
Hayes, Rutherford B., 130
Hendren, Jim, 169
Herring, Mark, 282, 297
Higgins, Clay, 107
Holley, Yvonne Lewis, 226, 235
Hood, Jim, 113, 125
Hood, M. V., 248
Hoover, Herbert, 208, 247
Hosemann, Delbert, 114
Huddleston, Walter (Dee), 209, 215
Hudson, Richard, 234
Huffmon, Scott H., 41
Humphrey, Hubert, 263
Hutchinson, Asa, 169

Hutchison, Kay Bailey, 264
Hyde-Smith, Cindy, 111, 112, 115–18, 123–25

Information Technology & Innovation Foundation (ITIF), 308–9
In God We Trust Flag Commission, 118–19
Ingoglia, Blaise, 197
Insure Tennessee, 250
Isakson, Johnny, 85
ITIF. *See* Information Technology & Innovation Foundation (ITIF)

Jim Crow era, 302
Johnson, Lyndon B., 247, 263
Johnson, Mark, 226
Johnson, Mike, 107, 226
Jones, Doug, 54–57, 61, 62, 303, 311n1

Kaine, Tim, 284
Kapeluck, DuBose, 4
Kash, Jeffrey, 3
Kefauver, Estes, 246
Kemp, Brian, 78, 85, 86, 90, 91
Kennedy, John F., 77, 131, 263
Kentucky: AP VoteCast data, 214, 215, 217; composition of U.S. House delegation, 209; counties with largest relative Democratic trend, 1996–2020, *210*; exit-poll results, 215; general election, 217; governorship, 211; killing of unarmed black woman, 207, 214; pattern of supporting Republicans, 208–9; post–Civil War activities, 207; Republican domination, 210; Republican party share of two-party vote 1976–2020, *212*; Senate Bill 228, 218–19; Tea Party primary challenge, 216; Trump factor, 217–18; Trump's easy victory, 213–16; 2020 results, 218; vote pattern trends, 211–12
Kerry, John, 280

Key, V. O., 2, 71, 240, 246, 261–62
Kilgore, Ed, 306
King, Martin Luther Jr., 156
Klobuchar, Amy, 56, 135, 137, 156, 157, 253, 286–88
Knotts, Gibbs, 240

Lasley, Scott, 3
Letlow, Luke, 107
Let Mississippi Vote, 119
Lewis, Ron, 209
Lindell, Michael J., 69
Loeffler, Kelly, 78, 84–86
Lott, Trent, 111
Louisiana: campaigns, 99–100; COVID crisis, 105; differences across parishes, 103; differences in turnout, 99, 100; election results, 101–6; gender gap in voting, 105; general election, 99–100; history, 95–97; impact of congressional elections, 107–8; late primary date, 97–98; other elections, 106–8; party identification, 103; poll results of likely voters in 2020, *104*; primary elections, 97–99; race, 104–5; State law, 108n1; statewide elections, 106; support for GOP in 1980–2020, *96*; support for Republicans by population, 97, *102*; 2020 presidential primary results, *98*; U.S. Senate seats, 107; voter turnout presidential elections 2012–2020, *100*; votes for present by region, *101*; voting patterns assessment, 103
Luebke, Paul, 240
Lunsford, Bruce, 216
Luria, Elaine, 284, 289, 294

McAuliffe, Terry, 297
McBath, Lucy, 90
McCain, John, 78, 250, 281
McClellan, Jennifer, 297
McConnell, Mitch, 208, 209, 213, 214–16, 218–19, 231

McCrory, Pat, 234
McCullough, Tippi, 157
McDaniel, Bill, 125
McDaniel, Chris, 112–14, 117, 119
Mace, Nancy, 146
McGlennon, John J., 1, 227
McGovern, George, 263
McGrath, Amy, 213, 217
McGuire, John, 289
McKee, Seth C., 245
McKinley, William, 208
McMaster, Henry, 129
McWherter, Ned, 247
Mahoney, Josh, 167–68
Manning, Kathy, 227, 233
Martin, Mark, 235
Maxwell, Angie, 302
Mayer, Jane, 216
Meacham, Jon, 253
Meadows, Mark, 226
MEC. *See* Mississippi Economic Council (MEC)
Medicaid, 25, 113, 117, 177, 283
medical marijuana issue, 119
Medicare for All (MFA), 25, 116
MFA. *See* Medicare for All (MFA)
Midlands, 132
Minter, Patti, 218
Mississippi: congressional races, 124; constitutional amendment proposal, 114; County-level aggregate data, 120–21; election results and analysis, 120–25; election returns in federal elections, 2020, *121*; flag, 118–20; In God We Trust Flag Commission, 118–19; House Concurrent Resolution 47, 119–20; medical marijuana issue, 119; political context, 111–14; presidential and Senate voting patterns comparison, 121, 124; presidential campaign, 115–16; presidential Election results for county-level 2020, *122*; presidential voting patterns, 121; racial justice

protests, 114; Republican dominance, 125–26; Senate election, 117–18; Senate election results for county-level 2020, *123*; special U.S. Senate election, 2018, 111–12; state elections of 2019, 113; state legislative session, 2020, 114
Mississippi Economic Council (MEC), 114, 117, 119
Mississippi Votes, 119, 124–25, 310
Mondale, Walter, 35, 263
Moody, Ashley, 177
Moore, Roy, 53, 58, 62, 71
Moreland, Laurence, 3
Morton, Thurston, 209
Mucarsel-Powell, Debbie, 194
Mueller probe into 2016 campaign, 54
Mulvaney, Mick, 145
Musgrove, Ronnie, 120

Natcher, William, 209
National Center for Health Statistics classification scheme, 108n2
National Voter Registration Act, 175
Navarro, Peter, 69
Nelson, Bill, 176, 177, 197
Newby, Paul, 235
new economy, 308–9; index, indicators, 308; score and support for Biden, *309*
Nixon, Richard, 131, 173, 263, 302
nomination process: Biden and Sanders cumulative delegate count, 38–41, *41*; characteristics of voters, *45*; COVID-19, impact of, 37; democratic primary results, 37–41; percentage of Black voters, *44*; percentage of demographic group support for Biden, *47*; polling data are from Real Clear Politics, 49n12; pool of candidates, 48n1; primaries and conventions, 34; Republican National Convention in 2020, 34; role of South Carolina in 2020 nomination contest, 41–44; for southern states-pledged delegates, *40*; for southern states-popular vote, 38, *39*; timing of Primaries and Caucuses, 35–37, *36–37*; winning nomination, 34–35; women, 45
Norquist, Grover, 249
Norrell, Mandy Powers, 147
Northam, Ralph, 282, 289, 291, 296
North Carolina: absentee by mail voting, 225, 238; absentee one-stop (AOS) voting, 238; analysis of precinct election data, 231; before and after 2008, 223–24; congressional districts, 227; COVID-19 and voting, 238–39; democratic primary election results, 225; dynamics, 241; early in-person voting, 225; election, 2012, 224; Election Day voting, 225; Federal Election Commission (FEC) data, 231; general election, party registration turnout rates and vote method distribution, *240*; general election two-party results by vote methods, *229*; governor's COVID-19 response, 234; governor's race, 234; indicator of Republican interest, 228; justices and judges in partisan elections, 235; March Primary, 224–27; methods for casting ballots, 225; nomination contests, 226; percentage of total ballots cast by vote methods, 2004–2020, *236*; presidential election, 227–31; progressive plutocracy, 240; public opinion polls, 228–29; racial dynamics, 237; regional divide, 230; resources committed, 228; results, for Republican Presidential And Congressional candidates, *233*; result pattern, 228–29; Robinson-Holley contest, 226; state elections, 234–36; Tea Party insurgency, 224; ticket ballot races, 235; top-three contests, 227; Trump and Biden two-party vote totals and percentages,

230; turnout among generational cohorts, 238; U.S. Senate and House elections, 231–33; vote methods by party registration percentages, 2004–2020, *239*
Nunn, Louie B., 209

Obama, Barack, 35, 78–80, 82, 87, 100, 117, 138, 155, 156, 173, 175, 197, 216, 223, 250, 280, 281, 283, 287, 290, 292
Ocasio-Cortez, Alexandria, 232
the "Old 5th," 211
O'Rourke, Beto, 157, 286
Ossoff, Jon, 1, 2, 78, 87–89, 302

Paris Climate Agreement, 25
Patrick, Deval, 118
Patronis, Jimmy, 177
Paul, Rand, 208, 209, 216, 219
Pelosi, Nancy, 112, 113, 160
Pence, Mike, 82, 113, 181, 227
Perdue, Beverly, 223
Perdue, David, 78, 84, 86, 87, 89, 91
Perkins, Adrian, 107
Perriello, Tom, 282, 284
place type, 16–17
political dispositions: FNVA respondents, 10–12; ideological self-labels, 12; partisanship/Partisan loyalties, 10; party preferences, 12
post–World War II Republican belief system, 1
Prather, Joe, 209
Putnam, Adam, 176

racially polarized voting, 12, 14, 28
"racial threat," 304–35
racism, *24*, 27, 55, 192, *193*, 232
radical socialists, 87
Raffensperger, Brad, 84–86, 89–91
Ramsey, Dave, 249, 257, 258n1
Ramsey Solutions, 245
Reagan, Ronald, 77, 117, 124, 131, 175, 210, 227, 263

Reeves, Tate, 113, 125
religion, 16, 191, 249
Republicanism, 57, 120, 240, 246, 261–67, 270
Republican National Convention in 2020, 34, 54, 159, 214, 228
Resistance at All Costs (Strassel), 253
Riggleman, Denver, 284, 290
Rim South and Deep South, division, 2
Rispone, Eddie, 97, 106
Robertson, Trav Jr., 134
Robinson, Mark, 226, 235
Roby, Martha, 57
Roe v. Wade, 26
Rogers, Mike, 68
Romney, Mitt, 85, 95, 101, 131, 138, 210, 250, 267
Ross, Deborah, 233
Rubio, Marco, 198–99
Rutledge, Leslie, 160, 169

Sanders, Bernie, 7, 33, 35, 37, 38, 41–44, 46, 48, 55, 56, 98, 99, 115, 135, 137, 157, 159, 169, 177–79, 213, 225, 226, 253–55, 282, 286–88, 308
Sanders, Sarah Huckabee, 159, 169
Sanford, Mark, 146
Sasser, Jim, 246
Scalise, Steve, 107
Schumer, Chuck, 87, 112, 113
Scott, Frank, Jr., 156
Scott, Rick, 156, 176, 177, 198
Sewell, Terri, 56, 68
Shalala, Donna, 194
Sheheen, Vincent, 147–48
Shelby, Richard, 58, 68, 70
Shelton, Jason, 116
Shields, Todd, 302
Shumer, Chuck, 226, 231
Sink, Alex, 197
Smith, Erica, 226
South Carolina: Clyburn's endorsement of Biden, 43; construction of the BMW plant, 132; County-level Trump percentage of vote in 2020,

144; Democratic nominating primary exit poll, 135–37, *136*; democratic primary, 134–37; Democrats in the Midlands, 133; downticket race, 146; exit poll results, 2020, 44, *143*; "First in the South" presidential primary, 131, 146; general election, 137–46; impact of absentee ballots, 137; Midlands and the Low country, 132–33, 138; new residents in the Charleston, 133; nomination contest, 41–44; Palmetto State, 131–32; political background, 129–32; political landscape, 132–34; real clear politics poll average-South Carolina, *42*; Reconstruction, 129–30, 130; reelection, 145; Republican dominance in the past, 131; Republican regions, 134; results of presidential and congressional elections, *139*, *139–40*; Senate and House contests, 147–48; South Carolina democratic primary, *43*; voting by region and county in 2020 general election, *141*; voting patterns, 130

Southern democratic primary electorate: characteristics of voters, *45*; percentage of Black voters, *44*; percentage of demographic group support for Biden, *47*; women, 45

Southern distinctiveness, 27–28

Southern electorate, 2020: attitudes about voting, *22*; Biden's win, 8; Biden vote share by demographic group, *13*; campaign issues, 23–27, 24t; COVID-19. *See* COVID-19 pandemic; data, 8–10; education gap, 15–16; election security, 23; Fox News Voter Analysis (FNVA) survey, 8–12; gender gap, 15; ideological self-labels, 12; partisanship/Partisan loyalties, 10; party preferences, 12; patterns and attitudes, 21, *22*; place type, 16–17; race, 12–14; religion, 16; southern distinctiveness, 27–28; state electorate characteristics, *10*; state voting and turnout patterns, 8, *9*; turnout and election security, 21–23

Southern Politics in State and Nation (Key), 246, 261

Southern (Five) States: college-educated voters, 306–8; "Contract with America," 302; diversity score, 305; GOP takeover of the south, 302–3; ground for Democrats, 310–11; groups to increase voter turnout, 310; high level of Republican success, 301; impact of voter turnout, 309–10; national trends, 307; new economy, 308–9; new economy score and support for Biden, *309*; organizations, 310; percent Black and support for Biden, *304*; percentage college and support for Biden, *307*; positive signs for democrats, 309–11; positive signs for democrats, 309–11; race, 302; racial threat, 304–35; Republican congressional success, *303*; Republican region, 301; return of African Americans, 303; Southern Strategy, Nixon's, 302; state diversity and support for Biden, *306*; suburbanization, 302; technology hubs, 308; Trump's economic populism, 308–9; voting patterns differences, 306; younger voters support Democrats, 309

Southern Strategy, Nixon's, 302
Spanberger, Abigail, 284, 294
special election, 2017, 53, 57, 145
state electorate characteristics, *11*
state voting and turnout patterns, 8, *9*
Steed, Robert, 3
Stennis, John, 111, 113, 124
Stewart, Corey, 282, 284, 289
Steyer, Tom, 286
Strassel, Kimberly, 253

Sundquist, Don, 247, 248
superdelegates, 75
Super PACs, 87, 159
Super Tuesday, 33, 35, 38, 47, 54–56, 135, 137, 156–58, 178, 224–26, 286–88
Symposium on Southern Politics, 3–4

Tax Cut and Jobs Act, 2017, 216
Tax Revolt chronicles, 248
Taylor, Breonna, 26–27, 208, 214, 215, 220n1
Taylor, Scott, 284, 289
Tea Party movement, 57, 248
Tennessee: Affordable Care Act, 250; Biden's win, 254; black voting registration, 246; competition at presidential level, 247; democratic primary, 2020, 253–55, *254*; general election, 2020, 255–57; GOP's conservative supermajority, 250; "grand divisions" of Tennessee, 254; Insure Tennessee, 250; Mountain Republicanism, 246; partisan advantage in most populated counties, *256*; political diversity, 246–48; power of fusionism, 249–50; presidential election results, 2016–2020, *255*; racial demographics, 255; religious traditions, 249; "Republicanization" of evangelical Protestants, 249; Senate race, factors (2018), 252–53; taxes and traditionalism, 2000–2020, 248–50; tax revolts, 248–49; "Trumpism," 251; Trump's victory, 2016, 250–51; Trump's vote margins, 245–46; war against the GOP establishment, 250
Texas: Anglo Republican vote for statewide offices before and during Trump, *273*; Anglo voters participation, 275; "Big 12," 270; "Big Six" counties, 262; changes in congressional districts, 276n3; drop in GOP officeholders in 2018, 266; exit-poll data, 273; GOP dominance, 263; GOP in Trump era, 267–72; GOP vote cast by Anglos, 273; Latino support, 275; non-white (non-Anglo) residents, 270–71; population growth, race, and Republican vote, *271*, 271–72, 277n8; Republican affiliation of Anglo Texans, 2010–2020, *274*; Republican growth, 264; Republicanism, 262–66, *266*; Republican Presidential vote and population growth, *262*, 264, 267–69, *268*; Republicans in district-based elections, 1998–2020, *265*; rural-urban Anglo division, 273–74; statewide elections since 1998, 266–67; Texas Democratic coalition, 263; Trump's presidency and Republican Party, 275
Thompson, Bennie, 111, 115, 124, 126
Thompson, Fred, 247
Thurmond, Strom J., 130, 131, 262
Tillis, Thom, 225, 231, 232, 241
Timmons, William, 145
Timmons-Goodson, Patricia, 234
Truman, Harry S., 130, 183, 262
Trump, Donald: Alabama, 53–55, 57–61, 63–70, 71n1; Arkansas, 155–62, 166, 169–70; five Southern states, 301, 303, 305–8; Florida, 173–83, 185, 187–88, 190–95, 198–99, 199n5, 200n20; Georgia, 78–86, 88–91; Kentucky 2020, 210–20; Louisiana, 95, 97–108; Mississippi, 112–13, 115–18, 120–24; nomination process, 33–34, 37, 41, 48; North Carolina, 225–31, 233–34, 237–38, 241; South Carolina, 129, 133–34, 137–38, 140–42, 144–47; Tennessee, 245–46, 250–53, 255–57; Texas, 262, 267–75, 277; Virginia, 279–87, 289–96, 298
"Trumpism," 169, 251
Tuberville, Tommy, 69, 70, 303
Turner, Joel, 3, 208

Valentine, Phil, 248, 249
VEP. *See* voting-eligible population (VEP)
Vindman, Alexander, 253
Virginia: abolition of death penalty, 297; access to mail ballots, 289; accommodation to voting in a pandemic, 291; Biden's performance, 288; congressional nominations, 289–90; congressional outcomes, 295; conservatism, 279; early stages of national nominating process, 286; election (2020), nomination, 287–88; election for governor and House, 283; elections (2017), 282–83; exit-poll results, 292, *293*; factors for Democratic success, 279; gender gap, 292; general assembly elections, 2019, 285–86; general election, 290–96; general election polls, March–November, *291*; GOP's district plan, 283; impact of race and sex scandals, 296–97; impact of Trump, 281; increased turnout, 295; legalization of marijuana, 297; locality and region, 294–95; midterm congressional elections, 2018, 283–84; notable GOP nominations, 289; Obama's candidacy, 280–81; pattern of succession to the Executive Mansion, 297; politics in 21 century, 280–81; preference for "Someone Else" over Trump, 290; promotion of traditional values, 280; Republican contests, 290; results, 292; shift in voter preferences, 287; significant Republican contest, 290; social conservatism, 280; state GOP dispute, 298; statewide election years, 282–83; transformation by trump, 281–82; triangle of support in NOVA, 295; Trump's campaign and his presidential administration, 282; U.S. Senate and House races, 296
Vitter, David, 97
voting-eligible population (VEP), 8, 183

Walker, Robert, 126
Warner, Mark, 282, 285, 289, 296
Warnockk, Raphael, 2, 78, 86–89, 92, 302
Warren, Elizabeth, 55, 56, 115, 122, 123, 135, 157, 212, 220, 247, 286, 288
Webb, Cameron, 290
Webb, Jim, 285
Weld, William, 34, 55, 99, 157
Wetherby, Lawrence, 209
Wexton, Jennifer, 284
Whitfield, Ed, 209
Wicker, Roger, 111
Wildmon, Walker, 116
Woodfin, Randall, 56
Wright, Jeremiah, 87, 130

Yarmuth, John, 209
Young, John, 116
Youth Empowerment Project, 97

About the Contributors

Scott E. Buchanan is professor of political science and chair of the Department of Government and Sociology at Georgia College and State University. From 2009 to 2020, Professor Buchanan was on the faculty at the Citadel and served as the executive director of the Citadel Symposium on Southern Politics. His research focuses on Southern politics and elections, and he is the author of the only published biography on former Georgia Governor Marvin Griffin. From 2019 to 2020, Dr. Buchanan was the Fulbright Finland Bicentennial Chair in American Studies at the University of Helsinki.

Branwell DuBose Kapeluck is professor of political science at the Citadel. Since 2004, Professor Kapeluck has been codirector of the Citadel Symposium on Southern Politics. He is the author and editor of a number of publications, including *The Future Ain't What It Used to Be: The 2016 Presidential Election in the South*.

Patrick R. Miller is an associate professor of political science at the University of Kansas. His areas of specialization include American politics, political behavior, survey and experimental methods, and quantitative research methods.

Aaron A. Hitefield is a Ph.D. candidate in the Department of Political Science at the University of Georgia. He is broadly interested in the U.S. Congress, Congressional elections, the U.S. presidency, presidential elections and primaries, American political development, and separation of powers.

M. V. Hood, III is professor of political science and director of the SPIA Survey Research Center at the University of Georgia.

Shannon L. Bridgmon is a former associate professor of political science at Northeastern State University. Her primary teaching and research areas are Southern politics and state political party issues. Some of her work has appeared in the *American Review of Politics*, the *Criminal Justice Policy Review*, and the *Presidential Elections in the South* series. She is currently researching as an independent scholar.

Charles S. Bullock, III, is the distinguished professor of public and international affairs, Josiah Meigs Distinguished Teaching Professor and Richard B. Russell Professor of Political Science at the University of Georgia.

Robert E. Hogan is the R. Downs Poindexter Professor of politics and chair of the Department of Political Science at Louisiana State University. He conducts research on electoral politics in the American states. His most recent projects examine candidate decision making and representation in state legislatures. Professor Hogan's published works have appeared in a variety of academic journals, including the *American Journal of Political Science*, *Journal of Politics*, and *Political Research Quarterly*.

Anna R. Elinkowski is an undergraduate student at Louisiana State University majoring in political science. After graduating she plans to attend law school.

Stephen D. Shaffer is professor of political science at Mississippi State University. He publishes extensively on Mississippi's political campaigns and parties, and also teaches in the fields of southern politics, public opinion, political parties, and political leadership. Professor Shaffer directed the twenty-four-year Mississippi Poll project, and is coauthor of *Mississippi Government and Politics: Modernizers versus Traditionalists* and the V. O. Key Award-winning *Politics in the New South: Representation of African Americans in Southern State Legislatures*. Recipient of two NSF subcontracts, he has also published in such journals as *American Journal of Political Science*, *Social Science Quarterly*, and *American Review of Politics*.

Jay Barth is M.E. and Ima Graves Peace Distinguished Professor of politics, Emeritus, at Hendrix College. Barth has written and taught on state politics, the politics of education, political parties and elections, and LGBTQ politics. In addition to teaching awards, Barth was awarded the Southern Political Science Association's Diane Blair Award in 2014 and the Arkansas Political Science Association's Distinguished Scholar Award in 2018.

About the Contributors

Janine A. Parry is professor of political science at the University of Arkansas and has directed the Diane D. Blair Center's annual Arkansas Poll since its inception in 1999. With particular interests in voter behavior, public opinion, gender and politics, and state politics, she teaches introductory to graduate-level courses and has earned numerous teaching honors. She was awarded the Arkansas Political Science Association's Distinguished Scholar Award in 2020.

Jonathan Knuckey is an associate professor of political science at the University of Central Florida. His research interests include Southern politics, voting behavior, and race and politics. His research has been published in journals that include *American Politics Research*, *Party Politics*, *Political Research Quarterly*, *Social Science Journal*, and *Social Science Quarterly*.

Aubrey Jewett is an associate professor of political science at the University of Central Florida. He is author of *A Concise Introduction to Florida Politics*, coauthor of *Politics in Florida*, 5th edition, and coeditor, with former Florida Congressman Lou Frey, of *Political Rules of the Road*. Jewett has published numerous book chapters on Florida politics and scholarly articles in various journals, including *Presidential Studies Quarterly*, *Legislative Studies Quarterly*, *Political Research Quarterly*, and *American Politics Review*. He served as an American Political Science Association (APSA) Congressional Fellow in 2003–2004 and received the Leon Weaver Award from the Representation and Electoral Systems section of the APSA for his study of ballot invalidation in Florida during the 2000 presidential election. Jewett cofounded the Lou Frey Institute of Politics and Government and has helped to bring in more than $1 million in external grants to support civic education. In 2020, the Florida Political Science Association honored Jewett with its Manning J. Dauer Award for his "sustained exemplary record of research, teaching, mentoring and service related to Florida politics and policy."

Joel Turner is professor of political science at Western Kentucky University. Professor Turner's research interests include Southern politics, public opinion, media and politics, and political psychology. His work has appeared in *Political Psychology*, *Political Behavior*, *Social Science Quarterly*, *Social Science Journal*, and the *American Journal of Media Psychology*.

Scott Lasley is professor of political science at Western Kentucky University, where he serves as the head of the Department of Political Science. His research interests include Kentucky politics, public opinion, and the intersection of sports and politics.

Jeffrey P. Kash is professor of political science at Western Kentucky University. His primary research interests are political psychology, public opinion, political communication, and public policy. His work has appeared in the *American Review of Politics*, *Social Science Quarterly*, and the *Policy Studies Journal*.

Michael Bitzer is professor of politics and history and the T.P. and J.C. Leonard Chair of political science at Catawba College in Salisbury, North Carolina, where he serves as chair of the politics department. Bitzer's teaching and research interests are in American politics and history, public law, public administration and policy, and genocide in the twentieth century. He researches and analyzes North Carolina's politics and manages a blog on the topic, OldNorthStatePolitics.com.

Vaughn May is professor and chair of political science at Belmont University. His research interests include Southern politics, Tennessee politics, and the interplay of politics and popular culture. His work appears in a range of journals, including *Urban Education*, *Southeastern Political Review*, *College Teaching*, *Tennessee Historical Quarterly*, and *Studies in Popular Culture*.

Seth C. McKee is professor of political science at Oklahoma State University. His primary area of research focuses on American electoral politics and especially party system change in the American South. He has published numerous articles on such topics as political participation, public opinion, vote choice, redistricting, party switching, minority representation, strategic voting behavior, and state legislative voting behavior. McKee is the author of numerous works on the American South. His most recent publication is *The Dynamics of Southern Politics: Causes and Consequences* and is working on forthcoming book (University of South Carolina Press), *An Untold Story: Rural Republican Realignment in the Modern South*. McKee serves on the editorial boards of *American Politics Research* and *Political Behavior*, and is the editor-in-chief of *Political Research Quarterly*.

John J. McGlennon is a professor of government and public policy at the College of William & Mary in Virginia. He has published widely on political party activists, politics in the American South and politics in Virginia. His work has been published in more than twenty edited volumes, as well as journals such as *The Journal of Politics*, *The International Review of Political Science*, *The Australian Political Science Review*, and *The American Review of Politics*. A participant in the Citadel Symposium on Southern Politics since its inception, he has been a member of two major National Science

Foundation-funded research projects on party activists and activism in the South.

H. Gibbs Knotts is professor of political science and dean of humanities and social sciences at the College of Charleston. His research focuses on Southern politics, political participation, public administration, and the scholarship of teaching and learning. His most recent book (coauthored with Jordan M. Ragusa) is *First in the South: Why South Carolina's Presidential Primary Matters* (University of South Carolina Press, 2020).

www.ingramcontent.com/pod-product-compliance
Lightning Source LLC
Chambersburg PA
CBHW021342300426
44114CB00012B/1053